CASING INTERPERSONAL COMMUNICATION

Case Studies in Personal and Social Relationships

SECOND EDITION

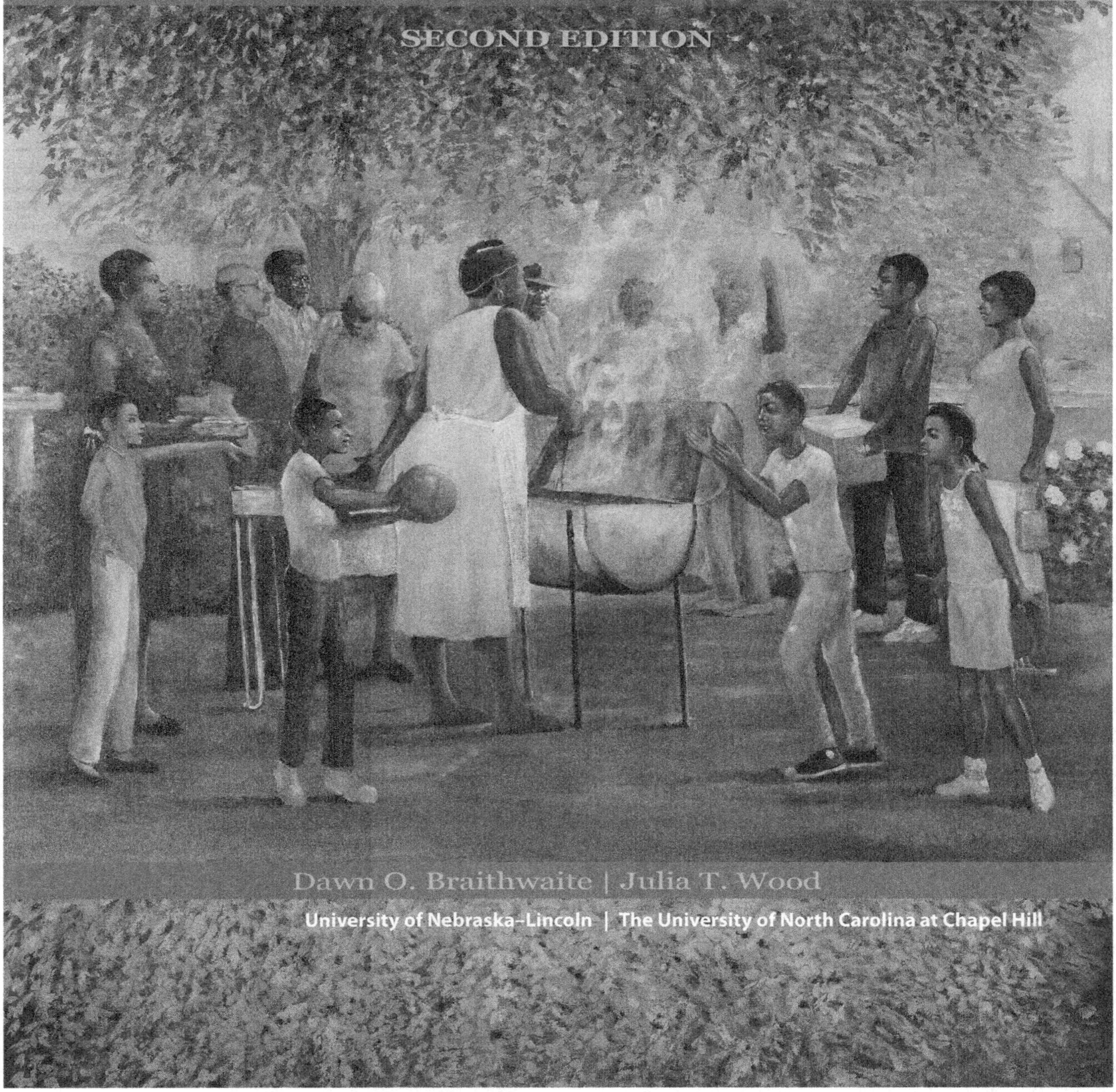

Dawn O. Braithwaite | Julia T. Wood

University of Nebraska–Lincoln | The University of North Carolina at Chapel Hill

Kendall Hunt
publishing company

Cover art of Family Reunion courtesy of Lavarne Ross, www.lross.com

Book Team
Chairman and Chief Executive Officer *Mark C. Falb*
President and Chief Operating Officer *Chad M. Chandlee*
Vice President, Higher Education *David L. Tart*
Director of Publishing Partnerships *Paul B. Carty*
Product and Development Supervisor *Lynne Rogers*
Senior Developmental Editor *Angela Willenbring*
Vice President, Operations *Timothy J. Beitzel*
Permissions Editor *Kathy Hanson*
Cover Designer *Faith Britt*

Kendall Hunt
publishing company
www.kendallhunt.com
Send all inquiries to:
4050 Westmark Drive
Dubuque, IA 52004-1840

ISBN 978-1-5249-4686-9

Printed in the United States of America

CONTENTS

Part IV
Series Challenges in Interpersonal Communication 123

Part V
Change and Continuity in Long-Term Relationships 161

ACKNOWLEDGMENTS

Although our names appear as the Editors of this collection of cases, we could not have completed this project without the help of many people. Our greatest debt is to the scholars who made time to write the cases included in this book. The research they have undertaken and the insights they bring to interpersonal communication make their cases as rich and vital as human relationships themselves.

We also thank Paul Carty and Angela Willenbring at Kendall Hunt, whose enthusiasm and support made it a pleasure to work on this project. Throughout the development and production processes they embodied the key principles of effective interpersonal communication.

We are especially grateful to our students. They are unfailing sources of ideas for cases. In our classes, they tell us about issues they are facing in their relationships. In addition, they let us know which concepts and theories they find particularly difficult to understand without concrete illustrations.

Finally, we thank our families. For both of us, our families include two-footed and four-footed members with whom we have blood or legal ties as well as those who are family for other reasons. Dawn thanks Chuck Braithwaite for his unfailing support, his incredible meals, and thirty years together. She appreciates her step-family, dear friends, and voluntary family members who make life worth living (and communication even more worth studying), and sweet beagles who bring joy to life. Julia thanks her sweetheart, Robbie Cox, her puppy Cassidy, and her kittens Rigby and Always Rowdy. Our family and friends are ongoing case studies in our lives!

Dawn O. Braithwaite, *University of Nebraska–Lincoln*
Julia T. Wood, *The University of North Carolina at Chapel Hill*

ABOUT THE CONTRIBUTORS

Jenna Stephenson Abetz (Ph.D., University of Nebraska–Lincoln) is an Assistant Professor in the Department of Communication at the College of Charleston. Her research focuses on the communicative construction and negotiation of identity, particularly during times of transition and challenge. Her work has included explorations of communication in emerging adulthood, dual-career couples, and mother-daughter relationships and has been published in outlets including *Western Journal of Communication* and *Women's Studies in Communication.*

Brenda J. Allen (Ph.D., Howard University) is a Professor of Communication and Associate Vice Chancellor for Diversity and Inclusion at the University of Colorado Denver. Her research and teaching areas are organizational communication, social identity, and critical pedagogy. Her publications and presentations often center on issues related to communication and diversity in higher education.

Betsy Wackernagel Bach (Ph.D., University of Washington) is a Professor of Communication Studies at the University of Montana. She explores communication and identification in organizational entry and exit and communication in voluntary kin relationships. She has served as Associate Provost, Dean of the Davidson Honors College, and Associate Director for Research at the National Communication Association. She has published over thirty articles and one book. She is Past President of the Western States and National Communication Associations.

Leslie A. Baxter (Ph.D., University of Oregon) is a Professor of Communication Studies and Collegiate Fellow in the College of Liberal Arts and Sciences at the University of Iowa. Her scholarly interests include studying relational dialectics in relating, especially in non-traditional families. She has published over 160 articles, book chapters, and books. She has been fortunate to be the recipient of many awards for her research, including recognition by the National Communication Association as a Distinguished Scholar.

Denisha Biggers is an undergraduate student in the Department of Communication at Christopher Newport University in Newport News, Virginia. Denisha's scholarly interests center on interpersonal communication within cross-sex romantic and platonic dyads.

Dawn O. Braithwaite (Ph.D., University of Minnesota) is a Willa Cather Professor and Chair of Communication at University of Nebraska–Lincoln. She studies communication in discourse dependent families, rituals, and dialectics of relating, publishing 100 articles and five books. Braithwaite received National Communication Association's Brommel Award in Family Communication and was named a Western States Communication Association Distinguished Scholar. She is a Fellow of the Council on Contemporary Families, Past President of the WSCA and National Communication Associations.

Carol J. Bruess (Ph.D., Ohio University) is Professor of Communication and Journalism, and Director of Family Studies at University of St. Thomas, Minnesota. She studies relationship ritual and construction of co-cultures in families and close relationships, focusing on communication in the digital age. She has published four books and dozens of articles and chapters. She is deeply committed to translational scholarship and is editing the book, *Family Communication in an Age of Digital and Social Media.*

Patrice M. Buzzanell (Ph.D., Purdue University) is a Professor in the Brian Lamb School of Communication and the School of Engineering Education by courtesy at Purdue University. Co/editor of three books and author of over 140 articles and chapters, her research centers on the everyday negotiations and structures that produce and are produced by the intersections of career, gender, and communication, particularly in STEM (science, technology, engineering, and math).

Jeffrey T. Child (Ph.D., North Dakota State University) is an Associate Professor at Kent State University in the School of Communication Studies. His primary research explores communication technology and human interaction. His most recent work focuses on social media interactions and effective online privacy management. This social media and privacy research includes examining issues in interpersonal, family, and organizational settings. Dr. Child has published more than thirty journal articles in these research areas.

Jennifer L. Cronin (Ph.D., University of North Carolina at Chapel Hill) is an instructor of communication at UNC–CH and Elon University. She works with newly engaged couples on building communication skills, and examines identity management, disclosure processes, and relationship implications when difficult information is shared among family members. Cronin received the Robert Bostrom Young Scholar Award for her dissertation research and has served as a reviewer for the *Journal of Social and Personal Relationships*.

William R. Cupach (Ph.D., University of Southern California) is Professor emeritus in the School of Communication at Illinois State University. His research pertains to problematic interactions in interpersonal relationships, including such contexts as embarrassing predicaments, relational transgressions, interpersonal conflict, social and relational aggression, obsessive relational pursuit, and stalking. He is a past President of the International Association for Relationship Research (IARR).

Suzy D'Enbeau (Ph.D., Purdue University) is an Assistant Professor in the School of Communication Studies at Kent State University. Suzy specializes in feminist theorizing, work-life issues, and popular culture. Her work has appeared in leading journals such as *Communication Monographs, Human Relations, Journal of Applied Communication Research, Qualitative Inquiry,* and *Women's Studies in Communication*.

Belle A. Edson (Ph.D., University of Denver) is Director of Undergraduate Studies and teaches at the Hugh Downs School of Human Communication at Arizona State University. Her research and teaching interests include feminism and communication, rhetorical theory and criticism, and social-movement theory. She was awarded the College of Liberal Arts and Sciences Distinguished Teaching Award in 2006.

Karen A. Foss (Ph.D., University of Iowa) is Regents Professor and Professor of Communication & Journalism at the University of New Mexico. The focus of her scholarship is feminist perspectives on communication, the discourse of marginalized groups, and social change. Her awards include Gender Scholar of the Year, Presidential Teaching Fellow, Francine Merritt Award, and Scholar of the Year. In 2006, she served as Fulbright Senior Specialist to the University of Southern Denmark.

Kate Lockwood Harris (Ph.D., University of Colorado Boulder) is an Assistant Professor in the Department of Communication at The University of Missouri in Columbia. She studies the communicative and intersectional aspects of gender, violence, sexuality, and organizing. Her publications have appeared in journals such as *Discourse & Society, Management Communication Quarterly, Women and Language, Women's Studies in Communication*, and *thirdspace: a journal of feminist theory and culture*.

Amanda Holman (Ph.D., University of Nebraska–Lincoln) is an Assistant Professor in the Department of Communication Studies at Creighton University. Her research focuses on challenging family and peer relationships to better understand how communication shapes individuals' identity, attitudes, and behaviors. In this, her primary efforts have focused on adolescents' perceptions of their parents' communication about sex and sexuality. Her work has been published in outlets including *Health Communication* and *Journal of Family Communication.*

Haley Kranstuber Horstman (Ph.D., University of Nebraska–Lincoln) is an Assistant Professor in the Department of Communication at the University of Missouri. Her research focuses on health outcomes of communicated sense-making in the context of family diversity and/or difficulty. She grounds her work in narrative theorizing to study relational contexts including adoptive families, mother-daughter relationships, and married couples regarding miscarriage. Her work has received several top paper awards and has been published in regional and national journals.

Naomi R. Johnson (Ph.D., University of North Carolina–Chapel Hill) is an Associate Professor and Chair of Communication Studies at Longwood University. She teaches coursework related to organizational, interpersonal, mass media, and gendered communication practices. Her research related to novels popular among teen girls has been reviewed in *The New York Times, Newsweek, NPR, The Richmond Times-Dispatch,* and other regional media outlets.

Douglas L. Kelley (Ph.D., University of Arizona) is a Professor of Communication Studies at Arizona State University. His research and teaching focus on interpersonal communication and forgiveness as represented by two books, *Marital Communication* and *Communicating Forgiveness*. He has published in various academic journals, is coordinator of educational initiatives for the *Family Communication Consortium*, and is a recipient of the *2012 Centennial Professor Award* at ASU. He also hosts *RelationshipArt.com*, a website encouraging healthy relationships.

Kendra Knight (Ph.D., Arizona State University) is an Assistant Professor in the Department of Communication at Christopher Newport University in Newport News, Virginia. A major focus of her research is the experience of noncommitted sexual interaction among emerging adults. She has published nine journal articles and book chapters, and recently received the National Communication Association's Gerald R. Miller Outstanding Doctoral Dissertation Award. She currently serves on the board of the International Association of Relationship Research.

Andrew M. Ledbetter (Ph.D., University of Kansas) is an Associate Professor of Communication Studies at Texas Christian University. His research examines how relational partners use mediated communication to maintain relationships, with over thirty-five articles in peer-reviewed journals. He has developed graduate and undergraduate courses on social networking sites. He received the Outstanding New Teacher Award from the Central States Communication Association and the Early Career Award from the Interpersonal Communication Division of the National Communication Association.

Jennifer A. Linde (M.A., Arizona State University) is a senior lecturer in the Hugh Downs School of Human Communication at Arizona State University. Her scholarly and teaching interests include performance studies, adaptation of traditional scholarship to the stage, education through performance, civil dialogue as public communication practice, and feminist criticism.

Kristen Lucas (Ph.D., Purdue University) is an Associate Professor in the Management Department at University of Louisville. She specializes in organizational communication with emphases on social class and workplace dignity. She has conducted research on how family communication influences ongoing socialization experiences of people from blue-collar families as they pursue white-collar careers. She has published in *Management Communication Quarterly, Women's Studies in Communication, Communication Monographs,* and *Journal of Family Communication.*

Joseph P. Mazer (Ph.D., Ohio University) is an Assistant Professor and Associate Chair of Communication Studies at Clemson University. He is the Director of the College of Architecture, Arts and Humanities' Social Media Listening Center, an interdisciplinary research lab providing a platform to listen, measure, and engage social media conversations. He has published work on virtual social networking, social and academic support, and measurement issues. He has been recognized for outstanding teaching, research, and service.

Sandra Metts (Ph.D., University of Iowa) is a Professor emeritus in the School of Communication at Illinois State University. Her research focuses on emotion experience and expression in both traditional and nontraditional dating relationships, as well as in family transitions during parental divorce and remarriage. She has served as the editor of *Communication Reports,* Associate editor for *Journal of Social and Personal Relationships* and *Personal Relationships,* and as President of the Central States Communication Association.

Paul A. Mongeau (Ph.D., Michigan State University) is Professor and Associate Director at the Hugh Downs School of Human Communication at Arizona State University in Tempe. His research focuses on modern sexual and relational norms on college campuses, communicative conundrums, and social influence processes. He has served as editor of *Communication Studies* and the *Journal of Social and Personal Relationships*. He has published over fifty journal articles book chapters and coauthored a book on persuasive communication.

Tim Muehlhoff (Ph.D., University of North Carolina at Chapel Hill) is a Professor of Communication at Biola University. He is the author of *Authentic Communication: Christian Speech Engaging Culture* and *I Beg to Differ: Navigating Difficult Conversations with Truth and Love*. His research interests include marital communication, social justice, civility, and gender. He is currently involved in a project focusing on the often devalued and silenced narratives of rural Indian women in New Delhi, India.

Sayaka (Sai) Sato Mumm (M.A., Illinois State University) completed her doctoral candidacy in Communication Studies at the University of Nebraska–Lincoln. She is interested in communicative and redemptive aspects of close relationships, such as relational transgressions, hurtful events, forgiveness, and reconciliation.

Kristen Norwood (Ph.D., University of Iowa) is an Assistant Professor in the Department of English and Communication at Fontbonne University. Her teaching and research interests lie in the areas of interpersonal, family, and gender communication. Her work has examined connections between relational and cultural communication in the contexts of adoption, transgender identity, and motherhood and has been published in journals such as *Communication Monographs*, *Journal of Family Communication*, and *Management Communication Quarterly.*

Clark D. Olson (Ph.D., University of Minnesota) is a Professor in the Hugh Downs School of Human Communication where he has taught for thirty years. He regularly teaches interpersonal theory and research and has published over forty articles and book chapters, winning the National Communication Association's *Golden Monograph* award for his research. He is a Founding Director of the Institute for Civil Dialogue and active as a Master Docent at the Phoenix Art Museum.

Loreen N. Olson (Ph.D., University of Nebraska–Lincoln) is an Associate Professor of Communication at the University of North Carolina–Greensboro. Her publications explore the dark side of close relationships, the communication of deviance, and the luring communication of child sexual predators. Currently, she is examining the relationship between battery and traumatic brain injury and polyvictimization and teen parenting. Olson is co-author of *The Dark Side of Family Communication* and editor of the *Journal of Family Communication.*

Sandra Petronio (Ph.D., University of Michigan) is a Professor in the Department of Communication Studies and the Fairbanks Center for Medical Ethics at Indiana University–Purdue University, Indianapolis, and a National Communication Association Knapp Interpersonal Scholar. Her expertise includes health, interpersonal, and family communication. She has published five books, received NCA's Brommel Award in Family Communication, and published over 100 scholarly articles on privacy, confidentiality, and disclosure. Petronio is the creator and author of Communication Privacy Management theory.

Emily A. Rauscher (Ph.D., University of Missouri–Columbia) is an Assistant Professor in the Department of Communication at Texas A & M University. Her primary research interests include investigating privacy and information management in health and family communication. Her recent work has explored family communication regarding genetic cancer risk, assisted reproductive technologies, and family health history.

Mary E. Rohlfing (Ph.D., University of Iowa) is the Assistant Dean of Social Sciences and Public Affairs at College of Western Idaho. She has studied the role of women in popular music, long-distance friendship, and conflict resolution. For a decade, Rohlfing took a break from academia to start an organic farm. She is excited to be back in higher education as an administrator for a new community college.

Paul Schrodt (Ph.D., University of Nebraska–Lincoln) is the Philip J. and Cheryl C. Burguières Professor of Communication Studies and Graduate Director at Texas Christian University. He studies communicative cognitions and behaviors that facilitate family relationships, focusing on stepfamily functioning. He has authored more than eighty journal articles and book chapters, and received the NCA Brommel Award for Family Communication, the Early Career Award in Interpersonal Communication, and the Dean's Research Award from TCU.

Debra-L Sequeira (Ph.D., University of Washington) is a Professor of Communication and Dean of the College of Arts and Humanities at Seattle Pacific University. Her research focuses on culture and language studies, with articles published in *Text and Performance Quarterly* and *Research on Language and Social Interaction*, among other journals. She has also contributed book chapters in interpersonal communication, interpersonal communication, family communication, cultural communication, and spiritual/religious communication.

Jordan Soliz (PhD, University of Kansas) is an Associate Professor of Communication at the University of Nebraska–Lincoln. His research investigates communication and intergroup processes primarily in family relationships, with a current emphasis on multiethnic-racial families, interfaith families, and grandparent-grandchild relationships. His work has been published in journals such as *Communication Monographs, Communication Quarterly, Journal of Marriage and Family,* and *Journal of Language and Social Psychology*. He is the editor-elect of the *Journal of Family Communication.*

Brian H. Spitzberg (Ph.D., University of Southern California) is Senate Distinguished Professor in the School of Communication at San Diego State University. His primary areas of research involve interpersonal communication skills, jealousy, conflict, coercion, violence, and stalking. He was named a Distinguished Scholar of the Western States Communication Association.

Elizabeth A. Suter (Ph.D., University of Illinois at Urbana–Champaign) is an Associate Professor in the Communication Studies Department at the University of Denver. Keenly interested in family interactions with the social world, her program of research focuses on interactions at familial exterior borders—where family intersects with culture, outsider relationships, and context. Recently she received the Monograph of the Year Award from the GLBTQ Division and Caucus of the National Communication Association.

Paige W. Toller (Ph.D., University of Nebraska–Lincoln) is an Associate Professor in the School of Communication at the University of Nebraska–Omaha. She has been studying communication and grief since writing her masters' thesis in 2000. She teaches courses in interpersonal, family, and small group communication as well as a graduate course in qualitative methods.

Tiffany R. Wang (Ph.D., University of Nebraska–Lincoln) is an Assistant Professor and Basic Course Coordinator in the Department of Communication at the University of Montevallo. She explores communication surrounding college transition within instructional and family contexts. She has authored and co-authored articles in *Communication Education, Communication Reports, The Journal of Continuing Higher Education, Journal of Divorce & Remarriage*, and *Journal of Family Communication*. In 2012, she received the International Communication Association's Outstanding GTA Award.

Sarah E. Wilder (Ph.D., University of Nebraska–Lincoln) is an Assistant Professor of Communication Studies at Luther College. Her research centers on the role of communication within interpersonal relationships during times of unpredictable, stressful, or transitional life events, recently including topics of supportive communication during divorce and widowhood. She has several publications in communication and interdisciplinary journals and enjoys her current service in at-large positions with the Iowa Communication Association and the National Communication Association.

Erin K. Willer (Ph.D., University of Nebraska–Lincoln) is an Assistant Professor in the Department of Communication Studies at the University of Denver. Her research focuses on the communicative management of relational difficulty, including social aggression and reproductive challenges. She has received Top Paper awards from the National Communication Association and the Western States Communication Association and was honored with the Central States Communication Association's Outstanding New Teacher Award in 2013.

Julia T. Wood (Ph.D., University of Pennsylvania) is the Caroline H. and Thomas S. Royster Distinguished Professor of Graduate Education, Emerita and the Lineberger Distinguished Professor of Humanities, Emerita at the University of North Carolina at Chapel Hill. She studies communication in personal relationships and gender, communication, and culture. She has published 100 articles and chapters and authored or edited 25 books. She has received fourteen awards for distinguished scholarship and thirteen teaching awards.

Introduction: Teaching with Case Studies

Julia T. Wood
The University of North Carolina at Chapel Hill

Dawn O. Braithwaite
The University of Nebraska–Lincoln

Imagine two scenarios. First, imagine that you are in an interpersonal communication class and your teacher tells you this: "Romantic partners often experience tension between the desire to be independent and the desire to feel connected."

Now imagine a second scenario. In it, your teacher asks you to read this story: Cecile feels really confused about her relationship with Josh. They've been dating exclusively for six months and for most of that time, they couldn't get enough of each other. All they wanted to do was see each other, talk to each other, be together. But that's changed in the last two weeks. Lately Cecile has sometimes felt crowded by Josh, and she is starting to resent the way that being with him keeps her from being with other friends. She knows they love each other, but she's confused by also wanting time apart. Cecile wonders if it's possible to love someone and not want to be with him all the time. Isn't it inconsistent to want to be with Josh sometimes and to want to be away from him at other times? Cecile wants to tell Josh what she's feeling, but she's not sure what it means or how to talk with him.

Which scenario was more effective in giving you insight into the tension between autonomy and connection that occurs in most interpersonal relationships? In the first scenario you were given the statement that romantic partners often experience tension between wanting independence and wanting connection. You understood the idea and felt confident that you could recall it for a test.

In the second scenario, you read about Cecile's relationship with Josh. Perhaps you could identify with her confusion because you've had similar feelings at times in your own relationships. Perhaps you've wanted some private time or time with other friends while still knowing you love another person and want to sustain an intimate relationship with that person. Perhaps you empathized with Cecile's concern that she wanted to talk to Josh but didn't know how to do so without hurting him.

Did you understand the tension between desires for independence and connection better from the statement in the first scenario or the story in the second one? If you're like most people, each approach offered you distinct insights. The first scenario presented you with conceptual information that is essential to analyzing dynamics of interaction. The second scenario provided you with a rich example of how this tension surfaces in a concrete relationship. It allowed you to see how the abstract idea of tension between desires for connection and autonomy plays out in a real relationship with real people. The story provides a context for understanding conceptual information about tensions between desires for autonomy and connection. It also invites you to participate actively in learning by identifying with Cecile's situation and thinking about what she might do to communicate effectively with Josh.

This book is designed for people who want to learn by exploring conceptual information in real-life situations. The cases in this book invite you to use abstract and conceptual knowledge that is drawn from theory and research to analyze and address concrete circumstances. This is active learning because it requires you to understand how concepts, theories, and principles apply in actual situations. Studying interpersonal dynamics in practical situations develops your skill in applying what you learn to your own relationships. It also helps you expand your personal repertoire of communication choices so that you can adapt effectively to diverse contexts, individuals, and relationships.

This book provides you with case studies that are based on research and theories in the field of communication. Each case was written by one or more people who have studied extensively the particular issues covered in the case. Analyzing the cases allows you to apply concepts, theories, and principles you've read about to concrete, real-life issues, problems, and processes in human relationships. In this opening chapter, our goal is to explain the role of case studies in learning about interpersonal communication. We first describe the tradition of case study as a method of teaching, and we identify distinct pedagogical values of case studies. In the second section of this chapter we link the case method of teaching and learning to narrative theory. Our discussion highlights the richness of a narrative approach to knowledge. The third section of this chapter describes ways you can approach the case studies in this book to enhance your knowledge of interpersonal communication. Finally, we preview the organization of this book, so that you understand why we've arranged cases in a particular sequence, and so that you can decide how you can most effectively learn from case studies in this book.

Case Studies as a Means of Learning

There are many ways to teach and to learn. The most conventional method is lecture. This method is effective in presenting concepts, principles, theories, and research and is most valuable when there are efforts made to *apply* concepts, principles, theories, and research to real-life communication situations. Thus, presentational methods can be effectively supplemented by case studies, which foster rich understandings and practical skills in how to use knowledge.

Robert Diamond, Assistant Vice Chancellor of Syracuse University, asserted that conventional methods of education do not prepare students to function in the real world after they leave college. According to Diamond (1997), students must not only learn information; they must also learn how to *apply it effectively.* According to experts at the Eberly Center for Teaching Excellence & Educational Innovation at Carnegie Mellon University (2014) it is important for students to practice using knowledge from their classes and apply what they learn. In other words, education should help students develop skill in applying knowledge in practical ways. When we really know something, we know how to use it to improve our effectiveness in personal, social, and professional interactions. Management professor Larry Hartman advocates teaching methods that "enable students to learn by doing" so that students leave college with experience in applying "individual communication skills, intellectual skills, and interpersonal skills" (p. 41). Knowledge consists not just of information, but also of insight into how to use it effectively.

Case studies are one means to foster skills in applying knowledge effectively. Case studies are extended descriptions of particular events, situations, and people. A case tells a story, complete with the kinds of details and intricacies that characterize real life. Because cases are narratively rich, they allow us to see the complexities that mark human behavior and to appreciate the different ways that given behaviors might be interpreted. William Naumes, a management professor the University of New Hampshire who teaches about case writing, tells us that a case presents a good story, with a theme that we can think about when we have finished reading it. A good case will help us apply concepts or theories to our everyday lives and teach us about ourselves. Cases also encourage us to identify options for interpretation and behavior and to generate understanding and effective action.

The Case Study Tradition

The case study method of education enjoys a long and distinguished history in many fields. Perhaps the most familiar use of case studies is in religious and moral education. For centuries religious instructors of Ancient Chinese, Hebrew, and Greek used parables to teach moral principles. This tradition persists in contemporary religious teaching—parables figure prominently in Christian, Jewish, Islamic, and Buddhist religious education.

Case studies also have an established place in secular education. Larry Hartman notes that since 1908, law schools have featured case studies prominently in teaching. Cases allow law students to discover how legal theory applies to the intricacies of particular situations. The same is true of business schools, which rely on case studies to teach students how to assess organizations and develop plans for managing public relations, improving efficiency, boosting employee morale, and so forth. Intercultural workshops and training programs also rely heavily on case studies to teach people about diverse customs, assumptions, and expectations in different cultures. Public Administration Programs, such as those at Harvard and the Kennedy School of Government, feature case studies prominently.

The principles that make cases appropriate for training in law, business, and intercultural relations also render cases ideal for learning about communication. Professor Beverly Sypher first published *Case Studies in Organizational Communication* in 1990, which featured realistic cases that allowed students to apply communication concepts to organizational processes. Eileen Berlin Ray, a professor of communication at Cleveland State University, led the way in introducing case studies in teaching about health communication. She edited a book of case studies in health communication in 1993 and three years later she edited a book of case studies in communication and disenfranchisement within the health-care system. The cases in Ray's books give readers complex and useful understandings of multiple and interacting issues in health contexts. Dawn O. Braithwaite and Julia Wood, the editors of this current collection of cases, first published a book of interpersonal communication case studies in 2000, as they wanted to put into action principles of learning by doing in interpersonal communication classes. Teaching with case studies has definitely caught on in the communication discipline, for example, Erika Kirby and Chad McBride (2009) edited *Gender Actualized,* a book of case studies on gendered dynamics in human interaction.

The collection of essays presented herein extends the case study method to the study of interpersonal communication and we note that most of these cases shed light on family communication as well. In it, our goal is to show how theories, concepts, and principles of interpersonal communication operate in realistic situations and relationships.

Values of the Case Study Method

Case studies are widely used educational tools because they have distinct values—ones that are less prominent in conventional methods of education. Three primary values of the case study method are a focus on application to specific situations, ability to represent real-world complexity, and practice in problem solving and management of tensions in human communication.

Application to Specific Situations

A key value of case studies is that they allow students to apply concepts. Doing so allows students to learn how to adapt general principles to specific circumstances in their own and others' lives. For example, contract courses in law school teach students that a contract is "a meeting of minds." That abstract definition, however, cannot teach students what contracts mean—or even when they exist—in particular cases. Is there "a meeting of minds" if one person is intoxicated when a contract is signed? What if a person who signs a contract feels coerced by others? What if a person doesn't understand the binding nature of a contract? Is "a meeting of minds" possible when one person doesn't understand the obligations inherent in a contract? Working with the particularities of specific cases allows law students to appreciate the nuances and complexity of the abstract definition, "a meeting of minds." Working with cases helps law students realize that the abstract definition of "meeting of the minds" must be interpreted to fit multiple details of concrete situations.

Let's consider an example of how case studies can help us learn about communication in interpersonal relationships. Interpersonal communication scholars define self-disclosure as revealing information about oneself that others are unlikely to discover on their own. Yet, knowing this abstract definition doesn't show us what self-disclosure means, or how it takes place, in specific contexts.

Going beyond abstract concepts, a case study helps us analyze self-disclosure within particular settings and under specific conditions. Is it self-disclosure if a woman unintentionally reveals something about herself? Is it self-disclosure if a man who is told something personal by a friend doesn't realize the information is private and not to be shared with anyone else? Is it self-disclosure if a person routinely reveals what most of us would consider very private information to others? Is self-disclosure equally common and does it mean the same thing in cultures that emphasize privacy and in those that emphasize revealing oneself to others?

A case study allows us to look at self-disclosure in particular circumstances. This encourages us to recognize that what self-disclosure means and how it affects relationships across time and contexts. We learn not only what self-disclosure is in an abstract sense, but also how it operates and what it means in specific settings. As a result, we gain a more sophisticated appreciation of self-disclosing communication.

Real-Life Complexity

Another virtue of working with case studies is that they can highlight interaction among aspects of communication. Traditional methods of education introduce students to concepts individually—one concept at a time. This makes it difficult to appreciate how multiple concepts interact, and how they work together to shape what happens in human interaction. Realistic case studies can give us insight into multiple processes and issues that are simultaneously present and interacting in interpersonal communication.

A good case study of self-disclosure provides insight into how self-disclosing and the meaning of doing so are shaped by issues such as trust, relationship history, and self-concepts of communicators. We gain concrete understanding of how people decide when and to whom to reveal private information. We might also learn how self-disclosing affects those who disclose and those who are recipients of disclosure. Does learning another person's secrets increase feelings of closeness? Does disclosure by one person encourage reciprocal disclosure by another person? We might also discover how different responses to self-disclosures—acceptance, disapproval, betraying confidence, reciprocating—affect trust, self-esteem, and willingness to invest more in the relationship.

Because case studies provide layered narratives, they compel us to recognize the complexity of interpersonal communication. They help us realize there are links between self-disclosure and previous interactions in a relationship, as well as what is likely to follow. Case studies can illuminate other issues such as timing, context, and style of communication, and trace how these issues affect self-disclosure and responses to it.

Practice in Diagnosing and Managing Problems

A third value of case studies is that they encourage us to think about how communication can help us deal with interpersonal problems and challenges and improve our relationships. When you examine a case thoughtfully, you can identify patterns of communication that lead to conflict, misunderstanding, or other problems. For example, you might ask whether Cecile and Josh should bring up their feelings with each other instead of trying to understand individually. Are they being dishonest not to share their feelings of wanting time apart? Is the lack of direct communication about feelings fueling resentment toward each other? Once you recognize patterns and their likely consequences, you are able to make more informed choices about which patterns to foster and avoid in your own relationships.

Cases invite you to figure out a way or ways to address problems and deal with the conflicts and tensions that are inevitable in human relationships. You might ask how Cecile could meet her needs for independent time without jeopardizing the relationship. What could she say to Josh to assure him that her desire for time apart doesn't mean she doesn't love him? Thinking about how Cecile and Josh might work out their problem helps you generate practical strategies and skills for analyzing and improving communication in your own interpersonal interactions.

Narrative Theory as a Foundation for Cases

The case method of education is built on the assumption that knowledge can be gained from detailed accounts of people, situations, and events. This assumption is shared by narrative theory, which is well established in the communication discipline. One of the scholars who developed this theory is Walter Fisher, who was a professor at the University of Southern California. Fisher believes that humans are naturally storytelling beings. We tell stories to make sense of our experiences and to share them with others. We listen to others to understand who they are and what their lives are about. According to Fisher, we continuously learn about ourselves, others, and the world through the process of telling and hearing narratives. Interpersonal communication scholar Jody Koenig Kellas (2015) of the University of Nebraska–Lincoln explains that narratives help us understand the ways human build and make sense of their identities (who we are), our relationships, and our lives.

What is a narrative? Most simply defined, it is a good story. A good story involves believable characters who experience events that are organized in a deliberate way to give them coherence and meaning. In addition to providing an ordered presentation of events, stories also involve characters and plots. We encounter people and learn about their motives—why they do what they do. We learn about their backgrounds, goals, fears, and dreams, and all of this information helps us understand their actions. We also see plot lines develop as particular events and interactions make certain lines of future action likely and foreclose others. We see where a character's choice at one point in a story sets the stage for what can and cannot happen later.

Narratives are not just interesting stories. They are carefully constructed accounts, or explanations of human action. They give us insight into why certain things and not others happen and why characters act in particular ways. Narratives are not objective or true in an absolute sense. Rather they make sense from—and only from—particular perspectives. Many narratives are told from one person's point of view, so our insight into the account is shaped by that subjective point of view. Sometimes narratives switch between more than one character's point of view so that we gain insight into different, sometimes conflicting outlooks on what is happening and what it means. Because narratives reflect particular points of view, they teach us about individuals' perspectives on life and interaction. When we really enter into a narrative on its own terms, we gain understanding of how the narrator or character(s) sees the world.

Because narratives reflect specific points of view they have the power to increase our understanding of multiple perspectives and some of the reasons for them. For example, suppose you read a story about a woman who avoids conflict in her relationships. Told from her husband's point of view, the narrative portrays her as closed and unwilling to work through tough issues. His story highlights his frustration when his wife refuses to deal with conflict. The husband's point of view reveals that he has had conflicts in his friendships and in past romantic relationships and he is comfortable confronting them in dialogue.

Told from the wife's point of view, however, the story tells us that she feels paralyzed and profoundly scared when conflict threatens to arise in her marriage. Her story enlightens us about the abuse and violence that regularly erupted in her parents' marriage. We learn how helpless and scared she felt as a child watching vicious episodes between her mother and father. This insight, in turn, might make us more sympathetic to the woman and her reasons for avoiding conflict at all costs.

Which narrative is more accurate—the one reflecting the husband's or wife's point of view? It's not useful to ask whether one story is more accurate in some objective sense. What we need to appreciate is that each narrative gives us insight into how one person feels and why that person acts as she or he does. If we can discover the reasons for each person's feelings, actions, and desires, then we can better understand unsatisfying patterns of communication and how they might be changed.

Case studies allow us to examine how events unfold and how relationships are affected by the choices that people make. What we learn enlarges our understanding of a range of people and the ways they communicate.

In addition, what we learn develops our abilities to analyze communication patterns and processes in our own interactions, so that we can create relationships that are healthy and productive.

Learning from Case Studies

If you have not had classes that feature cases, you may wonder how you should approach this book. Human Resource Management professor George Stevens suggests a three-stage process. First, he advises you to read a case in its entirety to gain an overall understanding of the characters, issues, and context. Set the case aside for a while, then reread it, this time making notes to yourself—perhaps in the margins of the pages. You might use notes to identify communication concepts, principles, and issues, as well as ways of approaching the case. Then put the case aside again so that it's on the back burner of your mind. Finally, read the case a third time and refine the notes that you made on the second reading. Now is the time to elaborate conceptual issues and applications.

After you have thought about a case and made notes on your own, it's a good idea to discuss a case with others. You will discover that you can learn a great deal by exploring others' views of a case—how are their perspectives similar to and different from your own? What do their experiences allow them to see that you didn't notice? Differences in how people perceive cases remind us that the interpretations of communication are personal and subjective. Discussion of a case also allows you to refine your skills in presenting your ideas and responding to those of others. Finally, discussing a case provides an opportunity to broaden your own perspective and your repertoire of communication choices by learning from the unique experiences, insights, and approaches of others.

You may find it useful to let three questions guide your individual analysis of cases and your discussion with others. These questions direct your efforts to apply theories, principles, and concepts. First, ask what each case teaches you about interpersonal communication. Second, ask how and why various people in the case might interpret the situation differently and how each point of view makes sense from a specific individual's perspective. Finally, ask how you might respond to each case if you were in that situation. We'll elaborate how to use each of these questions when reading the cases in this book.

What Does This Case Teach about Interpersonal Communication?

The initial question to ask as you read a case is what it teaches you about interpersonal communication. George Stevens asserts that case studies are extremely effective in providing opportunities to learn how theories and research findings apply to actual situations. As you read each case, ask whether it emphasizes a particular theory, concept, or set of concepts, communication principle, or relational process? When you can identify the conceptual focus of the case, ask what you learn. Do you gain a better understanding of a concept such as self-disclosure? How is your understanding enlarged? What do you now know that you didn't before reading the case? What questions remain unanswered?

When thinking about what you learn from a particular case, also ask yourself how issues in this case relate to ones presented in other cases and to other topics you've discussed in your class. As we noted earlier in this chapter, in interpersonal communication multiple issues are simultaneously present and interacting. Looking for connections among issues and concepts will lead you to recognize the complexities of interpersonal relating. For example, Case 1 focuses on decisions about keeping or changing names upon marrying. How might this topic be linked to issues of managing the desire for privacy with openness that a newly married couple faces that are covered in Case 13? Can you identify connections *between* patterns of development in stepfamilies, covered in Case 10, and efforts to balance needs for family and work that are discussed in Case 15? Having the cases available to you electronically may facilitate your ability to search between and compare different cases and different concepts highlighted in the cases.

Can I Understand Alternative Perspectives on Interpersonal Communication in This Case?

The second question that should guide your reading of cases is whether you can understand alternative perspectives presented in the case. This is critical because understanding different, sometimes conflicting perspectives is one of the main skills of effective interpersonal communicators. You may not *agree* with all perspectives, and that's okay. The point is for you to understand different points of view and the reasons behind them. This gives you insight into people who think, act, and feel differently than you do. Thus, it enlarges your understanding of human communication.

Understanding alternative perspectives on situations also helps you communicate more effectively, especially with people who differ from you. In our earlier example, did you identify more with the husband who was frustrated by his wife's avoidance of conflict or the wife who perceived conflict as frightening and dangerous? Can you stretch to understand the perspective with which you didn't originally identify? If so, then you increase your ability to recognize, respect, and deal constructively with orientations to conflict that are unlike your own. In turn, this makes it more likely that you can communicate effectively with people who do not share your views of what conflict means and how to deal with it.

How Might I Address the Problem in This Case?

The case studies in this book offer you opportunities to generate concrete ways to address common problems in interpersonal relationships. As you read the cases, ask how you might deal with the tensions or problems presented. What would you tell Cecile she should do about her feelings of claustrophobia in the relationship with Josh? What would you advise the husband and wife about how to manage their conflicts constructively?

Your ideas for approaching interpersonal communication problems should reflect what you've learned in the course this book accompanies. Thinking about how to address the issues in cases is an opportunity for you to apply the concepts you've learned and to see how they can be used to improve interpersonal communication.

Your ideas for managing or resolving problems should also respect the perspective of each person in the case. Interpersonal literally means *between* people. Thus, interpersonal communication problems occur between people. They involve more than one person. By extension, effective resolutions of problems must also involve more than one person. We would be unwise to suggest the wife should simply recognize that couples need to deal with their conflicts. This advice ignores her deep-seated fear of conflict, so it's likely to be ineffective in changing conflict patterns. That advice might even make her feel guilty, which could create further problems in the marriage.

For the same reason, it's not helpful to suggest the husband should simply accept his wife's inability to confront conflict, since that neglects his need to talk about problems in the marriage. This would do nothing to relieve his frustration and would not help the couple learn to deal with their conflicts constructively. A good approach to the situation would begin with respect for both the husband's and wife's feelings and perspectives. Following that, it would be effective to make communication choices that reflect respect for both perspectives.

It's important to realize that there is seldom only one good way to address problems in interpersonal communication. Usually there are multiple, potentially constructive approaches to addressing problems in human relationships. An important value of discussing cases with others is that you increase your awareness of alternative ways of resolving tensions and keeping relationships healthy and enjoyable.

Extending Cases in the Classroom

There are additional ways you can work with the cases in this book to sharpen your skills in applying your conceptual knowledge to real-life situations. One option is to rewrite a case so that choices made early in it are revised to lead to different outcomes later in the case. How might a different response to anger or disclosure affect what happens between people in a case? A variation on this is to enact a case and to stop it at key points, so that you can create alternative trajectories for the story. You might stop a case at a key juncture and have one or more characters make different choices about how to communicate. Then you can follow through by enacting what might happen given the different choices. A third option is to write a continuation of a case. Working individually or with others in your class, you might compose the next chapter in a case to explore what is likely to happen, given what you know about the characters, situation, context, and choices made so far in the case.

The Organization of This Book

The cases in this book reflect current theories and research about human communication processes. The cases are organized into five topical areas that represent major foci of research and theory in the communication field. Within each area, the cases follow a standard format that is designed to facilitate your analysis.

Grouping of Case Studies

The cases in this book are organized into five major sections. The first set of case studies focuses on how we use communication to announce, negotiate, and alter personal identity. Each case in this section of the book presents you with a specific situation in which identity is at stake. One chapter, for example, explores the issue of whether to change one's name upon marrying. Another case explores how families deal with a member who changes her or his gender identity. These two cases, as well as others in Section I, ask you to think seriously about how communication shapes and reflects personal identity, and to consider how communication changes in response to changes in our identities over our lifetimes.

The second section of the book presents cases involving communication during the process of developing closeness. How does communication help us define our relationships, negotiate needs for autonomy and connection, and deal with gender-related differences in interaction style? These are among the issues that we examine in the section focused on the evolution of friendships and romantic intimacy.

In the third section of the book we consider common communication processes in established and ongoing relationships. One case highlights some of the issues involved in balancing career and family commitments. Another case illuminates the ways in which intimates use rituals to sustain intimacy in long-term relationships.

The fourth section of the book focuses on the dark side of interpersonal relationships. The cases in this section deal with issues such as acquaintance rape, stalking, and racial-ethnic biases. Each case allows you to appreciate complex communication processes that operate when relationships are troubled by major crises. These cases also invite you to think about ways to avoid serious problems in relationships you are building and how you might deal with problems and their aftermath in other relationships in your life.

In the final section of the book we provide cases that show how communication changes over time in long-term relationships. The case of caring for a parent reveals how parent–child communication patterns alter when a child assumes the role of caregiver for a parent. Another case in this section illustrates some of the communication patterns that are typical in long-lasting friendships. These cases provide insight into the dynamics of enduring bonds.

The five sections in this book provide you with in-depth narratives of communication processes and problems that are common in the various relationships in our lives. Studying them will help you make sense of your own past and present interactions, and to anticipate ones that may be part of your future. In addition, studying these cases should enhance your understanding of others' perspectives so that you gain an appreciation of the multiple ways people communicate and interpret what happens between them.

Format of Individual Case Studies

Each case is written by one or more scholars who have expertise in the particular topic of the case. This means that although the cases are presented as stories, they reflect theory and data from research. Thus, in reading the cases you will learn what has been discovered by scholars who investigate human communication.

To facilitate your study, all of the cases in this book follow a standard format. The authors open the cases with a list of keywords to alert you to communication concepts, theories, and principles that are embedded in the case. Then authors present a focused narrative that sheds light on a particular topic in interpersonal communication. Typically, the authors create a story that allows you to understand what different people in the story feel, think, or perceive what is happening, and how they interact in that particular circumstance.

Following the case, the authors pose a few questions to guide your analysis and discussion of the case. The questions that follow each case need not limit your reflection and discussion. In other words, the questions at the end of each chapter should stimulate your thinking, but not restrict it. Feel free to explore issues beyond those raised in the questions we pose.

Each case concludes with a short list of references. These references are not comprehensive bibliographies of research in an area. Instead, they highlight primary research that is reflected in the case they accompany. These references will lead you to further information about particular topics that interest you.

We hope that studying the cases in this book will prove valuable to you as you seek to learn more about human communication in your life and the lives of others.

References

Ambrose, S., Bridges, M., DePietro, M., Lovett, M., Norman, M., & Meyer, R. (2010). *How learning works: Seven research-based principles for smart teaching.* San Francisco, CA: Jossey Bass.

Diamond, R. (1997, 1 August). Broad curriculum reform is needed if students are to master core skills. *Chronicle of Higher Education,* p. B7.

Eberly Center for Teaching Excellence & Educational Innovation (2014). Theory and research- based principles of learning. Carnegie Mellon University. Downloaded May 8, 2014, from: http://www.cmu.edu/teaching/principles/learning.html

Eisenhardt, K. M. (1989). Building theories from case study research. *Academy of Management Review, 5,* 501–508.

Fisher, W. (1984). Narration as a human communication paradigm: The case of public moral argument. *Communication Monographs, 51,* 1–22.

Fisher, W. (1987). *Human communication as narration: Toward a philosophy of reason, value, and action.* Columbia, SC: University of South Carolina Press.

Hartman, L. D. (1992). Business communication and the case method: Toward integration in accounting and MBA graduate programs. *The Bulletin, 55,* 41–45.

Kellas, J. K. (2015). Narrative theories; Making sense of interpersonal communication. In D. O. Braithwaite & P. Schrodt (Eds.), *Engaging theories in interpersonal communication: Multiple perspectives* (2nd ed., pp. 249–262).Thousand Oaks, CA: Sage.

Kirby, E., & McBride, C. (Eds.). (2009). *Gender actualized: Cases in communicatively constructing realities.* Dubuque, IA: Kendall Hunt.

Naumes, W. (2006). *Art and craft of case writing.* Armonk, NY: Sharpe Reference.

Ray, E. B. (1993). (Ed.). *Case studies in health communication.* Mahwah, NJ: Lawrence Erlbaum.

Ray, E. B. (1996). (Ed.). *Case studies in communication and disenfranchisement: Applications to social health issues.* Mahwah, NJ: Lawrence Erlbaum.

Stevens, G. E. (1996). *Cases and exercises in human resource management.* Chicago, IL: Richard D. Irwin.

Sypher, B. D. (Ed.). (1990). *Case studies in organizational communication.* New York, NY: Guilford.

Thomas, G. (2011). A typology for the case study in social science following a review of definition, discourse and structure. *Qualitative Inquiry*, *17*, 511–521.

PART I

Negotiating Personal Identity in Relationships

1

What's in a Name? Negotiating Marital Name Changes

Karen A. Foss

Belle A. Edson

Jennifer A. Linde

Keywords

commitment, decision making, marriage, names, relational perceptions, self-disclosure, self-identity, conflict styles

Madeline Anderson took a sip of her iced tea and sighed. It still amazed her that this man who sat across the table smiling and speaking casually in Spanish to the server was going to be her husband in less than six months. "Husband" seemed like such a strong label to assign him. Did that automatically make her a "wife"? Weren't they more like "partners" in this new phase of their relationship? What did all these words mean? She gazed absentmindedly at the closed menu in front of her, certain that she could order the Frontier Special in Spanish if she really wanted to try. Perhaps it was easier to let Martín do the ordering and save herself the embarrassment of sounding too much like a Minnesota girl trying to roll her "r's." She missed the time that she and Martín had when they first started dating: time for impromptu Spanish lessons, time for easy conversation, and time for lots of flirting. But Madeline also cherished the changes in their relationship over the last two years. Martín Romero had become many things to Madeline—classmate, friend, Spanish teacher, confidant, lover, and partner—and soon he would be her husband.

Another sigh escaped her lips, and this time, Martín caught her eye and winked. Madeline wondered how he could read her mind so easily. She wondered how he knew her as well as he did. It seemed to her that her parents were such strangers to one another, even after 26 years of marriage, even after living in the same house together for all that time. She marveled that she and Martín already had a way of relating that seemed absent from her parents' marriage. Madeline knew that her ability to share her feelings with Martín and to listen, argue and work at communicating had not come from her upbringing; she wondered where she had learned it. She certainly had discovered herself in these four years of college, and she felt a twinge of sadness (and maybe fear?) that graduation was just a month away. Soon she'd be saying good-bye to the routine of the University of New Mexico and the beautiful Albuquerque sunsets. There were so many changes on the horizon.

Martín: Is it that serious? (Madeline was startled out of her thoughts.)

Madeline: What?

Martín: You stopped smiling a few minutes ago, and now you look far too preoccupied for a Friday night. Is everything OK?

Madeline: Yup. What am I eating tonight?

Martín: Cartón y plátanos. [Cardboard and bananas].

Madeline: That sounds delicious. Does it come with jalapeños?

Martín: (laughing) Your Spanish is awful—remind me again why I'm marrying you.

Madeline: I'm going to make a lot of money.

Martín: That's right! Within a year, you'll be the head of engineering for some big company, and I'll get a job in a nearby school district. Then we'll have four babies, and my mother will come to visit frequently.

Madeline: Do you expect me to make a mother-in-law joke now? I'm sorry, sweetie, but I like your mother. She can come visit us anytime she wants.

Martín: That's good—because she and Dad are coming up from Socorro next weekend.

Madeline: Cool. Are they staying with us?

Martín: No, they'll stay at Aunt Yolanda's. Mom doesn't want to acknowledge that you and I are living together, and this is her way of dealing with it.

Madeline: I can stay with a friend for the weekend if it bothers them.

Martín: I've told you I'm not going to lie to them. Besides, I don't think it really offends them; it's just all that Catholic guilt.

Madeline: How come *you* don't have it?

Martín: I'm just a weekend Catholic.

Madeline: I still don't understand what you mean by that.

Martín: Do Lutherans go to mass on Wednesdays and Saturdays?

Madeline: We don't have mass.

Martín: (laughing) You engineers are so literal. My point is that if I were a full-fledged Catholic, I'd be in church a lot more during the week. (After a short pause) Sometimes I actually miss it.

Madeline: Martín, are you really okay about getting married in my church?

Martín: I'm okay with everything, *mi amor*: a chilly fall wedding in St. Paul, hoards of passionate Romeros doing the wedding dance to the rhythm of a polka band, *mi abuelo* bonding with your grandfather and inviting him to come spend winters in Española, and a quaint Norwegian wedding cake made by your cousins Uffda and Lefse.

Madeline found herself laughing loudly at Martín's descriptions. She knew that it was his way of letting her know that he intended to make the best of this Midwest-meets-Southwest wedding. They had been planning the wedding since January, and both were tired of the stress. At times it seemed like more hassle than it needed to be, and she and Martín had certainly had a few arguments because of it.

Madeline hated conflict. She remembered their first huge fight and how sick to her stomach she had felt. Martín seemed so comfortable with expressing emotion, probably a result of being raised by parents who encouraged their children to talk and work through problems. Martín still called his sister every weekend in San Francisco and often drove to Socorro during the week to go to his little brother's baseball games. In both relationships, she had noticed open displays of affection and displeasure. Madeline wondered if it bothered Martín that she often side-stepped disagreements. He was pretty good at drawing her out, and she was working on being more direct about expressing herself—but she hated to make him responsible for guessing her feelings.

And that made her remember something she had been avoiding. For several weeks, she had been wondering how to talk to him about keeping her family name, Anderson, when they married. In her typically conflict-avoidant style, Madeline had not told Martín that she had made her final decision about this topic. The first time she had mentioned it, he had been angry and hurt, and Madeline had no reason to believe that he would have changed his mind from that initial conversation. Madeline grinned at Martín as he finished his entertaining description of their wedding and decided that now was as good a time as any to bring up the name issue.

Madeline: Martín, since we're on the subject of the wedding, there's something I want to talk to you about, something that's been on my mind.

Martín: Okay.

Madeline: I know we talked about this briefly before, and I know how you feel about it, but I've decided to keep my name when we get married.

Martín: (pausing) Okay . . .

Madeline: It's not that I don't like your name—you *know* that I really love the name Romero. It's just that it's not *my* name.

Martín: All right.

Madeline: (pausing) Is that all you're going to say?

Martín: I'm just a little surprised. I thought that we had made a decision about this when we talked about it before. Is it because you want to keep your name for professional situations?

Madeline: Yes, that's part of it. But, honestly I don't want to change my name at all. I've given it a lot of thought, and I've talked to a lot of my friends about it. I hope you're not hurt by this.

Martín: Yeah, it hurts a little but that's not really the point, Maddy. I'm just trying to figure out why. Why don't you want to have my name?

Madeline: We've had this conversation before! It isn't about not wanting *yours*; it's because I don't want to give up *mine*.

Martín: Why? Because it's a hassle to change your driver's license, credit cards, and passport? Sorry if taking my name is such a hassle.

Madeline: God, Martín, I'm not *that* shallow! This has nothing to do with convenience. I don't want to change my name because I don't know who I would be if I wasn't Madeline Anderson.

Martín: You'd be Madeline Romero.

Madeline: Exactly. I don't know who that is.

Martín took a deep breath and tried to control the fear that was creeping into him. The idea of Madeline not changing her name bothered him more than he wanted to admit. If she didn't want his name, what else didn't she want? His mind was racing with a thousand questions and a thousand reasons not to ask them. Maybe Madeline wasn't ready for this commitment, maybe he had rushed her into getting married too soon, maybe they didn't know each other as well as he thought. He really thought that they had made this decision together. Why was she suddenly changing her mind?

Martín's love for Madeline was very much a part of his wanting to marry and raise a family with her. He felt lucky to have grown up with parents who still laughed together and played and held hands in public. He liked the idea of marriage and the goal of building a life together. He had met Madeline in a rock climbing class at UNM during their sophomore year, and he could still recall how funny and smart and beautiful she was to him that semester. There was no doubt in his mind that she was the one he wanted to be with for life.

His family had been very supportive, and even his abuela had gotten past the idea that he was going to marry an Anglo. Martín's stomach dropped at the thought of having to explain this to his mother and grandmother. He didn't want them to think that Madeline did not love him, or that she did not fully embrace his family. He knew that he needed to ask Madeline a very difficult question.

Martín: Madeline, do you really want to spend your life married to me?

Madeline: Of course I do! Martín, this isn't about *us* and our future together. I simply want to keep my name because it represents who *I am,* just as your name represents who you are.

Martín: So you think being an individual is more important than being in a relationship?

Madeline: I didn't say that! I want our marriage to be a partnership of two individuals; our relationship adds to who we are without taking anything away. I'm just trying to tell you that I've worked hard to create Madeline Anderson, and I don't want to throw all that away.

Martín: By marrying me?

Madeline: (loudly) That is ridiculous! I'm having a hard enough time talking about this without your questioning my commitment to you. My name is simply important to who I am—that's all. You don't even have to think about your name—you know you'll keep it. Why should it be any different for me?

Martín: Don't get so angry!

Madeline: Well, I think you're being pretty selfish.

Martín: Ditto.

Madeline: (after a pause) Let's just talk about this, okay?

Martín: Maddy, I'm trying very hard not to let this bother me, and I'm not really sure why I feel so upset—but I do. I guess there are a few issues around this that we need to talk about.

Madeline: (taking his hand across the table) I'm ready to listen.

Martín: I'm worried that my family will see this as you not accepting our culture. My grandmother thinks women should use the traditional Spanish "de" when they get married.

Madeline: Madeline de Romero?

Martín: (laughing) No, you would be called Madeline Elaine Anderson de Romero. See, you could keep Anderson! Don't a lot of women just keep their family name as their middle name? Is that an option? Madeline Anderson Romero.

Madeline: It would take me forever to sign checks!

Martín: I love my *abuelita*, and I want her to accept you.

Madeline: (speaking softly) Just like I love my grandparents. Do you see how remaining Madeline *Anderson* is one way I can honor them? What else are you concerned about?

Martín: I'm wondering what our friends will think. Won't they think it's pretty weird?

Madeline: Some might, but most of my girlfriends agree with me about this—at least my college friends do.

Martín: You're kidding! What is this, some kind of female conspiracy? How come guys aren't in on the conversation?

Madeline: (with a smile) It's just our way of taking over the world. Keeping our names is simply the beginning. Our next move will be to stop wearing make-up and tight shoes . . . maybe we'll even stop shaving our legs!

Martín: Hmmm . . .

Madeline: Seriously, though. Women think about it because they have to make a decision about it—and men don't. Well, I guess gay men do now that marriage is legal in so many states. I wonder what gay and lesbian couples do with their names? Do they just pick one? That gives us an interesting choice—you could become Martín Anderson!

Martín: Very funny.

Madeline: Actually, I'm serious. It is an option, just as both of us taking a completely new name is, or both of us hyphenating our names.

Martín: Rob and Paul are hyphenating their names when they get married in New York this year, but the big difference is that they don't plan to have children. What about our children? Whose name will they have?

Madeline: Yours, or maybe both of ours. Or we can give the girls my name and the boys yours. Or we can give our children a totally different name than ours, like Elizabeth and Jonathan did. Can't we figure that out when we have them? Or maybe they could choose a name when they get older? What do you think?

Martín: Madeline, as much as I want to swallow all this and tell you I understand, I just can't. I don't think this is just your decision to make, and I don't think you've considered all the angles. I'm sorry.

Martín wondered if Madeline truly wanted to know what he was thinking. He took pride in the fact that he was open and honest with her most of the time, but on this occasion he was beginning to feel that raw honesty was just going to get him into trouble. He wanted Madeline to have his name; it was that simple. Yet, he also understood her desire to stick with Anderson. He had taken a gender and communication class last semester where this very topic had come up. His professor had talked about how men had an invisible male privilege that felt attacked by gains that women were making in society. Some of the women in the class talked about how they felt that keeping their name was a way of keeping their marriages more equal. He remembered being a bit confused by the idea that privilege could be "invisible." He also recalled thinking that those women were pretty radical thinkers and that he was really happy that Maddy planned to take his name. Funny how life comes back to bite you sometimes!

Martín was having a hard time sorting out his feelings. He certainly didn't want Madeline or anyone else to think that he associated marriage with ownership or that she was not important as an individual, but he also saw this move as one that would destroy yet another tradition that men and women were used to sharing. Martín hated that. He thought that the loss of rituals was a danger to modern society, and he didn't want to participate in such a loss.

Madeline and Martín sat silently eating their meal. Each felt hurt and confused, and neither felt closer to a solution.

For Further Thought and Reflection

1. In what ways do Martin and Madeline use language to persuade or influence one another?
2. What are the reasons Madeline and Martín give for their married-name preferences?
3. Considering both Madeline's and Martín's perspectives, what are the possible decisions this couple might make? How might they best communicate about this situation?
4. In what ways do married-name choices suggest different styles of marriage relationships? Identify the characteristics of marriage for Martín and for Madeline.
5. To what degree do cultural influences affect married-name choices?

6. Why do "most" but not all of Madeline's girlfriends support her decision? How might demographics such as age, geographical location, and educational level influence this decision?
7. What issues of power and control are playing out between the couple in their relational decision-making process? What influence might "invisible male privilege" have on Martin's position?
8. How might current changes in same-sex marriage laws affect heterosexual marital name change decisions? Are there other societal practices and laws that may have an effect on these decisions?
9. How have the women (and men) in your family handled the issue of married names? Are there particular practices in your family that have become traditional for women when they marry?

References

Boxer, D., & Gritsenko, E. (2005). Women and surnames across cultures: Reconstituting identity in marriage. *Women and Language, 28*(2), 1–11.

Clarke, V., Burns, M., & Burgoyne, C. (2008). Who would take whose name? Accounts of naming practices in same-sex relationships. *Journal of Community & Applied Social Psychology 18,* 420–439.

Duggan, D. A., Cota, A. A., & Dion, K. L. (1993). Taking the husband's name: What might it mean? *Names 41*, 87–102.

Foss, K. A., & Edson, B. A. (1989). What's in a name? Accounts of married women's name choices. *Western Journal of Speech Communication 53*, 356–373.

Goldin, C., & Shim, M. (2004). Making a name: Women's surnames at marriage and beyond. *Journal of Economic Perspectives 18*, 143–160.

Gooding, G. E., & Kreider, R. M. (2010). Women's marital naming choices in a nationally representative sample. *Journal of Family Issues* 31, 681–701.

Kerns, M. (2011). North American women's surname choice based on ethnicity and self-identification as feminists. *Names: A Journal of Onomastics 59,* 104–117.

Kline, S. L., Stafford, L., & Miklosovic, J. C. (1996). Women's surnames: Decisions, interpretations and associations with relational qualities. *Journal of Social and Personal Relationships 13*, 593–617.

Lillian, D. L. (2009). Social and regional variation in women's marital surname choices. The LACUS Forum, *34,* 147–156.

Scheuble, L. K., & Johnson, D. R. (2005). Married women's situational use of last names: An empirical study. *Sex Roles 53*, 143–153.

Suter, E. A. (2004). Tradition never goes out of style: The role of tradition in women's naming practices. *Communication Review 7,* 57–87.

2

The Whole Package: Commodifying the Self

Naomi Johnson

Keywords

self-concept, consumption, marketing, mass media, celebrity culture

Ashley swept through her bedroom door, saucily placed her hand on her outthrust hip, and turned sideways for her best "red carpet" pose. She had learned the pose from her older sister Rachel's sorority pictures that were posted on Facebook. Rachel told Ashley the "tea cup" pose helped create a "skinny arm" and made you look thinner in pictures.

"What do you think, girls?"

Ashley's best friends Suzie, Brittney, and Heather gazed at her and considered her question.

Brittney nodded in affirmation and sounded her approval. "Hot. Definitely a 10. That'll get Jake's attention!"

Suzie bit her lip. "I'm not so sure. Don't you think the skirt is a little . . . short? And maybe the stockings are a bit . . . over the line."

Ashley stomped her foot and sighed. "But, I'm not wearing them with heels, so it's not skanky. Look, it's Homecoming, so you're allowed to be a bit 'over the line,' Suzie! How else will I get Jake's attention?"

Ashley personally thought Suzie's Japanese parents made her a bit too conservative when it came to dressing.

"Yeah, it's just like in Cinderella—a little wave of the wand and *booya* —a sparkly dress, new shoes, and, then *bam*—the love of a prince!" proclaimed Brittany.

Suzie rolled her eyes. "That's a movie. This is real life in Columbus, Ohio. Not exactly Disney. Besides, don't you remember that stupid Taylor Swift 'You Belong to Me' video that played over and over while we were in middle school? You get more attention for being an everyday girl in jeans than by trying to look like all sexy."

Heather finally piped up. "Is that your new Abercrombie skirt? That is fetch."

Ashley felt a small surge of pleasure from Heather's approval. She had just found the skirt with *the tags still on* at the Goodwill, but felt no need to let her friends know that it wasn't brand new from the store. Ashley didn't like for her friends to know that she couldn't keep up with their spending. Ever since her parents had gotten divorced, Ashley's mom had cut back on how much Ashley could spend on clothes. Her mom was always lecturing her about how it was all marketing anyhow, that Wal-Mart's clothes were the same as anyone else's. Ashley didn't care how many Miley Cyrus and Max Azaria lines of jeans there were at Wal-Mart. It still didn't make it *cool* to shop there.

Ashley's family's newly reduced financial status was why she had suggested this sleepover with her friends to celebrate her 14th birthday. Before the divorce, one of the girls' favorite activities had been shopping and a movie. But now it was streaming Netflix movies and listening to Pandora at home. Ashley mentally shrugged. She didn't mind it much really. The girls had spent the evening watching funny YouTube videos and chatting about high school life and the boys they liked, which had led to discussions about what to wear to Homecoming. This was the girls' first year of high school and they were looking forward to their first *real* dance with high school boys instead of a bunch of middle-school nerds.

Heather, suddenly distracted from the discussion, turned up the volume on the first *Twilight* movie that was playing on Ashley's laptop on the corner of the dresser. "Shhhh . . . this is my favorite part, where Edward carries her up the tree and they almost kiss!"

Ashley suffered a small pang of envy as Heather's attention moved away from her to the boy on the screen.

"See, Bella is a simple jeans kind of girl, and both Jacob *and* Edward want her." Suzie interjected, unwilling to relinquish the point.

Brittany jumped in, "Oh my God! Aren't you *sick* of the whole *Twilight* thing by now? I mean, Bella has no personality. She just walks around getting rescued by Edward all the time when he's not threatening to hurt her until she gives up her life to become a vampire. Doesn't sound like a good relationship to me."

Heather laughed and pointed to her old, but still favorite, Hot Topic hoodie emblazoned in glitter with the words "Stupid Lamb," referencing Bella's characterization of herself from the first novel.

"Put me firmly in the Team Edward camp," Heather said with a grin, alluding to the popular "Team Edward" or "Team Jacob" Burger King advertising campaign that had sparked hot debates at their school about whether Bella should date Edward or Jacob. "Give me a boy that sparkles. I'd wear jeans and become a vampire anytime to be with him."

Brittany snickered and threw a pillow at Heather. "You *would* say that!"

Ashley smiled and looked over her friends. They were all different, but she loved how their differences didn't pull them apart. They had been best friends since the sixth grade. They all teased each other over these differences at times, but they also shared their deepest secrets, laughed together, and supported each other when times were rough.

Suzie, whose real name was Setsuko, had been Columbus Middle School's top sprinter. She and her mother currently were training to run in a marathon later in the fall, and Suzie was hoping to make the high school track team. A sporty girl, Suzie favored Nike tennis shoes and Under Armor workout gear over the type of sparkly shirt that Heather preferred. However, underneath all that, Suzie liked to be a little bit girly, too. Ashley knew for a fact from their shopping expeditions that Suzie favored Victoria Secret's Pink line of bras and underwear. "After all," Suzie had once reasoned to the group during a shopping expedition, "even though nobody sees them, I still like to feel pretty." She merely ignored it when Heather had wisecracked back in a sing-songy voice, "Sure it's not so you can look sexy for Kelvin?"

Thinking back on it, Ashley realized that this was a perfect example of how much Heather had changed over the last year. Among themselves, she, Suzie, and Brittany had voiced some worries about this change in their friend. Heather didn't know this, but some of Suzie's friends from the track team had received a picture yesterday on Snapchat of Heather walking into school with the caption "Heather the Hussy."

Ashley had admired Heather's beautiful figure ever since they were 12 and Heather's curves started filling out. To the envy of her friends and the often not-so-subtle admiration of some of their male classmates, Heather had the largest breasts of the four girls—a 34C cup, in fact. (Ashley knew this from that Victoria Secret shopping trip and late night girlfriend chats.) Lately, Heather had taken to showing her breasts off in form fitting t-shirts as she had gone quite "boy crazy" (as she herself termed it). At the moment, Heather was especially fond of her latest t-shirt acquisition from Aeropostale that proclaimed, "Hello, My Name is Hottie." Actually, the older, more generously proportioned Hot Topic hoodie Heather currently was wearing showed how much her tastes had changed. Now, Heather typically preferred the "preppy," yet "sexy" looks of Aeropostale or Abercrombie. "If I mix a little naughty with nice, it shows that I'm unpredictable!" she had once confided to Ashley.

Heather's reputation for her clothing choices at school was spreading beyond just the students. Even the teachers were noticing. Just last week, Heather had been sent home to change because she was in violation of the school dress code with her lacy black shirt over a red cami. Ashley had been nervous because she just so happened to have worn a similar lace shirt that day, but hers was white over a more modest blue cami. No one had made a remark about Ashley's choice of an outfit, but maybe that was because she didn't have half the bod that Heather had to fill it out. Really, it didn't seem fair at all, Ashley thought. No one cared about how much flesh the boys could show, but the girls had to wear shorts or skirts that were longer than their fingertips, and couldn't wear "revealing" tops.

Brittany took a bite of the Atkins diet bar that appeared to be her dinner for the evening. "Hey, don't you have some *Seventeens* or *Cosmos* or something? They might have some ideas for how to do our hair," Brittany suggested, interrupting Ashley's reverie.

Brittany, the fashionista of the group, could always be counted on to be "on trend." Brittany was going places. She was writing for the school paper's Style section regularly, even though she was only a first year student. An aspiring fashion designer, Brittany read fashion magazines and followed websites like gURL.com and teenvogue.com religiously for the latest celebrity looks (and gaffes!). Brittany's work had paid off in a big way. Recently, a local marketing company called Ally had started asking for *her* opinion on their latest teen tastes. Once a month, Brittany met with other "cool hunters" (as Ally termed them), talked about the latest teen trends, and gave opinions on new lines of clothing and electronics. Ally even let her keep some of the products as a thank-you for her expertise! Then she would post her inside knowledge, pictures, and videos on her Tumblr account, "All Girl." Even though she had only set up the account a few months ago, Brittany already had nearly 400 followers! Brittany wasn't just about fashion, though. Ashley could always depend on her for good advice on everything from parents to school to relationships.

"Suzie, since Heather is *obviously* busy, why don't you see what you can pull up on your iPad? Try gURL.com—they've got some good quizzes that'll be just what we need."

While Suzie started searching on her iPad, Ashley pulled out her magazines. Miley Cyrus, Selena Gomez, Ashley Benson, Taylor Swift, and other stars gazed back at her with perfect hair, make-up, and features. The covers promised some answers to match these looks: "Diet Makeover: 10 Ways to a Healthier *Hotter* Body!" "5 Secret Celebrity Beauty Tips!" "Kissing 101—Get smoochable lips!"

"Which boob is bigger?" Suzie seriously intoned, staring at her cell phone screen.

"What!" shrieked Ashley.

"Oh, my God. What is up with you?" giggled Heather.

"Hey, Brittany said she wanted to take a quiz. That's what gURL.com wants to know. Is it right, left, or I don't know?"

Brittany grabbed the iPad. "Stay focused here, girls. We've got a mission to make Ashley Jake-presentable."

Brittany ignored the ads for Spanx body shapers, Playtex Sport tampons, and a *Seventeen* magazine contest entry for a shopping spree that appeared on the screen. She paused to check out the newest Miley Cyrus video that began playing in the corner of the screen with information about the latest song downloads. Brittany liked the lace-up Chloé boots that Miley was sporting. She made a mental note to look them up on celebritystyle.com and post the link to the store that sold them on her next Tumblr post.

"Oh, ew. I am soooo over Miley!" protested Suzie when the laptop began playing the song.

"I like her!" countered Ashley. "You're just mad because that app I sent you last week said that the Disney star that you're most like is Hannah Montana, and now that she's grown up, she's totally different. She can't be Hannah Montana forever you know."

"Yeah, well, she was only 16 when she was dancing on a pole at the Teen Choice Awards. Never mind her whole twerking and tongue-wagging thing at the VMA's. That's just nasty!" Suzie retorted.

"You know, my Mom takes twerking and pole-dancing classes at her gym. It's not like it's just for strippers or celebrities or something. It can be for exercise for us ordinary people too," Heather chimed in. Just for effect, she jumped up, straddled a nearby floor lamp, and thrust her hips a few times while sticking out her tongue. "There, my workout is done!"

Suzie looked uncomfortable. Ashley's pulse jumped a beat, and she quickly looked away.

"Okay, this will work," Brittany declared with satisfaction and entered the "gURL games" section that asked "Which celebrity hairstyle best fits your personality?" She logged into her gURL account so that the site would automatically send her the results with links to e-coupons on the various companies' websites for the products necessary to create the ideal look.

Meanwhile, Suzie contemplated the latest *Cosmopolitan.* As usual, most of the models were white and didn't look anything like her.

"Hey, Ashley, what do you think of this? It says here that they recommend L'Oreal Perfect Curves cream to make smooth waves. You can use it to do this 'party ponytail.' That would look cute, but not like you're trying too hard." Suzie pointed to the product reviews and styling tips in the "Celebrate your Inner Diva" article while Ashley glanced at the Pantene ad on the adjoining page.

Ashley frowned and contemplated the choices her friends were laying out.

Getting Ready for the Dance

Ashley stared into her closet, but nothing seemed quite right. Her mom always talked about how good girls didn't need to look trashy to get a date. But, on the other hand, her mom was kind of old-fashioned. Did she really want to get fashion advice from her *mom,* of all people? Ashley thought about the products that Brittney had recommended for a sleek, smooth ponytail and pulled out the Spanx slimmer that Brittney had lent so that she could avoid "unsightly bulges" or the dreaded VPI (visible panty line). Of course, Ashley hadn't told her friend that she couldn't afford to buy the more expensive Bumble and Bumble hair glaze that Brittney swore by and recommended.

As she stared into her closet, Ashley contemplated the outfits and hairstyles the girls had worked out during the slumber party. Now that she actually was getting ready, Ashley felt less confident that she would stand out from the other girls. Not that she wanted to stand out *too* much, she quickly thought. Ashley wondered if Heather would listen to the girls' urging to wear a shrug over the low-cut, strappy red dress Heather had chosen. Heather had worn the dress once before when she and Ashley attended a wedding with Ashley's mom. Ashley remembered her mom's quickly hidden look of surprise when Heather entered the car. Privately, Ashley had thought Heather looked pretty sexy—not that Ashley would ever *say* that to anyone!

She quickly turned her thoughts away from Heather and toward her other friend's choices. Working from an inspiration garnered from an old *Seventeen Prom,* Brittney had found the ideal dress for Suzie online. After a bit of begging, Suzie's parents had agreed to buy the sleeveless, high-necked dress that perfectly showcased her toned arms and slender athletic build.

As for Brittney, Ashley admired her friend's creative flair and knew that she would look amazing, as always. Brittany planned to combine a simple, vintage Audrey-Hepburn-style dress, spiced up with a chunky rhinestone necklace and two secretly purchased items: Victoria's Secret stockings with a seam running up the back and tall silver heels! Brittney confided to Ashley on the phone that she would don the last two items only *after* she left home and her mother could no longer stop her.

Now Ashley's Abercrombie skirt ensemble that the girls had collaborated on no longer seemed right. It's just not *me,* Ashley thought to herself. All the other girls had found outfits that expressed their identities.

Of course, maybe the real problem was that Ashley just wasn't sure who she was anyhow! When it came down to it, Ashley admitted to herself, she didn't really care about Jake or what he thought of her outfit at all. She even didn't care about clothes all that much. But, she wasn't a sporty girl like Suzie, or a fashionista like Brittany, or certainly not a boy-crazy girl like Heather.

So, who was she? A loyal friend to her girlfriends? A good girl, like her mother always said, who studied hard so she could go to college one day? Would she someday be Jake's girlfriend? Or was she someone else entirely? Perhaps . . . dare she dream . . . could she join the drama club and someday star in a TV show like her favorite, *Pretty Little Liars?* Even now, Ashley still loved the show because of many good memories of sneaking in episodes with her friends when their parents weren't around. They had many whispered conversations about Aria, Spencer, Hannah, and Emily's scandalous and fashionable lives and loves!

Quit dreaming, Ashley thought to herself dejectedly. You just don't have style, money, or a bod like any of the Liars.

She pushed her clothes hangers aside in frustration. Whoever she was, whoever she was becoming, Ashley doubted any of those answers were in her closet. She turned away in confusion.

The author wishes to thank her nieces, Alisha and Amanda, for their invaluable suggestions for the storyline in this case.

For Further Thought and Reflection

1. In this story, how does marketing move beyond simple magazine or television ads? Do the girls themselves promote consumption through the interactions and activities that they do for fun?
2. List the products like beauty brands, music, and movies that are referenced from print, broadcast, or online media through this case. How do entertainment mass media *content* and celebrity worship complement and enhance marketing messages?
3. Looking at your product list from the second question, what do marketing messages about these products directly state or imply about socio-economic class, sexuality, and femininity? How does this influence each girl's self-concept, feelings of self-worth, and decision-making? How do the girls in this story both resist and embrace these messages?
4. What messages about idealized body types and sexual appearance are present in the marketing messages you identified in the first question? Identify two instances where one of the girls accepts the message. Identify two instances where one of the girls rejects or challenges the message. What interactions have led to this rejection or challenge? How do mass media messages and messages from other sources about sexuality and attractiveness contradict one another in this story?
5. Keep a log of marketing messages you encounter in one day of your everyday life including traditional ads, peer-to-peer marketing, product placement, "advertorials" (brand names included as creative content in magazines or programs), viral marketing (e.g., funny video on YouTube), and other forms of online and digital (e.g., video games) marketing. Then answer the following: What types of idealized femininities, masculinities, socio-economic classes, and sexualities are portrayed? How might these repeated messages influence identity?

References

Bailey, J., Steeves, V., Burkell, J., & Regan, P. (2013). Negotiating with gender stereotypes on social networking sites: From 'bicycle face' to Facebook. *Journal of Communication Inquiry, 37,* 91–112.

Duits, L., & van Romondt Vis, P. (2009). Girls make sense: Girls, celebrities, and identities. *European Journal of Cultural Studies, 12,* 41–58.

Durham, M. G. (2012). Blood, lust, and love. *Journal of Children and Media, 6,* 281–299.

Jackson, S., & Vares, T. (2013). 'Perfect skin', 'pretty skinny': Girls embodied identities and post-feminist popular culture. *Journal of Gender Studies, 4,* 1–14.

Marion, G., & Nairn, A. (2011). "We make the shoes, you make the story" Teenage girls' experiences of fashion: Bricolage, tactics, and narrative identity. *Consumption Markets & Culture, 14,* 29–56.

Mazzarella, S. R., & Atkins, A. (2010). "Community, content, and commerce": Alloy.com and the commodification of tween/teen girl communities. In S. R. Mazzarella (Ed.). *Girl wide web 2.0: Revisiting girls, the Internet, and the negotiation of identity.* New York: Peter Lang.

Pattee, A. (2009). When in doubt, choose "B": Encoding girls' magazine quizzes. *Feminist Media Studies, 9,* 193–207.

3

Moving Up: The Challenges of Communicating a New Social Class Identity

Kristen Lucas

Keywords

social class mobility, identity work, organizational socialization

ESPN SportsCenter was on, but Jim Morgan wasn't listening. Instead he was lying on his couch in an otherwise dark room, the light from his television screen flickering across his blank face. His phone was buzzing with text message alerts, but he was ignoring those too. He had a rough week—a rough couple months, to be exact—and he needed some time alone to gather his thoughts.

Since being hired as an entry-level attorney at one of the most prestigious law firms in the city, Jim was nagged by a little voice inside his head saying he didn't quite belong: *Kids from his working-class neighborhood grew up to work on the auto assembly line or to manage grocery stores or to enlist in the Army. They didn't become attorneys at high-powered law firms.* Whenever that pesky voice chimed in, Jim would do his best to silence it. He was smart, he graduated in the top 10 percent of his law school class, and he had an indefatigable work ethic. His logic just about licked that little voice until Monday afternoon.

Monday: The Performance Review

As he commuted into the city on Monday morning, Jim contemplated his to-do list for the day: conference call with his major client, file a couple motions in the case, spend a few hours researching case law, and put the finishing touches on a brief one of the senior partners had requested. The life of a young attorney was not nearly as glamorous as all those John Grisham novels made it seem. But it was definitely a good career with a lot of potential.

Jim kept busy all day, crossing items off of his to do list and racking up billable hours for the firm. As usual, he ate lunch at his desk. He figured he could eat leftovers *and* put in another hour of work while everyone else ate out at some overpriced downtown restaurant. Eventually, the alarm on his watch beeped: 2:55 p.m. In only five minutes he would have his 60-day performance review with his immediate supervisor. He took a deep breath and headed over to his boss's office. His secretary, Carolyn, was out front. "Hello, Mr. Morgan. I'll let Mr. Hughes know you are here."

The hierarchical culture of the firm made Jim uneasy. The secretaries, paralegals, and other clerical workers were required to address attorneys by title, but attorneys addressed everyone in the firm by their first names. That rule didn't sit well with Jim. In the case of Carolyn, it just didn't seem right that a woman nearly 20 years his senior had to address him formally. Yet after many failed attempts, he had given up asking Carolyn to call him by his first name. "Thank you, Ms. Jackson," he said with a mix of respect for Carolyn and a twinge of defiance to the organization's rule. Carolyn smiled warmly back at Jim.

Marc Hughes opened the door, "Come on in, James." They started their meeting by making some small talk about the previous night's game and Jim updated Marc on his caseload. Then they got down to the real reason for the meeting, the performance review.

Jim was relieved to hear Marc's initial feedback. "We are impressed by you, James. You are a hard worker. You're billing an impressive number of hours. Your research and writing skills are top-notch. And you've got a good analytical mind." Jim breathed a sigh of relief. This review was going better than he had expected. Perhaps all the rumors that this firm chewed up and spit out new attorneys were just that—rumors. Marc continued, "In these respects, we could not ask for more." Jim took notice of his words—"in these respects"—and he could feel the proverbial tide turning.

"Listen," Marc said to him, "We've got to talk about a few things. We know that you're a bright guy and a hard worker, but your success at the firm relies on some of the intangible things as well."

"What do you mean?" asked Jim.

Marc took a deep breath and shifted in his chair. "I don't know how to say this gently, so I'm just going to come out and say it directly. You're not projecting the image we need our young attorneys to project." Hearing the words out loud startled Jim, but the little voice inside his head said, 'I told you so.' Although Jim was prepared for a critique of his writing or his productivity, he wasn't prepared for the litany of little things that came his way in that performance review.

According to Marc, the senior partners thought that Jim was too rough around the edges. For starters, his language was not polished enough. *What does that mean? They already said that he had excellent writing skills. So what if he occasionally slipped up said "good" instead of "well" in casual conversation? And maybe he cussed a little here and there. But he really watched it around clients.* He did not dress well enough. *But he wore a suit and tie to work every day. He was never disheveled or in violation of the dress code. It shouldn't matter that his suits are off the rack at JC Penney. He didn't need a whole closet of fancy clothes to do this job, right?* His car was not sending the right message to clients. *Are they serious? His Chevy? That thing got him through undergrad and law school. Maybe it was showing signs of its age, but he worked in an office building—not his car, for crying out loud.* He was too friendly with the wrong people and not close enough with the right people who could get him somewhere in the firm. *Wrong people? Like Carolyn? The partners should be glad to know that one of their attorneys has taken time to get to know everyone in the firm and establish good working relationships with people from the janitorial staff who clean the offices, right up through the senior partners.*

It was a lot to take in. Marc ended the meeting by asking Jim to make a more conscientious effort to "fit in" to the culture of the firm. Shell-shocked as he was, Jim agreed to try. After all, this job was an excellent opportunity. He would be hard-pressed to find something comparable, especially having only a couple months of experience.

Tuesday: Dressing for Success

After his morning run, breakfast, and a shower, Jim got dressed. This was normally the easy part of the day. He owned two suits—a dark grey one and a blue one—that he alternated. He also owned 10 shirt-and-tie "sets," the kind that come matched in a box. He hung each set together on the same hangar so he wouldn't have to worry about coordinating his clothes each morning. All he had to do was blindly grab one of the hangars. But today was different. Marc Hughes's comments were booming in his head and Jim could not help but look at the contents of his closet with despair. There was not much he could do about his wardrobe this morning. So he made do the best he could by mixing up one of his shirt and tie combos, hoping that it actually matched.

Rather than his usual mental to-do list preparation, Jim thought about suits, shirts, and ties his entire commute. It may be superficial, he reasoned. But if that is what is needed to be successful, then maybe he could try dressing a little differently. He promised himself that he would go shopping soon. A couple new suits might actually be a good thing. Maybe he would even try coordinating shirts and ties on his own instead of buying another box set. The thought of replacing his favorite watch was not as easy to swallow though. He could see Marc's point about an expensive metal watch—one like all the other attorneys wore—looking more professional. But his digital watch was so practical. It had a timer and an alarm and a light. Instead of getting upset about it, Jim reminded himself that with a new position come new expectations. He should appreciate his boss raising these issues with him early so that he could make the necessary adjustments. If a new watch was what is needed to be successful at the firm, then a new watch it would be.

At the office, Jim found it more difficult than usual to concentrate on his work. Typically, he jumped right into it. But today he found himself surveying what other men in the office were wearing. Jim was hoping that he'd be able to pick up on a couple trends and go shopping with a specific checklist. But maybe this clothing thing was trickier than he originally anticipated. Their suits looked pretty standard: blue, grey, black, and brown. Their shirts and ties were a variety of colors. How exactly did these guys look any different from him? More importantly, how was he going to figure out how to look more like them if he couldn't see the difference?

Jim was in the break room pouring himself a fresh cup of coffee when he heard a familiar voice ring out. "What's on your mind, Jim? You look like you're a thousand miles away." It was Kendra, a woman from Jim's law school class and his only real friend at the firm. He wanted to confide in Kendra about his review and the long list of things that Marc wanted him to change. But he also didn't want to expose himself too much.

"Oh, I don't know. Just tired, I guess." Kendra commiserated with him. The long hours were taking their toll on all the new hires. "Well," Jim started, "There is one thing I could use your advice on."

"Sure thing," Kendra said.

"Now that I've had a few paychecks roll in, I've been thinking about going shopping for some more clothes. But I'm at a loss for where to start. Any suggestions?"

"Finally!" The enthusiasm of Kendra's voice made Jim realize that maybe he stuck out more than he originally thought. "If I were you, I'd get...." Jim found a pen and carefully wrote down the list in as much detail as possible, trying not to dwell on much this would cost.

By 4 p.m., Jim knew he was just spinning his wheels and not making any real progress. He logged off his computer, grabbed his shopping list, locked his office door, and headed out to tackle the wardrobe problem head on.

Wednesday: Networking with the "Right" People

Jim had gotten behind on his caseload, especially because he had been so preoccupied the first couple days of the week. But bolstered by his recent purchases—which totaled more than what he paid for his beloved Chevy—he was able to concentrate again. He felt almost like his old self and began making up for lost time. In fact, things were going so smoothly that he completely lost track of the hour until Kendra came by his office at 8 p.m. "Hey, Jim, nice tie," she said as she leaned in his doorway.

Jim smiled and glanced admiringly at his new brightly colored silk tie, smoothing it against his heavily starched shirt. "Wait until you see my new suits. It'll be a couple more days until the alterations are complete. But they are going to look real sharp! At least that's what the salesperson told me. Thanks, Kendra. You're a lifesaver. I couldn't have done it without you."

"A bunch of us are heading out right now for drinks and a bite to eat. We were thinking of going to that new sushi bar a few blocks from here. I know it's not your style to hang out after work, but why don't you join us?"

Jim briefly pondered why they never went out for beer and wings. It's all about the company, he reminded himself. "Know what? I'd really like to go this time."

The gathering at the sushi bar was nice. The firm really did have some incredible people working there. They were all young, intelligent, and driven. And they also were a lot of fun. He appreciated how the banter flowed between college rivalries, to political debate, to crazy law school stories, to talking about the firm. Marc was right. Hanging out with these people really could be an advantage. Maybe he could even learn from them how to project this so-called image. So he decided to take on more of an observer role and to really figure out how they presented themselves: how they told stories, what kinds of jokes were appropriate, what topics of conversation were taboo.

Thursday: In a Jam

By late Thursday afternoon, Jim had wrapped up most of his work for the week. When he walked past the copy room, he saw Carolyn struggling with the copier. "Hey, can I give you a hand with that?"

Carolyn waved off his offer to help, but Jim could tell that she was stressed out. She was flipping all the trap doors open and shut, twisting hidden knobs, and peering between gears. But the copier still was blinking "Error—Paper Jam." "Really, it's no problem at all," Jim said as he took off his suit jacket and rolled up his sleeves. "These copiers can really be a pain in the…" Jim paused momentarily to adjust his language, "… neck."

"You can say that again," Carolyn said. "I've been working on this paper jam for 40 minutes and now I'm right up against the deadline for Mr. Hughes." Jim saw the panicked look on Carolyn's face and saw tears welling up in the corner of her eyes.

"I bet you didn't know I have a black belt in paper jam removal." Jim had a knack for finding humor in stressful situations. "Give me five minutes and I'll have this copier begging for mercy." He opened, closed, twisted, and pulled until he found the offending piece of paper stuck in the rollers. "Ta da!" Jim waved the crumpled white sheet in front of Carolyn, then shot it basketball-style into the nearby recycling basket.

Just then, Marc Hughes walked by. "Excuse me, Carolyn, do you have those files ready?" he asked sternly.

"Yes, sir."

"Good. And James, may I see you in my office?" It was unusual for Marc to call spontaneous meetings. He looked serious. And he slapped the doorframe as though to indicate there was some urgency to his request. Jim's curiosity was piqued.

"Well, my work here is done," Jim said to Carolyn. "You can handle it from here, I assume."

"Absolutely. And…" She waited until Marc was out of eyeshot and earshot, then quietly mouthed, "Thank you, *James*." Jim smiled to himself as he walked towards Marc's office.

Marc quickly knocked Jim back to reality. "James, can you tell me what was going on back there?"

"Sure. I walked past the copy room and saw Carolyn wrestling with the copier. I figured because she looked so stressed out and I was winding down for the day, I'd give her a hand."

Marc was not impressed by Jim's team spirit. "When I see a problem, James, I feel the need to nip it in the bud. That way, the problem doesn't get out of control. Remember our talk on Monday?" How could Jim forget? It had consumed almost all of his energy the rest of the week. "Well, we need you to be focusing on being the best attorney you can be. And just now, it looked like you were working on being an *assistant* to a *secretary*. We didn't hire you to fix our copiers. We have people like Carolyn for that. You're too important to be stooping to that level."

Jim interjected, "But I wasn't stooping. I was helping. It was a job that needed to be done."

"Well, if you're looking for work, come talk to me and I can get you additional assignments. But from now on, leave the paper jams to the little people. Okay?"

Up until that point, Jim was handling Marc's critique quite well. He adjusted his wardrobe, watched his language a little more carefully, and even made a point to network with other associates at the law firm. But this was going too far. "Little people"? What did Marc mean by the comment? Jim thought of his own mother who worked as a secretary while he was growing up. He knew how hard she worked and was infuriated to think about anyone considering her a "little person."

Friday: Going Home

Jim parked on the street in front of his parent's house. The familiarity of the neighborhood was comforting and a welcomed relief from his stressful week at the office. The front porch light was on and he could hear laughter. He opened the door without knocking and joined the festivities. "Jimmy!" a chorus of voices rang out. His parents, brother, Aunt Mary, and Uncle Frank greeted him. The adults squeezed their chairs a little closer to make room for Jim at the small kitchen table.

"Can I get you a beer?" his Uncle Frank boomed.

"I'd love one," said Jim.

"So what took you so long?" Jim's dad asked.

"I stayed late at work tonight," Jim said as his mother warmed him a plate of leftovers in the microwave.

"They better be paying you overtime for that, Jimmy," his dad said.

"No, dad, I'm on salary. So I don't get any overtime." Jim wolfed down the pot roast and potatoes his mother served.

"I just don't get why you'd work for them for free," Jim's dad shook his head in dismay. He worked as a mechanic in a union shop his whole life, so he genuinely didn't understand working without overtime pay.

Jim's brother chimed in, "You know, if you worked down at the factory with me, at least we'd pay you overtime. And with these 70-hour work weeks you're putting in, I'd be surprised if ya weren't seeing bigger paychecks than you are now as a lawyer. Of course, you'd have to get those delicate little hands of yours dirty." Jim cringed—not at the thought of manual labor, but at the twinge of resentment he sensed in his brother's words.

"So how's life as a big shot?" asked his Uncle Frank, diverting the conversation.

"Big shot? I'm no big shot."

"Yeah, right. You're the only big shot this family's got." Jim knew that his family was proud of him. His father had been calling him the "family lawyer" since his first semester of law school. His mother cried through his entire law school graduation. He couldn't let them down. He really needed to make the job at the law firm work out.

"Yeah, Jimmy, you were always the smart one in the family," said his Aunt Mary.

"The smart ass, anyway," his brother good-naturedly retorted, and the whole family erupted into laughter.

* * * * *

Jim arrived back at his condo by about midnight. He picked up his remote control and mindlessly turned on the television. His head was swimming. How could so much happen in only a week? He had barely begun implementing the changes Marc wanted to see. He still had friendships to establish, mentors to seek out, communication habits to break and others to make. He had a long road ahead of him.

Even if Marc thought he still had a long way to go, Jim knew that he was far from the starting line, too. Looking back, his transformation began in college when he started getting exposed to new ideas and a new worldview. Law school prompted even more changes, as it prepared him for life as an unequivocally white-collar professional. No one understood these changes more intimately than his family. Yes, they were proud of him for all of his successes. But he knew that they also lamented the distance that was growing between them. It wasn't for a lack of love. It was the difference that sprung up between them the further he went along this road to becoming the ideal professional Marc and the senior partners were grooming him to become. He no longer fit in with his family. They didn't understand his new world. So should he work harder to fit in with his coworkers? Or should he back off and revert to some of his old ways? How can he possibly reconcile these feelings of limbo he was experiencing? How could he prove to his boss that he is cut out to be an attorney? And how could he reassure his family that he is the same old Jimmy?

For Further Thought and Reflection

1. Kaufman (2003) explains that in order to earn reciprocal middle class membership, people from working class backgrounds must engage in conscientious identity work, involving changing how they speak, attending to the nonverbal messages they use to represent themselves to others, and adjusting their relationships (e.g., prioritizing friendships with other middle class people). What specific examples of identity work did Jim engage in? What kind of identity work do you think might be required of you in your chosen career field? What identity work is acceptable to make for the sake of a career? How much is too much?
2. Throughout the case, different people called Jim by different names. How might these names have signaled different class-based expectations? What influence do you think these names had on Jim's ability to perform class-based identity work? Have you conscientiously changed your name or adopted a nickname to fit in to a new work environment?
3. How might family dynamics influence social mobility? What messages did Jim receive from his family that encouraged social mobility? What messages may have hindered his mobility? What impact do you think family support has on a person's ability to be successful in a new social class role?
4. Social class mobility is often marked by feelings of being in "limbo" (Lubrano, 2004), in which someone feels that he or she belongs a little to two social classes, but not fully to either. What evidence do you have that Jim is experiencing limbo? Do you think that limbo is a legitimate feeling to experience during social class mobility?
5. In what ways might Jim's working class background be a hindrance for his success? In what ways might it be an advantage?

References

Alvesson, M., & Willmott, H. (2002). Identity regulation as organizational control: Producing the appropriate individual. *Journal of Management Studies, 39,* 619–644.

Kaufman, P. (2003). Learning to not labor: How working-class individuals construct middle-class identities. *The Sociological Quarterly, 44*, 481–504.

Lair, D. J., Sullivan, K., & Cheney, G. (2005). Marketization and the recasting of the professional self. *Management Communication Quarterly, 18,* 307–343.

Lubrano, A. (2004). *Limbo: Blue-collar roots, white-collar dreams*. Hoboken, NJ: John Wiley and Sons.

Lucas, K. (2011a). Socializing messages in blue-collar families: Communicative pathways to social mobility and reproduction. *Western Journal of Communication, 75,* 95–121.

Lucas, K. (2011b). The working class promise: A communicative account of mobility-based ambivalences. *Communication Monographs, 78,* 347–369.

Wieland, S. M. B. (2010). Ideal selves as resources for the situated practice of identity. *Management Communication Quarterly, 24*, 503–528.

4

The Whole Truth and Nothing but the Truth? Negotiating Face and Revealing Difficult Information

Jennifer Lynne Cronin

Keywords

face negotiation, roles, self-disclosure, relational dialectics, computer-mediated communication

Elaine had just gotten home from working a double shift. It had been a grueling day of caring for patients at the hospital and she could not wait to put her feet up, catch up on her favorite late-night sitcom, and drift off to sleep. Her husband, Mac, was still swamped at the hospital. Just as his shift was about to end, a family of four involved in an accident with a tractor-trailer was airlifted to the ER and needed his attention. He was the best traumatic brain surgeon in the area, so Elaine knew that her husband was the family's best chance of survival. She presumed that he'd be forced to get a few hours of sleep in the hospital's resident's room tonight and she would just have to see him at work in the morning.

As soon as she dimmed the lights and plopped down on the couch, she heard her phone vibrating in her purse—a text message. "So much for relaxing just yet," she sighed. She debated briefly whether to ignore it, but her curiosity got the best of her. Who could be texting her at this hour? Almost delirious from exhaustion, Elaine tossed her blanket aside and used her last bit of energy to hoist herself up and aimlessly sift through her oversized purse. It was a message from her 19-year-old daughter, Sarah.

The following conversation that night over text messenger between Elaine and Sarah would change both of their lives forever.

Sarah: hey mom. u home?

Elaine: Yep. Just walked in. How's school?

Sarah: fine. u busy? I need to tell u something

Elaine: OK. What's up? You alright?

Sarah: sure, yeah. I'm ok. Ummm, I really don't know how to say this

Elaine: Just tell me honey. I'm listening. Are you hurt?

Sarah: no, nothing like that. I'm just worried u'll be disappointed.

Elaine: Whatever it is, we will get through it. What's going on?

Sarah: Id really rather tell u in person. Can we meet up?

Elaine: Of course…putting my shoes on now. Where are you?

Sarah: My dorm room.

Elaine: All right. Stay put. I'm on my way. I love you, Sarah.

Three Weeks Prior

Sarah's heart was racing and her hands were wringing with sweat. She felt light-headed, dizzy, and hot, prepared at any moment for the anxiety to make her pass out. She cowered alone in the back corner stall of her dorm community bathroom waiting on the pregnancy test to reveal her results. The two-minute wait duration seemed to drag on for an eternity. She glanced down at her watch. Forty-five seconds to go. She clinched the test stick tightly and closed her eyes. She immediately started praying—if she could just get out of this one… then what? She wasn't sure. She was not religious, but she was desperate enough to try anything. "Please just let the test be negative," she whispered to herself.

Finally her watch beeped, alerting her that the test was complete. "This is it," she thought. "My future rides on this very moment." Reluctantly, she opened her eyes one at a time, afraid of what she would discover. She looked down at the test. A bright pink plus sign glared up at her. Her heart sank as her fears were confirmed; she was indeed pregnant. She thought she was going to throw up. It was as if she had developed tunnel vision—there was no sound and time had stopped. Sheer panic flooded her body and the dizziness intensified. What was she going to do now? She had just gotten into one of the most prestigious universities in the country. She had been valedictorian of her class in high school, and her entire future was riding on getting good grades, keeping her scholarship, and attending medical school just like her parents. Becoming a single mother at 19 certainly had not been a part of the plan.

Of course, she knew other girls who were single moms; it was not like this never happened, but it was not supposed to happen to *her*. She was "Miss Jackson County," Homecoming Queen, a straight-A student, captain of the rowing team, and a role model for her two younger siblings. She had never been in trouble a day in her life and she did not intend to start now. She wrapped the test in tissue and hid it under her shirt, terrified that her news would be discovered by one of her hall mates. Wiping the sweat from her brow and the tears from her eyes, she took a moment to pull herself together. She walked back to her room and quickly locked the door. Luckily, she didn't bump into anyone she knew.

For the next two weeks, Sarah kept to herself. She constantly thought about other women she knew who had unplanned pregnancies and the choices that they had made. Just last semester a sorority sister, Aliyah, had decided not to return to school from summer break because she couldn't (or perhaps didn't want to) simultaneously manage being a single mom and a full-time student. Instead, she decided to move back in with her parents and enroll in night classes at her local community college. "At least Aliyah was still going to get a degree," Sarah thought, desperately searching for something positive to make of her situation.

She thought about Claire, another woman who had become unintentionally pregnant. She didn't know Claire well—they had only hung out on occasion—but she knew about her abortion. Sarah was not supposed to know that piece of information about Claire, but a mutual friend had slipped during dinner one night and made Sarah "swear on her life" not to tell anyone else. Claire seemed like a perfectly normal, happy, college student and never mentioned her abortion, but then again the topic of pregnancy had never come up. Sarah wondered if Claire might be willing to talk with her about the abortion procedure, but doubted it because they weren't really that close. "Besides," she thought, "it would be next to impossible to bring up the abortion without Nancy getting in trouble for telling me."

And finally, there was Elise, a classmate from her History class who had gotten pregnant as a teenager and had given up her baby for adoption. Unlike Claire, Sarah was certain that Elise would be more than willing to talk with her, but there was no need because she already knew what she would say. Elise was constantly volunteering in the local high schools and organizing campaigns for teen pregnancy prevention. It was the pregnancy *prevention* part of her work that made Sarah uneasy and hesitant to seek out Elise. She was already pregnant and didn't want to feel judged by Elise (or anyone else for that matter). "Ugh," Sarah groaned as she tried to sink lower in her bed. "There are so many options, but none of them seem quite right for me!"

Thinking about what others had done just made her more confused and depressed. It was all she could do to get out of bed and make it to class, but even that was becoming a rarity. She was having trouble sleeping so her eyes were puffy and bloodshot, and the thought of eating made her sick to her stomach. She avoided phone calls from her parents and shrugged off her friends' concerns that something was wrong. She received e-mails from two of her professors inquiring about her absence from their classes. It was not like her to miss class or fail to turn in assignments, and even her teachers were beginning to notice her strange behavior.

She told no one about her pregnancy—not even Jeff, her boyfriend of two years and the father of her baby. So far, it had been easy to avoid telling him because he attended school more than 200 miles away and they were not planning a visit until next month. She was only a few weeks along and definitely not showing yet, so concealing her pregnancy symptoms during their late night FaceTime chats was not all that difficult. She was, however, gravely conflicted about whether or not to go ahead and tell him about the baby. She hated keeping things from him, but he was just as focused on school as she was, and she anticipated that this was not going to be particularly welcome news. Playing college baseball and trying to get into the Business School left little available time for her, much less a baby. Although this baby was technically his child, too, it was her body and she felt protective of her secret and her decision. She wanted to be sure of her decision—whatever that may be—before complicating things by bringing Jeff into the situation. What would she do if he did not want to make the same decision about the baby that she did?

As far as telling others, that was out of the question. She was already feeling down on herself for getting into this mess and was not ready to feel judged and criticized by her (so-called) friends. She remembered the whispers, mocking, and stares that Aliyah had received behind her back from the women in their sorority after she announced her pregnancy. Although Sarah regretted it now and would never admit to it, she too had been a participant in the questioning of Aliyah's moral character when she heard the news. She felt wretched about that given her current situation and wished that she had been more supportive of what Aliyah was going through. She thought about how hard it must have been for Aliyah because now all Sarah wanted was for someone to comfort her and tell her that everything was going to be okay. She desperately wanted to tell someone, but she was not willing to risk the perfect image that she worked so hard to uphold. She knew it was a terrible thought, and she felt guilty for thinking it, but she kept hoping that the pregnancy would just "go away" and life could go back to normal. If she ignored it long enough, perhaps it would. She just could not be "one of *those* girls."

A Friend Comes to Visit

The next day, Sarah was woken by a knock at her door. Groaning, she rolled over to look at her alarm clock. It was 2:00 in the afternoon and she had slept through her Wednesday morning classes. She wondered who was on the other side of the door because most of her friends had stopped coming by. She knew that her repeated refusals to answer the door or return phone calls would eventually turn them away so she didn't blame them at all. She wanted to be left alone to go back to sleep—at least when she was sleeping her mind stopped reeling—but something made her open the door anyway. Her best friend, Julie, appeared in the doorway with a look of concern spread across her face. "I think we need to talk," Julie said insistently. At the sight of her friend, Sarah could not hold back the tears and folded herself into Julie's arms. It was the first time that she had outwardly expressed emotion about her situation; she felt numb up until now. Julie hugged her tight and guided her friend over to the couch. "It's going to be all right, Sarah," she began. "It's going to be all right. Now, tell me what's going on." In between sobs, Sarah recounted the events that had taken place over the past few weeks. It was the first time that she had told another person and verbalized the words, "I'm pregnant." It was the first time that the pregnancy seemed real.

Letting her finish, Julie began asking her questions. She inquired about all sorts of different topics (e.g., what she planned to do about the pregnancy, if she had been to the doctor, what was she planning to do about finishing school, and if she had told Jeff or her parents). Sarah realized that she had not given a lot of thought to her situation or the implications that could result from different decisions she could make. She was obviously at a standstill, paralyzed by anxiety regarding her situation. Her temporary solution was to simply do nothing at all and pretend that it was just a bad dream. As a good friend, Julie was helping Sarah take the steps she needed to move forward—in whichever direction that might be.

For the next few hours, Julie and Sarah discussed her options and determined what she should do next. They ultimately decided that telling Jeff was probably a good place to start. Sarah felt obligated to tell him first because he was the baby's father after all. Concealing the news from Jeff allowed Sarah to only make sense of her situation through her (and Julie's) perspective. However, Jeff was an important person in this and Sarah needed to know what he thought, too. Her best-case scenario was for the two of them to talk this out and decide on a course of action that they could pursue together. Unfortunately, the long distance between Sarah and Jeff's schools prevented her from telling him in person, but she wasn't ready to see the look on his face anyway. So, she decided on the telephone. With Julie sitting by her side and squeezing her hand tightly, Sarah picked up her phone and dialed his number. With every ring, her longing for his voicemail grew.

Jeff: Hello?

Sarah: Hey, hon.

Jeff: Hi sweetie! I'm actually right in the middle of something that I need to finish. Can I call you back a little later?

Oh thank goodness! Sarah was relieved at Jeff's offer to give her way out. Unfortunately, Julie (who was listening in) narrowed her eyes and shook her head, encouraging Sarah to continue. They both knew that if Sarah did not tell Jeff now, she might never gather up the courage to tell him!

Sarah: Actually, no, I kinda need to talk to you about something now. It's pretty important.

Jeff: Oh, OK. Hang on just a second. Just…let…me…type…this…last…thing. OK, got it! What's up, babe?

Sarah: Well, there is something that I've been needing to tell you, and I'm really not sure how you're going to react.

Jeff: Oh, God. This doesn't sound good, Sarah.

Sarah: Well, it's not. I mean, I'm not sure if it's good or not.

Jeff: Okaaaay…well, what is it?

Sarah: Jeff, ummm, I think—no, I *know*—I'm pregnant.

There was a long silence. Neither of them said a word. Sarah removed the phone from her ear and looked down to make sure that the line had not gone dead.

Sarah: Are you still there? Jeff?

Jeff: Yeah, I heard you. Are you sure?

Sarah: Of *course* I'm sure! Why would I not be sure?!

Jeff: How did this *happen*? You said you were on the pill!

Neither Jeff nor Sarah was a yeller, but their tempers flared, words were curt, and their tone became stern as the conversation heated up. Sarah could tell that Jeff was starting to panic, which only made her want to panic as well. She kept reminding herself that this was the first time Jeff had heard the news, so he was probably experiencing the same anxiety that she did when she found out.

Sarah: You know *how* this happened, Jeff, and you also know the pill isn't 100% effective! Don't you dare blame this all on me. It's just as much your fault as it is mine.

Jeff: I'm not, Sarah. I'm just not really sure what to do right now. I mean we *can't* be parents! That much I do know. We both have two years of school left, not to mention four more years of graduate school. We don't have the time or the finances to take care of a kid. Damn it, Sarah! This is terrible!

Jeff's reaction was pretty much on par with what she had anticipated, and his certainty about the pregnancy was exactly what she was worried about. She wasn't sure what she wanted to do yet, but Jeff sure seemed convinced that he did not want any part in this. She had prepared herself for him to push her into a decision that she was not ready for, but she hadn't considered him not being a part of this at all. That seemed worse.

Sarah: Well, I'm not sure what to think or what to do right now either. I think we both need to take some time and think about it. Maybe next weekend you can come up here and we can talk?

Jeff: All right. I don't think I have a game that weekend, so I should be able to make it. I gotta go. I'll call you later.

The phone clicked as Jeff hung up without the usual closing of "I love you." Sarah began to cry and Julie comforted her, reassuring her that Jeff just needed some time to sort things out. After an hour of trying to analyze Jeff's reaction, Julie knew it was time to bring up another big question: *how to tell Sarah's parents*.

This question had Sarah's stomach tied up in knots—the very thought of telling them made her cheeks flush and heart race, especially because things had just gone so poorly with Jeff. She had always been "daddy's little girl" and "the good kid." She had a promising future ahead of her and she had worked hard to get herself here—now her life was coming to a screeching halt right in front of her eyes and she did not know how to control the chaos that had become her life. Her younger sister, Alex, was the wild one; the one who was always in trouble. They might expect something like this from Alex, but not *her*. This was the worst thing she could do: let her parents down and disappoint them. She worried that telling them the news might change their view of her forever (and *not* in a good way). She could never again be the perfect child that they had always known her to be and their hopes and dreams for her life would be shattered.

Although she was not exactly sure what her parents would say, she knew they were not going to be happy that she was pregnant. Just last weekend she was at home watching television with her parents as a news story covering teen pregnancy aired. She recalled her mother's reaction, word-for-word: "How devastating for parents to find out that their child is an unwed mother! I'm just so glad that *my* girls don't make bad decisions like that!"

Devastating—that's how her mother had described it. They would be *devastated* by her news. She started to panic yet again.

Telling Mom

For the next four days, Julie visited Sarah's room each afternoon after class. She talked with Sarah, helped research her pregnancy options online, located medical care providers in their area, and crafted out a plan for telling her parents. The women believed that telling Sarah's mother first (and soon) might be an important factor in gaining the help and support of other family members should she need it. To curtail Sarah's feelings of insecurity, Julie reassured Sarah that she was an adult and more than capable of making these decisions for herself. The plan, therefore, for telling her parents, was to portray a sense of confidence and being in control of her situation. She wanted to appear strong, capable, and knowledgeable about the implications of her choices—these characteristics would at least be consistent with the image of Sarah that her parents had always had. Perhaps if she seemed positive and sure of her decisions, they would be, too. Now, all she had to do was gather up the courage to tell them.

"I don't think I can do it!" Sarah sobbed.

Julie handed her the cell phone. "Start with a text message. That's how y'all usually talk, right?"

She was right, *again*. Text message was the way she and her mother normally communicated, but this was no ordinary conversation. Whichever way she ultimately decided to unveil the pregnancy, Sarah had to first see if her mom was available and off work. She picked up the phone and typed "Mom" into the message search bar. "Here goes nothing," she sighed.

For Further Thought and Reflection

1. Although Sarah decided to tell her mother in person and not to reveal her news via text message, there are many advantages of revealing difficult information via this medium. What are they? What are the disadvantages? Which medium (e.g., in person, telephone, video conference, e-mail, letter, text message) do you believe is most effective and appropriate for revealing different types of difficult information?
2. Privacy and disclosure are often conceptualized as a unified dialectical (or oppositional) process (Petronio, 2002). Consider the risks and benefits associated with revealing personal information. What risks and benefits of disclosure can you derive from Sarah's story? In your opinion, did Sarah make the right choice by disclosing to Julie, Jeff, and her mother? Should she tell anyone else? If you were to find yourself in Sarah's situation, how would you assess the risks and benefits of telling others? What types of information would you not reveal to your parents?
3. Our perceptions are shaped by the roles we inhabit. In what role do you think Jeff sees himself, and how does this affect his perception of the situation? What rights and responsibilities does he have? If you were in his position, how would you react to the news? Whose views should prevail if he and Sarah disagree about continuing the pregnancy?
4. Face negotiation theory (Ting-Toomey, 2005) asserts that all people have a desired image (or face) they want to project in front of others and they work to maintain that image in all communicative encounters. What was Sarah's desired image, and how did she work to maintain that image when revealing her news? How (and why) did her facework differ when telling Julie, Jeff, and her mother?
5. How do you think Elaine (Sarah's mother) reacted once she learned her daughter's news? In other words, if you were to write the conclusion of this case study, how would it read?

References

Cronin, J. L. (2014). *Speaking the unspeakable: Adult children's revelations of unwed pregnancy to parents*. (Doctoral dissertation). Retrieved from ProQuest Dissertations and Theses. (University of North Carolina at Chapel Hill).

Greene, K., Derlega, V. J., & Mathews, A. (2006). Self-disclosure in personal relationships. In A. L. Vangelisti & D. Perlman (Eds.), *The Cambridge handbook of personal relationships* (pp. 409–427). New York: Cambridge University Press.

Metts, S., & Cupach, W. R. (2008). Face theory: Goffman's dramatistic approach to interpersonal interaction. In L. A. Baxter & D. O. Braithwaite (Eds.), *Engaging theories in interpersonal communication: Multiple perspectives* (pp. 203–214). Thousand Oaks, CA: Sage.

Petronio, S. (2002). *Boundaries of privacy: Dialectics of disclosure*. New York: State University of New York Press.

Ting-Toomey, S. (2005). The matrix of face: An updated face-negotiation theory. In W. B. Gudykunst (Ed.), *Theorizing about intercultural communication* (pp. 71–92). Thousand Oaks, CA: Sage.

Wright, K. B., & Webb, L. M. (2011). *Computer-mediated communication in personal relationships*. New York, NY: Peter Lang Publishing.

5

Why Has *Finding God* Changed My Relationships? Managing Change Associated with Religious Conversion

Douglas L. Kelley
Debra-L Sequeira

Keywords

conversion, forgiveness, self-forgiveness, identity, looking-glass self, peer relationships, turning points, uncertainty reduction

John stood in front of the mirror. He turned his body to one side and then the other trying to get the best view possible of his lats. This morning, like every morning since he had joined the Kelleira College football team, the mirror confirmed John's own thoughts—he was a stud. He was the key component of the Eagles' defense and one of the most popular students on his small college campus. With the delivery of his lunch in his hospital room, John was jolted out of his daydream memory. In the flash of a second, everything that had happened over the last year came flooding back to him.

One year ago during the Homecoming game, John intercepted a pass in the final seconds and ran it back for the winning touchdown. The next day at school he found himself in the men's bathroom at lunch, looking in the mirror to make certain that he was the same guy who had come to school the day before. His friends seemed friendlier; seniors who had never so much as given him the time of day before, gave him the subtle head nod that said, "You're in," and he suddenly seemed a topic of interest for girls in his classes.

John's sophomore year also brought some new experiences in the form of partying with the guys on the team. Here, as well as on the football field, he expanded his popularity by being seen as a risk-taker. Football, drinking, and the willingness to try just about any new substance, allowed John to live life on the edge. His new personalized license plate: YOLO. It was this edge that provided him with the "rush" that he increasingly needed to feel good.

The winter following his star season, the rush John needed came in the form of driving 65 miles per hour on an icy mountain road near his home. Beer, weed and tequila shots subtly blurred his vision and dulled his senses. Lulled into a false sense of control, John ignored his sister's pleas to slow down as he careened out of control and rolled his jeep two and a half times over an embankment. A Douglas fir was the only thing that kept the car and its passengers from cascading 210 feet to the bottom of the ravine. This silent sentinel was the difference between death and life.

Death was more what it felt like to John, however, when he awoke from a five-day coma to find himself in a hospital bed, his mother by his side. Her bright eyes were a comfort to him at first, but her troubled smile betrayed the truth. The doctors were sure he would once again walk normally and regain full mobility.

However, playing college football was out of the question. Life as he had known it was gone. Suddenly he remembered his eighteen-year old sister, Katie, and her pleas for him to slow down. John paused, afraid to ask, "Is…is Katie okay?"

His mom paused, tears in her eyes. "Katie is fine. She was bruised up a bit, but she's going to be okay."

* * * * *

John's first conscious week in the hospital was brutal. His friends were encouraging and uplifting, but he could sense their uncertainty about how to treat him. They tried to joke as they had before, but somehow it seemed forced and unnatural. The look in their eyes, the distance they kept, and their short stays were like a mirror reflecting John's changed identity. Secretly, he felt like they blamed him for screwing up his own life and putting his sister in danger.

Following surgery on his neck and right leg, John was moved to a rehab facility where an intense physical therapy regimen brought the ex-Eagle football star to the point where he could get out of bed on his own. As he moved slowly around the room with a walker, he paused and stood silently before a full-length mirror, taking in what others' eyes had told him—his hopes dashed, his spirit crushed. "Why me?" he whispered. "Why me?" He heard no reply. John was still standing in front of the mirror when his physical therapist, Mark, knocked on the door, "Hey, lookin' good. You've come a long way."

Looking down at his legs, John didn't think so. "Yeah, a long way to nowhere," he snapped sarcastically. "I've lost everything."

"Listen, man, you can't afford a pity party now. You've still got a lot of work to do. The doctors and I can help you learn to regain use of your legs, but the real healing is up to you."

John looked quizzically at Mark. What did he mean, "the real healing is up to me?" Each and every day since regaining consciousness, John had punished himself for ruining everything. Katie had come to visit him shortly after he had regained consciousness. She still had bruises and cuts on her face. It could have been so much worse. When he found out that her face would always be slightly scarred, he felt even more strongly that he had no right to be healed himself.

Mark could sense John's mental resistance to healing, so later in the exercise room he asked John to come to the center of the workout area. With the aid of his walker, John slowly worked his way out until he stood eye to eye with Mark. "Give me the walker."

John recoiled. "I can't! You know that."

"Give me the walker, John."

Mark slowly began to pull John's walker away from him. "John, you're trying to do this with only upper body strength." Mark put his hand firmly on John's shoulder, "John, you need to trust me." John paused, then slowly let go of the walker. He stood silently, staring in disbelief at his legs that somehow were now supporting his body. When he finally raised his head, Mark was looking straight at him. "A little faith goes a long way, John." John could see a mixture of strength and compassion in Mark. This man seemed so certain, so assured. Yet, in the heaviness of John's shame, and guilt, he wasn't sure others could ever forgive him for what he'd done, or that he could forgive himself.

After the session, Mark took John back to his room. "Good workout. I'll leave you alone to think about what happened today—especially how faith and trust might be part of your recovery. Oh, and here's some reading material that might help." Mark dropped a small book on John's lap, entitled, "God's Forgiving Love."

Over the next few days John devoured the book. His family wasn't religious; he'd never attended church; he'd never heard that God could love someone, even if they had made some huge mistakes. One night, after finishing the book, John prayed and wept and told God that he wanted His forgiveness. John had never been much for forgiveness, he believed that each person should earn their way and "pay the price" for the choices they make. Yet, after praying and, for the first time in his life, feeling free from having to be perfect, John felt like a physical weight had been taken off of him.

The next morning he was ready for Mark to walk through the door. "So John, what's up with you today? That's the first real smile I've seen from you since we started your physical therapy."

"Is it?" John felt slightly embarrassed. "I've been reading that book you gave me. I, uh, um, decided to forgive myself for what I've done. I mean, if God can forgive me, I guess I can, too."

"Great," said Mark enthusiastically. "Now that's progress. If you're up for it, I have some challenging exercises planned for today."

From that point on, John began to feel like it was okay for him to finally work full out on getting better. He began to look forward to his physical therapy and his talks with Mark. In fact, the change was so dramatic that his family and friends remarked on how quickly his recovery was going.

One day Katie unexpectedly showed up. She hadn't visited John very often since that first day because of her own injuries and because she was going to a college that was about two hours from home. "Sorry I haven't been by."

"Well," John said sheepishly, "I wouldn't blame you if you never wanted to see me again."

"No way. You're still my brother. We all make mistakes. You know, you may find this hard to believe, but I was afraid I'd lost you."

"I guess you'll always have a reminder of me"—John pointed to Katie's face.

"John, the scar will improve over time. I just want you to know. . . I mean. . . I just want us to forget that it ever happened. You know? Back like old times."

John exhaled with relief at Katie's apparent forgiveness. After a long time of talking and catching up on the latest news about friends and school, Katie ventured into new territory, "So, John, I see you have a Bible on your bedside. It's like you're preparing to have the priest read you your last rites." With this she gave a somewhat uncomfortable laugh, trying hard to sound natural.

"Yeah, I thought that I'd better be ready in case you all have been kidding me about my actual improvement."

Both laughed this time, yet Katie couldn't decide if John didn't pick up on her discomfort or if he simply decided not to acknowledge it. She pressed on.

"You know, Mom told me last night that you had mentioned God quite a bit yesterday when talking to her."

"Yeah! I pretty much decided to give my life to God. I mean think of it, if it wasn't for that one tree I would have been a goner. And my physical therapist, Mark, is a Christian. We've had some really great talks."

"John, you know…um…Well, it's great if that's helping you, now. You've been through a lot, but when you come home . . . I mean, well. . . ." Katie rose to go. "I guess what I'm trying to say is that . . . well . . . we all go through phases, and, well . . . well, when you get home, everything will be able to get back to normal." With this she tousled his hair and headed out the door.

* * * * *

After being released from the rehab facility, John started attending church with Mark. It was after church one Sunday, when Katie was home for the weekend, that John burst with excitement into her room, "Katie, you've just got to hear what we talked about today in church."

Plunking down on her bed next to her, John could feel the tension in Katie's body and see the stressed look on her face. "Are you all right?" he asked.

"John you know I think you're the best brother ever, even when you're a total dork. And, I know you have just gone through the most traumatic time of your life, but you've changed, and I want my old brother back."

"Look, I'm still me. The only difference is that God is part of my life, now."

"It's just that we used to fight and argue all the time, but there was always this real connection between us. I felt like we were so similar, you know? I mean, we could talk about anything."

"That's exactly what I'm still doing," John replied. "I'm still sharing with you what's most important to me. It just happens that God is a big part of that."

"I know," said Katie reservedly, "I mean, I guess I'm glad for you and all, but somehow it's just different between you and me now."

"It doesn't have to be that way," John quickly retorted. "I'm still sharing with you. It seems to me that you're the one who's changed. You're the one who isn't sharing with me!"

"But . . . look, never mind."

"Never mind what?"

"It's just that I'm not so sure that you really approve of me and my friends anymore."

"What do you mean?" John asked in confusion.

"Well," Katie began hesitatingly, "I mean, you don't really think drinking and getting high is cool anymore and, well, I know what you think about Jennifer and Amy."

"Well, Jennifer and Amy aren't good influences on you. You wouldn't party so much if it weren't for them. And, remember, it was getting high and drinking that caused that scar on your face. Besides, I really do want you to experience God's grace like I have."

"See what I mean!" Katie suddenly exploded. "What is this 'God's grace' crap? It's like you're talking in secret code. And, regarding getting high and drinking, it was *your* behavior, not mine, that gave me this scar. Just because you're still feeling guilty doesn't mean I shouldn't have fun. Look, I've gotta go. Oh, and by the way, Tyler called and wants you to call him back."

As the door shut behind her, John sat staring at the full-length mirror that hung on the back of the door. Had he really changed? He knew that his encounter with God was real and that he wasn't the same person, spiritually, that he had been before. But, wasn't he the same brother he had always been? And, why was Katie so resistant to hearing about how God had changed his life? As he stared in the mirror longer, he thought, "I'm still the same. I just have God now, that's all. Katie just needs some time to get used to it. I'll show her I'm not so different. I'll call Tyler and get together with the guys." The call to Tyler lifted his spirits. They laughed, and he found out some friends wanted to get together that very night.

Later that evening, John walked nervously up the steps of Tyler's apartment. The reality of rejoining his former life raised all kinds of doubts and questions: Would he still be accepted now that he could no longer play football? Had someone else taken his 'star' status? What about his faith? He already knew his family wasn't very open to it. And, since injuring himself and his sister, he was committed to drinking less, or not at all—would his friends be okay with that? He took a deep breath and opened the door. As John entered the room, eyes lit up and a barrage of voices said how great he looked and how they had meant to call. The warm air, moving bodies, slaps on the back, and blur of faces was almost numbing.

Suddenly, John was being jostled over to the dining room table—ten cups of beer were set up on each end. Tyler put his arm around John's shoulder and proposed a toast in his honor. "Friends, we've gathered here tonight to bring one of our own home. John's life has taken a few unexpected turns lately, but he's finally back with us." Tyler raised his beer high. "Here's to John! Our beer pong champion has returned!" With this, beer cans clanked all around the room and John took his first sip of beer in ten weeks.

The next two hours of conversation and beer pong went as well as could be expected—mostly shallow and surface stuff, no risks—and John basically tried to let his teammates do most of the drinking. But finally, what he feared most, happened. He heard Tyler's voice and felt his arm around him, again, "John, let's step outside for a few minutes." The two of them walked into the backyard and sat down by a fire pit that was popping and spitting sparks.

"So, how are you, dude?"

"Good, I guess. It's been pretty crazy but, really, I'm happier than I've ever been."

Tyler paused. "I'm glad to hear that, because...you don't seem like yourself."

"What do you mean?"

"I just mean," Tyler paused again. "I just mean that you seem, like you're holding back. You know? You used to be crazy, John. But, tonight, I could tell you weren't in to the whole beer pong thing."

"Hey, you know they don't let you drink much in the hospital so I'm kind of out of practice," John said weakly.

"Dude, this is me, Tyler. Don't B.S. me. What's going on?"

"Well, it's just that. . ." John began.

"Just that John has found religion, that's all," came a familiar voice from behind the two men.

John wheeled around quickly, only to see Katie and her friend Amy. "Katie, what are you doing here? You're stoned. After all that's happened how could you...?"

"Amy and I were just crashing a few parties, oh Pong Meister," Katie said mockingly.

John slowly became aware of Tyler's voice, "Is this true? You're religious, now? I thought you were acting weird all night. Why didn't you just tell me?"

John stared at Katie's face, and at the mark that would be there forever because of his choices. "No. I haven't exactly found religion. . . ." John started.

"Good!" Tyler interjected.

"It's more like God just grabbed hold of my life. I just don't need drinking, and pot, and, well...whatever, anymore."

The fire was still crackling and popping, but John couldn't hear anything but his own heart pounding wildly in his chest. Tyler got up and he, Katie, and Amy, walked slowly toward the house. Before going through the door, Tyler turned and said, "What the hell, man. We were friends. We were tight." As the door slammed shut, John had never felt so alone.

The drive home was painful. Why was this so hard? Had he really changed? Why couldn't they accept him with this new part of his life? And, most importantly, how could Katie have humiliated him like that in front of his best friend?

When Katie came home a little after midnight, the light was still on in John's room. She knocked lightly on the door. "I'm not here!" John called. Katie slowly opened the door. "I told you, I'm not here. Isn't that what you said to me earlier? If I'm not me anymore, then I'm really not here, am I?"

"John, I'm sorry."

"Sorry for what? That I'm not here anymore or that you humiliated me in front of my closest friend?"

Katie shot back, "Look, you're not exactly innocent you know. You stood there and made all of us feel that you are better than we are because you don't need to drink anymore. I guess God's grace and forgiveness only works one way, huh?"

For Further Thought and Reflection

1. Write the end of this story. Is reconciliation possible between John and Katie? How can they more productively communicate to rebuild their relationship?
2. Early in the story John had to accept forgiveness from God for his choices. How does one try to gain self-forgiveness?
3. It appears that both John and Katie need to forgive one another. Forgiveness is *not* excusing "wrong" behavior, it is a process of recognizing that something hurtful happened and choosing to move ahead by honestly dealing with the emotional impact and trying to make sense of the situation. Forgiveness doesn't require reconciliation, but in John's and Katie's relationship it seems like it could be a desired outcome. Describe how you think John and Katie might constructively move toward forgiving one another.
4. Several times in this story people mention "getting back to normal." What do people want in their relationship when they talk about this? Is this a realistic goal for John, Katie, or Tyler?
5. Have you ever taken a position or held a belief that put you at odds with the majority of your peers? If so, how did you handle it? What are possible positive or negative outcomes when someone stands firm in their beliefs?
6. Following the accident, what were the turning points in John's relationships with his family? His friends? What types of turning points could occur that would strengthen or weaken his current relationships?

References

Afifi, W. A., & Matsunaga, M. (2008). Uncertainty management theories. In L. A. Baxter & D. O. Braithwaite (Eds.) *Engaging theories in interpersonal communication: Multiple perspectives*. 117–132. Thousand Oaks, CA: Sage.

Baxter, L. A., & Bullis, C. (1986). Turning points in developing romantic relationships. *Human Communication Research, 12*, (4), 469–493.

Carr, K., & Wang, T. R. (2012). "Forgiveness isn't a simple process: It's a vast undertaking": Negotiating and communicating forgiveness in nonvoluntary family relationships. *Journal of Family Communication, 12*, 40–56.

Fisher, M. L., & Exline, J. J. (2010). Moving toward self-forgiveness: Removing barriers related to shame, guilt, and regret. *Social and Personality Psychology Compass, 4,* 548–558.

Mead, G. H. (1934). *Mind, self, and society*. Chicago, IL: University of Chicago.

Sherif, M., & Hovland, C. I. (1961). *Social judgment*. New Haven, CT: Yale University Press.

Waldron, V., & Kelley, D. (2008). *Communicating forgiveness*. Newbury Park, CA: Sage.

6

When a Daughter Becomes a Son: Negotiating Gender, Identity, and Ambiguous Loss in Families

Kristen Norwood

Keywords

transgender identity, gender, ambiguous loss, relational dialectics theory, presence-absence

It's 4:00 p.m. on a Sunday afternoon at the O'Hara house. Anne, a college freshman who attends a school a short drive away, is home for the family's weekly Sunday dinner. This week Anne, her mother, Catherine, and her sister, Maureen, will be joined by Maureen's new boyfriend. Anne has been meaning to have an important conversation with her mom for some time now, but has been struggling to work up the nerve. Knowing there won't be an opportunity over dinner and that it will be time to get on the road back to school after that, Anne decides now is the time.

Anne: Mom, can I talk to you about something?

Catherine: Of course, Annie. What's wrong?

Anne: Nothing…or, I guess something, depending on how you look at it. (Anne pauses and takes a deep breath). Okay, there's something I've been struggling with for a long time and I didn't know how to talk to you about it because I didn't really understand it myself. But, I've done a lot of research and I've reached out to other people who struggled with the same thing and I finally feel like I understand who I am.

Catherine: Annie, are you trying to tell me that you're lesbian?

Anne: No. I'm not trying to tell you something about who I'm attracted to; I'm trying to tell you something about who I *am*.

Catherine: I know who you are—you're Anne Carter O'Hara—my brilliant, capable, funny, talented, loving daughter. Why would you need to do research to figure that out?

Anne: Thank you, mom, but that's just it—I don't see myself as your *daughter*. I know this is not going to be easy to hear, but I'm transgender.

Catherine: What? What does that mean? You mean like Cher's daughter?

Anne: Yes, like Cher's *son*.

Catherine: Oh, Annie, how could that be? You've never said anything about this before! You've never been a confused kid! You never hated your body! Now you suddenly want to become a man? That doesn't make sense!

Anne: Mom, I'm sorry. Please calm down. (Both Catherine's and Anne's eyes fill with tears). I know this is a lot to take in and I know it might seem sudden to you, but it isn't. I've felt this way for a really long time and it has taken me years to come to terms with it. I need you to try to understand that just because I didn't express what I was feeling doesn't mean I wasn't feeling it. Please, try to be there for me because this is hard enough as it is.

Catherine: Well, that's just it, Anne! Why would you want to make things hard on yourself like this? Do you even understand what kind of life you're setting yourself up for?

Anne: I know you care about me and you don't want me to be stigmatized or whatever, but I can't deny who I am just to save myself from some uncomfortable experiences. I mean, can you imagine someone asking you to live as something or someone you're not? Can you imagine society saying that you can't act the way you want to act or look the way you want to look or be the person you are?

Catherine: Oh, Annie. Society *does* tell me those things! As a woman I'm *expected* to do all kinds of things that I'm not prone to doing—bake, clean, be submissive, wear high heels—and you know I'm not very into makeup or girly clothes. Hell, I'm the only female mechanical engineer in my entire company!

Anne: I know, mom.

Catherine: When your dad died, I filled the role of mother and father for you. I think I've always provided you with a model of how to be a woman without conforming to some traditional ideal. So, why is it that you can't just do the same? I mean, you've already been that way for years now. You were always a rough and tumble kid. You didn't want to wear dresses and I didn't force you. You never wanted to be a princess for Halloween and nobody made you. You didn't want to take dance lessons like your sister did and I certainly never tried to talk you into that. You're a tomboy, plain and simple. Why can't you just be happy being that?

Anne: Mom, you've always been a great role model. You've definitely shown me how to break gender barriers and that's one reason I feel like I can face what I'm up against. But, the barrier that I have to break is different from the ones you broke. It's not about not wearing high heels or not having a typical female career – I mean, those things are important to me, but it's more than that. When you call me Anne it doesn't *feel* right even though it's been my name for 18 years. When someone says 'she' or 'her' when they're talking about me it makes me uncomfortable. When I look in the mirror I see someone who isn't quite me. I have to break through this female identity that doesn't reflect who I really am. I know it must be almost impossible for someone who isn't transgender to understand, but I also know that I cannot be happy if I have to continue to live as a female. Can you understand that?

Catherine: Honestly, I don't know. It's very hard for me to wrap my mind around it. I don't know what to think or feel right now. Of course, you're my daughter, so I—

Anne: Mom, please.

Catherine: What? I can't call you my daughter anymore? You just told me you don't feel like a female and within five minutes I'm supposed to be calling you my son? I'm sorry, Anne, but this is not just some switch I can flip! I love you and I will always love you, but you're going to have to understand that I need time to process this. And, in the meantime I think you should see a therapist.

Anne: I've been seeing a therapist, for four months, actually.

Catherine: Oh. Well, what did the therapist say?

Anne: He supports my decision to transition and is willing to recommend me for hormone therapy. And, actually, he suggested that you come with me to my next appointment.

Catherine: I'm sorry, wait, what is hormone therapy? How can this person who has only known you four months support this decision? I'm your mother, for goodness' sake! I've known you for almost 19 years now—I'm the one who has supported you, loved you, and raised you, mostly on my own. Don't I get a say in all this? (Tears run down Catherine's face).

Anne: Mom, please don't cry. Of course, I want you involved. I want you there with me every step of the way. When I transition it will be a transition for you, too, and for Maureen. My therapist is very experienced with this. He's been a gender therapist for 25 years and I trust him. I'd love for you to come to my next appointment. You can meet him and we can talk about this together.

Catherine: Oh, Anne, this is just all so fast. I feel like I'm losing you. How could you not be my daughter, my Annie, anymore?

Anne: Mom, please don't think of it that way. You're not losing me. I'm right here. (They share a long hug).

Catherine: Listen, we need to pull ourselves together. Maureen and her boyfriend will be here any minute. We'll talk about this again soon, though.

Anne: Okay, but one more thing. I brought some things for you to read about transgender identities and transitioning if you feel like learning more.

Catherine: Oh, okay. Thanks honey. That's very thoughtful of you. You've always been a very thoughtful person. So, I do want to ask you to please just give this more thought before you take any steps that are irreversible.

Anne: (Anne exhales loudly). Okay, I will give my transition choices more thought, but more thought won't change the reality that I'm transgender. I want to ask you to please try to understand that as best you can. Is that a deal?

Catherine: (Catherine exhales loudly). I'll certainly do my best.

Six months have passed since Anne came out to Catherine. Catherine has struggled to adjust as Anne, now called Carter, has begun to physically and socially transition to a male identity. Carter's transition has included not only a name change, but also pronoun changes and physical changes, some of which have been brought about through Hormone Replacement Therapy. Catherine and Carter are in a session with a therapist who specializes in LGBT family issues.

Dr. Mertz: Catherine, let's hear more about what you've been feeling in the last few months.

Catherine: Well, I feel happy to see my child happier. I honestly hadn't realized before all this that she—sorry, he. I slip sometimes. I hadn't realized that he wasn't very happy. But, I also feel (she looks down, her voice breaks) grief. That's the best way I can describe it. I feel something like I felt when my husband died. It's not nearly as bad, but it's similar. I know that doesn't make sense, but I've felt like I was losing Anne from the moment she told me about being transgender. Things only got worse when he started to transition. The feeling of loss grew when he cut his hair and began dressing in more masculine clothes. Then it was even worse when he started taking testosterone; his voice changed and his face looked different to me. I couldn't see much of Anne anymore. One of the hardest things has been making the switch to male pronouns and a new name. And, I think we've been interacting differently since those changes have happened, which might be my fault. I feel like I'm not supposed to have a mother-daughter relationship with Carter, so I've been trying to establish a mother-son relationship, but I don't have experience with that (she chuckles and then takes a deep breath). It feels like Anne has fallen away piece by piece and now Carter is here. It's like he's replaced her. I love Carter very much, but I feel like I've lost a daughter. I've lost someone...but no one has died. My child is still here, of course. It's very difficult and confusing.

Dr. Mertz: Catherine, what you're feeling is very normal, actually. A lot of families I've worked with have said that for them transition feels like a living death—that the transitioning family member is somehow present and absent at the same time. Actually, there's a term for what you're experiencing, it's called *ambiguous loss.* It's a kind of grief that we feel when we're not quite sure what it is that's lost. The object of grief is ambiguous and/or there's no sense of closure. This kind of grief can result from other circumstances, as well; for example, families who have a loved one with dementia can experience ambiguous loss. The person suffering from dementia is there in body, but not in mind, in a sense. It also happens in the reverse; some families struggle with a loved one's ongoing psychological presence when there's a physical absence. For example, when a military family member is missing in action the family might struggle to reconcile the physical absence of that person with the lack of confirmation of death, which can create an ongoing psychological presence.

Catherine: Wow, I had no idea there was a name for that. That sounds like what I'm experiencing in some ways, but different, too. I mean, my child is still here beside me *and* my child is still here psychologically, so that's different from what you're describing, right?

Dr. Mertz: I think it is in some ways. Like you said, your child isn't gone and yet you feel you've lost a person, in a sense, so although it's a different variation of ambiguous loss, I think the resulting feeling of grief is very much the same. So, maybe a good question for you to pursue is "What is it that is lost?" Consider the fact that you say "my child" is still here, rather than my *daughter* is still here. That seems to me to be very important.

Catherine: Right. I say that because it wouldn't make sense to me to say that my daughter is still here. My daughter—the little girl I raised, the little girl I imagined would be a mother herself someday—she's *not* still here.

Carter: Can I say something?

Dr. Mertz: Of course.

Carter: Mom, I'm so sorry you feel this way. I wish I could take this feeling away. I hate that I'm causing you pain. I'm doing what I can to ease it, you know. I thought it would help for us to choose my new name together. Did it?

Catherine: It did, honey, and it helps that the name isn't completely new. I do feel like Carter (she turns to Dr. Mertz), which is my maiden name, has always been a part of you, so there's something nice about that. There's a kind of continuity that I like about that.

Dr. Mertz: From what you've said, Catherine, and from what other families have said it seems that continuity, or the lack of it, is key to this issue. You say that you see *Anne*, your daughter, as gone and *Carter*, your son, as here. Carter replaced Anne in a sense. Anne and Carter are two *different* people for you. Does that seem right?

Catherine: Yes. I mean, I guess that's what I'm struggling with. I know they're not, but it seems like it in many ways.

Dr. Mertz: Mmm hmmm. I believe that at the core this is a contradiction in how you are constructing the meaning of Carter's transition. This version of the presence-absence dialectic, or meaning struggle, seems to stem from what we might call the gender binary. As a society, we see people as falling into one category or the other. We think of males and females as distinct, opposite, and even incompatible *types* of people. We see the difference between male persons and female persons as a *fundamental* difference, so it seems to us that one person cannot transition from female to male or male to female and still be the same person. Our identities are so intertwined with ideas about sex and gender that we have trouble separating personhood from them.

Carter: Hmmm. Yeah. That must be why people seem to always be trying to figure out what I am—male or female. It seems to really bother people when they're not sure. It's like they don't know how to interact with me if they don't know whether I'm male or female.

Dr. Mertz: Yes, I think we're compelled to sort people into categories and sex is one of the most basic categorization systems we have. I wonder, Catherine, are there ways that we can try to reconstruct the meaning of Carter for you? Is there another way of constructing meaning for what personal identity is or who this person—your child—is, in particular, that would relieve this struggle for you?

Catherine: I'm not sure what you mean.

Dr. Mertz: Sorry. That did sound pretty academic, didn't it? Let me try again. For example, can we think of persons as separate from sex and gender? Can a person just be a person and not a *male* person or a *female* person? Or, can you reconcile maleness and femaleness such that one person can be both male and female in a lifetime? And, are there things that can be done to facilitate continuity of the identities of Anne and Carter so that the transition seems like less the transition from one *person* to another and more like one person's transition? Stop me if I'm not making sense.

Carter: Yeah, that's what I've tried to tell you, mom. I'm the same person on the inside. It's just outside stuff that's changing and that shouldn't matter so much. The hair, the name, my voice—they're important to my identity, but that's not *all* of who I am and it's not the core of who I am. I'm me, whether or not you see me as male or female—whether or not I *am* male or female.

Catherine: I get what you're saying. I guess I can try to do some work to reframe things, but it won't be easy. You have to understand that even before you were born, once we knew your sex, I was thinking of you as a girl, you know? I guess I have associated that sex with what you call "the core" of who you are, so it will take some effort to rethink that. And, actually, it's not just your identity I feel like I'm undoing, but mine too. I've always been the mother of two daughters. That's very much a part of who I am, so there's that adjustment, too. I guess that's what you meant when you said this would be a transition for me, too, and for Maureen.

Carter: Yeah. And, mom, you and Maureen have been so awesome through this. I know it's been hard sometimes to be there for me because you're struggling with these feelings, but you've made things so much easier for me and I want to do the same for you, however I can.

Catherine: Thanks, sweetie. You're such a good kid. You must have been raised right (they laugh).

Carter: Definitely.

Catherine: Actually, I know one thing that would help me, I think.

Carter: Name it.

Catherine: Well, ever since you started transitioning, I've felt like I had to almost erase Anne. Out of respect for you, and maybe out of fear that I would offend you, I've put old family pictures away, I've been careful not to say your old name, and I've tried not to reference the past. That's been very hard. I think maybe if I felt like I didn't have to completely close the book on Anne then I could feel a little less loss.

Dr. Mertz: That sounds reasonable and helpful to me. Do you agree, Carter?

Carter: I do, actually. I hadn't thought of it from that perspective. I mean, at first, part of becoming the real me meant wiping away the old identity. You know, like getting rid of the girl people saw me as for so long was really important to me. Honestly, though, it doesn't bother me anymore when I do see old pictures of myself. I just kind of see it as who I used to be and this is who I am now, like, I grew out of that phase or something. I know for a lot of transgender people it's not that simple, but I think I'm okay with not completely erasing Anne, especially if it helps you, mom.

Catherine: Really? Well, wow. Okay. I feel a little bit better already just being able to talk about things like this with you. How about we do more of this? Maybe we can work on reframing things together by talking about stuff more openly and more often. Is that a deal?

Carter: We'll certainly do our best!

Dr. Mertz: Good. This is great progress, I think.

The author gratefully acknowledges the contributions of Jes Stevens who offered experiences and insights that informed and improved this case study.

For Further Thought and Reflection

1. West and Zimmerman (1987) argue that gender is a performance or something that we do, but that unlike other social roles we perform (e.g., student or teacher), gender functions as a *master identity* in social interaction because it has no specific context. In other words, the roles of *man* and *woman* are different from others because they are not as easy to relinquish. In what ways can we see this idea at work in the case of Anne/Carter's identity and Catherine's difficulty with her child's transition?
2. Catherine and Anne have a conversation about the difference between Catherine not conforming to traditional feminine expectations and Anne's desire to engage in an identity transition based on an internally felt gender identity. Do transgender identities and identity transitions support, challenge, or complicate the argument that gender is socially constructed through communication? What does this mean to you?
3. Dr. Mertz suggests that a gender binary may be at the heart of why Catherine struggles with Carter's transition. Do you agree? Are your sex and/or your gender central to who you are? Is it true that we see men and women as fundamentally different people? If so, how does this affect your own sense of identity and your communication with others?
4. What do you think Catherine is grieving over? What does it mean that her feelings of grief worsened each time she perceived change in Carter's behavior, physicality, or the gendered relationship between them? What does this tell us about the importance of communication to identity and vice versa?
5. Dr. Mertz suggests to Catherine that a reconstruction of meaning might be the key to moving past her struggle with the idea that her child is both present and absent. Relational Dialectics Theory (Baxter, 2011) posits that meaning struggles are central to the process of relating. In addition to presence-absence, some of the more commonly identified relational dialectics include contradictions between autonomy and connection, privacy and expression, and stability and change. Have you ever been in a relational situation where you felt caught between any of these or some other opposing viewpoints? If so, what did you do or say to manage that struggle?

References

Baxter, L. A. (2011). *Voicing relationships: A dialogic perspective.* Thousand Oaks, CA: Sage.

Baxter, L. A., Braithwaite, D. O., Golish, T. D., & Olson, L. N. (2002). Contradictions of interaction for wives of elderly husbands with adult dementia. *Journal of Applied Communication Research, 30,* 1–26.

Boss, P. (1999). *Ambiguous loss*. Cambridge, MA: Harvard University Press.

Granucci Lesser, J. (1999). When your son becomes your daughter: A mother's adjustment to a transgender child. *Families in Society: The Journal of Contemporary Human Services, 80*, 182–189.

Norwood, K. (2012). Transitioning meanings? Family members' communicative struggles surrounding transgender identity. *Journal of Family Communication, 12*, 75–92.

Norwood, K. (2013). Grieving gender: Trans-identities, transition, and ambiguous loss. *Communication Monographs, 80*, 24–45.

Norwood, K. (2013). Meaning matters: Framing trans identity in the context of family relationships. *Journal of GLBT Family Studies, 9*, 152–178.

West, C., & Zimmerman, D. H. (1987). Doing gender. *Gender & Society, 1*, 125–151.

Zamboni, B. D. (2006). Therapeutic considerations in working with the family, friends, and partners of transgendered individuals. *The Family Journal, 14*, 174–179.

PART II

Coming Together:
Developing Closeness with Others

7

Talking Family: The Discourses of Voluntary Kin

Dawn O. Braithwaite
Betsy Wackernagel Bach
Sarah E. Wilder
Haley Kranstuber Horstman
Sayaka Sato Mumm

Keywords

fictive kin, voluntary kin, discourse dependent families, turning points

Miriam scurried around the kitchen, working on Thanksgiving dinner. She checked the dining room table and decided it was lovely, with her grandmother's linens and china that she used only for special dinners. She straightened the tall candles and the little Thanksgiving Pilgrim couple, figurines that had always graced her mother's table when Miriam was growing up. Her mom, Esther, had given the Pilgrim couple to her when Miriam and Mike were newly married. Seeing them on her table brought back great childhood memories, despite the fact that Franco, the man she called "Little Bro," teased her every year since he and his partner Steve had moved in next door, claiming that the man Pilgrim was gay. "I mean, come on, look at those pants, those boots with the big buckle, and that hat," he'd say. Now Miriam's son Matt was joining Franco in poking fun at the Pilgrim figurines. *Little does Matt realize, he'll inherit those Pilgrims*, she thought, smiling to herself.

Miriam loved Thanksgiving and all the traditions associated with it—the turkey roasting in the oven, the cranberry salad, the wild rice dressing, and even Franco's jokes about her little Pilgrim man. She looked forward to the following day, as their tradition was to continue the festivities at Franco and Steve's and watch the final football game of the season against their arch-rival. Miriam always contributed a big pot of turkey soup from Thanksgiving leftovers.

Miriam counted the place settings around the dining room table one last time. There was a place for herself, Esther, Yuki, Franco, Steve, Dejon, her new friend at work, and Dejon's wife, Krista. Miriam had a lot of trouble deciding how to place everyone at the long table—Mike always sat on one end and she on the other. This was the first time she had hosted a formal dinner since he left. Their divorce was final just two weeks ago. "Stop it. Don't start thinking about it," she told herself. She switched the places around one last time. At first she planned to have her mother sit in "Mike's chair," but was afraid that Esther would not be able to hear well, so she switched her work friend Dejon to the end of the table. This way no one in the family would have to sit somewhere new this first Thanksgiving without Mike.

Miriam returned to the kitchen and checked the "kids' table" in the corner. The boys would enjoy eating in the kitchen where they could cut up and have a good time. Miriam hoped that Mike would get their son back home on time. Matt had spent the night with his Dad and Mike promised to get him home well before dinner. *Mike had better not get him back late like he did on Matt's birthday*, she muttered to herself.

Miriam forced her attention back to more positive thoughts. She basted the turkey and put a large pot of water on the stove to boil potatoes. The cranberry dish was done and she checked the clock; everyone would be arriving soon. She decided to wash up some of the dishes before she changed into that beautiful new sweater Yuki had given her. As she worked her way through the pile of pots and pans, her mind wandered. How many holidays, birthdays, homecoming games, and other events they had all spent together—Miriam, Mike, and Matt with Yuki, Esther, Steve, Franco, and their sons. They were inseparable, or so she had thought, and had often referred to themselves as "the family" when they were talking with each other. Steve and Franco's boys called Esther "Grandma" and had always called her "Auntie Miriam." Esther referred to Steve and Franco as "my boys" and always gave their sons Christmas and birthday presents, like she did for all her grandkids.

"Thank goodness for Mom," Miriam said out loud as she washed the last of the dirty pans. Esther had been a rock since the day Mike announced that he was leaving. Her financial support had kept Miriam afloat until she could refinance the house to cover the payments on her own. Then of course, there was Yuki—what would she do without the woman who was like a sister to her? She and Yuki became close almost immediately since meeting during sorority rush. Yes, all the women were technically sorority sisters, but Miriam's relationship with Yuki was definitely closer right from the start. When she brought Yuki home for Thanksgiving during freshman year that seemed to change things between them and quickly they felt like real sisters. Because Yuki did not see her family in Japan very often she joined Miriam's family for holidays and special events. After college, their relationship continued and Miriam was certain they would be sisters for life. Miriam was an only child, and she could not imagine any sister closer than Yuki.

Even though she lived just a couple of miles away, Yuki had spent the night at Miriam's. She was upstairs taking a shower before everyone else arrived. Yuki often stayed with Miriam the night before a holiday. In fact, Yuki, Miriam, and Mike had a long tradition of making blueberry pancakes for breakfast and reading the newspaper together. This year Miriam was especially glad to have Yuki stay over so she wouldn't wake up alone in a too-quiet house on a holiday. In light of Miriam and Mike's recent divorce, Miriam and Yuki decided to skip the pancakes and start a new tradition of home-made yogurt and granola. She and Yuki had Skyped with Yuki's parents in Tokyo last night. Even though they do not celebrate Thanksgiving in Japan, Yuki liked to talk with her parents on her American holidays, and Miriam was glad to join in and say a quick hello too—very quick, since they do not speak English!

Franco and Steve would be arriving any moment as Steve had promised to come and help make the mashed potatoes and the gravy, since Mike had always prepared them in the past. *They'll probably be late*, Miriam laughed to herself. Although Franco was always on time, Steve was perpetually late, trying to fit in one more task, editing one more manuscript, putting the final touches on a gourmet dish that he was making, or picking out the perfect bottle of wine to bring along. Miriam's thoughts turned to Steve and Franco's 20th anniversary celebration just this past Spring. Steve made his famous homemade lobster ravioli and set an elegant table for all of them. It was the last time that the whole family was together. Steve and Franco's two boys looked so handsome, and so uncomfortable in dress shirts and slacks. It was the first time Miriam had ever seen the boys out of jeans since they had bought their house seven years ago when the boys were in preschool. Mike joined the celebration, arriving late and leaving early. Miriam appreciated that he made the effort to be there, and recognized that it took some courage, as he knew that Esther, along with Steve and Franco, were furious with him for leaving Miriam. Everyone was on their best behavior for Steve and Franco's sakes, trying just a little too hard to make jokes and outdo each other with funny stories, like the family had always done.

* * * * *

As Yuki got dressed after her quick shower, she thought back to the Skype conversation she and Miriam had with her parents in Japan. Yuki could not believe how much time has passed since she had come to the U.S. for her college education. She still vividly remembered how helpless and lonely she was at first, surrounded by strangers, and struggling to get a good grip on English as her second language.

Once she became more comfortable speaking in English, Yuki joined a sorority in order to acculturate herself further and make friends. In the sorority, Yuki did make many friends, but more importantly, she found her "Big Sister," Miriam. Miriam and Yuki were assigned to be "Big Sister" and "Little Sister" during Yuki's first week in the sorority, and their sisterly bond grew from there. Yuki quickly thought about Miriam as her "sister in America," and Yuki's family in Japan had been more than grateful that Yuki developed such a solid and special bond in the United States. Since Yuki was very close to her family, despite living thousands of miles away from them, she was excited to have Miriam talk to her parents on Skype. This, in Yuki's mind, kept Yuki's parents happy and assured about how Yuki and her sister in America were doing.

Although Yuki felt blessed overall, she was not entirely without worries. Last night was the first night Yuki stayed overnight at Miriam's place since Mike moved out. As Yuki developed a strong sisterhood with Miriam, Miriam's other close ties, like her friends Steve and Franco, naturally became a part of Yuki's American family as well. Mike was no different. Now that Mike was gone, Yuki honestly was unsure about how this first Thanksgiving without him would unfold. Several questions ran through her mind. *How will the conversations go if everyone talks about past holidays, trips, and other occasions, when Mike was still one of us? Where are we going to sit at a Thanksgiving table without Mike? Who will make Mike's legendary pumpkin pie and mashed potatoes and gravy?* Yuki was concerned about Miriam's feelings, and was sure that Miriam would be nervous about how this Thanksgiving would play out. She couldn't help but imagine that the whole family would feel a void this Thanksgiving without Mike.

On Monday, Yuki had stopped over at Steve and Franco's on the way home from work to get their perspectives on Thanksgiving dinner. Yuki had met Steve and Franco through Miriam at one of Miriam's infamous Cinco de Mayo parties. She felt very close to Steve and Franco right away because of Miriam's strong bond with them, but soon developed a warm relationship of her own with them. Yuki considered Steve and Franco her "museum buddies," and they attended museum and gallery events in town frequently. The three of them had become closer in the last months since Miriam and Mike split up. They devised plans for getting Miriam out of the house and having fun, or called to consult each other on how Miriam was coping.

During their talk on the Monday before Thanksgiving, Steve and Yuki came up with ideas for keeping Miriam's mind off of Mike, while Franco chimed into the conversation from the kitchen as he was making dinner. They decided to suggest some new games to play after dinner to establish new traditions. Because of their close relationship with Miriam, the three of them felt a responsibility to support Miriam as she adjusted to the divorce. They knew Miriam would drop anything to help them in a time of need, and they were committed to doing the same for her. While taking care of one another was something they all did on a voluntary basis, during tough times like this they felt an especially strong sense of obligation to take care of her. Without Miriam knowing it, in fact, Yuki had turned down a trip to Chicago the day after Thanksgiving in order to stay with Miriam. Even though she regretted missing the new exhibit at the Art Institute, she knew that staying with Miriam was the right thing to do and what she wanted to do.

Still contemplating the upcoming day, Yuki headed downstairs to check in with Miriam. Miriam was still bustling around working on final details. Even though Yuki could see everything was ready to go, she easily fell into place next to Miriam in her efforts to straighten the candles and the table settings until all was perfect. Knowing Miriam had a lot on her mind, Yuki decided to just make a simple statement to her, "Miriam, you know I love you, I'm so grateful you are my family and I'm happy we can spend this holiday together, no matter what." Miriam looked at Yuki with moist eyes and smiled, and they kept working in silence. Both women continued to tidy up the house as they waited for Steve and Franco.

* * * * *

Steve and Franco were indeed running late when they arrived with their sons in tow. Even though they just lived down the street, they drove to Miriam's because they had decided to make extra dishes for the dinner in addition to helping with the mashed potatoes. Sensing Miriam's plight at hosting her first Thanksgiving alone, Steve had been cooking up a storm since yesterday. All four of them barged into the house like they always did, without waiting for Miriam to come to the door, each carrying something to add to the meal. Miriam was delighted, as she had confessed to Steve that since Mike had always planned their holiday dinners, she was at a bit of a loss at how to proceed without him. As usual, Steve delivered. Since Mike's departure, Miriam had come to depend upon Steve for moral support. They got together weekly just to drink wine and talk, and Miriam was most grateful for his friendship. He was always there for her when she needed to vent.

Miriam had known Steve and Franco since they arrived in the neighborhood. They had moved in down the street and their two boys were close in age to Miriam's son, Matt. The boys had all gone to preschool together, and now were all attending the same elementary school. Miriam, Mike, Steve, and Franco spent many warm summer evenings together at the baseball field. They would often bring a picnic dinner and eat when the boys finished their game. Miriam smiled when she thought of these times, because watching Little League games was always much more palatable when accompanied by the bottle or two of wine that the four adults shared with appetizers. Often, the two families and sons would stay at the field talking and eating until long after the game was over. Franco knew the constellations, so they would lie on their backs in the grass by the field and star gaze well into the night. They would always have a contest to see who could find Orion's Belt first. She was pleased that she, Franco, and Steve continued the picnic tradition this past summer despite Mike's departure, particularly for the sake of the boys, as all three had suffered in his own way when Mike moved out. The three boys were like brothers, and in fact often referred to each other as, "my fake-real brother" when talking with others. Thankfully Mike had gotten Matt back home on time and he was eagerly waiting for the boys to arrive.

As Steve, Franco and the boys entered Miriam's home, Steve looked at Miriam and whispered, "See if you can cheer Franco up. He's had a rough morning." Miriam threw Steve a quizzical look, and he responded, "Since it's Thanksgiving, Franco called his parents. I warned him—but he was too stubborn to listen to me."

Exasperated, Miriam replied, "Good grief! What happened this time?"

Steve rolled his eyes and said, "The usual. He should stop being such a faithful son to those people. They treat him so badly. They just won't acknowledge the fact that he is in a healthy, strong relationship and is a father to two beautiful boys. It drives me crazy since his sister has been married three times and had a string of failed relationships, but they treat her like royalty. Franco tries his damndest and always calls his parents to wish them a happy holiday and say that he misses them, but they just won't engage in any meaningful conversation. They are polite, but that's about it. They give a very cursory report about what they are doing, ask about the law practice, and hang up. As usual, they never ask about me or about the boys. It's as if we don't exist."

Steve continued, "I don't know why he keeps doing this to himself; he's just so sad after he talks with them. He says he believes he must keep some contact with them. I understand that he loves his family, and I know he thinks if he keeps at it, someday they'll come around, but I doubt it, I really do. Every holiday it's the same thing, over and over. I keep telling him not to call, but he still does. We have a lovely family here with you all. I just hate to see Franco get so torn up. And, it always wrecks our holiday for an hour or two until he snaps out of it. Thank God for you, your mom, and Yuki."

Nodding in agreement, Miriam replied, "Yes, I feel bad for Franco. I can certainly understand why he would want to try to keep contact with his family, and I know that it's hurtful and frustrating—for all of you. That being said, I am so glad that we're here for each other, particularly around the holidays." "That settles it," Miriam told herself, "I'll be sure to sit next to Franco at dinner; I can always make him laugh."

* * * * *

"Goodness, the house smells wonderful with this great meal spread out before us," Dejon exclaimed from the head of the table. "Miriam, it is so kind of you to invite Krista and me for Thanksgiving. We are so far away from our families and it would not feel like a holiday with just the two of us. You have all been so welcoming and we appreciate the cooks. You can count on us for dish duty afterward!"

"I am glad to abandon my post!" Esther added.

Dejon continued, grinning "You bet. And, hey, I didn't expect you to ask me to sit in the 'seat of honor' at the head of the table!"

Dejon's last statement was met with dead silence around the table. Everyone had noticed Dejon was seated in Mike's chair and no one quite knew what to say. Finally, Franco broke the tension, "OK, I'll say it, We all miss Mike. It's better to say it, rather than pretend nothing has changed. Dejon, you had no way of knowing that this is where Miriam's former husband Mike sat for our dinners. This is the first holiday he hasn't been here." Everyone sneaked a peek at Miriam who had tears sliding down her cheeks, as did Yuki. Dejon looked embarrassed, "Oh, I, I am so sorry, Miriam!"

"You didn't say anything wrong, Dejon," Yuki said. "It's just that we've had this little family going for a number of years, since college for many of us. This is our first holiday without Mike and it is tough." Yuki turned to Miriam. "We are so sorry. We wanted everything to be just like it was, and a good day for you above all."

Miriam paused. She had dreaded facing these feelings of missing Mike and she had vowed to herself she would not cry and ruin everyone's dinner. But actually, it seemed worse to have Mike gone and pretend everything was normal. Acknowledging his absence felt like the right thing to do. "Hey, guys, it's okay. I appreciate that you are all trying to make this a good day for me. And this first holiday without Mike is, of course, rough. But I am also aware that this is a loss for all of us. We have long called ourselves a family. So this is a loss for our whole family. Things are not the same, but here we are. I love you guys. Matt and I are both so grateful for your place in our lives. You've made these last months much more bearable. And it is good to have Dejon and Krista here too." Miriam managed a smile and wiped her eyes.

Franco rose from his chair and held his wine glass high. He looked around the table at these people he loved. "What is it about holidays that bring out all these strong feelings? Well, all I know is that we are family. A changed one, but family nonetheless. So, I propose a toast to family and to new friends." With that everyone stood, raised their glasses and joined in the toast. Steve chimed in, "And to the turkey too." Franco laughed and sat down, exclaiming, "Okay, people, let's dig in!"

Steve carved the turkey and Yuki poured the wine. The kids came in to the dining room, plates in hand, and the parents dished out their food and helped them carry their plates back to the kitchen and get settled in. They could hear giggles and silliness coming from the kitchen. "You kids be sure to eat some vegetables too," Esther called after them. "Last year I think all Matt ate was pie."

Miriam looked around the table and was grateful for all the people here with her today. She took Franco's hand and squeezed it. "Thanks Little Bro. Today's not easy, and, of course, Christmas is right around the corner. Mike is talking about wanting to take Matt to visit his girlfriend's family in Los Angeles." Franco looked her in the eye, "One day at a time, Miriam, one day at a time." He turned to Esther to his right "Hey, Esther baby, pass the potatoes and prepare for a major defeat in our Scrabble tournament after dinner!"

For Further Thought and Reflection

1. How has communication changed among the different members of this voluntary family since Mike moved out?

2. Braithwaite and colleagues (2010) identified several types of voluntary families: (a) substitute (replacing family), (b) supplemental (long-term relationships that form due to lack of emotional closeness or geographical distance, or in addition to blood and legal family), (c) extended (two families become one), and (d) convenience (family-like relationships in a particular time or place in life, that may not continue beyond that time). How would you categorize relationships of the different voluntary family in this case study?

3. What are major turning points (important points of positive or negative change) in the experiences of this voluntary family?

4. Galvin (2006) talks about non-traditional families as "discourse dependent," in that without cultural models and set roles, they have to interact and figure out how to be a family. How did these people come to regard themselves as family? How do they know what is expected of them?

5. Do you regard Miriam, Esther, Yuki, Steve, and Franco and their children a *real* family? Explain.

References

Braithwaite, D. O., Bach B. W., Baxter, L. A., Hammonds, J., Hosek, A. M., Willer, E., Wolf, B. (2010). Constructing family: A typology of voluntary kin. *Journal of Social and Personal Relationships, 27,* 388–407.

Braithwaite, D. O., & DiVerniero, R. (2015). "He became like my other son": Discursively constructing voluntary kin. In L. A. Baxter (Ed.), *Remaking "family" communicatively* (pp. 175–192). New York, NY: Peter Lang.

Galvin, K. (2006). Diversity's impact on defining the family: Discourse-dependence and identity. In L. H. Turner & R. West (Eds.), *The family communication sourcebook* (pp. 3–19). Thousand Oaks, CA: Sage.

Muraco, A. (2006). Intentional families: Fictive kin ties between cross-gender, different sexual orientation friends. *Journal of Marriage & Family, 68,* 1313–1325.

Nelson, M. K. (2013). Fictive kin, families we choose, and voluntary kin: What does the discourse tell us? *Journal of Family Theory & Review, 5*, 259–281.

Weston, K. (1991). *Families we choose.* New York: Columbia University Press.

8

He Says/She Says: Misunderstandings between Men and Women

Julia T. Wood

Keywords

gendered communication patterns, speech communities, instrumental communication

Ginger walks out of her last class of the day to find Luke waiting for her, as he usually does on Tuesdays and Thursdays. She greets him with a hug and they fall into a matched pace that soon will lead them to the library.

"Becky got an offer from BellTech—her first choice," Ginger says, knowing Luke will be interested because Becky is a mutual friend of theirs.

"Yeah? That's great." Luke says, raising his voice to compensate for a nearby student who is talking loudly on his cell. "We'll have to take her out to celebrate."

"Well, she hasn't accepted yet."

"What's she waiting for? A red carpet? BellTech is one of the coolest companies around."

"Chicago is pretty far away, you know, so it's a big decision," Ginger explains. She thinks how hard it would be for her to move away from Luke and all her friends and family. She adds, "And Ben doesn't want her to leave. He's not comfortable with a long-distance relationship. He's encouraging her to turn down the offer."

"That's selfish. They can visit and skype and do FaceTime. Lots of people have long-distance relationships."

"Maybe, but it's not the same as being together. Besides, I think she's worried that taking the job might end the relationship with Ben."

"Let's focus on the job offer, not the relationship," Luke suggests. "That's the issue for her right now."

"But the two are connected. How can Becky decide about the job without making a decision about Ben?" Ginger thinks about all short-term relationships Becky has had. "In the three years we've known Becky, she's never stayed with anyone for long. Whenever a relationship starts to get serious, she bolts. The question is whether she's going to do that again with Ben."

"So you think she won't take the job?" he asks, glancing at construction where a campus building is being renovated.

"What I really think is that this offer may be an easy way to end the relationship." Ginger tries to make eye contact with Luke, but his eyes remain focused on the surroundings. "I think her pattern of bailing out of relationships is because her parents divorced when she was 12. Maybe she doesn't trust a relationship to last."

"Maybe a job is more trustworthy," Luke says. "Besides, this is the time for her to launch her career. She can settle down later if she wants, but opportunities like BellTech don't come along every day."

"Neither do relationships," Ginger says sharply.

"Well, I think she should take the job. It's a sure offer, and who knows if she and Ben will last."

Ginger is irritated by Luke's assumption that his answer is the right answer. It's not his business to say what Becky should do. Ginger wonders how she would feel if her parents had divorced. Would she be wary of committing to a relationship? Wanting to share her thoughts with Luke, Ginger asks, "Do you think people whose parents divorced are less able to form commitments?"

"Beats me," Luke replies, only half listening to Ginger. He gets frustrated when she starts a conversation on one topic and then wanders onto another and another. He finds it hard to follow her thinking and there's never any closure on the topic that started the conversation.

Ginger looks at Luke and asks, "If your parents had divorced, do you think you would shy away from relationships? Do you think we wouldn't be together?"

"I don't know," he replies. How is he supposed to answer a hypothetical question? His parents didn't divorce, so he has no idea how he'd feel if they had. And what does any of this have to do with Becky's job offer? Why can't Ginger ever stick with just one topic? "I don't have any idea. They didn't split up, so how can I tell you how I would have felt if they had? Can you get back to the point?"

"This *is* the point. The point is about Becky's feelings about relationships," Ginger snaps.

"You started it by telling me Becky had an offer from BellTech, and now we're talking about hypothetical family dynamics. Can we focus on whether she should take the job?"

"It's not my place to say what she should or shouldn't do, and it's not your place either. I'm trying to consider all of the issues that are connected to deciding about the job offer," Ginger says crossly. "Why can't you ever let a conversation evolve naturally?"

"There's a difference between a conversation that evolves and one that rambles all over," he growls. "I'd just like for you, for once, to stay on topic."

"I am on topic! Lots of things are linked together. Do you think what Becky does about BellTech's offer is irrelevant to her relationship with Ben or her parents' divorce?"

"It's a job offer. She takes it or she doesn't," Luke replies. "Whether or not her parents divorced and whether or not she is serious about Ben, she has to decide about the offer. She's 21 years old. She should get her career started."

Ginger lets out an exasperated sigh. She is so tired of trying to have a real talk with Luke and having him try to force the conversation into some narrow cubby hole or flood her with advice she hasn't asked for and doesn't want.

"Let's just drop it," she says.

"Fine with me," Luke replies. He is happy to drop this conversation—one more in a long line of ones where he and Ginger wind up irritated with each other. He loves her but gets frustrated when she wanders all over in their conversations. If she would just stick to the point . . .

* * * * *

Michelle drops by Luke's room that afternoon and says, "Hey, guy, what's happening?"

He smiles, glad to see Michelle. They first met during first year orientation and became fast friends. They share core values, root for the same teams, and have similarly wicked sense of humor, leading to many pranks played on each other. In the three plus years since they met, Michelle and he have seen each other through academic anxieties, minor medical problems, and many, many relationships. He finds it so easy to talk with her about whatever is on his mind. He doesn't have to put up a false front and hide feeling afraid of things, like he does with his guy friends. Michelle always takes him as he is and empathizes with his feelings.

"Nothing much, really. I'm just kind of aggravated with Ginger," he replies, clearing his clothes off a chair so Michelle can sit.

"Trouble in paradise?" she teases. When Luke doesn't smile, Michelle asks, "So, is there a problem between you two?"

"No, not really—just a problem that keeps coming up when we talk. She starts a conversation about one thing and the next thing I know we're all over the map. She's unable to stick to a topic. The minute I try to respond to one thing she's said, she's bouncing off somewhere else." Luke describes what happened today to Michelle and then says, "I mean why bring up the job offer if she wants to talk about how divorce affects children?"

Michelle laughs, "Oh, that's easy. She wasn't just trying to talk with you about the job offer or divorce."

Luke's face reflects his confusion. "Huh? She brought up those topics. What do you mean she didn't want to talk about them."

"Well, she did and she didn't," Michelle explains. "She was talking about them because they were on her mind, but mainly she just wanted to be in touch with you and share herself with you. It could have been other topics. It could have been plans for graduation day or anything. Talking with you about what's happening in her world makes her feel closer to you. Or it would if you would let her talk about all of the stuff that's connected."

"That's crazy."

"No, it's just not how you think and talk."

"But it's incoherent," Luke insists. "You can't have a conversation about one thing, like a job offer, if you're jumping to relationships and divorce and everything else."

"But, Luke, in Ginger's mind what Becky decides to do about the offer is related to her relationship with Ben and what she does about Ben is related to her parents' divorce. Ginger probably feels that Becky would be less likely to take the job in order to stay near Ben if her folks hadn't divorced. If you understand that, then you understand why Ginger would bring up those other things."

"Is that why she got angry when I offered advice?"

"She probably was more interested in having you tune into what she was thinking and feeling than in any advice. You don't always have to fix things, you know."

"But the only reason I give her advice is because I care about her," he protests.

"I get that, but I wouldn't bet that giving advice feels caring to Ginger. Maybe you two should talk about what you want in conversations," Michelle suggests. "It sounds to me as if there are times, like in this situation, where you are really talking past each other."

* * * * *

That evening Ginger is hanging out with her roommate, Cassandra. She describes the earlier conversation with Luke and expresses her frustration that he never seems willing to talk in a free-flowing kind of way.

"I know what you mean," Cassandra says, nodding vigorously as their eyes connect. "The same thing happens with me and Aaron. I'll start talking about something and that will lead naturally to something else, and then he's all over my case for what he calls 'rambling.' But it's not rambling to deal with a lot of issues that are all so related."

"Exactly," Ginger says. "And no matter what I bring up, Luke's first response is to give advice. That drives me crazy—like I need his advice or something. Mr. Answer Man."

"It used to drive me crazy, too," Cassandra agrees. "But in my Gender and Communication course I learned why this happens. It's not just you and Luke and me and Aaron. It's a problem a lot of women and men have when they talk."

"Really?"

"Yeah, really—we're not alone," Cassandra laughs. "When we were kids and learning how to interact with others, we mainly played with other girls and Aaron and Luke mainly played with other boys. Boys and girls play differently and communicate differently, so we learned different ways to interact."

"Such as?" Ginger prompts.

"According to an article I read for one of my classes, most girls learn to weave issues and people together in conversations, but guys generally learn to compartmentalize topics and people. So to them it feels logical to deal with one topic at a time, but to us it feels logical to mix everything together. Some researchers who study this think this happens not only because of socialization but also because women and men tend to have different brain specialization."

"What does that mean? Like math or English preferences?" asks Ginger.

"Well, how we use our brains might explain why some people have more aptitude or interest in math and others in English, but I was talking about the fact that women are more likely than men to use both sides of their brains, so they tend to connect things."

"So it's a basic gender difference?"

"Well, not entirely. Gender isn't the only thing that affects how we communicate," Cassandra qualifies. "We've read some research that shows there are differences between how, say, Black and White and Asian people communicate, so ethnic communities also affect how we interact. Like, men are more assertive verbally than women are, but Black women tend to be more assertive than White women. That's what I mean about gender not being the whole story. You can't say 'all women do this, and all men do that,' but you can say there are some general patterns."

Cassandra thinks back to her class. The teacher used the term "speech communities" to describe the different ways women and men generally communicate. Her teacher explained that researchers had observed young boys and girls playing, and had discovered that the boys and girls played in different ways. The boys tended to play games like football and war that were structured by rules (what counts as a touchdown; what counts as victory in battle), whereas girls tended to play games like house and school in which there were no clear-cut rules. The girls had to talk with each other to work out how to play their games—who would be mommy and who would be daddy, what they would do in the game. As a result, girls were more likely to learn that talk builds relationships and is a way to link people together. In their games, the boys used communication mainly to define events (calling out a foul) and to plan strategy (the huddle). The researchers also noticed that games boys typically played were more competitive whereas games girls more typically played were cooperative. After a lot of observations, the researchers concluded that boys learn to use communication to achieve specific things whereas women learn to use communication to create relationships. Thinking back over what she has learned in her class, Cassandra tries to translate it for Ginger.

"I think it's like this: You were talking to Luke about Becky's job offer more to connect to him than to report on the job offer, right?"

Ginger shrugs. "Well, yeah, I wanted to connect with him about her job offer and all of the stuff related to it."

"Exactly," Cassandra says. "But Luke probably saw the conversation as about the job offer, so he addressed that. For him, the point was to solve the problem of whether or not Becky should take the job. He didn't understand talking about the issue as a way for you and him to relate."

"Weird." Ginger shakes her head. "Why would you talk to someone if you weren't trying to relate to them?"

"If you were a guy, you might talk to resolve an issue or accomplish something like telling news or solving a problem or giving directions or offering advice."

"But I didn't ask him for advice. I was just trying to talk with him about Becky and the connections between the job offer and her relationship with Ben and her parents' divorce. Why does he feel compelled to give advice instead of just listening or talking with me?"

"He was trying to help, trying to support you and Becky by figuring out what she should do."

"But why won't he connect with me first and then offer advice, if he feels he has to do that?" Ginger asks. "I mean, isn't that the point of talking, anyway?"

"To you, it is, but it may not be to Luke, because he may not perceive the point of conversation the same way that you do," Cassandra reiterates. "And he may find your way of talking just as confusing as you find his. He probably thinks it's really weird that you don't stick to just one topic. And he probably thinks it's really strange that you didn't want his advice. He was trying to help, after all."

"Do all straight couples have this problem?" Ginger asks.

"Probably not all, but what we are studying in my class shows that an awful lot of them do. My teacher says the biggest problem is not that girls and guys approach conversations differently, but that they judge each other's way as wrong or inadequate or something like that."

"You mean like when I say it's weird that he doesn't see conversation as a way to connect?"

"Just saying….." Cassandra smiles.

Ginger laughs, "Boyfriends!"

"Amen to that," Cassandra agrees.

* * * * *

After class the next Thursday, Ginger finds Luke waiting in the usual spot. She walks over to him and hugs him hello. "Becky turned BellTech down," Ginger announces.

"Wow, that's news," he replies as they start walking.

"She decided to stay because of the relationship with Ben. We had a long talk about how she always ends relationships, and she said she didn't want to continue that pattern."

"So does she think it's because her parents divorced?"

Ginger stops and looks at him. "What's going on? You don't sound like yourself."

"Well, I'm beginning to understand a bit better why you put all these things together in a conversation, and I'm trying to follow the connections you make instead of always telling you what ought to happen or to stay on topic."

"That's so strange, because I talked with Cassandra the other night and she helped me understand why you like to tackle one topic at a time and that when you give me advice you are trying to help, rather than saying you think you have all the answers or that I can't solve my own problems."

"I thought you knew that I was trying to help. Why else would I offer advice if I didn't care about the problem and you?"

"I sort of get that now," says Ginger.

"So Becky really turned BellTech down, did she?" he says to resume the conversation. "Is she interviewing with other companies now?"

"Right now she wants to focus on the relationship with Ben and see where it might go," Ginger replies. "I think making the relationship a priority is a real breakthrough for Becky. She's never done that before in all of the time we've known her."

"But this is prime time for interviewing. She shouldn't delay that or she might not get a job at all."

"So your advice is that she should be interviewing?" Ginger asks with a mischievous smile.

He grins and says, "Even when you start to understand gendered patterns of communication, it's hard to break out of them, isn't it?"

For Further Thought and Reflection

1. Reread the conversations between Ginger and Luke, Ginger and Cassandra, and Luke and Michelle. What gendered patterns of communication can you identify in the three conversations? How similar are the conversations in these cases to your own experiences communicating with women and men?
2. Why do you think Luke talked with a woman friend instead of a man friend? Whom do you talk with when you are upset or frustrated? Why?
3. How much does understanding the sources of gendered conversational patterns help men and women to avoid misunderstandings and frustrations in their interactions?
4. In this case Cassandra noted that gender is not the only aspect of identity that affects communication. Drawing on your experience and observation, can you point out ways in which communication is influenced by race, ethnicity, religious and spiritual values, economic class, and other aspects of social identity?
5. To what extent have you experienced gendered patterns in conversation similar to those in Ginger's and Luke's relationship? If you have experienced these patterns, how did you respond and feel when they happened?

References

Maltz, D., & Borker, R. (1982). A cultural approach to male-female miscommunication. In J. J. Gumperz (Ed.), *Language and social identity* (pp. 196–216). Cambridge, UK: Cambridge University Press.

Metts, S. (2006). Hanging out and doing lunch: Enacting friendship closeness. In J. T. Wood & S. W. Duck (Eds.), *Composing relationships: Communication in everyday life* (pp. 76–85). Belmont, CA: Wadsworth-Cengage.

Wood, J. T., & Inman, C. C. (1992). In a different mode: Masculine styles of communicating closeness. *Journal of Applied Communication Research, 21,* 279–295.

Wood, J. T. (2014). *Gendered lives: Communication, gender, & culture,* 11th ed. Belmont, CA: Wadsworth-Cengage.

9

Traversing Racial and National Boundaries: Adopting Transracially and Internationally

Elizabeth A. Suter

Keywords

White privilege, intrusive interactions, online support groups, protector vs. educator roles, racial derogation, topic avoidance

ANN'S STORY

Announcing Our Plans to Adopt

I come from an all-White family. No one is adopted and no one has married across racial lines. Raised in a primarily White and largely Catholic Midwestern city, I have a series of troubling memories about race from growing up. The worst happened when I was walking with my paternal grandfather in his recently racially-integrated neighborhood. A large Black family was hanging out on their porch, barbecuing on the front lawn, playing music, and simply having a grand ol' time. I still feel sick remembering hearing my grandfather calling them "jungle bunnies" and going on and on about how the Blacks were bringing down his neighborhood.

With hindsight, I now realize that announcing to a family like mine one's plans to adopt a child of a different race and from a different country should have been fraught with anxiety and negative anticipation. I guess I wanted to believe that my parents were less prejudiced than they really are. I was just so excited to share my big news. I simply couldn't wait to let my family in on it.

My spouse, Charles, and I shared our adoption plans in my parents' dining room with my parents, siblings, their spouses and children all seated at the table. With tremendous excitement I proudly announced: "Charles and I have wonderful news and we wanted you to be the first ones to know. We have decided to adopt a baby girl from China!" My nieces and nephews immediately shouted "Cool!" In their young eyes this was simply an alternate path for the arrival of a long-overdue cousin. The only reaction from my dad was a cleared throat. Not usually a positive sign. After a short-while, he began with what I now refer to as the "Why" questions: "*Why* would you *adopt*? Don't you want your *own* child?" (pause) "Why *China* of all places?" (even longer pause) "And why not adopt from America if you are set on adopting? Don't you want the chance at a White child?"

I was quite taken aback by his questions and the lukewarm reactions of the other adults in the room. I kept saying to myself, *What just happened? I have taken all the required pre-adoption classes. I have taken 'Race in America,' 'Being a Multicultural Family,' 'Chinese Culture.' I thought I was armed and ready. What just happened?*

In retrospect, I realize I should not have been surprised.

I now recognize that my naivety came from my failure to realize all the privileges my family and I get from being White in America. Sure, I had taken all the pre-adoption classes, but these classes had stopped short of forcing me to fully consider my own race as a White person. The class materials had focused on the racial and cultural background of our internationally adopted child. Not my racial and cultural heritage. In the classes we learned how as parents we can help our child to grow up with a positive cultural and racial identity. The instructors suggested ideas such as enrolling our child in Mandarin language lessons, attending Chinese culture camps, staying in touch with our adoption travel group so our child could be raised around other transnational and transracial families like our own. Ultimately, like my experiences growing up, these classes left unexamined my own racially privileged status as part of the White majority race in America. Race and culture mattered; it just didn't matter for me.

Adopting MeiLin

At the time, I figured my father's remarks and the other adults' less-than-enthusiastic responses were unique to my family. I envisioned other parents announcing their plans to the joyful receipt of friends and family members. So, I sucked it up and moved on. Frazzled by adoption paperwork and preparing for our adoption trip to China, it was easy to think about other things.

We flew the nearly 7,000 miles from Chicago to Beijing to adopt the most amazing 11-month-old girl. Our chubby-cheeked, almond-eyed, brown-skinned, jet-black haired daughter was all mine—despite my blond curls, blue eyes, and alabaster skin.

Returning to the Midwest, we quickly settled into a new family routine. My spouse returned to work while I began the process of acquainting MeiLin with her new community. Thrilled to introduce MeiLin to my favorite local grocery stores, parks, restaurants, and shops, we began making the rounds. My enthusiasm, however, was quickly tempered. Everywhere I turned it seemed like someone had a new question or comment. In public I felt like we were on display. Different versions of my father's initial questions seemed to appear everywhere: "Are you her *real* mother?" "Didn't you know that there are 400,000 children in the U.S. foster care system needing homes?" Or, the worst one: "How much did she cost?"

I turned to the Internet for advice. I found a myriad of online adoption support groups with adoptive parents discussing similar issues. Others were struggling with my same need to better understand these intrusive encounters. Parents were posting questions just like those running through my own head: "Why had I and my family suddenly become open to outsider comment and judgment?" "What is driving people to make such remarks?" "Why do people feel entitled to ask and receive answers to such blunt and personal questions?" "Don't they realize the impact of their comments and questions?" I quickly realized that I was not alone in this struggle.

Fortunately one of the online support group participants was both an adoptive mother and an adoption researcher. She often posted findings from her own research and that of others that provided some guidance. Her online messages provided me tremendous insight. Perhaps most importantly she helped me understand how adoption is viewed in America. She explained how adoption is still seen as "second-best" to the first choice option of having children biologically. Adoption is seen as a lesser than, last resort version of family turned to when the "natural" or "normal" way to have children fails.

Her posts helped me to begin to examine my own racial privileges as a White person in America. For the first time in my life, I began to see White as a racial category. I began to understand that race doesn't only matter for people with darker skin, but that it also deeply matters for me. I saw that my own previously unexamined White racial privilege was a big part of the reason that outsider remarks had felt so troubling and invasive to me. Prior to adopting MeiLin, I had passed unnoticed in my mostly White community. But now, as a transracial family, we call attention to ourselves. This unsolicited negative attention from strangers had forced me to confront my own racial privileges—for the first time in my life.

The researcher helped me to understand that people stare and make remarks not usually because they are intentionally trying to be hurtful. They are not trying to be intrusive or to challenge our identities; they are usually just trying to reduce the uncertainty and ambiguity created by my family's visible differences. Strangers are often unaware of the underlying negative messages, oblivious to how their remarks question the authenticity of adoptive family relatedness (e.g., "Are they *really* sisters?"), reinforce biological normativity ("Just wait. Now you will get pregnant and have your *own* child") reflect nationalism (e.g., "She is so lucky to have been adopted into America"), commodify adoption (e.g., "Was it worth all the money?"), objectify the adopted child (e.g., "She looks just like a china doll"), position the adoptive parent as "wonderful" savior for "rescuing" this "poor" adopted child, disparage children's birth cultures ("You know, in Asia they KILL girl babies"), and question parental decision-making (e.g., "Why *China*?").

Present Time

MeiLin is now 15 years old. Across the years, I have learned a lesson or two myself—particularly how to best respond in these situations. I used to react much more defensively. I thought my role during these public encounters was to protect our family identity. I thought, as a mother, that it was my job and my duty to defend and shield our family from potentially harmful outsider remarks. I reasoned that being confrontational was a justifiable response to these inappropriate remarks. Particularly when remarks had racist or anti-adoption overtones, it was like my wall would just go up. To me, it would literally feel like our family was under attack. The part I probably regret most was that I was always watching when we were out in public. I could never really relax when we were out and about as a family. I was always on guard.

I am now embarrassed to admit it, but I used to spend much of my time trying to come up with real zingers. Since we received certain remarks over and over, particularly about cost, why we didn't look alike, whether or not I was her *real* mother, and why in the heck we chose China, I worked on sassy comebacks. My favorite response when people asked me why I adopted from China was to say, "Because I like Chinese food." Or, when they asked me if I was her *real* mother to respond by saying, "Don't I look real? I am standing right here." I hoped that my comebacks would shock people into realizing the negative meanings underlying their remarks and to think, even just for a moment, about how what they say impacts us as a family.

I now realize that this was a defense mechanism. I was just trying to cope with the emotional costs of these recurring, unsettling encounters. What is more, my chronic protection of our adoptive identities came at a price. I was losing a part of myself. Unfortunately, I wasn't able to change for a long, long time. I wasn't able to change until I found myself trying to "toughen up" MeiLin. One day I actually heard myself trying to prepare MeiLin for coping with a "tough" world inhabited by "cruel" people. This woke me up. These were not the messages I had intended to communicate to my daughter. Something simply had to change.

I began wondering if I could stop worrying so much about protecting our identities and shift toward using these interactions as opportunities to *build* family identity. Outsider remarks weren't going away. We would always be a conspicuous family and that wasn't changing. But what if I began to change? What if I changed what I did before, during, and after these interactions? I began shifting how I was preparing MeiLin. I stopped trying to toughen her up and started trying to empower her instead. I found this great book about the "W.I.S.E. Up Method." It was intended just for adopted children. In the book, a very wise old owl explains to the child that she or he can *choose* how (and if) to respond to others' questions. The book gives the options of **W**alking away, saying "**I**t's private," **S**haring (e.g., "I was born in China"), or **E**ducating (e.g., "Many children are available for adoption from China because of China's One-Child-Policy"). MeiLin could be W.I.S.E. MeiLin learned that it was entirely up to her how to respond and that she could choose her response depending on who was doing the asking, her relationship to him or her, and the person's tone of voice.

Not only did I shift what I was doing to prepare MeiLin, but I also changed my own responses during actual encounters. Over time, I learned to better manage these intrusive interactions—even with my family. I now answer with increased sensitivity. As MeiLin got older, she began to understand the nature of outsider remarks. And even if she didn't quite yet fully understand everything that was said, she certainly was beginning to take her cue more and more from the way I reacting as a parent. I began to craft my responses with MeiLin in mind, worrying less and less about my own snappy comebacks. I began to realize that how MeiLin feels in these interactions is of upmost importance—particularly when outsider remarks have racist or anti-adoption overtones.

But perhaps most importantly, I started doing something after the interactions. Before, I would just come home and ruminate about what they had said, what I had said, and how next time I was gonna have an even better comeback. But now, I started holding what I came to call debriefing sessions with MeiLin. MeiLin was maturing, and I too was maturing as a parent. These debriefing sessions allowed time and space for us to unpack challenging remarks removed from the emotional charge of the interactions. I came to think of myself more as MeiLin's educator rather than her protector. These debriefing sessions became a safe space for MeiLin to express her feelings. Up to now, it hadn't really dawned on me to be concerned about what was going on with her. Under the guise of protection, I was caught up in firing back the zinger of the day. But when I made the space and took the time to listen to MeiLin, I realized how little I actually understood about her perspective.

But, quite frankly as MeiLin has gotten older, I seem to receive these comments and questions less and less. Remarks were near-constant when MeiLin was younger. But, ever since she started school, remarks and stares have decreased. I don't know if people have changed or if our community has just adjusted to us. All in all, I am feeling much better and relieved that these challenging interactions seem to be fewer and further in-between.

MeiLin's Perspective

If I had to sum up how I feel about these interactions with strangers who make comments or ask inappropriate questions about me or our family, I would say one word—frustrated. Hang on. I need two words—frustrated AND angry. One thing that really peeves me is how everyone is always staring at us all the time. What's up with that? I feel like I am this beautiful, expensive china doll in a glass display case. When people walk by, they just can't help themselves. They stare. They gawk. It's like they can't keep their eyes off of me. It's like my parents are the people at an art museum that direct you through the exhibit and remind you to keep your voice down. But people can't stay quiet. It's like this china doll is the most beautiful, exotic thing they have ever laid their eyes on. So they ask the people working at the exhibit. "Oh my gosh, where did you ever get her?" "She is so beautiful!" "I want one too!" You might think I am kidding here, but people really say this stuff. I just want to scream back, "Hello . . . I am a REAL person. I am not some object you can just buy and sell." One time, back when my mom was more sassy, I heard my mom respond to the "How much did she cost" question with, "You can't BUY people, that is human trafficking, by the way." You should have seen the other lady. She glared at my mom and shot back, "That is not what I meant." My mom said, "Oh really? Then what exactly did you mean?" The lady just turned on her heels and stomped away. My mom asked me if I had overheard. I told her I didn't, but I really did. I felt so proud of my mom. That she would stick up for me made me feel so close to her. I hope that lady learned her lesson and will think twice the next time.

As I have gotten older, some really gross and creepy things have started happening when my dad and I are out together by ourselves. I don't know if he has told mom about this stuff, but I sure know I am not gonna be the one to tell her. The first time it happened I was with my dad who was in the checkout line at the liquor store. My mom waited in the car, but I came in to help him carry the wine for our annual neighborhood Christmas party. So I'm standing there while my dad is fussing about whether or not he has enough red wine and the sales clerk actually asks my dad, "Where did you get a pretty young thing like that?" The clerk starts going on about being a Vietnam war vet and all the women he saw over in "'Nam" and I'm like, "Dad, I'm out of here. You can carry your own stuff." I walked out to the car. My mom was like what's up. I just said nothing. In a few minutes, my dad got in. The ride home was very quiet. That was way gross. We've gotten some other weird stuff since, like when we are being seated at a restaurant people assuming I am his girlfriend, which I totally hate. Kinda ruins my appetite.

And the stuff that goes down on the bus on the way to school. No WAY am I telling my mom about that. The worst was during middle school on the bus or in gym class, you know, times when we were less supervised. No one ever tried to trip me or "accidentally" knock into me like I saw them do to the boys. It was always making fun of how I looked and calling me names, which was bad enough. I have been called every name in the book: "Chink," "Jap," "Chigger," "banana," "gook," a "Nip," a "Charlie," just to name a few. Kids used to pull back their eyes to mock the almond shape of my eyes. One boy on the bus used to say how he could blindfold me with a piece of dental floss. Tons of jokes about my flat nose. I gave up trying to wear sunglasses because they would always joke when they slid down my face.

I don't know why I don't tell my mom about all this stuff. It's not that I avoid telling my mom about the teasing, the name-calling, and the mistaken identities because I don't think she is capable of helping me with my problems. Having heard and seen her in action before, I actually think she would help me come up with some pretty cool stuff to say back. It's just that I want to fit in. I mean, geez, I just want to blend in with my mom and dad, with my friends. My friends at school don't have to deal with this crap. No one thinks they are their dad's girlfriend. No one asks them if their mom is their *real* mom. I hate being different. I wish people just wouldn't notice that I am not White. It does make me feel lonely and isolated not to be able to tell my mom about this stuff, but I don't know. I think it would make me feel even more different from everyone if she and I talked about it.

For Further Thought and Reflection

1. What advice would you have for people who are curious about adoption but are not sure what to do or say?
2. As MeiLin has gotten older, people address their remarks directly to MeiLin rather than to her mother, Ann. How would you explain this shift?
3. In Ann's narrative, we see Ann realizing it was more important to pay more attention to MeiLin and worry less about having the perfect comeback. Unfortunately, this is coming at a time when MeiLin prefers to avoid the topics of racial and cultural derogation. What suggestions might you have for Ann for how she might get MeiLin to open up? What might you say to MeiLin to persuade her to disclose to her mother?
4. While Ann is trying to change her communicative style to be more responsive to MeiLin, MeiLin remembers with fondness times when her mom shot back sassy comebacks. Her mom's zingers were affirming to MeiLin; they made MeiLin feel particularly close to her mother. Which do you think is a better parental response style: Protector or Educator? Explain the reasoning behind your choice.

References

Docan-Morgan, S. (2010). Korean adoptees' retrospective reports of intrusive interactions: Exploring boundary management in adoptive families. *Journal of Family Communication, 10,* 137–157.

Docan-Morgan, S. (2011). "They don't know what it's like to be in my shoes": Topic avoidance about race in transracially adoptive families. *Journal of Social and Personal Relationships, 28*, 336–355.

Jacobson, H. (2009). Who's watching?: Interracial surveillance and biological privilege. In M. K. Nelson & A. I. Garey (Eds.), *Daily practices of surveillance among contemporary families* (pp. 73–93). Nashville, TN: Vanderbilt University Press.

Suter, E. A. (2008). Discursive negotiation of family identity: A study of U.S. families with adopted children from China. *Journal of Family Communication, 8,* 126–147.

Suter, E. A., & Ballard, R. L. (2009). "How much did you pay for her?": Decision-making criteria underlying adoptive parents' responses to inappropriate remarks. *Journal of Family Communication, 9,* 107–125.

Suter, E. A., Reyes, K. L., & Ballard, R. L. (2011a). Adoptive parents' framing of laypersons' conceptions of family. *Qualitative Research Reports in Communication, 12*, 43–50.

Suter, E. A., & Reyes, K. L., & Ballard, R. L. (2011b). Parental management of adoptive identities during challenging encounters: Adoptive parents as 'protectors' and 'educators.' *Journal of Social and Personal Relationships, 28,* 242–261.

10

Becoming a *Real Family*: Turning Points and Competing Discourses in Stepfamilies

Dawn O. Braithwaite
Leslie A. Baxter
Paul Schrodt

Keywords

stepfamily development, turning points, relational dialectics, rituals, caught in the middle

Lonnie was lugging the last of her clothes down the stairs. The large trunk made a loud "thump!" as she dragged it down the worn steps. "Which of you kids is making all that racket?" her mother, Gail, called brightly. Lonnie smiled to herself. Even though she was 18 years old and off to college, she still loved to bug her mother. "Where are Tim and Celia? I want to get going soon so baby Emily will sleep while we're on the road." Lonnie pointed out to the driveway where Tim and her sister, Celia, were waiting next to the van, packed with Lonnie's treasures.

As she stood at the bottom of the stairs, Lonnie felt strangely sad. It didn't seem that long ago that she hated this house. Now the day to leave for college had come and all Lonnie could do was think back to all her family shared in this old yellow house. In some ways, it was even hard to remember what life was like before they lived there, but as she stood waiting, she remembered other moving days.

Dad Moves Out

Lonnie had known this day was coming. It was just two weeks after her 12th birthday. Her parents, Gail and Gene, had a huge fight the night before, the worst Lonnie and her nine-year-old sister, Celia, had ever heard. Things had been bad between her parents for some time. For many years, the family had enjoyed a weekly family dinner at a local diner, Flo & Mo's. For nearly a year now that ritual had degenerated with her parents bickering all the way back from the restaurant.

Finally, one warm July night, Gail and Gene called Lonnie and Celia together after dinner and explained that they had tried to work things out, but that "sometimes moms and dads just can't make things work." Their father was moving out. They had decided that the girls would be better living with their mom, and they would have dinner with him on Wednesdays and spend every other weekend and part of each summer with him. Lonnie was not unfamiliar with this arrangement, as several of her friends whose parents were divorced had similar schedules. Despite this, Lonnie and Celia were devastated by the news.

The Single Years

For the next two years, Lonnie and Celia lived with Gail in their house on Evergreen Street. They didn't have much money, and they missed having their mom and dad together. The only good part was that they did not miss their parents arguing all the time. Once their dad got on his feet and bought a condo, Lonnie and Celia shared a huge bedroom with their own flat screen TV and Netflix. In contrast, things were tight financially at home with mom. They turned their dad's old office into a bedroom for Celia and painted a second-hand bed and dresser for her. Each sister had her own room at least, and Lonnie relished her time alone.

Gail was working hard to support them, while also going to night school. Lonnie knew about their financial problems, as her parents did fight about money whenever that subject came up. They passed messages back and forth through Lonnie, for example, "Tell your mom your sister needs new skates" or "Bring a check from your dad for the dentist's bill. I just can't cover it." Lonnie liked to be in the know on what was happening, but talk about money made her feel uncomfortable and she did not like being the messenger for her parents. And she hated it when one of her parents criticized the other. All too often her parents took their anger out on her when she delivered a message, which just didn't seem fair. Sometimes she felt like a bone caught between two dogs when this happened.

Lonnie took on a lot of responsibility and learned to cook. She often had dinner waiting when her mom dragged herself home. The three of them enjoyed really talking when they went out for pizza on payday and then went window-shopping. As they walked along looking in the shop windows, their mom asked them about what was going on in their lives, and they shared their concerns and questions. At times, as Celia skipped ahead of them, mom also began to share a lot of her own worries, and Lonnie began to feel as though her mom treated her more like a close friend than a daughter at times. In one sense, this made her important and closer to her mom, yet it also felt uncomfortable now and then. Sometimes her dad would text or call during these outings and, even though she felt bad doing it, Lonnie would not answer during their special times with mom. She struggled, as it was hard to please both parents at the same time.

Tim Moves into the Scene

That summer Lonnie and Celia had spent a month with their dad and his parents at the lake. It was great to see her dad and grandparents, but Lonnie missed her mom. They texted and Skyped a few times, but the wireless connection at the lake was limited. When they arrived home, Gail ran out to meet them, and Lonnie noticed that her mom had a new hairstyle. When she asked about it, Gail blushed and said, "Oh, we'll talk about it." They went out to Flo and Mo's and on the way home, mom said, "Well, girls, I hope that you don't mind, but I am going to the movies later tonight." Lonnie was surprised and asked, "Going out? With Betty?" "No, well, um . . . with Tim." Mom stammered, "Tim Bartino, a man I've been seeing." Lonnie felt sick. "You mean you've been dating someone and you didn't tell us?" "No, Lonnie, well, yes I, I met Tim at school last spring. We had coffee a few times, but the last couple of weeks we have been going out. Don't worry—it's nothing serious." Lonnie and Celia didn't say anything, because they didn't want to hurt their mom's feelings, but as the two of them talked that night they shared their anger and disappointment that their mom wasn't home on their first night back. Both of them wondered how their dad would react when he found out that their mom had met someone else.

Over the next few months, "nothing really serious" became "something serious" as Gail and Tim began spending more time together. Lonnie and Celia were wary of Tim at first—unlike their dad, he was a quiet man. He was divorced with two children—Tony, who was a high school junior, and Tina, who had dropped out of high school in her senior year. Tony and Tina lived with their mother, three hours away, and it was six months before Lonnie even met them.

Tim was spending much more time with them; in fact, he was staying at their house most of the time now. At first, all of Lonnie's conversations with Tim were brief, awkward, and filled with small talk. However, once they had worked through some of the initial nervousness, like seeing Tim at breakfast, things fell into a fairly normal routine. For the first time, life seemed kind of like it was before her parents' divorce. She knew something had changed in their lives the first time Lonnie found herself telling a friend that she had to be home for a "family dinner." It was nice and, well, just normal to have the four of them together, and their mom seemed so happy. At the same time, this bothered Lonnie too. Had their mom been unhappy with just the three of them? Were her old family and her dad really that replaceable? One evening when Tim asked her what time she would be coming home from a party, she blurted out, "Hey you're not my dad! I am not ready to trade dads this year!" He looked very hurt.

On Thanksgiving weekend, Tim moved in for good. Her mom called a "family meeting," and the four of them discussed the move. Tim said he had already spoken with Tina and Tony and said, "they are looking forward to spending our first Christmas together." At first Lonnie felt strange when her mom used the term "family meeting"—were they a family? She didn't feel the same as she had with her real family, yet, as Tim moved in, it seemed like a new period had started in their lives. Family-like routines had developed, and things began to feel different. As she got to know him, Tim was a little easier to talk with. Lonnie began to open up a little more with him and to share with him what was going on with some of her friends at school. Lonnie started watching football with Tim on Sundays, as they both loved sports. She didn't tell her dad about getting closer to Tim because she didn't want him to feel bad.

Things changed in their household. Whereas Lonnie was used to taking care of her mom and making dinner, now Tim often made dinner, and she had to admit he was a great cook. One of the things that really irked Lonnie was that Tim now went along on their payday dinner and window-shopping nights. Celia and Lonnie missed talking with just their mom, and both felt like they had to compete with Tim for their mom's attention. When Lonnie brought it up, Gail seemed irritated, "Now, Lon, Tim is just trying to be part of the family. Give him a break!" Pretty soon they stopped having their nights out altogether.

The Wedding and Move to a New Home

Spring and the summer after her first year of high school were a busy and happy time. Gail and Tim announced their engagement in April and planned an August wedding. Lonnie was glad to see her mom so excited, and she had to admit she genuinely liked Tim and the way the family was going, especially when it was just the four of them. Tony seemed OK, but things were tense when Tina was around. Since they would not be living with them, Lonnie figured it really didn't matter.

Before he asked Gail to marry him, Tim took Celia and Lonnie out to lunch and asked how they felt: "I don't ever intend to replace your dad, but I love your mom and I know we can have a good life together." It meant a lot to Lonnie that Tim respected them enough to consult them. Nonetheless, Lonnie had some mixed feelings about it all and she worried how her dad would react. She had to admit that she certainly felt much more at home with Tim and mom these days than she did with her dad. She liked Tim a lot, and it was hard to imagine their family without him now. The younger Celia didn't seem to be bothered by any of it and was excited that all four kids were to serve as attendants at the wedding. Lonnie felt kind of lucky when she compared herself to some of her friends who described how upset they had felt attending a parent's second wedding.

In June, Tim and Gail began looking for a larger house. Just before the wedding they bought a big old yellow farmhouse on three acres of land. It was definitely a fixer-upper, and Gail was excited about the huge kitchen and told the girls they would finally be able to have a garden! The problem was that the house was 20 miles away from their present home. Lonnie protested, "Mom, this means I will have to leave all my friends and start a new school for my sophomore year! I don't want to attend South High!" Gail seemed too busy to even hear her concerns.

As the wedding day approached, Lonnie felt mixed emotions, "How can I feel so happy and so sad at the same time?" The night before the wedding Lonnie told Celia, "I know this sounds stupid, but I guess till today I always thought mom and dad might get back together." Celia agreed, "I know what you mean—I wish Tim and mom weren't getting married! And I am not going to call Tony and Tina my brother and sister!" Despite these mixed feelings, it was a nice wedding and, as Tim and Gail exchanged their vows, Celia and Lonnie cried—for all they had lost and for all they had gained.

On Saturday they had the wedding, on Sunday they moved to the yellow farmhouse, and on Monday, the girls started at new schools. These were among the darkest days of Lonnie's life. She missed her friends, and she absolutely hated the farmhouse. Most importantly, she resented Tim and her mom's time alone together when she desperately needed her mom's attention and support. Tim and Gail put off their honeymoon to work on the house. During the home repair period, Lonnie and Celia had to share a room, and they fought constantly. The low point was when Tina came for the weekend and slept in their already crowded room. Time alone was starting to be a distant memory for Lonnie.

The First Christmas

By the holidays, things had settled down. Lonnie had joined the choir at her new school and had a date for the Holiday formal. Christmas had always been special in their household and Gail promised, "I plan to make it very special for us all." Her family had always come together on December 24th to decorate the tree with all their family ornaments and sing Christmas carols. They went to Christmas Eve Mass and then spent a quiet Christmas Day at home—just the family—opening gifts and enjoying a huge turkey dinner.

Gail had everything ready for Tony and Tina's arrival the morning of the 24th. When they arrived—late—Tina said, "Geez, it doesn't look much like Christmas around here. Don't you people even have a Christmas tree?" They filled her in on their plans for the day's activities, but Tina did not seem interested. As Gail, Lonnie, and Celia decorated the tree, Tim and Tony sat and watched and Tina texted her friends. Tony and Tina refused to go to church. On the bright side, Tim had gone shopping on his own to buy a special present for each of the four kids. Tina complained that "my dad does this every year and comes home with the most goofy stuff," but Lonnie was touched by his efforts and the gift he chose for her.

On Christmas Day Lonnie, Celia, and their mom worked on the traditional Christmas dinner and Tim joined in. Tony and Tina were trying to get everyone to go to the movies, "C'mon you guys—let's get out and *do* something!" Lonnie tried not to show it, but she was really pissed off at those two. "Mom, why can't they just join in and give our traditions a chance?" Gail ran interference, saying to Tony and Tina, "Look why don't you two go to the movies, and we'll hold dinner so we can all eat together, OK?" Lonnie hated to admit it, but she felt much more comfortable when Tony and Tina were gone and just the new family was there.

Tim and Gail spent all their free time throughout the winter and spring months working on the house. Tim made a special effort to finish the interior of Lonnie's and Celia's bedrooms first so they could move into their own rooms. Tony came to visit much more than Tina, and Lonnie appreciated appreciated that he was starting to feel like a brother to her. Tony and Tim had a long-standing routine of watching sports together on Sundays. Lonnie started to join them and soon Tim and Tony started calling her "one of the guys." Although she could never bring herself to say it to their faces, Lonnie often referred to Tim and Tony as "her dad" and "her brother" to her friends.

Dad Remarries

After the first of the year Lonnie and Celia learned that Gene was seriously dating Victoria, a divorced woman with a four-year-old son. They met Victoria a few times at elegant but very formal dinners in her immaculate home. Gene and Victoria married in a ceremony at the courthouse in the late Spring. In fact, Lonnie and her sister didn't even find out about their marriage until afterward and, although she felt guilty admitting it to herself, Lonnie just could not get all that excited.

Dad said that they would now "be a family," but it certainly did not *feel* like a family. Not like what she felt as a child with her mom and dad, or what she felt with mom and Tim. In fact, it surprised her to see how strongly she felt about her new family with Tim. Lonnie had grown close to Tim over time and he knew way more about her than her own dad did. In fact, Lonnie thought about her mom and Tim as her main or primary family.

Lonnie could not say that she truly disliked Victoria, but she could not warm up to her. As time went on, Lonnie and Celia found reasons to miss their weekends with them or go home early. They loved their dad, and didn't want to hurt him by telling him how they felt.

Tina Moves In

As her junior year began, Lonnie was surprised at how happy she was. One good thing was that Gail and Gene were getting along better and had started meeting alone for coffee once a month to talk about the girls. What a change that was, and Lonnie was relieved not to always be the messenger between her parents. Shortly after the school year began, Gail called a family meeting. At the meeting, Gail and Tim announced that Tina would be moving in with them for "a while until her money problems were under control."

Tina was very rude and demanding. She smoked constantly and got into fights with Lonnie in particular. When Lonnie complained to her mom and Tim, they took Tina's side: "Look, Lonnie, Tina is adjusting to a lot here and has her own problems to work through right now. Let's try and keep a lid on things, OK?" Finally, Tina got on her feet financially and was able to move out. Lonnie was really glad Tina was gone and the family went back to normal. Lonnie viewed Tina as an outsider to their family and she always felt uncomfortable when she had to introduce her to friends. She could not describe Tina as her "sister," so she usually just tried to avoid the whole matter or introduced her as "Tim's daughter."

A Second Dad

Things were going pretty smoothly by Fall of her senior year. Tony had moved to the city to attend community college and lived in an apartment close by. He spent a lot of time with the family now and was a great big brother. School was going well, and Lonnie was making college plans. Tim was especially helpful with her college applications. Her dad and Gail had negotiated and each agreed to pay 40 percent of her expenses at the university if Lonnie would cover the other 20 percent with jobs and loans. Lonnie was surprised when Tim told her, "Let's keep this between the two of us and I'll cover some of your extra expenses when you need help."

The big family news was that Gail was pregnant and expecting a baby around Easter! Tim was ecstatic, and Lonnie had to admit that she was surprised at her own reaction—she was really excited! Celia was less certain about the whole thing and worried that "they will only have time for the baby—what's going to happen to me?"

The weekend before the Homecoming dance, Lonnie was out shopping when she suddenly felt hot and queasy and had stabbing pains in her side. When she called home, Tim answered the phone and said he would be right there. It was all she could do not to pass out. Tim took one look at her and raced her to the emergency room. He held Lonnie's hand as he drove like a wild man. Gail showed up soon thereafter and called Gene. Lonnie's appendix had burst and she was rushed into emergency surgery.

Tim barely left Lonnie's side while she was in the hospital. She had always known he cared about her, but she never realized just how much. When her friends stopped by, Tim told them, "You better get going soon, my daughter needs her rest." Lonnie had never heard him call her "daughter" before. Just as the words left Tim's mouth, her dad called to check in. Lonnie did not tell him how she got to the hospital and said that her mom had taken good care of her.

Baby Emily's crying pulled Lonnie back into the present. Tim shooed them into the van. "We've got to get to the university by noon," Tim reminded them. Lonnie shoved the last of her stuff into the van and they were off. Gail exclaimed from the front seat, "Oh geez, I was supposed to call your dad and let him know where to park for the parents' orientation. He'll be upset I forgot. Lonnie, honey, give your dad a call and tell him it's Parking Lot F4, will ya? It will be better coming from you." Lonnie sighed. Today of all days, she did not want to cause a stir. *It's never simple,* she told herself and dialed the phone.

For Further Thought and Reflection

1. Compare and contrast the changes that occurred in the communication between Lonnie and her stepfather, Tim, and that occurred between Lonnie and her dad, Gene. In what ways did the conversational patterns of these dyads become more or less personal and intimate?
2. What are major turning points (important points of positive or negative change) in the development of Lonnie's original family, single-parent family with Gail, and two stepfamilies?
3. Relational Dialectics Theory explains that relationships are organized around competing discourses—opposing systems of meaning or worldviews. Discursive competition can unfold between the value attached to openness and the value attached to nonexpression. How do Lonnie and her parents deal with openness and nonexpression, and how does Lonnie end up "caught in the middle" between them at times? What other competing discourses can you identify in Lonnie's relationships in this case?
4. Rituals (routines and traditions) are important recurring communication practices that honor some aspect of family life. How did family rituals change as Lonnie's families changed? Why were they able to adapt some rituals and not others, as family circumstances changed? Sometimes, rituals are empty, failing to satisfy their participants. Are there any empty rituals in this case study?
5. What is a "real" family? How does society define what a "real family" is? What are the communicative practices that make a family "real"? Do some families have an easier time of it than others in feeling like a "real family"? Why so?

References

Baxter, L. A. (2011). *Voicing relationships*. Thousand Oaks, CA: Sage.

Baxter, L. A., Braithwaite, D. O., Koenig Kellas, J., LeClair-Underberg, C., Lamb-Normand, E., Routsong, T., & Thatcher, M. (2009). Empty ritual: Young-adult stepchildren's perceptions of the remarriage ceremony. *Journal of Social and Personal Relationships*, *26*, 467–487.

Baxter L. A., Braithwaite, D. O., & Nicholson, J. (1999). Turning points in the development of blended family relationships. *Journal of Social and Personal Relationships, 16,* 291–314.

Braithwaite, D. O., Baxter, L. A., & Harper, A. (1998). The role of rituals in the management of dialectical tension of "old" and "new" in blended families. *Communication Studies, 48,* 101–120.

Braithwaite, D. O., Toller, P., Daas, K., Durham, W. & Jones, A. (2008). Centered, but not caught in the middle: Stepchildren's perceptions of contradictions of communication of co-parents. *Journal of Applied Communication Research, 36*, 33–55.

Schrodt, P. (2015). Discourse dependence, relational ambivalence, and the social construction of stepfamily relationships. In L. A. Baxter (Ed.), *Remaking "family" communicatively* (pp. 157–174). New York: Peter Lang.

Schrodt, P., Braithwaite, D. O., Soliz, J., Tye-Williams, S., Miller, A., Normand, E. L., & Harrigan, M. M. (2007). An examination of everyday talk in stepfamily systems. *Western Journal of Communication, 71,* 216–234.

11

No Strings Attached: Friends with Benefits on a College Campus

Kendra Knight
Paul A. Mongeau
Denisha Biggers

Keywords

friends with benefits, hookups, dating, relational uncertainty, emerging adulthood

First Year Orientation

At eleven o'clock on a Friday night in September, a popular college bar called Josie's Grill has a line out the door and snaking down the block. Inside, men in polo shirts and women in stilettos crush against the bar, vying for the bartenders' attention. Whitney, a first-year college student, who got into the bar using her older sister's ID, wraps her small hands around six shot glasses full of a pink liquid and squeezes through the mob back to her table. She sets the shots on the high-top table to cheers and feigned groans from her friends.

Her roommate Lindsay, who also entered the bar using a fake ID, holds her shot glass up in the air and turns a clumsy pirouette, shouting "Woo-hoo!" The gang downs the drinks in unison.

Lindsay stumbles and yelps in pain as a guy at the next table steps back onto her foot.

"Ow! Look out!"

The young man reaches toward Lindsay, spilling half his beer trying to catch her. "I'm so sorry!" He shouts over the roar of the crowd.

"No worries!" Lindsay shouts back over the music. "Here, let me buy you another beer!"

"Okay, thanks! What's your name?"

"Lindsay."

"Nice to meet you Liz."

"No, *Lindsay*!"

"Sorry! *LINDSAY.*" He bends his face close to her ear: "I'M JEROD."

Homecoming

Whitney opens her eyes on a Saturday morning. Because she has lived in her dorm room only a few weeks, some mornings it still takes her a little while to remember where she is. The room is completely dark except for a ribbon of light glowing around the door frame. Her roommate Lindsay holds the door ajar with her foot while she whispers to someone in the hallway. Lindsay is saying goodbye to Jerod, who has shared her tiny dorm room bed the last three Friday nights. Whitney clicks on her bedside lamp as Lindsay squeezes back through the door.

Lindsay says, "Oh, sorry, I hope I didn't wake you up."

Whitney replies, "No, I woke up because my stomach is growling. What time is it?"

"Almost ten. We've gotta hurry if we're going to make breakfast at the dining hall." The two of them slip on sweats and flip flops and shuffle down the hallway toward the stairwell.

Whitney is glad for Lindsay's company because most days, she eats breakfast alone. She and Lindsay hit it off right away as friends, but Lindsay declared right away that she is not a "morning person." And whereas Whitney was raised in a big family in which every day started with family breakfast, Lindsay's parents both had high-powered careers that meant they were typically at the office by 7 a.m. To Lindsay, therefore, a Diet Coke and a granola bar is typically as good a breakfast as any. But on weekends, Whitney can usually drag her roommate out of bed at least in time for brunch.

Whitney teases Lindsay about her overnight guest, "So, this is the third weekend in a row with Jerod? Getting pretty serious, huh?"

Lindsay rolls her eyes, "Not even *close*. We're not even dating."

Whitney says, "Well, something is going on! I hope you didn't lock me out of our dorm room until 3 a.m. because you were just talking!"

Lindsay says, "Well yeah, we *are* hooking up... but we're not dating. We're...I don't know...friends with benefits."

"I thought you had to be *friends* before you could be friends with benefits? You just met him a month ago."

Lindsay laughs and says, "Well, I think that for some people, you have to be friends to be friends with benefits, but I just mean that we're not *in a relationship* or anything like that."

"Okay," Whitney shrugs.

"We're still getting to know each other," Lindsay offers.

"Well, it seems to me like you know each other pretty well!"

"Yeah..." Lindsay absentmindedly chews on the inside of her cheek. "It's kind of the opposite of a typical relationship, I guess. We definitely clicked right away physically, but we're still sort of on the superficial level in other ways. Like I don't know anything about his family or anything."

Whitney nods, "Yeah, I think a lot of college relationships are like that. Or more than I expected when I first came here..."

"Well, we talked about it last weekend," Lindsay replies, "He said he wasn't looking for a relationship. He just got out of a long-term thing with his high school girlfriend, and he just wants to be single. His fraternity and his career are more important to him right now."

Whitney asks, "Is that what *you* want? You seemed pretty into him after that first night."

"Well, he's not looking for a relationship...and I guess I don't really want that either. I'm just having tons of fun hanging out with lots of different people. That's the most important thing to me right now. Jerod and I just have fun when we're together, and then we do our own thing the rest of the time. When you stop and think about it, it's really the best of *both* worlds."

Whitney says, "Well, if that's what you want, then I'm happy for you! Anyway, what are we having for breakfast? I'm starving!"

Midterms

At 2 a.m. on an early Sunday morning, the Phi Zeta Theta frat house is a wreck. Last year, as a first year pledge, Jerod would have been up until dawn picking up beer bottles and keg cups while the upperclassmen crashed. Thankful to be a sophomore, and free from cleanup duties, he lounges in an armchair in the front room. One pledge, who escaped cleanup duty by volunteering as a designated driver, pulls his car into the circle driveway to haul a group of the guys for a late-night run to Luigi's Pizza. Jerod squeezes into the back seat next to his frat brother Matt and opens his phone to text message Lindsay.

Matt says, "See if you can get some girls to meet us back at the house!"

"Yeah right," Jerod says sarcastically, "You have a girlfriend."

Matt says, "Relax. I'm just talking about hanging out! Besides, you have a girlfriend too."

"Who are you talking about? Lindsay?"

"Don't play dumb. You haven't hung out with another chick this whole semester."

"Maybe, but she's not my girlfriend."

"Yeah well, does she know that?"

"Yes."

"Did you have '*the talk*'?"

"Yeah, actually I told her from the beginning that I didn't want a girlfriend."

Matt says, "The *very* beginning?"

Jerod says, "Well, almost the beginning—after we'd hooked up like twice."

"How did that go over?"

"Um, fine. I think she may have wanted to date at first, but once we talked, she knew that wasn't going to happen. She's cool with it now. We just hang out when it's convenient for both of us."

"Like right now."

"Yup." Jarod clicks a message into his phone: "going to luigis rt now then back to the house u coming over?"

* * * * *

Lindsay, Whitney, and their friends shuffle out of a bar called Moose's at last call. Their high heeled shoes click an irregular cadence on the cement sidewalk as they cling to each other for balance and warmth against the chilly autumn night. More than a little tipsy, and with their ears ringing from bar music, they trudge up the long hill back to campus. Lindsay's phone buzzes to life and a picture of Jerod appears on the screen. Actually, it's a picture of him and Matt, drunk at the Homecoming game. Whitney says, "Let me guess...it's Jerod."

Lindsay replies, "Good guess..."

Whitney asks, "Is there an after-party at Phi Zeta tonight?"

Lindsay says, "I don't know. He says they're picking up Luigi's and asked if I want to come over."

Whitney says, "Well, let's go then. Text him and tell him to get us a large supreme with extra cheese!"

"Oh, pizza sounds so good right now! But... I don't know if I want to."

"Eat Luigi's or go to the house?"

"*Whitney...*"

"Okay. Why not?"

"Well, it kind of bugs me sometimes that he doesn't call or text until two in the morning. Or, if we go to the bars or a party, we just get drunk, hook up, and then pass out.

"And that's a bad thing? I thought that's what you said you wanted." Whitney says.

"Well, it is...it was...I don't know...in some ways it's good—perfect really. I usually get to hang out with you guys and then see him later. But it wouldn't kill me if we hung out more often, outside of parties and stuff."

"Okay..."

"I guess I'm just a little confused about Jerod's and my relationship."

"But a few weeks ago, Linz, you said there wasn't any relationship," Whitney says.

"Well, there isn't. Or there isn't *supposed* to be anyway. But sometimes I feel like... I feel like I want something *more*, almost as if I *like* him or something."

"Yeah?"

"I don't know," Lindsay shrugs, "I guess I shouldn't make a big deal out of it. I should just enjoy it while it lasts."

"So are we going to meet the guys at Phi Zeta or not?" Whitney asks.

"Sure, why not? The night is young!"

Finals Week

Jerod kicks open the large oak front door of Phi Zeta Theta, holding two 10-pound bags of ice in each hand. He holds the door for Matt, who inches past him carrying a folded up gaming table.

Jerod says, "You're setting up beer pong on the porch tonight? It's going to get cold later."

Matt replies, "Yeah, I don't want a bunch of people spilling beer in the house—we don't want another deep clean before winter break."

Jerod sets the ice down in the foyer, blows in his hands to warm them up, and follows Matt onto the porch. Matt's phone vibrates in his shirt pocket. "That's probably Kristin." Matt hands the table to Jerod and slides his thumb across his phone to read a text message.

Jerod says, "Is she coming tonight?"

"Yep. She finished her finals today so she's driving down for the weekend with one of her roommates from State."

Jerod leans the table on its side and unfolds the collapsible legs. "That's cool. I invited this girl Jenna from my Spanish class so I'm hoping it's not all guys here tonight."

"Oh *really*. What about Lindsay?"

Jerod shrugs. "Um, I don't know what she's up to tonight. Probably hanging out with her friends or something."

Jerod and Matt stand the table upright. As they walk back into the house, Matt says, "I'm surprised you didn't invite *her*."

Jerod replies, "I don't know...I hadn't really thought about asking Lindsay. We don't have to hang out every weekend. Plus, I think I like this girl Jenna. I want to try to get to know her a little better, maybe ask her out."

Matt says, "Whatever happened to Mr. 'I just want to be single and not tied down?'"

Jerod replies, "First of all, it's just a date. Second... it depends on the person. Lindsay is cute and cool and we have fun, and I think our arrangement works fine. But with Jenna... I don't know, I think there's just something *more* there. She's more like the kind of girl I could see myself with."

Matt says, "What if Lindsay comes over anyway? How are you going to explain all of this?"

"I don't think I have to *explain* anything. Lindsay and I don't really get into each other's business—it's not like we're in a relationship. On the other hand, though... well, I really don't know."

* * * * *

By 11:00 p.m., Josie's Grill is packed for the last party night before winter break. Whitney and her friends watch a basketball game on the big screen; their college team trails in a holiday tournament game. As the game's final seconds tick away, the group drowns its sorrows with a round of tequila shots. Whitney's phone buzzes on the table. She flips open her phone and reads a text from Lindsay: "omg im freaking out where are u"

Whitney clicks back: "josies what happened"

Lindsay's reply: "tell u when i get there"

Twenty minutes later, Lindsay arrives, teary, her mascara smeared beneath red-rimmed eyes. Whitney nods toward the bathroom, and the women elbow their way through the mob toward the back of the bar. In the relative quiet of the bathroom, Lindsay fixes her makeup and tells her story to Whitney's reflection in the mirror.

"So, I told you before that I hadn't heard from Jerod all week, but I saw on his Facebook page that there was a party at Phi Zeta."

"Yeah."

"Well, I decided to go over there, just to check it out. I knew they'd be watching the game or whatever."

"Okay."

"So, when I showed up, Jerod was talking to some other girl. At first I just blew it off and talked to some of his frat brothers for a little bit. Matt and his girlfriend Kristin were there, so we played beer pong on the porch for a while."

"Uh-huh."

"Then, when I went back into the living room, the other girl was sitting on Jerod's lap!"

"Oh geez. What did you do?"

"Nothing; I just left. What *could* I do?"

"Well…"

"It's not like I'm his *girlfriend* or anything. We're just hanging out and hooking up. What was I supposed to say, 'I know we agreed two months ago that we were just friends with benefits and not in a relationship, but it hurts my feelings when another girl sits in your lap?' I don't think so…."

"But if you didn't talk to Jerod about it, how do you know it was anything? It could just be flirting and nothing else."

"Maybe, but I *can't* talk to him about it. I definitely can't bring up my feelings. I shouldn't even have feelings about him because we're not dating. I don't have a *right* to be hurt. And if I bring it up, then I'm just '*that* girl.'"

Whitney says, "Yeah, I see your point. It sucks to look like the uptight one who needs 'define the relationship'."

Lindsay adds, "*OR* the crazy girl who said she was cool with just being friends with benefits but is suddenly all emotional now."

"True. I guess you like him more than you thought you would," Whitney says.

Lindsay sighs and thumps her head back against the bathroom wall. "Ugh. There was never supposed to be this kind of drama. That's exactly what I was trying to avoid since I started hooking up with Jerod. If I wanted to feel jealous and emotional, I would just have a *real* relationship."

Whitney leans against the wall beside her friend and says, "Maybe so Linz, but you're pretty deep in it now. So what are you going to do?"

"Spring" Semester

Lindsay shifts her old SUV into park and hops down from the seat into the frozen slush and snow in her dorm parking lot. Under her breath, she mutters "Ugh, I am so ready for warm weather."

She opens the SUV's tailgate and drags out a large duffle bag and a backpack. She swings the duffle on her shoulder and, just as she closes the hatch again, her phone buzzes in her jacket pocket. She pulls off her glove and opens a text message from Whitney: "U back yet?"

She replies, "just parked."

Then a second later, "b there in 5."

When Lindsay reaches her dorm room, the two roommates reunite with a hug and compare winter break stories.

"So, how is your family?" Lindsay asks.

"So good," Whitney replies, "I hadn't even realized how much I missed my little brother until I saw him. How about you?"

"It was a really good break," Lindsay says.

After a few minutes, Whitney asks: "Have you talked to Jerod at all?"

Lindsay drops a load of clean laundry and new clothes out of the duffel and onto the bed. "Not really. I texted him at midnight on New Year's but otherwise we haven't talked."

"Do you think you'll see him again?" Whitney asks as she runs her hands over the new sweater on Lindsay's bed.

"Honestly, knowing us, we'll probably hook up again. I see him all the time around campus. But I think I'm over whatever feelings I had last semester. I think if we keep it to just occasional sex, and nothing else, we'll be fine."

Whitney asks, "And you're comfortable with that?"

"Honestly, it's not really about comfort—it's about priorities."

"What do you mean?"

"Over break, my dad told me that he thinks I should aim to have an internship every summer of college."

"Okay…"

"But I need real experience…[imitating her father's deep voice]… 'You need to show what kinds of skills you can bring to an internship.' So I'm trying to get involved with as many activities and clubs as I can to build my resume. And, my dad thinks that I should go to grad school."

"That's great, but what does that have to do with Jerod?"

"If all that is going to happen, I don't think that this is the time in my life when I should have a boyfriend. First, I'm too busy with classes and all these activities. Second, what happens when we graduate? I could go *anywhere* and do *anything*. But not if I'm attached to some guy. Hooking up every once in a while fits best with all the other stuff I need to do."

"Aren't you worried you'll get hurt again?"

"Not really, no. I understand how to play the game now. I'm way more worried about risking my future and my career by getting too involved with a boyfriend. I could really miss out on a lot if I got distracted."

Whitney nodded, but sitting on Lindsay's bed, she suddenly felt a profound difference between herself and her roommate. She recalled that Lindsay was the only child of wealthy parents, both of whom were alumni donors to the University. In contrast, Whitney was the first from her family to go to college. Both families had high hopes for their daughters, but it was funny to Whitney how that came across differently. *Over break, no one pestered me about internships or graduate school. My parents and aunts and cousins mostly gushed over how proud of me they are. In a way, I feel bad for Lindsay. First, she had had her heart broken by Jerod, and now she is under so much pressure from her parents. But she is probably right about getting internships and building a resume…and I really would not know how to do all that and find time for a boyfriend.* To Whitney, it just all felt a little overwhelming. Lindsay seemed to have it all figured out, but she was also from a world that lived by slightly different rules from a world that Whitney hadn't really been exposed to. And although she couldn't quite put her finger on what was bothering her, Whitney couldn't shake the feeling that they each could potentially miss out on something very important.

For Further Thought and Reflection

1. How does communication help to create relational uncertainty or ambiguity in this case? How do the characters communicate in an effort to handle or manage that uncertainty? What opportunities and obstacles for interacting arise when uncertainty is present?

2. How well do theories of relationship development apply to friends with benefits and other types of noncommitted sexual involvement (e.g., hookups)?

3. In this case, we see some examples of how friends with benefits relationships are more difficult to maintain than the label implies. What factors (psychological, communicative, biological) might contribute to this difficulty?

4. In this case, Lindsay implies that there is a "life stage" in which friends with benefits or casual sexual relationships are preferred. Do you agree or disagree with this view? Why or why not?

5. At the end of the case, Whitney reflects on how the different family circumstances seem to influence Lindsay's and her approach to college and relationships. What do you think is the role of social class in making decisions about college relationships?

References

Bisson, M., & Levine, T. (2009). Negotiating a friends with benefits relationship. *Archives of Sexual Behavior, 38,* 66–73.

Epstein, M., Calzo, J. P., Smiler, A. P., & Ward, M. (2009). "Anything from making out to having sex": Men's negotiations of hooking up and friends with benefits scripts. *Journal of Sex Research, 46*, 414–424.

Mongeau, P. A., & Knight, K. (in press). Friends with benefits. In C. Berger & M. Roloff (Eds.), *International Encyclopedia of Interpersonal Communication*. New York: Wiley-Blackwell.

Mongeau, P. A., Knight, K., Williams, J., Eden, J., & Shaw, C. (2013). Identifying and explicating variation among friends with benefits relationships. *Journal of Sex Research, 50*, 37–47.

Paul, E. L., Wenzel, A., & Harvey, J. (2008). Hookups: A facilitator or barrier to relationship initiation and intimacy development? In S. Sprecher, A. Wenzel, & J. Harvey (Eds.), *Handbook of relationship initiation* (pp. 375–390). New York, NY: Psychology Press.

Shulman, S., & Connolly, J. (2013). The challenge of romantic relationships in emerging adulthood: Reconceptualization of the field. *Emerging Adulthood, 1,* 27–39.

12

Opening Closed Doors: Managing Identity and Privacy with Social Media

Jeffrey T. Child

Keywords

communication privacy management, disclosure, impression management, mediated communication, social media interaction

Religion and Sexuality

From an early age Scott was raised in a deeply religious faith community. Multiple generations of his extended family had been devout and faithful members of his church. Scott was no different. Being raised in the church, Scott knew from an early age that he wanted to do missionary work and live his life according to the standards and practices of his religious faith. In his youth, religion brought comfort and guidance. It taught him how to treat others and live a virtuous life. Eventually, Scott served a mission for two years in a foreign country and helped many people learn more about living faith-filled lives.

Scott discovered something else about himself as he went through puberty that would eventually become a deep source of contemplation and friction in reconciling the religious, sexual, and personal aspects of his identity. He had never been attracted to women, as his faith, church, and culture at large taught him he should be. Rather, he was attracted to men, even though he knew that being gay was not morally or socially acceptable in his religious community. Gay people were teased, bullied, and talked about by members of his different networks in very derogatory, discriminatory, and sometimes hateful ways. By age 12, Scott decided he would try to suppress his feelings to live the lifestyle he had been taught was acceptable.

Discussing any of the feelings about his sexuality with anyone seemed impossible, and he felt particularly vulnerable about the prospect of discussing these issues with his family members. Because of the way that gay people were perceived and treated within his community, he decided it would be wise simply to act straight, hoping that his faith would eventually correct or provide answers about finding a life-long partner. He would avoid any discussions of sex or sexuality, choosing not to share such private information even with close friends or family. The only discussion within his family on this topic was that religion provided all of the answers about sexuality; nothing further needed to be discussed.

Personal Identity Exploration

Scott successfully avoided any conflicts regarding his sexuality until after returning home from his two-year-long mission at age 21. He had hoped and expected that his same-sex attractions would be washed away following his mission, replaced with attraction to women because of his personal righteousness. He could then pursue the version of his life that he had been socialized to believe was morally correct, in the same way that most of his friends and mission buddies were getting married around that time. There was only one problem; his attraction to men had not dissipated upon returning from his mission.

One way to gain perspective and privacy was to move far away from his family so that they wouldn't be able to drop by unexpectedly to visit. Once he accepted the fact that his same-sex attractions were not going to disappear, he first thought he would always be alone. However, after a number of years, Scott longed to know what his life might be like with a partner who shared the same values that he did. He hoped to meet someone who was everything his faith taught he should have as a life partner, but simply a man instead of a woman. There was only one problem: Scott didn't know the first thing about gay people, gay culture, or even where to find a date that might be a good prospect for a future partner.

Since Scott viewed talking about sexuality as intensely private, he did not ask anyone for help, nor did he want to be seen in a gay bar. Furthermore, Scott assumed that guys he would have the most in common with would be unlikely to frequent gay bars regularly. Instead, Scott turned to online chat rooms to get to know more gay people and to understand gay culture, remaining anonymous while learning and exploring his identity within the gay community.

Understanding Gay Culture

Scott was able to use Internet chat rooms to conceal his identity while exploring new aspects of his personality. While it is relatively easy for a straight person to find prospective dates, it was much harder for Scott to know how to meet other gay people. Chat rooms allowed Scott to form friendships and ask questions about how others merged being religious with being gay, how they came out to family and friends, what was important to them in a relationship, and how they went about establishing and developing healthy gay relationships.

Chat rooms allowed Scott to chat with men who didn't live nearby before he felt comfortable enough to chat with others who lived nearby. Even then, he was able to control what they learned about him and even when they could see pictures of him as he built trust. Eventually, this led to meeting face-to-face to see how things went in person. Though several of those early meetings did not work out when guys were significantly different from their online personas, some of the online relationships turned into dates and others turned into great friends.

After several years of chatting and exploring, Scott met Mark, who made him light up and shared many of his same religious values. Mark was great for several reasons, but one of his greatest attributes was his supportive nature. Mark had come out of the closet years ago and reconciled his sexuality, religious convictions, and relationships with his family. Mark became a role model for Scott of how a gay person could be open about sexuality within a family.

In contrast to the close relationships among Mark's family, Scott's family lived very independent and separate lives. Simple updates every couple of months among family members was the norm in Scott's family, rather than deep involvement in one another's lives. In addition, Scott was the last sibling in his big family who wasn't married, so he did not have as much in common with them as they began their families. Scott was convinced that if his family ever found out he was gay, they would disown him, so he didn't mind the infrequent communication within his family. This allowed him to avoid discussing his sexuality while still maintaining some sort of relationship with them. Because he feared rejection by loved ones, Scott concealed both his sexual identity and his romantic relationship with Mark from his family.

Mark was comfortable openly discussing his sexuality with his family and friends because the most important people in his life had already lovingly accepted his sexual identity. However, Mark also did not require Scott to be more open about his own sexual identity or their relationship with anyone that Scott wasn't already ready to tell. Mark's identity was not affected by whether or not Scott was willing to talk to others about him. It was their actual bond and the life they shared together that mattered most to Mark. Scott and Mark decided to move to a new town together where they could start a new life, devoid of any pretense, and develop a community of support as a committed couple.

Careful Social Media Use

When Scott and Mark moved in together, they decided to be more out and open about their relationship with work colleagues, neighbors, and people around the area than had been the case where they had previously lived. This enabled them to establish a new network of people who could support their relationship. At the same time, Scott was able to protect his important relationship with Mark from any potential criticism from his conservative friends and family.

Scott was very careful and cautious about how he used social media to reach the simultaneous goals of maintaining relationships with conservative family and friends who lived far away and supporting this new developing network of friends who knew about his relationship with Mark. Scott didn't want these two groups of people interacting or even knowing about each other at all on social media like Facebook. To manage privacy effectively through social media, Scott initially disabled wall posts by anyone who wished to leave a public, open message to him that his entire network of friends could read. Scott also disabled people being able to look through his other social media friends and see the company he kept. Scott was very purposive in everything that he posted through social media. Scott managed his online communication so that he could interact with diverse groups while also safeguarding his privacy.

For instance, Scott established two primary groups that he interacted with through social media in different ways. The first group was for conservative family and friends connected to Scott's religious life and his family back home. This group included everyone Scott was concerned would judge him or his relationship with Mark in a negative way. None of these people knew Scott was gay or in a relationship. When Scott posted things to this group on Facebook he would be very careful in his use of adjectives, never referencing a romantic relationship or using words like "we" or "us". The second Facebook group that Scott established was for people who were either more liberal in their thinking and beliefs or accepting of Scott and Mark's relationship together. Scott interacted primarily with this second group, regularly posting photos of his home with Mark, their dog, or vacations they took together. Scott never posted messages on Facebook that all of his friends could read. If he had news to share that was important enough to share with both groups, he would post the information twice, once for each group, so that the networks would never comingle. Scott had about 250 friends in each Facebook group with approximately 500 total friends on Facebook.

Scott enjoyed interacting with his family and friends back home in this way. It allowed him to keep them at a distance and yet also provide important updates from time to time about his job and other things going on in his life. It also enabled Scott to protect his sexual identity and romantic relationship from his conservative family and friends. Scott's family back home enjoyed using Facebook because it allowed them to maintain the arm's-length connection that was typical of their family interactions.

Coming Out to the Family

Scott and Mark had been together for seven years and Scott's family still knew nothing about his sexual identity or their relationship. Scott and Mark had developed many friendships during their new life together, and Scott felt that he had an adequate support network to proceed with revealing his identity and romantic relationship to family members. Even if his family did reject him, which he sincerely hoped would not happen, Scott knew that he had enough supportive people in his life to help him through any hard times that might come. Mark supported this decision and helped Scott consider possible ways to talk about his sexuality more openly with his family.

Scott decided that this critical step required face-to-face communication. He didn't want to send an e-mail or text or reveal such sensitive information to his family and conservative friends through phone conversations, because he might be misunderstood or his family might even simply hang up on him. These media would also not allow Scott to use the full range of nonverbal communication that a face-to-face conversation would allow. Scott wanted to be able to look his family in the eye and see their facial expressions as the conversation progressed. Scott also thought a face-to-face conversation would allow the opportunity for questions or discussion that would ensue after the revelation. While difficult, Scott knew that this conversation needed to occur as a face-to-face conversation back home.

An invitation from Scott's brother presented a perfect opportunity for him to go home for a few days. His brother had invited him to attend the blessing of his newborn baby boy. Scott decided he could go to church and be with family before getting the entire family together for an open discussion about his life. While Scott had several family members in the area, he chose to get a hotel room and a rental car so that if things went badly with the discussion, he could easily retreat to a place of security and comfort before returning back to his life with Mark.

The day finally arrived and Scott had his entire family around the dinner table early in the morning. Scott had told everyone the night before that he wanted to have the morning left open to have a more serious discussion and spend time together without anything else planned. He figured there would be a lot of time to talk through things and process what he was about to tell them. Scott told his family that he had essentially kept the door to his life closed when it came to discussing his romantic relationships with them. He said that he wanted to open that door and be more open about himself and he told his family it would be up to them how they wanted to handle the opening of that door. They could slam it shut again, keep it open just a crack, or open it up even further, if they wanted to know more and be more involved. Scott told them that he was gay and had been in a significant relationship for seven years. He explained his difficulty with learning to love himself. He told his family he had learned he had to give up trying to change to become something he wasn't in order not to disappoint them. He discussed how he and Mark had a wonderful relationship and how all of the values he had been taught growing up were very much present within this relationship. Scott was scared but anxious to hear their response.

The response by Scott's highly conservative family amazed him. At first, they were shocked, of course. They wanted to know why Scott had kept this information from them for so long. His family members also admitted that they had discussed the possibility of this among themselves since Scott wasn't married yet but had decided not to pursue further questioning before this because it was a sensitive subject, given the family's religious values. They wanted to know more about Scott's struggle to come to terms with his sexuality, his partner Mark, how they met, and their life together. Scott was open with them and answered each of these questions. His family wanted to know how they could be more involved in his and Mark's lives going forward. From everything Scott could tell, his family wanted this revelation to signify a positive turning point in terms of openness in Scott and Mark's relationship and them being involved in their lives together. Scott's mom even said now they were a modern family. Scott was thrilled this had gone so well. His family even wanted Scott to call his partner Mark on the phone so they could welcome him to the family and let him know they were exited to get to know him further. In the end, the most difficult questions to respond to were why Scott had waited so long and what had the family said or done to suggest they might criticize and judge. Scott deflected these questions because rehashing past interactions with family members that stood out in his mind as discriminatory seemed counterproductive when they clearly were accepting him and his relationship with Mark.

The visit ended with Scott's family expressing a desire to visit Scott and Mark together at their home. Scott's mom also asked him to send her photographs of them together so she could display them in their home along with the families of his siblings. Many tears were shed. Scott realized that the same conversation did not go so well in all families, especially when religion is central to family functioning. He felt so very fortunate. Scott knew of many other LGBT friends where such discussions resulted in the end of family support and involvement. Scott had fully prepared himself for this type of rejection and was not prepared for his family to accept him and his partner so fully into their lives. Truly the door had been swung wide open.

Developing Family Bonds

In the days to come, Scott also explained to family how he had protected his relationship with Mark from the family through social media, purposely keeping them at a distance. The family asked to be placed in the group where they could learn more about Mark and Scott's "real lives" together. All of Scott's family members requested to be Mark's Facebook friend. Now the same technologies that were useful in keeping his family at a distance would be employed to achieve new family interaction goals of increasing closeness, mutual understanding, and connection.

Scott's brother and sister-in-law were the first to plan a visit. Upon arriving, Scott's sister-in-law immediately told her four-year old son, "This is Uncle Scott and Uncle Mark," normalizing their relationship in a very simple way for a young child. Scott's mom and dad have also visited since the revelation. Before coming out, Scott would probably talk to a member of his family every three or four months at best. Now, a member of his family interacts with him via phone or FaceTime video chats on at least a weekly basis.

Scott's family now expends energy catching up and being more involved in ways that were never characteristic of the family, and Scott is so gratified about how the family has changed. After the revelation, they are more supportive and mindful of how others might interpret what they said and did in ways that undermined closeness and caused anxiety. During the holidays, all of Scott's siblings used FaceTime for the first time to enable Scott and Mark to be a part of family holiday celebrations several states away from them. Use of FaceTime allowed Scott and Mark to watch their nieces and nephews open the first presents they had ever sent them and talk about their excitement during the holiday season. New interaction norms for the family are being facilitated and supported through communication technology in addition to their face-to-face interaction.

The increased openness in the family presents new challenges for the future, given the ultimate differences in some deeply-held convictions and values. Scott and Mark are happy to refer any difficult questions they may get about the morality of their relationship from Scott's nieces and nephews back to their respective parents. They are walking a fine line between wanting to be open and honest with family and yet also respectful of parents' rights to instill values in their children. As Scott is wrapping up a present for his new baby nephew he considers how much happier he and Mark are dealing with these difficulties going forward rather than continuing to hide their relationship from Scott's family or figuring out how to recover from the negative reaction that might have occurred from his revelations.

For Further Thought and Reflection

1. One assumption of Communication Privacy Management theory (Petronio, 2002) is that people decide for themselves what is private based on what makes them feel vulnerable. In this case, how did Scott and Mark's privacy boundaries regarding discussion of their sexuality differ? How does Scott's privacy boundary regarding the discussion of sexuality with his family change throughout the case? While Scott might identify issues of sexuality as highly sensitive private information, what sorts of topics might you or others you know identify as highly private?

2. Uses and Gratifications theory (Rubin & Haridakis, 2001) contends that technology itself is not as important as how it is used by different people and what motivations drive them to communicate in the ways that they do through technology. How did Scott use interactive communication technology in different ways to achieve different goals and outcomes? What goals are important to you as you interact through different forms of mediated communication?

3. Scott determined that communicating information about his sexuality was inappropriate to do through any mediated communication channel. What type of information would you freely communicate through mediated communication channels? Are there things that you would only discuss with others through face-to-face channels? What would that type of information be and why do you think use of a mediated communication channel would be inappropriate?

4. Walther's (1996) hyperpersonal perspective contends that there are situations where people get more fulfillment and enjoyment out of interaction through mediated communication channels. When would you characterize Scott's interactions through mediated communication channels as hyperpersonal communication? Have you ever experienced situations when utilizing mediated communication channels where you would classify your interactions as hyperpersonal communication?

5. Goffman (1959) used the metaphor of actors in a play to explain the ways we present ourselves in different social contexts. In the context of social media, the internal dialogue, not shared can be placed in the category of backstage. The images, messages, links, videos, and even friendships posted or made public are on the front stage. How did Scott exert caution in what information was presented on the front stage of his social media site? What information do you mark as private and leave backstage and away from social media?

References

Child, J. T., Haridakis, P. M., & Petronio, S. (2012). Blogging privacy rule orientations, privacy management, and content deletion practices: The variability of online privacy management activity at different stages of social media use. *Computers in Human Behavior, 28,* 1859–1872.

Child, J. T., & Petronio, S. (2011). Unpacking the paradoxes of privacy in CMC relationships: The challenges of blogging and relational communication on the Internet. In K. B. Wright & L. M. Webb (Eds.), *Computer-mediated communication in personal relationships* (pp. 21–40). New York, NY: Peter Lang.

Child, J. T., & Westermann, D. A. (2013). Let's be Facebook friends: Exploring parental Facebook friend requests from a communication privacy management (CPM) perspective. *Journal of Family Communication, 13*, 46–59.

Goffman, E. (1959). *The presentation of self in everyday life.* New York, NY: Anchor Books.

Petronio, S. (2002). *Boundaries of privacy: Dialectics of disclosure.* Albany, NY: State University of New York Press.

Rubin, A. M., & Haridakis, P. M. (2001). Mass communication research at the dawn of the 21st century. *Communication Yearbook, 24*, 73–97.

Tidwell, L. C., & Walther, J. B. (2002). Computer-mediated communication effects on disclosure, impressions, and interpersonal evaluations: Getting to know one another a bit at a time. *Human Communication Research, 28,* 317–348.

Walther, J. B. (1996). Computer-mediated communication: Impersonal, interpersonal, and hyperpersonal interaction. *Communication Research, 23,* 3–43.

PART III

Communication Processes in Established Relationships

13

Disclosing Private Information: Newly Married Couple's Embarrassing Dilemmas

Sandra Petronio

Keywords

privacy, disclosure, embarrassment, rules, boundaries, marital adjustment

On the way over to Matt's parents' home, Jennifer asked, "Matt, why do we go over so often?" "Because my mom likes to see us," said Matt[1].

"But, she is always asking me personal questions about our marriage. Half the time I don't know what to say—I feel embarrassed. And, why does she insist that I call her Mom? It makes me feel funny," Jennifer confessed.

"You can say anything to her; she's easy to talk to," Matt said encouragingly. "I think she wants you to feel like you are a part of the family; that's why she told you to call her Mom." Matt got the feeling that Jennifer didn't appreciate his mother, and he was confused about Jennifer's complaints. After all, he felt so happy when he saw them spending time together.

As Jennifer sat talking to her mother-in-law, Kelly, she realized how uncomfortable she felt. She wasn't used to talking with Kelly about personal things. When she stopped to think about it, she really didn't know Kelly. Jennifer wanted to get close to Matt's mother, but Kelly expected her to act as if they had known each other all their lives. Jennifer was torn. She wanted Kelly to like her, yet she also felt that her privacy was always being invaded.

Figuring this out was going to be tough, and Matt was not going to be much help. Matt just didn't see the problem Jennifer was facing. The strangest part was that Matt's openness had been the thing that attracted her. He had no trouble telling her all about his feelings. Now, the difference in how they regulated privacy and disclosure was beginning to be a problem.

Matt's Point of View

Matt loved his family. He found Jennifer's reluctance to talk to his parents and brothers difficult to understand. "Jennifer, all my life I have been open with my family, especially my mom. Why can't you just let it go and tell them the things you feel?" "Because they are not my parents," Jennifer complained. "Well, they are now," Matt pointed out. Matt was beginning to realize Jennifer needed a lot more privacy than he had growing up and one particular incident drove home that point. Right after they were married and moved into their new house Jennifer did something that confused Matt then, but it was beginning to make more sense to him now.

Their new bathroom had a separate shower with a clear glass door and large window looking out to the rest of the bathroom. The first time they were both in the bathroom together getting ready for work Jennifer was in the shower and Matt came in to shave. Jennifer yelled at him not to stare at her through the glass. She acted embarrassed—as if it wasn't appropriate even to glance her way. *We're married, for goodness sake,* thought Matt. From then on, Jennifer waited until Matt was through in the bathroom to take her shower. Matt found this hard to understand.

Matt has two brothers, and his parents are still together after twenty-seven years. They never expected too much privacy when they were living together in their parents' home. When they were growing up, his parents always assumed the children would talk to them if they were facing problems. They also really liked "family talk time" around the dinner table. In fact, everyone was supposed to be home at dinnertime, and the television had to be turned off when they were eating dinner. Matt had fond memories of the way he talked with his family during those times. It wasn't just during dinnertime that the family confided. He remembered one incident that happened with his brother Jamie.

"Say, I really need to talk to everyone about something. Could we meet in the family room after dinner? I need your help," Jamie said one evening. The family agreed. They were all curious, wondering what Jamie had to say, but they knew that it was up to him to tell.

Although they were an open family, they had their privacy rules about not pushing someone to talk. Jamie seemed edgy, as if he had the weight of the world on his shoulders. Matt was afraid of what Jamie might say. But, he was his brother and would always be there for him, no matter what.

Jamie finally announced to the family that his girlfriend was pregnant. "My stomach dropped out," Matt told Jennifer after they were married. "I thought his life was ruined. Everyone was great, though. I was worried that Mom would go ballistic, but she was just concerned about Jamie, as well as his girlfriend." Matt's family talked it out. Jamie and his girlfriend, Alicia, wanted to keep the baby. He was just finishing college and looking forward to being on his own and starting a career. Jamie and Alicia decided to get married.

"We always knew that we could come to our family with problems, but after the stuff with Jamie, I was really struck by how open our family really is with each other. Even my Mom and Dad would come to us and tell us when they were having some problems. I like the fact that they included us kids in their lives," Matt confessed to Jennifer.

"It gives me a sense of security that I know other kids don't have with their parents. My brothers are always telling me things about their lives, too. I really can depend on my family to listen when I need to talk. That's why I can't understand your reluctance to talk to them, Jennifer," Matt grumbled.

"Well, Matt, my family is completely different from yours," Jennifer replied.

Jennifer's Point of View

Jennifer grew up in a family that didn't believe in talking freely about problems. Her father, Lyle, always commented that discretion is a valuable lesson to learn in life. Likewise, Jennifer's mother, Kristen, believed that revealing too much to others would make a person vulnerable. She taught her kids that, even if you are talking to other family members, it is best to keep things to yourself and work them out on your own rather than bother everyone else with your troubles. Working your problems out showed strength. Jennifer, her two sisters, and her brother all recognized the merit in keeping things private, sometimes even from each other.

Jennifer's family respected privacy. They believed that having thick privacy boundaries was the best way to keep solid relationships with others. When growing up, they did not pry into each other's business. They did not touch personal property; nobody barged into another's bedroom without knocking; nobody borrowed clothes, bikes, or anything without asking first. Typically, they did not burden each other with problems.

Jennifer remembers learning a valuable lesson about privacy when she was young. Her mother always warned about going through other people's dresser drawers or closets. But, when Jennifer was a child, she found that those warnings made her curious.

On one particular afternoon she was home from school, not feeling well. She stayed in bed, but as a restless ten-year-old, she wandered around the house ending up in her mother's room. Her mother was down in the basement doing the laundry. One particular dresser drawer captivated Jennifer. She had been told that she should never open up that drawer. She wondered what was in there to make her mother warn the children so many times never to touch it.

Noticing earlier that her mother had a lot of laundry to do, Jennifer headed for that secret drawer. She quietly opened it and moved the papers around. "Hum," she thought, "only papers." Then she picked one up that looked kind of old. As she read the words on that paper, they did not make sense to her. She saw that it said "Birth Certificate" on the top. She remembered that she had seen her own birth certificate and it had her whole name on it. It read, "Jennifer Johnson" with her mother's name, "Kristen Johnson" and her father's name, "Lyle Johnson." This paper looked like it was her brother's birth certificate. Yet, she was not sure. It said "William," which was her brother's name. But, the last name wasn't Johnson. Instead, it said "Cramer." Jennifer didn't know what to make of this discovery. She realized that she had been in the room a long time. She was afraid her mother would find her. So, she stuffed the certificate back into the drawer and left the room quickly.

Even at Jennifer's age, her privacy dilemma was clear. She could not ask her parents about the information she found, because she knew how much they valued privacy. She was also worried that she would get into trouble for snooping in the dresser. Nor did she think it was okay to ask her brother. In fact, she wondered if he even knew about this information. She kept the secret to herself. She wondered at times why her brother's certificate had a different name on it. Jennifer knew, though, that she could never find out from her family. She was reminded of this incident as she thought about Matt's family. His family would have discussed this information at some length. But, she could not understand how they felt so free to disclose to each other.

Talking to Matt about Kelly's request to call her "Mom" was hard for Jennifer. Usually she tried to work out a way to handle unpleasant situations like this one. Jennifer was trying to be more like Matt, yet it was not easy. "Matt," Jennifer commented, "I'm not sure you know how hard it is for me to tell you how I feel about the fact you want me to be more open with your family. In my family, we don't complain to each other when we are facing problems. We just try to cope ourselves. So please know that this is very troubling to me."

"Jennifer," said Matt, "I really don't understand the fuss."

Incident with Matthew's Family

Jennifer wondered why she and Matt were so opposite in the way they thought about privacy. Part of her wanted to make Matt happy; part resisted being so open.

One Sunday afternoon, Matt and Jennifer were visiting his family. As usual, when they finished with dinner, the family joined in to clean up amid chatter about nothing and everything. Matt loved this time most when he visited—all the family doing something together, joining in on different conversations that seemed to be going simultaneously. They always were kidding and joking with each other about things. Yet, Matt was worried about whether Jennifer would fit into his family. She did not seem to welcome or understand that teasing was their way of loving each other. One family motto was "Why tease someone you hate—it is a waste of energy."

Jennifer liked a good laugh as much as anyone did. But, often Matt's family joshed about people she didn't know, or made "inside jokes" that were never explained. Many times when they teased her, she felt embarrassed. She really didn't like the teasing; it made her feel like they were picking on her and she felt exposed. This afternoon was especially bad for Jennifer. Matt's whole family was at his parents' house, including Matt's two brothers, Jamie and Ed, and Jamie's wife Alicia. After cleaning up from dinner, they all sat at the kitchen table talking.

Then Ed started to talk seriously about taking a job in another city. He wanted to change jobs so he could make more money. He also talked about a woman he was interested in, and asked for some advice from his parents. Jennifer wondered why someone would seek advice so openly in front of so many people. When the conversation died down about Ed's decisions, Kelly turned to Matt and asked how he and Jennifer were getting along. Matt quickly revealed that Jennifer was feeling uncomfortable about having to call her Mom. Kelly asked Jennifer why she felt that way. Jennifer wasn't sure how to respond. She had told Matt in confidence and thought that he would know not to tell his Mom. Jennifer thought that she and Matt had established a co-owned privacy boundary that made Matt responsible for "taking care of" private information that Jennifer told him. Jennifer assumed Matt would understand that he was to keep the information just between the two of them. Jennifer was embarrassed and hurt that Matt did not respect her need for privacy. Kelly realized that there was some tension between Matt and Jennifer, and saved Jennifer further embarrassment by telling her not to worry—she didn't have to call her Mom if she didn't want to. Nevertheless, Jennifer was concerned that Kelly was offended.

Just as she was thinking that she'd have to talk to Matt again about disclosing her private thoughts and putting her in an awkward position with his family, he surprised her by confessing that he and Jennifer had another, more serious problem. He told his family that he and Jennifer disagreed about when to have children. Jennifer wanted to pursue a career. She had studied hard and finished her BA degree. She was hoping to go to law school. Matt wanted to have children right away. Jennifer knew Matt's family was hoping they would have another grandchild soon. The intensity of her distress was greater because Matt raised this issue without even letting her know he was going to tell his family. His disclosure caught her off guard, because they never really fully explored all the options and now his parents were invited into the decision-making process.

Jennifer had already felt miserable about Matt telling his mother that she didn't want to call her "Mom." Now she wanted to scream and run away, maybe even be swallowed up by a big sink hole because he told his whole family they were having this problem. Jennifer's ears began to ring; she thought that she might become sick on the spot and lose the fine dinner she just enjoyed.

How could he be so insensitive, she thought. *The nerve of him to humiliate her like that!* When Jennifer calmed down enough to hear how the family was responding, she just couldn't take any more of it. Every member of the family had an opinion about their problem. Some of his brothers were mad at her for putting a career first. Jennifer tried to explain her feelings but the family was on Matt's side. She felt so mortified that she ran from the room.

Matt and his family were not sure why Jennifer reacted this way. They were trying to help Matt and Jennifer with their problem. However, to them, Jennifer seemed so unwilling to be helped and talk like they always did about a problem. "What's up with Jennifer?" asked Ed. "What is her problem?"

"I don't know exactly. I better go and talk to her," said Matt.

Time for Understanding

"Jennifer, why did you run out of the room?" asked Matt. "My family was only trying to help us with this decision."

"You just don't get it, do you, Matt?" said Jennifer.

"No, please help me understand," Matt responded.

"When you talked about our private life with your family, I felt betrayed because it's not just yours alone to control" said Jennifer. "Our private life belongs to you and me now. It's like you drew a circle or boundary around our private information and marked it only yours. Because we are both responsible for our private lives, I should have as much say as you do in how we reveal that information to other people. When we talk about our private lives, we are telling things about both of us, and the information belongs to us mutually. If one of us takes control over the information, it is unfair to the other. Neither one of us should make independent judgments about disclosing the information. We need to talk about it first. We need an agreement about the kinds of things we can say to others, even your parents."

"You are comfortable with your family—you've known them all your life," pointed out Jennifer. "I, on the other hand, just met them. I don't know them at all; they are strangers to me. My family has rules about not disclosing private information, even sometimes to other family members," noted Jennifer. "For me, talking about personal matters even with you is difficult. I have been working on this, but I can't deal with telling your whole family things that should be kept private between us."

"I still don't get it and now you want me to change the way I talk to my parents," said Matt.

"I think it's up to us to decide when we have children. Your family shouldn't be involved in the discussion. Tonight I felt embarrassed and like a villain. It was more than I could tolerate. I don't think I can look at your family, never mind have dinner with them anymore," said Jennifer.

From Jennifer's point of view, this information was something they both should manage together. Interestingly, Matt was not used to this kind of sharing. Although he is very open about his feelings, and expects Jennifer to be open as well, jointly agreeing on when to disclose and when to keep something private between the two of them is unfamiliar to him. His family privacy rule is to be open; that is the rule he has always used. Now, he is expected to consult Jennifer whenever something is about the two of them, before he tells anyone else.

Matt knows it is going to take a real effort for them to work this out in a way they both feel comfortable. He is worried about how this is going to affect his relationship with his family, and wonders how Jennifer will ever get close to them if she will not open up to them. But, from their discussion, he is beginning to see that they have very different ways of defining private information. He never thought about the possibility of families being secretive, even with each other. Having this conversation, though painful, is helpful in beginning the long process of negotiating some basic ways to mutually manage information important to both of them. Matt loves Jennifer and knows that, although this is going to be a lot of work, they both want to build a life together. Part of the building blocks is learning how to blend values and attitudes that are different. It is funny, because Matt never even thought that this kind of thing would be a problem. He is sure that Jennifer never questioned her family's way of dealing with privacy, or thought it would be a problem either.

Endnote

[1] This case represents a composite of experiences found in open-ended questions about private disclosures by newly married couples. The names and circumstance are fictional.

For Further Thought and Reflection

1. Many newly married couples do not talk about expectations or the values they have for disclosing private information. Privacy rules are often assumptions people make without confirming another's point of view. Beside the points raised in this case study, what other ways do you think Matt and Jennifer might have conflicts over privacy in the future? Do you think that their privacy rules for their relationship will change over time? In what ways do you think the rules might shift and their privacy boundaries change?

2. Why is managing private information so important in a marriage? What is the difference between remaining private and lying?

3. Matt and Jennifer grew up with different family privacy orientations that lead to having diverse expectations about private information. How do they differ and where do they have similarities in the ways they think about privacy management?

4. Why does Jennifer feel so embarrassed when Matt discloses private information about their relationship to his parent? Would you? Why?

5. Jennifer and Matt talk about privacy rules; can you find what those rules are in this case? How do the rules change for this couple as a result of the privacy turbulence that erupts in this case?

6. Can you identify privacy rules operating in your own relationships? How do people in these relationships know that these are your privacy rules?

References

Petronio, S. (2002). *Boundaries of privacy: Dialectics of disclosure.* Mahwah, NJ: Lawrence Erlbaum..

Petronio, S. (2010). Communication privacy management theory: What do we know about family privacy regulation? *Journal of Family Theory and Review, 2*, 175–196.

Petronio, S. (2013). Brief status report on Communication Privacy Management theory. *Journal of Family Communication, 13,* 6–14.

Petronio, S., & Durham, W. (2008). Understanding and applying Communication Privacy Management theory. In L. A. Baxter & D. O. Braithwaite (Eds.), *Engaging theories in interpersonal communication* (pp. 309–322). Thousand Oaks, CA: Sage Publications.

Petronio, S., Olson, C., & Dollar, N. (1989). Privacy issues in relational embarrassment: Impact on relational quality and communication satisfaction. *Communication Research Reports, 6,* 216–225.

Serewicz, M. C. M., & Canary, D. J. (2008). Assessments of disclosure from the in-laws: Links among disclosure topics, family privacy orientations, and relational quality. *Journal of Social and Personal Relationships, 25,* 333–357.

14

A Place for Connecting and Disclosing: Facebook and Friendships at the Dawn of College Life

Andrew M. Ledbetter
Joseph P. Mazer

Keywords

self-disclosure, social connection, warranting, Facebook

Ben barely noticed the soft July rainstorm fluttering against his bedroom window. On this late Friday afternoon, Ben knew many of his high school friends would meet together somewhere, doing something social. He'd been to several such gatherings during the summer—this intermission, this pause between the end of high school and the new life of college. Already he'd heard the beep of incoming text messages emitting from his phone. But tonight, as he clutched his Xbox controller, Ben was content to stay home and do some of the 'alone' things he loved most. *This game is so much more controllable than my world right now*, he thought.

His mom's familiar knock echoed from his bedroom door. "Come in," Ben yelled as he paused his game.

She cracked open the door. "Got the mail, and there's a letter for you from Lasher State."

"Really?" Ben said as his mom handed him the envelope. As he opened it, he sized it up—it looked official, like everything else from Lasher State, but felt thin, unlike the huge amount of promotional material they sent. During senior year. Every. Single. Week.

His eyes scanned the single sheet of paper inside. "What is it?" his mom asked.

"Looks like information about my roommate." Ben was surprised they'd sent the information this quickly. He had only completed the roommate preference form two weeks ago.

"Who is he?" his mom asked excitedly, stepping through the door and turning to see the paper. "David L. Bradford, from Hill City? I wonder if he knows the Woodsmiths?"

"Maybe," Ben shrugged. "Probably. There's only about 5,000 people living there."

"Well, his e-mail address and phone number are right here; maybe you should try to give him a call after dinner."

Ben felt his gut tighten. The last thing he wanted to do tonight was talk to anyone else. Much less talk about college. "I might e-mail instead. Or look him up on Facebook."

"Just don't wait too long. You'll have to make some plans with him before school starts!"

"I know," Ben said, picking up his Xbox controller again as his mom left. He unpaused, fired another shot, and dodged a missile. But then he paused again, curiosity creeping into his brain. *I wonder... what can I find out about this David guy online?* He moved to his computer, noticing he had new e-mails, but it took a moment for him to realize that one message was from David Bradford! But wait, it wasn't a "real" e-mail; the subject line read, "Dave Bradford added you as a friend on Facebook..."

The knot in Ben's stomach tightened a little bit. He had only created his Facebook account about a year ago, and mostly to keep in touch with a few close high school friends. At the time, he hadn't thought about how Facebook might help build friendships at college, but now it made sense that it could. He moved to click "accept," but then hesitated. This felt weird. *Honestly, it's strange to accept a request from someone I don't know... but I guess I will know him. But then again, what if we don't get along? Will he be upset if I don't accept the request?* For a moment, he stared at the screen, hovering in indecision. Then, with firm finality, he clicked the button. *Now, let's see what my new roommate is about.*

In Dave's profile picture, he was wearing a football uniform, hoisting a medium-sized trophy above his head, enthusiastic teammates and students cheering around him. Ben's eyes moved further down the left side of the page. *What? He has 932 friends? How did he get that many?* Last time he checked, Ben's friends barely numbered 100. *Obviously Dave likes football... Dave Matthews Band, of course... in a relationship but "it's complicated"?* Ben skipped reading the list of brainless comedy movies Dave seemed to like and started reading Dave's wall. The first post was from someone named Annabelle Watkins, a gorgeous girl with what looked like some kind of alcoholic drink in her hand. "Hey man!!! Life of the party last night!! Won't be the same in h-town w/o u!!" The next post was from Jason Vernum, also wearing a football uniform: "What you doing sending me a FB message at 3 AM?? Oh wait, it's you, ha ha." Most posts were written by girls.

Ben leaned back, looked up, and blew air between his lips. In his mind, he saw his dorm room, plastered with Dave's ridiculous football posters. He saw himself trying to get some sleep while Dave partied into the late hours of the night. He saw Dave trying to hit on every girl that passed down the hallway. And he could almost smell the lingering scent of beer and cigarette smoke Dave would surely bring into their room. This had been his nightmare about college life: A roommate who would derail his vision of studying hard and being the first person in his family to earn a college degree. How had the housing office messed up so badly? He had made it so clear he wanted someone who prioritized grades. Did Ben just happen to get the last roommate available?

He navigated back to his own Facebook profile. *I list myself as single, but I think there are still a few pictures up with my girlfriend from junior year. Some of the bands under "Favorite Music" seem a bit dated... I still list The Jonas Brothers? That's gotta go. And he's going to think I'm such a big nerd with "reading" as my first listed hobby. And, oh wow, the most recent post on my wall is even from grandma.* Looking up, his eyes scanned his "Religious Views" and "Political Views." *I kinda listed those reluctantly. Maybe I should take them down before the fall?*

With a level of intensity that surprised him, Ben closed the browser window and turned back to his video game. This was the last thing he wanted to think about on a summer night.

* * * * *

Ben felt a small burst of glee as he plugged his Xbox's video cable into Dave's huge TV. *This is going to be so much better than my old TV at home! And so far only one silly football poster. Maybe Dave won't be so bad after all.* He heard a knock behind him and turned.

"Hi. Looks like you have quite the TV there?" said a tall girl with straight blond hair.

"Yeah, it's Dave's," Ben replied, setting the cable down. He extended a hand. "I'm Ben Hamilton."

"Allison Wickman," she responded, shaking his hand. "I live across the hall and thought I'd say 'hi.' Have you met my roommate yet? Chloe Martins?"

"I think I saw her bringing some boxes up with her mom."

Allison laughed. "Yeah, wait 'til you see how many shoes she has! But I knew that; we went to high school together. How about your roommate? Don't think I've met him yet."

"Dave? He seems OK, but we don't really know each other—just talked on the phone a few times this summer. He seems pretty athletic; spends a lot of time with the football team."

Allison opened her mouth to reply as a girl with curly dark hair tumbled out of the stairwell. The bulk of her huge cardboard box dwarfed her tiny frame.

"Allison? Um, help?" she asked, bracing herself against the wall.

Ben turned with Allison to help steady the box. As Allison grunted under the weight, she said, "Ben, this is Chloe."

"Nice to meet you," Ben breathed, helping them shove the box through the doorframe. It barely fit. He heard his ringtone from his room. "I should probably get that; can you handle it from here?"

"Think so," Allison said. "Catch you later… look you up on Facebook?"

"Sure," Ben nodded, then dashed into his room. The phone had just finished ringing; the missed call was from his mom. Ben rolled his eyes; *third time she's called me today.* As he set the phone down, his hand brushed his laptop. He had been editing his Facebook profile before the urge struck to set up the Xbox, and it was still on the screen. *Whoops. I still have The Jonas Brothers listed. Oh well, I guess Allison will just think I have stale musical tastes.*

"Hey Ben," he heard Dave say behind him.

"Back from the weight room?" Ben asked, turning from the computer.

"Yeah," Dave replied. "Hey, thanks for setting up the Xbox!"

"Oh, I'm not quite done yet. A girl from across the hall stopped by and interrupted me."

"Yeah, I think I saw them when I came in. Pretty good looking chicks!"

Ben felt himself squirm inwardly. *Not exactly how I was raised to think about girls. Time to change the subject.* "What are you doing tonight? I heard some of the other freshmen are going to a late showing of *Titan Wars*. Want to come?"

"Oh man, I've been wanting to see that movie!" Dave closed the door and opened up his closet. "But I've got to hit the sack early tonight; I know class doesn't start until Wednesday, but ROTC starts tomorrow. Gotta be up by six, so I'm going to try to be in bed no later than eleven this semester. Been meaning to talk to you about that; hope that's OK with you."

Ben's brain took a moment to catch up with the sudden change in his expectations. "Wait… you're in ROTC? From Facebook, it looked like you stayed up pretty late last year!"

Dave chuckled, pulling some clothes from his closet. "Yeah… you probably got a strange mental picture of me from Facebook, huh? Like I'm some party animal or something?"

Ben looked down. "Well —"

"No need to pretend; I didn't realize until I saw your profile how it might look to you. It's pretty clear you care a lot about your grades, and your family." He paused a moment, looking uncomfortable. "I don't really want to go into too much detail right now, but I made some bad choices my junior year. I almost didn't get into Lasher State. But then some tough things happened with my family and on the football team, and I changed a lot my senior year. That's why I requested someone who studies a lot and goes to bed early on that form they sent out. Some of my old friends still post stuff on my wall, trying to make it sound like I drink and party a lot, but I haven't touched alcohol for about six months."

"Wow," Ben said, feeling stunned. "Yeah, that's not the impression I had of you from Facebook. But I'm probably not as nerdy as I sounded on Facebook, either."

"I don't know about that, buddy—Jonas Brothers? Is it still 2006 or something?"

"Getting removed right now," Ben chuckled, turning to his computer. He had a new Facebook notification—a friend request from "Allison Wickman."

Before he clicked "accept," he wondered: *When she reads my profile, what impression will Allison have of me?* Knowing that accepting friend requests would probably become a routine part of his new life at college, Ben clicked "accept." He began to explore Allison's Facebook profile.

In her cover photo, Allison wore a red and white high school cheerleading uniform; an older couple, perhaps her parents, stood next to her, as well as a few friends and football players. But the most prominent friend in the picture was Chloe, also in a cheerleading uniform, her arm tightly around Allison's shoulders. Except for a new haircut, Chloe looked pretty much like she did now. The picture appeared to be taken just after a team victory. The football players looked exhausted, but happy. Everyone was smiling. Ben looked to the left side of the page—*Wow! 1,285 friends? Are you kidding me? That's about 250 more than Dave! I don't even think I know that many people in person.* Allison's timeline was littered with postings from Chloe: "Hey gurl! I had an awesome time dancing last night. Call me la8er. xoxoxo." Another read, "what party are we going to tonight? Gotta see ya before we head to Lasher!" Ben scrolled up and clicked on the "About" tab. Under "Education," it read: "I'm heading to Lasher State in the fall with my girl, Chloe! Can't wait for college! We're going to be roommates! Yay!!!" *Wow. They seem pretty close. I bet it's going to be so easy for them to live together here.*

* * * * *

Ben looked up from his midterm study sheet and glanced out the window. "Dave, it's snowing!" he exclaimed, watching thin clusters of flakes fall toward the parking lot below.

He heard Dave blow air between his lips. "Too early, man! Too early!"

Ben chuckled. "I think you're just in denial about midterms."

A small knock sounded from their open door. "Aren't we all?" asked Chloe, peeking her head around the door jamb. "Hey, you guys almost ready for dinner?"

Ben glanced at his watch; it was 5:30. "Wow, it is that time already!" Ben thought about how he expected that, many nights, he would have dinner with Dave, Chloe, and Allison. Since the beginning of the semester, they had become pretty good friends. In addition to lunch or dinner several times each week in the dining hall, they watched movies during the week and texted each other all the time. *Or at least, we all did until about a week ago.*

As Ben grabbed his room key, attached to his sporty Lasher State lanyard, he thought about asking the unspoken question that had hovered among the three of them this past week. He was sure Dave and Chloe didn't see him open his mouth and close it in hesitation before he finally opened it to speak. "Hey, Chloe, where's Allison?"

Chloe looked down, shaking her head. "Ya know, Ben, lately I just don't know about that girl. She's never in the room anymore. She leaves early before I get up. She gets in late, sometimes after I'm asleep. And she never talks to me anymore. Ever. I mean, about anything more than basic stuff. Won't even text me back most of the time. I've been wondering if I pissed her off somehow, but I just don't know."

"Nah, it isn't just you," Dave chimed in, throwing his lanyard around his neck. "Allison's been ignoring me lately too. We used to always meet in the library on Mondays after lunch to study, but she hasn't been there the last two weeks. And get this: I was down at the health center yesterday for an appointment about my knee, and I saw her coming out. I just, like, asked her where she'd been, but she seemed upset and said she was just busy. But she also was talking really fast and hardly looked me in the eyes."

Ben fingered his keys idly, thinking. "Well," Chloe said, "I'm sure it's not a big deal; I'll just try to check in with her tonight, no matter how late she comes in."

"Wait a sec," Ben said, bending back over his laptop. "Have either of you checked her Facebook profile recently?"

"Hey—isn't that kind of, like, stalking our friend?" Dave protested. But Ben had already accessed her profile. Allison hadn't updated her status message in about two weeks, and hardly anyone had posted on her wall. The exception was a message posted about two minutes ago by an elderly woman named Donna: "Hi dear—Heard from your parents about what's going on—so sorry—love always." Ben read it out loud to Dave and Chloe as they huddled around him.

"Sounds kinda serious," Dave said, his usual levity gone from his voice.

Chloe shook her head. "Maybe, but I know Donna from home; she's friends with Allison's grandma. She sometimes exaggerates things. She probably just heard about how stressed Allison is about midterms. I mean, Allison and I have been best friends since fourth grade. If it were anything really serious, she'd tell me right away. Maybe before her family."

"Guys, I know this could be important, but the dining hall is going to get crowded soon, and I'm so hungry!" belted out Dave. "I hope they don't have that stinky greenish looking meatloaf again!" Ben returned his Facebook page to the news feed and turned to head for dinner.

* * * * *

By the time they returned to their dorm floor after, fortunately, a non-meatloaf dinner, the unseasonably early snow had stopped. "Watching *The Bachelor* tonight?" Ben asked Chloe.

"Yeah. You guys doing your post-dinner Xbox ritual?"

"Of course!" Dave exclaimed. "Study for the psych test later? About an hour?"

"Sounds good," Chloe replied as she walked past her room toward the stairwell to the basement lounge. As Ben loaded the Xbox game, he saw Dave check Facebook on his iPad. Just as the game finished loading, Ben heard Dave draw in a sharp, startled breath.

"What is it?" Ben asked.

"Um, it's Allison," Dave replied. "Dude, you've got to read this." Ben bolted from the papassan chair to his desk, tapping the keyboard to awaken his computer. Facebook had placed Allison's note at the top of his news feed. As Ben began to read, Dave said softly: "I don't believe it. I feel so…" Quickly, Ben snapped back, "Shhh, quiet. I'm reading." He read the first two lines:

> "I feel like I am ready to share some very sad and very personal news that's been hard for me to talk about. But I think it's good for me to share it here. I've been diagnosed with ovarian cancer. The doctors think they caught it early. So my prognosis is good."

Ben felt stunned, his stomach twisting in knots. "This must be why Allison has been so distant," he said. "Why didn't she just tell us and especially Chloe? I know it's really personal, and we haven't known her that long, but it feels like we're good friends . . ."

"Yeah, I know," Dave replied. "Maybe she didn't tell us because it's a 'girl thing'?"

"But it doesn't sound like she told Chloe, either."

Dave was already finishing a text message to Allison. "Wait, Dave, what are you writing?"

"Asking if she's seen the note."

"Don't hit send yet. Erase that. Just tell her to come up here. We should break this to her in person or she'll freak."

Dave nodded. "Good call, bro." When he was done, Dave silently returned to his desk chair and opened his psychology textbook.

Ben stood for a moment, staring at Dave, then back at his laptop, then to the Xbox, the game's militaristic theme song droning through the television speakers. *I can't believe how normal things felt earlier tonight*, he thought. Not feeling like playing a game anymore, he turned off the Xbox and the television.

Dave's phone played its text message chime. "What does it say?" Ben asked. He held up the phone to Ben: *Coming up—is something wrong? This Bach episode looks good…* "Sounds like she doesn't know," Ben said, then feeling stupid for stating the obvious.

"What should we say? You know how she's going to react. Should we tell her?"

"I… I don't know. Maybe Allison was going to tell Chloe later tonight? Maybe we should back off and let her talk when she's ready?"

"But she's going to see this next time she checks Facebook, which will probably be after *The Bachelor.*"

Ben leaned back and thought for a moment. "It just doesn't feel like this is our news to share."

Silence hovered between them for a moment—then was interrupted by footsteps running down the hall. Chloe swiftly entered her room. Ben looked at Dave, and then both followed behind her. She was already bending over her computer, a tear streaming down her cheek.

"Just when you texted, s—someone downstairs checked Facebook on her phone—" she stammered as she opened the note. Ben and Dave remained awkwardly silent as she read the first few lines, her eyes filling with fresh tears. "Why—why didn't she tell me?" Chloe breathed in, her voice trembling.

"I'm so sorry," said Dave, trying to comfort her, putting his hand on her shoulder; she violently shrugged it away.

"She should have told me," Chloe spat, tears still in her eyes. "We've been friends since elementary school. We've been through everything together! Why couldn't she just tell me to my face? But no, I get to hear about it after she posts it on Facebook for the whole damn world to see!"

"Well, maybe she just wanted to tell everybody at once," Ben said, not sure what else to say. "I bet it would be hard for her to tell the same story over and over. She must have so much going on in her mind, and I'm sure she didn't mean to hurt you."

Chloe collapsed on her bed. "Ben, just shut up. You have NO IDEA what things we've gone through together! She was there when my parents divorced, and when grandpa passed away suddenly, and so many other times. And I told her EVERYTHING. But—" She buried her face in her pillow, sobbing. Ben and Dave's eyes met for a moment; Dave's face mirrored Ben's concern for Chloe, coupled with an utter sense of futility at understanding her feelings, much less comforting her. Without a further word, they both turned to leave.

But before they could take a step, the door swung open noiselessly. It was Allison.

For Further Thought and Reflection

1. Ben's perception of Dave from Facebook was very different than how Dave presented himself in person. When, if ever, have you experienced a mismatch between someone's online persona and how they communicate when face-to-face?
2. Some communication research on the *warranting value of information* suggests that we are more likely to believe a Facebook member's wall posts than their own statements about themselves. Why do you think Ben so easily believed wall posts on Dave's profile? When might we believe a person's statements about themselves rather than those of their Facebook friends?
3. Why do you think Allison shared her personal information with everyone on Facebook, instead of telling Chloe, her close friend, to her face? More generally, what qualities of online communication might help some people feel more comfortable self-disclosing online?
4. Do you think Chloe should ask Allison why she did not directly share her medical problem? Why or why not? What do you think might happen next in this story?

References

Donath, J. (2007). Signals in social supernets. *Journal of Computer-Mediated Communication, 13*, 231–251.

Ellison, N. B., Steinfield, C., & Lampe, C. (2007). The benefits of Facebook "friends": Social capital and college students' use of online social network sites. *Journal of Computer-Mediated Communication, 12,* 1143–1168.

Ledbetter, A. M., Mazer, J. P., DeGroot, J. M., Mao, Y., Meyer, K. R., & Swafford, B. (2011). Attitudes toward online social connection and self-disclosure as predictors of Facebook communication and relational closeness. *Communication Research, 38*, 27–53.

Mazer, J. P., Murphy, R. E., & Simonds, C. J. (2007). I'll see you on "Facebook": The effects of computer-mediated teacher self-disclosure on student motivation, affective learning, and classroom climate. *Communication Education, 56,* 1–17.

Walther, J. B. (2008). Social information processing theory: Impressions and relationship development online. In L. A. Baxter & D. O. Braithwaite (Eds.), *Engaging theories in interpersonal communication* (pp. 391–404). Newbury Park, CA: Sage.

Walther, J. B., Van Der Heide, B., Kim, S., Westerman, D., & Tong, S. T. (2008). The role of friends' behavior on evaluations of individuals' Facebook profiles: Are we known by the company we keep? *Human Communication Research, 34*, 28–49.

15

Having—and Doing—it All? The Hidden Nature of Informal Support Systems in Career and Personal Life Management

Suzy D'Enbeau
Patrice M. Buzzanell

Keywords

work-life balance, informal support systems, coworkers, caregiving, choice

Janie bolted upright in bed and reached for her alarm clock. It was 3 a.m. Brad was snoring. She tried to gently push him onto his side but he was sound asleep and getting louder by the second. She took a deep breath and got out of bed. She eased her feet into her slippers and tip-toed down the hall. She peeked into the girls' room and sighed with relief to find them both fast asleep. Lately, Eden, her four-year-old, had been waking up in the middle of the night, and it sometimes took an hour of rocking and singing softly to get her back to sleep. Janie was grateful to see Eden contently sleeping—her right arm covering her forehead and her curly brown hair—but frustrated that she herself was not.

Guided by the Mickey Mouse nightlight in the bathroom, Janie continued down the hallway. She turned on the faucet in the bathroom and filled her cup to take a drink of cool water. She rubbed her eyes while she was drinking. Then she looked in the mirror and was surprised by the grey streaks in her hair. "When did that happen?" she thought to herself. She returned to bed and covered her head with a pillow to block out Brad's snoring. She hugged another pillow and tried to calm her racing mind…

"Mom….mom…..MOM!" Janie woke with a start to see the sun streaming through the windows. Eden and Lucy, her 2-year-old, were jumping up and down on the bed, their brown curly hair flying through the air. "We want breakfast! We want breakfast! PLEASE!" Janie looked around and realized that Brad was already in the shower and singing along with the radio. Janie closed her eyes one more time, imagining that if she kept her eyes closed long enough, she could go back to sleep and Brad would take care of breakfast for himself and the girls. "If I do go back to work," she thought to herself, "we will have to figure out a new morning routine." But not today. She yanked on her faded blue bathrobe and yelled into the bathroom to Brad that if he wanted breakfast, he'd better stop singing and get to the kitchen quickly. Janie was in no mood to linger over breakfast or delay the start of her morning routine with her daughters.

Janie followed the girls as they scooted down the stairs on their butts to the kitchen. Her eyes lit up as she saw the pot of coffee that Brad made her before jumping in the shower. She smiled while savoring her first sip of coffee for the day. As she started to pour the girls their Rice Krispies, Brad walked into the kitchen, tucking his button-down shirt into his pants.

"Good morning," he said as he kissed her on the cheek. "How did you sleep?"

"Another rough night," Janie admitted. She continued, "Although this time, it wasn't because Eden 'popped up,' as she puts it when she awakes during the night. I started making to-do lists around 3 a.m. Get the oil changed in the car, take Eden to tumbling class, take Lucy to the doctor for her check-up, update my resumé, and call Tia to see if she can come over at 6 instead of 6:30 tonight so that we can go and watch the Purdue basketball game with Mike and Sara. It's been over a year since we've seen them! And I really need some adult time. Thank goodness for Sitter.com!!"

Brad listened while he finished eating his toast. He nodded and added a dry cleaning pick-up to Janie's list. Then he remarked, "I hope that you can get some useful feedback at the Working Moms Meetup Group so that you can get started on your job search. I'm really excited that you decided to attend the meeting. We can make things work if you find a job right away. I know that you need adult conversation during the day and you've missed working in the 3 years since you left Global Laboratories."

"Well, I haven't regretted the time with the girls and I am glad we didn't have the craziness of trying to juggle everything when they were newborns," Janie responded. "Do you remember the incident that finally pushed me to 'opt out' of the labor force? It would have to be better this time, right? I mean, now that the girls are older!"

Brad smiled as he remembered how hectic their lives where then. "I remember showing up at work with milk stains on my trousers on the day of a presentation to our most important client. And the penalty fees for picking up the girls late from daycare! It seemed like it was almost every day that we had to rely on friends, family, and bonded people that my job provided to come to the house and take care of the babies when they were too sick to attend regular day care but also not sick enough to require them to be home."

Janie got an anxious look on her face. "I will never forget the sick feeling in the pit of my stomach when I was late turning in my annual sales report, knowing full well that all the other staff in my region would be impacted by my lateness. Everyone else had their own family and personal interests to which they should have or would have liked to attend. But the final straw was when I was negotiating flexible hours with my boss and project team. Dad called to say that mom had slipped on some ice in their driveway and was not going to be able to help out with the girls for several weeks. Aargh I'm getting that sick feeling in the pit of my stomach now just thinking about all of this," Janie replied.

"Do you remember the conversation we had that night?" Brad asked.

Janie nodded and replied, "I said, 'if you aren't going to stay home with the girls, then I am.' After all, we both made about the same amount of money but I figured that it was more socially acceptable if I stayed home with the girls. At the time, I thought that re-entering the work force after a time out would be easier for me because of my work as a pharmaceutical sales rep. But now I'm not so sure."

Brad and Janie turned to the kids just in time to watch Lucy dump her cereal bowl contents onto the dog waiting for crumbs under her chair.

Lucy smiled and said, "I done."

Janie groaned while Brad said, "That's my cue to leave. See you later." He quickly gathered his car keys, kissed Janie goodbye on the forehead, and practically ran out the front door. Janie smiled. She couldn't blame him for leaving so quickly. If she could, she'd do the same!

When Brad got to work, he was surprised to see an empty desk where his administrative assistant, Steve, usually sat. Brad stepped into his own office just as his phone let out a beep indicating a new email. He switched on his computer and loaded Microsoft Outlook. It was an urgent message from Steve. Steve was going to be a few hours late or he may not come in to work at all. On his early morning walk with his golden retriever, Schatzi, she cut her paw on a sharp stick. Steve had to rush her to the veterinarian's office. Brad knew that Schatzi was like family to Steve. Steve's desk was covered with photos of the two of them playing at the beach and hunting in the woods. But Brad still wondered how he would manage without Steve's help. They were in the middle of last minute preparations for a bridge inspection safety conference the company was hosting in less than two weeks. He hunkered down at his desk and prepared for a long day.

Later that evening, Tia knocked and then slowly pushed the front door open. "Hello?" she called out.

"We're upstairs! Almost ready," Brad shouted down to Tia. "How was class today?"

Tia took off her jacket and hung it up in the hall closet. She took the tie out of her long hair and shook it out. She smiled as she did so. Eden and Lucy would want to "style" it during their book reading and snuggling time.

Tia responded, "My communication class was interesting today, to say the least. My professor just had a baby three weeks ago and she actually brought the baby to class! She wore her baby girl in a sling the whole time during lecture. I couldn't believe the baby didn't make a peep. But some of my classmates were not pleased. They said our professor was very unprofessional for bringing her baby."

"Wow," Janie said as she came down the stairs. "Does the university not provide maternity leave?"

But before Tia could answer, Eden and Lucy came running into the foyer and jumped into Tia's arms.

"You're here!" the girls proclaimed as they dragged her into the toy room. Janie and Brad yelled goodbye and hightailed it out the door while the girls were distracted by the thought of pizza and playtime with Tia.

Janie and Brad arrived at The West End in downtown Chicago early and sat at their favorite table near the window that also had a great view of one of the big screen TVs. Janie ordered a glass of house Merlot and Brad ordered a seasonal microbrew and some chips. Brad rubbed Janie's leg as they both eased into their seats. Then Brad spotted Mike and Sara at the door and waved them over to their table.

"It's so good to see you two," Sara exclaimed as she gave Janie a big hug. Mike waved the server over to their table and ordered a stout for himself and a pale ale for Sara.

Janie turned to Sara and whispered gently, "I guess this means you haven't had any luck yet?"

"We've been trying for a little over two years now, and I can't seem to get pregnant. We've been seeing a fertility specialist, Dr. Kelley, at Robinson Memorial. She has been very optimistic but we've already had two failed IUI (intrauterine insemination) treatments. So now we are going to try IVF (in vitro fertilization). I had to miss a big presentation at work because my body was ready to try for a procedure. I know that my colleagues on the project team were upset that they had to cover my part of the presentation but we can't help the timing of it all. And the hormone treatments make me very emotional. The other day a teammate questioned me about one of my conclusions for the company report, and I started tearing up. When Mike and I are together, we don't even have normal conversations anymore; it's all about whether the procedure took this time and whether this is a good time to have sex. Lately though, the conversations are focused on when we should stop trying before we kill each other. It's been a long and grueling process," Sara brushed a tear away from her eyes. "Okay, enough about me. I want to hear about those gorgeous daughters. Do you think you will have any more kids?"

"More? We aren't sure. The girls are wonderful. They keep me very busy," Janie beamed. "But for the past few months, I've been anxious to get back to work. Eden and Lucy were just taken off the wait list for The Learning Academy, an excellent school with a preschool a few blocks from our house. So I feel like now is the time for me to think about going back. I miss work—interacting with colleagues and clients, the thrill of making a sale. But I hope I'm not too late. The global pharmaceutical industry changes fast. I need to figure out how to update my resumé so that potential employers don't think I have been sitting around doing nothing for the past three years. And I need to somehow demonstrate that I have kept up with the current changes and trends in the industry. I've been reading trade journals in my limited free time and been following relevant websites. I just hope that's enough."

Just then, Mike's phone lit up. "You promised me that you would turn your phone off during our night out," Sara reminded Mike.

"I'm sorry," Mike said. "But that's Ann texting me now. Her mom moved in with her and her husband Rick to help take care of the twins and help the family save money. But Ann's mom is also in the early stages of kidney disease and has lots of doctors' appointments. Ann and I were supposed to spend the weekend working on a proposal but it looks like she needs to take care of her mom."

Mike exited the table as the drinks arrived to make a phone call to Ann without disturbing others.

Mike wasn't gone long and just continued the conversation where he left off. "Ann and I had a discussion with our managers about our personal needs at this time in our lives. At first our bosses were concerned that we'd look like we were getting preferential treatment. But what we proposed was that we work out a way to cover the essentials strategically if one of us had to be out of the office. That way neither of us would feel as though we were doing more than our fair share and we also wouldn't have to impose on others in our work group. It's been a little bumpy at times—like when we both had to run out of the office. Ann had to deal with an emergency with her mom and Sara's body was the ideal temperature for reproductive sex. Or so we had hoped."

"This is so interesting," Janie chimed in. "I was just explaining to Sara that I'm thinking about re-entering the workforce. I'm already worried about being able to cover everything with the girls and with Brad traveling for work."

The server returned to take their meal order as a Purdue basketball player made a 3-point shot near the end of the second half to give Purdue the lead. The conversation drifted to the game and other things. On the way home, Janie remarked to Brad, "I'm beginning to feel more comfortable about applying for jobs."

The next afternoon Janie left the girls with Brad and drove to The Root coffee shop to meet the other members of The Working Moms Meetup Group. She found this group through a Google search of "Chicago moms return to work." She walked into the coffee shop, ordered her cappuccino, and saw a group of three women sitting at a table in the back. She gave them an inquisitive look and they immediately waved her over.

"Hi, I'm Jamie. I found your group through an Internet search and am so grateful to meet moms who also work outside the home. I've been staying at home with my girls for the past years but am ready to get back into the workforce. But I wonder how I will be able to do it?"

"You picked the right group! Hi, I'm Susan. We have three girls ages 9, 7, and 5. I'm the breadwinner in our family because of my position with US Bank. During the early years, my husband was finishing up his MSW (Masters of Social Work) degree in the evenings and taking care of the girls during the day. It was really important to us to have one parent at home with the girls full-time at least during the early years of their lives. Now that they are all in school all day, we are both working full-time, and it can be very hectic between work, school and athletic events, dance practice, music lessons...the list goes on and on."

"I'm Colleen. I have two kids. Our son Keegan is 5 and Kaia is 3. I'm 4 months pregnant with our third. My company offers three months paid maternity leave but I always find that is not enough. With Keegan, I just went back to work full-time after my leave ended but it was a very difficult transition. I couldn't keep up my milk supply through pumping at work, and I had to stop breastfeeding much earlier than I wanted to. With Kaia, I negotiated working from home three days out of the week until she was 9 months. But I know some of my colleagues were resentful that my manager allowed me to negotiate that schedule. Now I'm trying to figure out how to approach work-family balance when we have our third. I want to be a good parent and a good employee. I welcome any ideas!"

"I guess it's my turn. I'm Roslyn. We have one son who is about to turn 1. I'm a graphic designer and work full-time. My partner also works full-time as a professor of management. My pregnancy was complicated and I was put on bed rest during the last three months. Then Ethan was born prematurely and had to stay in the NICU (neonatal intensive care unit) for a month. It was a very rough time. I thought I was going to lose my job but some of my co-workers agreed to assist me with my accounts, in addition to their own accounts, so that we could meet all of our deadlines. Thankfully, Ethan is healthy now and attending the on-site childcare at my partner's university. I just returned to work. Now I need to figure out how to thank my colleagues."

The time flew by as the women elaborated on the challenges they have faced as working moms. Janie sipped the last drops of her cappuccino. The moms shared e-mail addresses and phone numbers and planned their next meeting for the following month at a new downtown wine bar.

Janie walked into the door and Brad motioned to be quiet. "Shhhh....the girls are finally napping. How was your meeting?" Brad asked.

"It was great but it was also eye-opening. Managing work and family doesn't necessarily get any easier as the kids get older. I always thought that was the case."

Brad could feel the anxiety emanating from Janie. "Don't worry," he assured her. "We'll figure out how to make it all happen. We always do. Maybe you can find time to go to a yoga class this weekend?"

"Of course I would love to get to yoga more. But it's not just about me feeling stressed. Now that we have kids, I want to make sure we have sufficient back-up systems to manage work and family," Janie said. "The only way to have it all is to figure it out for yourself and not let anyone at work know that work-family balance is an issue. To me, it's a source of pride to be able to work it all out. Let's see how the job search goes. And I think that I'll want to be prepared to negotiate like Mike did with Ann and with their bosses and coworkers. I'll want to work with you and with members of the mom's group that I just met to figure out solid arguments for the work-life considerations I'd appreciate such as flex-time or maybe job-sharing. Ideally, I would like to find solutions that might also be advantageous to my co-workers and boss."

Brad said, "I agree. We can't solve it all now but it looks like we're headed in a productive direction. Let's plan more tomorrow. I know that you are wide awake and excited but I'm tired from playing with the girls this evening."

Brad went upstairs while Janie put away some dishes and continued thinking about their future.

For Further Thought and Reflection

1. Tia mentioned that her professor brought her infant to class. Although the baby was not disruptive to class, some students voiced their objections about the professor's actions saying that bringing the baby was inappropriate. Would you think it inappropriate if one of your professors brought her or his baby to a class she or he was teaching?
2. In the situation mentioned in the question above, Janie started to ask about maternity leave policies at the university. What were the underlying issues in this incident? Is it simply a family leave policy issue or is there more to this incident than first appears?
3. Most of the people in this case consider career and personal life management to be their own responsibilities rather than shared responsibility with their places of employment. What do you think about the assumptions about responsibility, choice, and policy in this case?
4. What might be some arguments and steps that Janie could propose for her future workplace that would benefit her own work-life balance and that of her co-workers and bosses?
5. How would you analyze this case from the perspective of organizational dynamics and that of family dynamics? Would your solutions to the case differ based on the theoretical perspectives you chose?

References

Buzzanell, P. M. (2015). Work and family communication. In L. H. Turner & R. West (Eds.), *The SAGE handbook of family communication* (pp. 320–336). Thousand Oaks, CA: Sage.

Buzzanell, P. M., & D'Enbeau, S. (2009). Stories of caregiving: Intersections of academic research and women's everyday experiences. *Qualitative Inquiry, 15,* 1199–1224.

Buzzanell, P. M., D'Enbeau, S., & Duckworth, J. (2010). What men say about women: Fathers contemplate work-family choices and motherhood. In S. Hayden & L. O'Brien Hallstein (Eds.), *Contemplating maternity in the era of choice: Explorations into discourses of reproduction* (pp. 291–311). Lanham, MD: Lexington Press.

Buzzanell, P. M., & Dohrman, R. (2009). Bosses, coworkers, and direct reports: Everyday communicative acts and consequences. In W. F. Eadie (Ed.), *21st Century communication* (pp. 331–339). Thousand Oaks, CA: Sage.

Buzzanell, P. M., & Liu, M. (2005). Struggling with maternity leave policies and practices: A poststructuralist feminist analysis of gendered organizing. *Journal of Applied Communication Research, 33,* 1–25.

Correll, S. J., Benard, S., & Paik, I. (2007). Getting a job: Is there a motherhood penalty? *American Journal of Sociology, 112,* 1297–1338.

D'Enbeau, S., Buzzanell, P. M., & Duckworth, J. (2010). Problematizing classed identities in fatherhood: Development of integrative case studies for analysis and praxis. *Qualitative Inquiry, 16,* 709–720.

Wood, J. T., & Dow, B. J. (2010). The invisible politics of "choice" in the workplace: Naming the informal parenting support system. In S. Hayden & L. O'Brien Hallstein (Eds.), *Contemplating maternity in the era of choice: Explorations into discourses of reproduction* (pp. 203–225). Lanham, MD: Lexington Press.

16

Same Sex Marriage at any Age: The Enduring Struggle for Acceptance of Marriage Equality

Clark D. Olson

Keywords

coming out, same-sex marriage, privacy management, dialectical contradictions, self-disclosure

It was June 26, 2013 and thirty-two-year-old Jeremy was standing on the steps of the San Francisco City Hall building with Daniel, his partner of four years. They were amidst a throng of jubilant same-sex marriage enthusiasts who were rallying in support of the U.S. Supreme Court's decision to invalidate California's Proposition 8, which would allow same sex marriages in California to resume shortly. He had just snapped an Instagram photo of the two of them smiling and posted it to his Facebook account with the caption "Now we can get married." Just moments later his phone rang and he heard his Grandma Sophie from Minnesota on the other end, "Congratulations, you two. Just saw your post, when's the wedding?"

Jeremy had always been particularly close with Grandma Sophie. For most of his childhood growing up in rural Minnesota, he had felt like a loner and many times Grandma Sophie seemed like she was the only one who understood him. He certainly wasn't cut out for farming like most of his cousins. In fact, he had always had an interest in politics and social justice so it was just natural for him to go to grad school. He completed his Ph.D. in political science at the U of M which was where he met Daniel, who had been in law school. They met at the Minneapolis pride parade some four years earlier. Now Daniel was an assistant professor at Sacramento State University and Daniel had gotten a job with a local gay rights advocacy group there and they had just finished renovating their older home on N Street in Sacramento.

Today, Minnesota and his rural childhood seemed like light years in his past. Never the school athletic star, he was much more gifted academically and preferred model U.N. and playing in the high school band rather than roughhousing on the football field. In farming country that meant he really hadn't had a lot of friends growing up and spent a lot of time at Grandma Sophie's house since she was taking care of Grandpa Wally, who had had a stroke before Jeremy was even born. While Grandpa had a full-time caretaker, Grandma Sophie had been a dutiful wife spending most of her days at home keeping Grandpa company. That meant she had plenty of time to sit and talk with Jeremy, essentially being his best friend through high school. Grandma Sophie was different from most adults in rural Minnesota. She was a big advocate of helping those less fortunate, and had even been arrested in the 1980s for protesting in favor of allowing illegal immigrants to enter the U.S. She was an outspoken advocate for gay rights; even before Jeremy had confided to her when he was sixteen that he thought he might be gay. She had spent tireless hours campaigning for the legalization of same-sex marriage in Minnesota which had just passed the previous November. While she encouraged Jeremy to come back to Minnesota to get married once the ordinance took effect, he and Daniel were hopeful they could get married in their home state of California in the near future. "Love who you want," was Grandma

Sophie's motto, "and don't let other people tell you what's right and wrong." And here she was, on the other end of the phone, being the first to congratulate him on his new legal right to get married.

"We've got lots of planning to do, Grandma," Jeremy replied, "I never realized how many details there are to put on a wedding, but we'll let you know."

"You keep in touch, Jeremy, and say 'hi' to Daniel as well. How's he doing these days?"

"Just great, even better today. Gotta run, Gram. There's a celebration starting inside the courthouse that we don't want to miss, and we've got to drive back to Sacramento tonight. Say 'hi' to Aunt Peggy, will you? Bye." And with that Jeremy put his phone back in his pocket and he and Daniel headed into the courthouse, waving their rainbow flag all the way.

Aunt Peggy wasn't really Jeremy's aunt. She had been Grandpa Wally's caretaker after he had his stroke and began using a wheelchair. She had been an Army nurse and after putting in her twenty years, she was eager to use her skills to help others. She had moved into the spare room in Grandma Sophie and Grandpa Wally's house, where she made Grandpa's last years as comfortable as possible. She had even made sure that Grandpa got to visit Norway, wheelchair and all, as one of his last wishes. Quite often, Peggy helped get Grandpa to the family cottage on a lake in northern Minnesota. She was so patient and thoughtful; it was as though she had become a member of the family. Once Grandpa Wally passed away ten years ago, it just seemed natural for her to stay on at Grandma's house in the spare room, as she was able to draw a good military pension and seemed happy to stay in Minnesota.

Peggy was good company for Grandma Sophie as well. Though she was five years older than Grandma, the two of them had become fast friends, bonding over Grandpa's care, but also sharing their "liberal" interests as well. Peggy had been quite the feminist, needing to survive in a chauvinistic military environment. Now that she was retired, she joined Grandma Sophie in her causes and they often vacationed together as Peggy took Sophie to several spots around the globe where she had been stationed throughout her career. Never the world traveler, Grandma Sophie thrived on seeing these places and was a never-ending source of travel information whenever Jeremy and Daniel wanted to take a European vacation.

After the rally, Jeremy and Daniel began the ninety-minute drive back to Sacramento. "What an exciting day," Daniel remarked. "So, how soon do you think we can get married?" Their wedding was the only topic of conversation en route home. They discussed their ceremony, who their attendants would be, the guest list, their bachelor parties, who might give the toasts, and even speculated on taking a Baltic cruise for their honeymoon. They were both eager to begin the next phase of their lives. Each had a good job, they both wanted to start a family, and they had just finished the rehab on their house so the timing couldn't be better. "Guess we'll be a real part of history," Jeremy said as they pulled into the driveway.

While they were both tired, the excitement of their future kept them awake that evening. Eventually their conversation turned to Grandma Sophie. She was so up-to-date on the Supreme Court's decisions that day. Not only had Californians won the right to same sex marriage, the Court had also struck down the Defense of Marriage Act in *Windsor v. United States*, a case that held particular interest for Grandma Sophie. Edie Windsor had sued the U.S. for back payment of $371,000 in estate taxes after her lifelong partner Thea had passed away. While they were residents of New York, one of the states that allowed same-sex marriage, the federal government's DOMA didn't recognize their marriage. Now that penalty had been struck down, and soon, despite a raft of conflicting legislation, a bold new step had been taken to insure equality for same-sex marriage.

These latest developments on same-sex marriage were uniquely important for Grandma Sophie as well. About five years ago, she had confided in Jeremy that she and Peggy were more than just "friends," they had fallen in love. Growing up in the 1950s, Grandma had done her duty, married at an early age and become the housewife and mother as was expected of women of that period. She had two sons, Jeremy's father and his Uncle James who had each married and given her five grandchildren to boast of. Jeremy was the eldest. While Grandma had seemed happy enough growing up, she remained the eternal optimist once Grandpa Wally suffered his stroke, and had taken on the expected role of grieving widow once he passed. Jeremy's father and Uncle James couldn't seem to understand why Aunt Peggy stayed in the picture. They were worried that Grandma Sophie was being taken advantage of, and their statements became ever bolder at family gatherings at holidays. Despite liking Peggy on a personal level, since she had taken great care of their father for nearly a decade, they just didn't think it was right for her to still occupy a place in Grandma's home. While Jeremy knew Grandma Sophie's secret for several years, it was only last year that she had revealed to her sons that she was, and always had been, a lesbian, and that she and Peggy had been a "couple" for years.

This news was not well received at all by Jeremy's father. He thought it was bad enough that he had a gay son, but now a gay mother as well. Somewhere Jeremy had remembered reading that often the "gay gene" skipped a generation, and here his family seemed to be living proof of that. Jeremy's dad and Uncle James were furious. Jeremy sympathized with his father, knowing it must be difficult for a rural, conservative farmer to first accept a gay son, and then learn that after all these years his mother was a lesbian. He wondered how he and Daniel might be able to help his father be at least be a little more tolerant, knowing it was likely to take some time. No matter what his father and Uncle James thought, Grandma Sophie refused to let either of her sons tell her what was right and wrong for her. "Love who you want," she kept reminding them.

And today, the Supreme Court had in many ways validated her love for Peggy. While Peggy was older than Grandma Sophie, they had vowed to care for each other until death. Now that same-sex marriage was about to become legal in Minnesota, they planned a quiet wedding ceremony where they could pledge their love for each other officially and insure that they secured the legal rights marriage would bestow on them. But today had been even better than they could have anticipated. While Peggy was still relatively healthy she wanted to make sure that Sophie would be taken care of should anything happen to her. This fact seemed lost on Sophie's sons. Once they were married, Peggy's generous military pension could now transfer to Sophie, ultimately relieving Jeremy's father and Uncle James from the financial burden of having to care for their mother. Even Sophie's medical expenses would be covered at a military hospital should Medicare not cover her needs completely. This security allowed Grandma Sophie and Peggy to be able to spend their resources on travel and visits to Sophie's grandchildren, most of who had moved out of state. For senior citizens, they had a great life, experiencing abundant travel, companionship, and family. The only thing they needed was to feel some acceptance by Sophie's two sons of their long relationship and love for one another. Why was it that something that seemed so obvious to the two of them would be lost on their own family?

Jeremy and Daniel were thrilled for Grandma Sophie and Peggy. Grandma had even invited Jeremy to be her "best man" when they got married around Labor Day, when most of the family returned to Minnesota for their annual family reunion. This would be a particularly special day. Daniel speculated, "Maybe we could announce our upcoming wedding at the family reunion." Jeremy was quick to point out that this should be Grandma Sophie and Peggy's special weekend and that they shouldn't try and steal their thunder. After all, one gay wedding in the family at a time was probably all Jeremy's dad and Uncle James could handle. While his father had been cautiously accepting of Jeremy, and ultimately Daniel, Sophie and Peggy's relationship had been much harder for him to comprehend. After all, he had had a father and mother growing up, and now he was about to inherit a second mother. While Jeremy knew his father was still struggling, he was proud of him for keeping his previously snide comments to himself in Peggy's presence and he was even starting to treat her as the family member she was about to become.

Jeremy and Daniel finished their conversation and headed to bed. Jeremy paused and texted Grandma Sophie "Guess today has been good for both of us—congratulations!"

A moment later he could see Grandma Sophie had responded: "☺" was all he saw on his phone and he drifted off to sleep smiling.

For Further Thought and Reflection

1. What risks are involved in gays and lesbians "coming out" to friends and family? What communication strategies are essential to help this disclosure go well?
2. Which communication theories would be beneficial to help one understand the varying nature of sexuality and how it is communicated?
3. How do you imagine social norms are different for Jeremy and Daniel vs. Sophie and Peggy?
4. How can a GBLT person communicate to overcome family disapproval of same-sex marriage?

References

Badgett, M. V. L. (2009). *When gay people get married: What happens when societies legalize same-sex marriage.* New York: New York University Press.

Berger, R. M. (2011). *Gay and gray: The older homosexual man* (2nd ed). New York: Routledge.

Breshears, D., & Braithwaite, D. O. (in press). Discursive struggles animating individuals' talk about their parents' coming out as lesbian or gay. *Journal of Family Communication.*

Lannutti, P. J. (2011). Communication about marriage amendments: Same-sex couples and their extended social networks. *Journal of Social Issues, 67,* 264–81.

Lannutti, P. J. (2013). Same-sex marriage and privacy management: Examining couples' communication with family members. *Journal of Family Communication, 13,* 60–75.

Oswald, R. F. (2000). A member of the wedding? Heterosexism and family ritual. *Journal of Social and Personal Relationships, 17,* 349–368.

Petronio, S. (2002). *Boundaries of privacy: Dialectics of disclosure.* Albany: SUNY.

Polikoff, N. D. (2008). *Beyond straight and gay marriage: Valuing all families under the law.* Boston: Beacon Press.

17

Shallow Talk and Separate Spaces: Dealing with Relational Conflict

Sandra Metts

Keywords

latent conflict, conflict escalation, conflict strategies, rules for managing conflict

Sarah was frustrated as she drove home from work. Always too much to do and never enough time. She was working way too much and she knew it. But she didn't know how to say no when asked to do more. She was still not finished with the midyear report and, to make matters worse, she was facing an exam tomorrow night in the class she was taking for her Master's degree. She was tired and hungry, and hoped that Russell had started dinner. She turned onto the driveway and pushed the automatic opener for the garage door. By the time it was halfway up, she saw that Russell's car was not there. "Well, I guess Russell won't be helping with dinner again," she muttered. "Why is everything my responsibility?"

Just as Sarah entered the kitchen, she heard the ding from her cell phone signaling a text message. She went back and dug the phone out of her purse. The message read: *backed up at work. be home by 6. luv U.* "Oh, thanks," she said to the cell phone as she put it on the counter. "You couldn't have texted me sooner?"

Sarah felt her mood darken even more. No need to return the message. It was already 5:30 and she didn't feel like cooking or waiting to eat. But she looked through the refrigerator until she found the makings of a salad, some leftover meatloaf, and some aging potatoes. She washed the breakfast dishes that were in the sink as she prepared dinner. *Geez, he can't even do the dishes when he knows that I am under such pressure,* she thought to herself. *Tonight after dinner I am going to ask him to give me a little help around the house, at least until the end of the semester. Maybe he'd take care of dinner and dishes during the week and laundry on Saturday.*

A short time later Russell pulled into the garage. Sarah was putting dinner on the table when he came into the kitchen. He too was tired, and the residue of a stressful day still lingered. "Ugh, what a day," he said. "I thought James and Mark would never get out of my office. Get this—they want me to do a survey of the entire county by the end of the month!"

"Well at least you don't have the same stupid report from last week, still hanging around your neck like an albatross, and an exam coming up that you haven't even studied for."

"Of course I don't. But then I wouldn't let anyone walk all over me like you let those folks at C & G do to you."

Sarah bristled. "It's my job. I can't help it," she said.

"Well, you *can,* but you *won't,*" Russell responded. Then looking at the countertop by the microwave he remarked, "Meatloaf again? We had that last night."

Sarah tried very hard to control her anger, but her voice was sharp. "Yes, we are having meatloaf again. If you want something else, then you can fix it."

Russell answered without thinking, "Let's just go out for dinner."

"Go out?" Sarah snapped. "After I made dinner? Since when can we afford to throw away food? Or is my cooking just too awful?"

"I never said your cooking was awful; I just don't feel like meatloaf tonight. Lighten up."

"Lighten up? Easy for you to say. You don't have to work full time, take care of the house, do all the shopping, and work on your Master's degree."

Russell felt his fatigue turning into anger. "Oh no, it's the poor-me-routine; you give and give, and I do nothing. Aren't you forgetting that I mow the lawn, pay the bills, buy the groceries, cook as often as you do, and clean the house every weekend?"

"Oh? Since when? You never do anything around the house. It's work all week and golf all weekend."

"Oh, so it's my fault that nothing gets done? Maybe I work all week because I am not allowed to make noise in this precious house. All I ever hear from you is 'Please be quiet; I'm studying. You know, my Master's degree, my Master's degree.' It's your excuse for everything. 'I don't have time to shop, my Master's degree. Can't watch TV, I have homework. Can't go out, I have an exam. Can't have sex anymore, gotta work on my Master's degree.' At least I get a little peace and companionship on the golf course."

"Oh, you're exaggerating, as usual. I do not make you be quiet, I do more than my share around here, and we . . . we have sex. You're making me out to be a selfish monster."

"Well, frankly, that's about it. You have the patience of a gnat, and you're just about as much fun. We have sex when the moon is full, and we never make love any more. I practically have to beg you to come to bed, and a man gets pretty tired of begging for something from his wife that other women would be glad to give."

"What's that supposed to mean? Are you looking at other women now?" Sarah felt resentful. She knew that there were problems in the bedroom and acknowledged she was partly to blame. But she resented Russell for making her feel so guilty; it was certainly not all her fault. "Why are you saying this? I can't help it if I'm tired. Maybe if I got some help around here, I'd have more energy. I'm carrying a heavy load. You knew I was going to continue my education when we got married."

"Yeah, but I didn't know that it would consume your life and our marriage. Now I have to worship at the altar of the Heavy Load. The pressures of work and, oh, the pressures of that blessed Master's degree. All bow in honor to the Heavy Load."

Sarah felt pushed into a corner. Russell was attacking the very core of who she was—a good student, a hard worker, a high achiever. His sarcasm hurt and she wanted to hurt him back.

"Well, at least I'm capable of getting a Master's degree. I don't see you in a grad program, Mr. Einstein. In fact, you barely got out with a bachelor's degree. We had to drag you off the golf course for graduation—or did you even graduate? I can't remember."

Russell stood up so abruptly that Sarah was startled. "I know that you don't think I'm very smart—certainly I'll never meet your standards. I don't know why you married such a stupid guy. But I'll tell you, Sarah, I'm a good man with or without an advanced degree! I don't need a piece of paper to prove I'm worth something, but you sure do. We've been married almost two years and you're still not a wife. When are you going to grow up?"

He moved to the door before Sarah could respond. "I'm going out to eat," he said, "and enjoy my own ignorant company."

"Well, good," Sarah yelled back. "You are the only one who can!" Sarah was agitated as she picked up the dishes and tossed the uneaten food in the trash. As she cleaned the kitchen, she fought back tears. *Why does this always happen. I promise myself I will be rational, but I get defensive and, bang, we're on the downward slope. I didn't think marriage would be like this. We had so much fun when we were dating. Why can't he be a little more supportive of what I'm going through? 'Still not a wife'? What kind of crack is that? I'm more grown up than he will ever be.*

Later that evening Sarah was working at the computer when Russell returned. She heard him click on the television downstairs, and she thought about going down to talk to him. Instead, she decided that if he wanted to talk he could just as easily come up to see her. *But he probably won't,* she thought. *He's too stubborn. Besides, he said some hurtful things, and he owes me an apology, but he will never give in and admit he was wrong.*

Russell stared mindlessly at the television. He knew that he and Sarah needed to talk, but he just couldn't endure another heated argument. His thoughts wandered back through the conflict. He knew that he shouldn't have brought up the sex thing again, but she was never "in the mood" anymore. Every night was a struggle just to get her to turn off that darn computer and come to bed. She seemed to think that Master's degree was more important than he was. She was always so serious, about everything. Heaven forbid that a smile should cross her face. And then, oh that remark about his grades—maybe he wasn't the best student in the world but he graduated and got a good job. And he was doing well. Why didn't she ever acknowledge that? *Better to sit here*, he thought, *and keep my ego intact than to try another discussion.* He loved his wife, but lately all they seemed to do was argue. *I just can't deal with this anymore,* he decided. *Maybe if I just don't say anything about our problems for awhile, things will settle down.*

Russell eventually fell asleep in the recliner and woke up some time after midnight. He found Sarah already in bed asleep. As quietly as he could, he slipped under the covers. Sarah was awakened by his movements and thought about apologizing. But the last thing she needed to hear was about how selfish she was. He didn't even seem to care about her needs, only his own—sex, sex, sex. Sarah lay there in the darkness very still, pretending to be asleep. Both lay awake for some time—feeling frustrated, rejected, angry, and hurt.

The avoidance continued for several days. Sarah got through her exam and finished her company report. Russell also got caught up at work and tried to be more helpful around the house, but only when he didn't need to be in the same room as Sarah. The distance between them was chilling. Shallow talk and separate spaces. Neither one brought up any issue that might cause conflict. They showed no affection and closed each other out. Both were beginning to feel the strain in their relationship.

On Saturday morning Russell was golfing and Sarah was working on her next class assignment. The telephone rang. Her older sister, Betty, was in a good mood and began chatting about her family. The kids were doing this and that; Fred was refinishing some furniture. After a few minutes she paused. "Is something wrong? You seem sort of down?"

"Yeah, I guess I am," Sarah replied. "Russell and I had another fight."

"Oh dear. What about this time?"

"I don't know. Just the same old stuff. He won't help around the house, but when I bring it up, he gets defensive about my Master's degree and starts complaining that we never have sex anymore. How am I supposed to feel sexy when I have to do everything around here? Besides, even when I am willing to have sex, he still complains because we aren't "making love"—whatever that means. We just can't seem to discuss anything without a big fight."

"Oh, I know how that is."

"You do? But you and Fred never fight."

"Oh contraire, sister dear. Fred and I used to fight a lot, and we still have conflict, but we learned how to fight fair."

"What do you mean, fight fair?"

"Well, it seemed that most of our arguments began when we were stressed. I would complain about something he did or didn't do and instead of just saying, yeah, you're right, Fred would complain about something I did or didn't do. Then I would get defensive and say he was wrong. Then he would say I was too sensitive, and I would say he was selfish. I don't know why, but we just got into these dueling matches that accomplished nothing but hurt feelings. So now, we try to take turns. If I have a complaint, we deal with that complaint, and put it to rest. If Fred has a complaint at the same time, we wait and deal with it later. It's hard sometimes, but we try not to get the issues confused and we try not to hit below the belt. To call each other inconsiderate, or lazy, or selfish solved nothing. It made us both feel hurt or angry but did nothing to help the situation."

"Yeah, that's pretty much what happens around here," Sarah said. "Maybe we need some ground rules for our conflict. Thanks for listening and sharing your own experiences. Well, I need to get going. Tell the family 'hi' for me."

"Sure, will do. And good luck," Betty said as she hung up.

Sarah put down her phone and went to the kitchen for another cup of coffee. As she stood there looking out the window, she thought about the past week. The silence was deafening; the tension was painful. *Betty's right. We don't fight fair. We're like two snarly little kids who always hit below the belt.* As Sarah turned to go back upstairs, she noticed their wedding picture on the wall. She was suddenly overwhelmed by a disturbing mixture of emotions—feelings of love and joy but at the same time intense feelings of fear and anxiety. She realized at that moment that if this pattern continued, the wonderful future she had always imagined would become a black hole of regret. She thought about this throughout the day and did some reading on the Internet, particularly a blog from The Gottman Institute, based on couples' research they have done. As she learned more about conflict and fighting fair, her anxiety slowly passed and she began to feel more in control.

Late that afternoon, Russell returned home from his golf game, a bit more relaxed than when he had left, but still dreading the cold shoulder he was expecting from Sarah. He put his golf clubs in the closet and decided he had best find Sarah and offer to help with dinner. He expected some kind of vague or curt reply, but he wanted to get it over with. "Sarah," he called. "Are you upstairs?"

Sarah answered from the kitchen. She was already making dinner and Russell noticed that it was grilled chicken and pasta. He wanted to say thanks for not reheating the meatloaf again, but didn't dare risk trying to be funny. He expected her to criticize him for playing golf instead of staying home to help with chores. So without saying anything, he went upstairs to change, came back down and began setting the table.

During dinner, Sarah seemed particularly nice and even asked about his golf game. "It wasn't bad," he said. "I'm getting better with my putts. Gene's advice to keep my arms closer in, sort of under my shoulders, helped." Russell smiled and added, "No more shanks." Sarah smiled back and considered for a moment how much pride Russell took in his golf game. Not really very different from the pride she took in her academic accomplishments.

After dinner, Russell began to clear the table. But Sarah stopped him and asked him to sit with her for a few minutes and talk. "I want to apologize to you for my comment the other night about you not being capable of getting a Master's degree. I know you could if you wanted to. I was just angry and lashed out. But I really don't understand why you are so resentful of my efforts to get more education."

Russell's first impulse was to list again the countless times that her studies intruded on his plans, his needs, his pleasures, but instead, he paused, put down the plates he had picked up and sat down across from her. He realized that she was not complaining or attacking him. In fact, he could tell from the tone of her voice and the way she looked at him that Sarah's apology was sincere and she really did want to know why her studying bothered him so much. He wanted to show the same sincere effort to get these issues resolved. His first impulse, to be sarcastic, faded away and he said instead, "I guess I just feel left out sometimes. I need time with you, too. All I ever hear is you're so busy or so tired."

Sarah didn't respond immediately, but when she did, she chose her words carefully. "You're right. I have been complaining a lot lately about my pressures at work and school. I realize that I tend to close you out when I'm busy and I'm sorry for that. Truly, I am. But right now I need your support, not your resentment."

"Oh, Sarah, I'm just not as good with words as you are. I don't resent you, I'm proud of you. I suppose I should tell you that more often. I guess I just want to know that there is some line you can draw for us, some period to be placed at the end of the work day when you put it all away and relax. If it's not possible to do that during the week, couldn't you at least try to do it on the weekend? I want to be supportive, but I feel disconnected from you sometimes, like everything else in your life is more important than I am. I have a job too and I'm doing pretty well at it. I would like to know you are proud of me too, that my life matters, that I mean something more to you than a roommate who helps around the house."

Sarah was struck by the sadness in Russell's voice and realized that the burden had not been hers alone. She hadn't been physically or emotionally available to him for quite awhile. Perhaps more importantly, she had stopped showing how much she respected him, how much she enjoyed his wit, his humor, his energy, his accomplishments, and his ability to keep work and play in proportion—all the things that had attracted her to him in the first place. She had become much more likely to find fault and criticize than to give him compliments and tell him how much she valued him as her friend, her companion, her lover, and her husband.

Impulsively, she leaned across the table and kissed him. Russell looked a bit surprised, but Sarah smiled and touched his hand. "I love you," she said, and then she proposed a plan. "What do you think about this? What if we give a compliment now and then instead of just criticism? What if we agree that when we have a complaint, we try to keep it focused on an action or behavior, not on personality, and that we really try to listen and be supportive even when we are getting angry? And let's try to stick to one person's complaint at a time. We just keep dumping our own agendas on the table without really listening to each other's concerns."

Russell nodded in agreement. "That sounds good, but it won't be easy."

"I know, but I think we have to try," Sarah responded.

Russell nodded again. "You're right." Then he added, "And how about apologizing when we are wrong instead of going on the attack?"

"You got it, big guy. Now how about helping me with these dishes and then maybe we can work out something in our schedules so I can have more free time for us?"

Russell stood up and began collecting the plates again from the table. "Ugh, I guess that means making a list of household chores and dividing them up, huh?"

"Yeah, but this time, we'll have three lists: household tasks, our own tasks, and things we want to do together."

Russell would have preferred that their life be a bit more spontaneous, especially where sex was concerned, but Sarah was such a planner. Oh well, maybe that was a good thing right now, given the challenges of being a dual career couple. Maybe he could quit thinking so much about his own needs and show her more appreciation. He smiled, looked down at Sarah as he moved her plate and said, "Okay, I guess I need a bit of organization, but can golf be on my Saturday to-do list?"

Sarah laughed and replied, "Absolutely, if working on the computer can be on mine. We'll just take turns paying for the pizzas we have delivered for dinner."

For Further Thought and Reflection

1. John Gottman (1994) describes four communication behaviors of dysfunctional conflict that characterize unhappy couples. As you look at the list of these behaviors below, what examples for each do you find in the conflict of Sarah and Russell?

   Criticism: Attacking a partner's personality or character, rather than his or her behaviour

   Contempt: Insulting and psychologically abusing a partner's sense of self

   Defensiveness: Refusal to accept responsibility for one's actions, often done by meeting partner's complaint with a counter-complaint

   Stonewalling: Actions characterized by withdrawing from interaction and keeping an icy distance

2. Sarah seems to have good intentions when she first decides to ask Russell for more help around the house. However, several factors seem to derail her original intention, influence Russell's reactions, and ultimately contribute to the escalation of the conflict. What are some of those factors? Which might be attributed to the situation and which might be attributed to the way Sarah initiated the interaction?

3. Sarah and Russell come up with some rules to help them manage their conflict. What are these rules? Do you think their rules are good ones? Are there other rules you think they should add to guide their conflict, either before it starts or after it is underway?

4. What do you see in the future for Sarah and Russell? That is, do you believe they have resolved all of the important issues? Do you think there is any "latent" conflict (unresolved issues) that might influence future interactions, for example, if they have children? If so, describe the issues that might linger as problems in their relationship.
5. Conflict episodes have two "texts" or levels. One text consists of the messages that are exchanged; a second text consists of the emotions that prompt particular messages or result from receiving particular messages. Explain the emotions that you see in Sarah's and Russell's conflict, and try to associate these emotions with the messages produced and received. To what extent do you think that Sarah and Russell are competent in controlling their emotions?

References

Birditt, K. S., Brown, E., Orbuch, T. L, & Mc Ilvane, J. M. (2010). Marital conflict behaviors and implications for divorce over 16 years. *Journal of Marriage and Family, 72*, 1188–1204.

Busy, D. M., & Holman, T. B. (2009). Perceived match or mismatch on the Gottman conflict styles: Associations with relationship outcome variables. *Family Process, 48,* 531–545.

Cloven, D. H., & Roloff, M. E. (1993). The chilling effect of aggressive potential on the expression of complaints in intimate relationships. *Communication Monographs, 60,* 199–219.

Cupach, W. R., Canary, D. J., & Spitzberg, B. H. (2009). *Competence in interpersonal conflict* (2nd ed.). Prospect Heights, IL: Waveland Press.

Gottman, J. (1994). *Why marriages succeed or fail.* New York: Simon and Schuster. http://www.gottmanblog.com

Sagrestano, L. M., Christensen, A., & Heavey, C. L. (1998). Social influence techniques during marital conflict. *Personal Relationships, 5,* 75–89.

Zacchilli, T. L., Hendrick, C., & Hendrick, S. S. (2009). The romantic partner conflict scale: A new scale to measure relationship conflict. *Journal of Social and Personal Relationships, 26,* 1073–1096.

18

Yard Sales and Yellow Roses: Rituals in Enduring Relationships

Carol Bruess

Keywords

relational culture, rituals, intimate play, private language, secrets, dialectical tensions

The back-and-forth motion of the porch swing brought comfort to Martha; she was feeling a bit exhausted from hauling boxes and cleaning out closets for their annual yard sale—a joint effort by her, Jack, and their kids to clean, purge, and simplify—and she was feeling both the stress of preparations and the relief from making good progress that day. As she and her partner Jack sat together on their front porch swing, she thought back to their first little house rented during graduate school.

It had been 26 years since they had married and sat on a porch swing very similar to the one now greeting visitors to their home. During their early years of marriage, they regularly sat on that creaky old swing late in the evening, stealing a few moments of peace after chaotic, packed days of studying and attending classes. Mundane talk about the events of the day, as well as dreams about their future, saturated such moments. Now, many years later, Martha and Jack used "porch-swing time" to reflect on the past, discuss their three grown children, and imagine the next chapter in their lives.

"Porch-swing time," according to Martha and Jack, had a few not-at-all-elaborate but absolutely essential items. First: popcorn. Since their first date in college, Martha and Jack shared a love of those salty, fluffy white kernels. At Raymond Theatre, where they'd sink into the red velvety seats and attempt to watch a movie—distracted by their interest in looking at one another instead of the screen—they purchased the biggest bucket of popcorn and then playfully wrestled each other for each bite. During the early years of their marriage, as they prepared for their weekly (sometimes daily) gathering on the porch swing, they would prepare a huge pan of their own popcorn. Jack insisted on a mountain of sea salt. Grabbing a bottle of red wine and mismatched wine glasses secured at others' yard sales, they'd head for the swing.

"Those were the days, weren't they?" Martha recalled fondly as they'd adjust the hand-me-down pillows flanking them on the swing. The air was warm and moist on this August evening; the streetlight cast curious shadows onto the shakes of their early 20th-century home. They used to dream about owning the very home in which they now felt lucky to dwell. As the motion of the porch swing brought them in sync, Jack had no doubt Martha would mentally and verbally reflect on their early years of marriage and raising children; she often did so whenever one of their children had called home with some important news. Their youngest daughter Jill, now 23, had Skyped with Martha, thrilled to share with a huge, screen-wide grin the details of her new job, one that would take her to Japan!

Jenny, now 29, their oldest child, lived in Green Bay, Wisconsin (Go Packers!) and worked as a 4th grade physical education teacher. Their second child, Chad, 28, recently made a life-long commitment to his high school sweetheart and moved to Ohio.

Although both Martha and Jack loved their three children dearly, they weren't shy about admitting how much they enjoyed an empty nest! Along with finding new hobbies, they re-initiated activities once abandoned when they chose being fully present and active with their kids instead of meeting their own recreation or relaxations needs. Weekday mornings, for instance, there is now a sense of peace that begins the day, instead of a sprint-like beginning, which sometimes created unpleasant and tense mornings with young children in the house. Jack described those early years as "rushed and swirling." Martha would run frantically about the house packing lunches, filling bowls with Cheerios, making beds, and urging kids to brush teeth. Jack would be busy reviewing kids' homework, getting the car ready for the morning carpool, taking out the recycling, and attending to the family dog with a brisk walk, without which he'd literally tear apart the house during their absence. As a couple, Jack and Martha rarely had a chance to utter much more than a fleeting "have a great day, honey!" to one another on those manic mornings. Now, however, Jack started each day by rising early and preparing their home-espresso machine for making a strong cappuccino for himself, and of course Martha's favorite: a vanilla latte with 1% milk. When she awoke a few hours later, they would sip their coffees, sit in the early morning quiet, and log into their iPads—side by side—for the daily news. After work, because they had no kids to meet at home, no basketball games to attend, and no dance lessons to observe, they would meet for happy hour at a nearby pub, go grocery shopping, or simply take a walk. Sometime around 2:00 P.M. each day one or the other would text the other at work just to say "hi," make plans for dinner or the evening, or send a kissy-face or another silly emojicon (Jack once accidentally added the little green turtle emoji to a message; they immediately decided little green turtles should be their private ways of saying "I love you!"). If the two o'clock hour passed without the text check-in or a little green turtle text, they each felt something was missing. Martha explained, "I don't know, it's just something we do almost without even thinking about it. It's pretty much expected and automatic. It's comforting for sure."

Jack agreed, and reflected on life with three growing kids living at home. "Those *were* the days. Remember how many schedules and activities we would be juggling? I kind of miss those times.""It does seem to be true what people say: 'They'll grow up before you know it.' Where has the time gone?" Martha also misses some of the chaos, but frequently reminds Jack of how good life felt now too. Similar, but different.

As they inched their way to the bottom of the popcorn bowl, the warm summer air blanketed them and their fond memories like a warm hug. Neither needed to actually say much out loud in these moments; each quietly enjoyed the symbolic comfort of the porch swing—back and forth, forward and back—the bowl of popcorn nestled between them, and wine glasses held loosely in hand. In these moments, they couldn't help but recall where their lives began together.

The Yard Sale

Each spring Martha began thinking about the yard sale months in advance. "Could it really take nearly six months to get ready for a tag sale?" Jack would often joke. Although some years there wasn't much to purge from their tiny rooms or recycled/hand-me-down furnishings, the spirit of the sale was clear: connect with neighbors and refocus on their family's motto of "Live Simply; Love More." Preparations for and conversations about the annual tradition typically went something like this:

"Hey Jack, I was thinking that this year we should sell the *old twin beds* downstairs at this Spring's yard sale." (Item in italics was different each year, but Martha said almost precisely these words). Jack predictably and playfully then replies with a groan: "Do we really need to have another sale this year?" Martha ignores his insincere grumbling, knowing Jack enjoyed the haggling, selling, and friendly-shout-outs about "deals happenin' here!" and "low, low prices!" to cars rolling by. As a customer strolls up, Jack is fond of humorous tactics: "Only 10 cents for this entire box! And we'll throw that tire in for free. Buy one tie and get a dog kennel for ½ price!" More than even Martha, Jack loves yard sale day. It's an event, no question, with a long, shared history in their family.

During yard sale prep days Martha would often yell down to the basement from the top of the stairs: "Hurry up Jack! What's taking you so long?" After a pause she would think to herself "Why ask?" She knew exactly what it was. He had stumbled across an old letter, tool, or photo, and was now captivated as he surveyed it from all angles. Sure enough, Martha would round the corner of the basement storage room and find Jack sitting crossed-legged on the cement floor, surrounded by college photos and yearbooks, or a box of "goodies" (some would call it junk) from their childhood homes.

One time she found Jack halfway into reading an essay exam written for Fr. Murray's Christian Ethics class. He had gotten an "A!" "One of the few from your college days . . ." Martha chided. "I can pull out a few of yours if you'd like, Miss Martha Betcher!" Jack often used Martha's maiden name when he kidded her about her "smarts." Martha was academically the much better student of this couple, and they loved joking about it both privately and publicly.

Martha had nicknames and special phrases she used privately for Jack too. The most common was to call him "Fuzzy." Its origins lie in a private, playful game created between them early in their marriage called "belly button search." Even after 26 years of marriage, the game will emerge when one of them least expects it. Martha explains its origins: "I would check Jack's belly button for fuzz on a daily basis at bedtime. It originated when I noticed some blanket fuzz in his belly button one day and thought it was funny! We both found it fun and teased often about the fuzz. If there wasn't any fuzz for a few days, Jack would put some in his belly button for me to find." Although none of their friends or family knows of the "belly button fuzz game," the nickname "Fuzzy" is used publicly while maintaining a symbolic, private meaning for them as a couple. When asked by others where the nickname came from, they both innocently shrug their shoulders and say "Hmm. Don't really know." They love having little "secrets" from the rest of the world!

"This stuff is hilarious, Martha. Check out this photo of us with the kids at the beach!" Jack pointed to the image of their three young children, and his and Martha's young faces and not-at-all-hip-anymore hairdos. "Remember how we could spend nine hours on the beach and not even know we'd been gone an hour? Those were such great times. And look at this one of us on our honeymoon. Why is *this* in this box of junk?" Jack quipped.

Martha became outwardly irritated when Jack would complain about "disorganization" or the way things were "junked up." A perpetual argument in their marriage was about who was responsible for the daily tasks and managing the house cleaning, the organizing, and the purchasing of household items. Martha would say she was overburdened in this area of their marriage, while Jack would say he "pitches in quite a bit."

For most of their marriage, except a few years when their three children were very young, both Martha and Jack worked full-time: she as a professor at the local University and he as a high school principal. Despite their busy days, Martha, like most women in dual career marriages, took on a good majority of the "house" work (laundry, cooking, dishes, organizing kids' activities, remembering to schedule dentist appointments, etc). So, when Jack asked these kinds of questions, she got irritated. "It's in that box because you probably put it there, Mr. Organization, Mr. I-never-put-anything-away-that-would-take-some-time-and-effort! . . . Mr-I-don't-know-what-it . . ." Her voice and mild irritation trail off when she sees Jack trying to add a bit of lightness because neither of them was in a mood for the same old argument. He was having such a great time looking at the old memories in the boxes! "Was that 93 cents or 96 cents?" He asks with a grin. Martha instantly shoots him a big smile in return.

The statement "Was that 93 cents or 96 cents?" was another of their relationship secrets, a sentence that had meaning just between the two of them. Jack's parents would often correct one another and bicker over the most trivial details. One evening Jack and Martha watched them argue for hour upon hour about whether something had cost 93 cents or 96 cents. They adopted the question for use in their own marriage as a way to gain perspective when tension or conflict was emerging and/or escalating. When uttered, they'd often laugh at themselves and divert unnecessary conflicts. It had worked again today!

Their eyes and attention swiftly moved back to the honeymoon photo Jack had unearthed. Martha: "We look so young! That was such a great time of . . . Oh!" She interrupted herself. As she dug even deeper into the box of old stuff she thought she had lost, out fell the ribbon used on her wedding bouquet. It was yellow, just like the roses it held. Martha: "Awww. Look at this!" "Ewww" was Jack's response. "That's looking kind of moldy." Martha agreed. But she couldn't toss it. And Jack knew she wouldn't. Yellow roses and yellow ribbons, like those in her wedding bouquet, had become a means for Jack to express his adoration of Martha. Each year on their anniversary (26 and counting) he sent her one yellow rose with the same hue of ribbon attached. He vividly recalls about 10 years before when he painstakingly drove to multiple flower shops—even in neighboring towns—before he was able to locate a yellow rose. But he did, successfully. Martha looked forward to the gesture but always tried to act surprised when the rose arrives. "They remind me, every time, how much we love each other. How far we've come, together. It's very sweet of him to always do that."

"Look at this photo of me and the guys at 456!" Jack found a snapshot of his roommates posing with a gaggle of pink flamingo lawn art at 456 Western Avenue, their college rental. Although most of "the guys" had dispersed about the country since graduation, one of Jack's best friends was Tim. They not only had shared a room in that overcrowded, run-down house, they also shared many of their most personal thoughts and dreams about their futures in that space. It was during one of their late night chats at 456 Western, over a pizza and a pile of unfinished homework, that Tim had told Jack that he was gay.

Until that time, Tim had told no one—not even his own family. After settling in at college Tim had decided he needed to start telling people, to let people know who he really was. Jack helped Tim through some of the toughest days of his life: when he finally told his parents and his family; when his parents wouldn't speak to him or visit for over a year during his last year of college; when Tim began to experience some of the unthinkable, hateful actions and words from students and others at the college; and when he had seriously thought about dropping out. It was that time, during their last year of college, when Jack and Tim became the closest of friends.

"By the way" Jack said, interrupting his own wandering thoughts. "Tim called the other night and wants to add a few items to the yard sale. He said they have lots of junk to get rid of after the move!" Martha was always pleased to add others' stuff to their yard sale. "The more the better" was her yard-sale-philosophy. "He's going to drop it off Friday night. He said he'll have it all priced."

Since Tim moved back to town, Jack had been very happy. He and his partner Bart decided to move to the city where Martha and Jack now lived. It was just a short drive from where Jack and Tim had gone to college, so it was a natural choice. Jack and Martha couldn't have been more thrilled when Tim had called to share the news of their decision!

If Jack said it once, he had said it a hundred times: "It's so great having *Rock* back in the city." Rock was Tim's nickname, given to him by Jack. He didn't use it very frequently anymore, but it still had a special place in their friendship. It represented Tim's inner strength, something Jack always admired. Tim called Jack Doughboy because of his pasty white skin and blonde hair. Yet Tim was the only one who could call Jack that without distaste. Martha saw Tim as a brother; she loved him dearly. They had all grown close over the years and had a long, shared history—something that made their friendship stronger than some of the others in their adult lives.

Living in the same town again resulted in welcome changes in how they stayed connected. When separated by thousands of miles, Jack and Tim maintained a weekly skype ritual, or a call at minimum. Throughout graduate school, even after Martha and Jack moved another 600 miles away, Jack and Tim talked routinely; usually the conversation took place on Sunday nights, well after the kids were all asleep. If it wasn't on Sunday night, it was Monday for sure. They now traded in their skype/call for a monthly (sometimes weekly) dinner and drink. It most often included their partners, Martha and Bart. The four thoroughly enjoyed evenings together; they cherished the chance to reunite, reminisce, and get to know one another's families and interests. Their favorite spot was Luci's, a cozy, authentic Italian eatery at the edge of town where they could sit and chat for hours. The conversation flowed seamlessly from serious to silly to significant. Most often, it was just good old "talk." And that's exactly what they looked forward to most.

One of the things about Tim was that he had a contagious energy, and a great sense of humor! Upon returning from a two-week canoe trip to the boundary waters of Northern Minnesota a few years ago, Martha and Jack were greeted by 100 pink flamingos poking around in their front lawn. When they pulled in the drive, they simultaneously shouted in laughter "Tim!" Jack yelled into the phone. "We'll get you, buddy. And paybacks are hell!"

And so it began. Every so often, when someone least expected, the plastic pink flamingos on wire spokes would make their way into either Tim or Jack's yard. Sometimes they even dangle from the roof. They looked particularly funny on Tim and Bart's snow-covered boulevard last February. And as the prank evolved, other local friends and neighbors have happily joined in, borrowing the flamingo collection for placement in others' yards or gardens (sometimes even in living rooms!). A few years back someone even expanded the collection by adding new "ugly" objects (twirling plastic daisies, the rear-view of a female gardener, and bright green bugs with waving wings), making it a veritable and ever-growing plastic farm that—just when you least expect it—migrates around the neighborhood.

Looking back at their college photo, Jack laughed: "Pink Flamingos. Ah. The good old pink flamingos. Where it all began!" They both laughed. "Maybe we should sell them at the yard sale tomorrow?" Martha was not at all serious, and Jack knew it. But still, he couldn't resist: "You're nuts! Marty! Those things will be around until I die. Or if Tim goes first, we can use them at his funeral!" A frown came from Martha; she didn't think it was funny to joke about death, and Jack knew that about her since they first began dating decades ago.

"Okay—time to get my rear off this floor and start hauling up to the garage." Jack knew his reminiscing must end. Martha began to move an old rusty fan and a box of her mother's old linens toward the steps. "It's already five o'clock, and we don't even have everything cleared out yet." Yet Jack still felt a bit glued to the floor, and before he stood up initiated one more stall tactic: "I'm hungry, Marty. What do ya say we go over and grab a burger at the counter first, and then come back to finish the hauling and tagging?"

Martha couldn't resist an invitation to "the counter," the malt shop just down the street from their house. Since the kids had moved out, it had become a new dinner ritual for her and Jack. It reminded her of the Woolworth's counter she and her dad used to go to on Saturday afternoons. She and Jack also liked "the counter" because it was similar to the soda fountain they went to when they first dated ("Sodas were a quarter then!"). Martha's favorite flavor was lime; Jack preferred Cherry Coke. Suppressing her urge to just push through and keep working on the yard sale, she said "Great idea. Let's go. But let's make it quick, eh?"

Back (and Forth)

The porch swing slowly rocked her and Jack back and forth, back and forth. She loved these "porch-swing" moments more and more as the years went by, as their children grew older, and as their relationship grew stronger. It wasn't that either of them thought they hadn't had a strong relationship from the start, but each session of remembering seemed to add clarity to the way their lives together—of memories, yard sales, nicknames, shared friendships, photos, stories, secrets, burgers, and popcorn—gave them a unique and irreplaceable history.

"Ouch" snapped Jack. "Darn mosquitoes! They're out in force this summer. I'm heading in the house." "Meet you inside," Martha responded as she gathered the empty popcorn bowl, and two glasses which had tiny red rings left at the bottom where the last drips of wine had settled. She glanced back with a peaceful smile as the swing slowly came to a halt.

Endnote

This case represents a composite of experiences from couples participating in a research study conducted by the author and her co-researcher, Dr. Judy Pearson. All names and identifying details have been changed.

For Further Thought and Reflection

1. Members of relationships create their own "relationship culture" in and through their communication. A relational culture weaves partners together not through the activities or interactions themselves, but in the meanings partners assign to these activities and interactions. How would you describe Martha and Jack's relationship culture to someone who had not read this case? How would you describe the relational culture of one of your own relationships? What kinds of interactions contribute to the relationship maintenance of the couple and the friends in the case? What kinds of interactions sustain a relationship of yours?

2. Rituals are defined as recurring interaction patterns that pay homage to something symbolically significant to relationship members. What rituals—large or small, mundane or celebratory—can you identify in this case, both between Martha and Jack and those they have with Tim and Bart? Make a list. After doing so, describe what Jack and Martha's relationship might be like without any of the rituals they enjoy. Referring back to question #1, how would their relational culture change if they had no rituals?

3. What do your answers to question #2 reveal about the importance of rituals in relationships? Researchers believe rituals serve a multitude of functions for relationship members. What functions did they serve for Martha and Jack? How about for Jack and Tim? How do some of the rituals in this case simultaneously serve the contradictory needs of novelty and predictability, openness and closedness, autonomy and connection?

4. Researchers report nicknames and private language serve a number of functions in our personal relationships. What examples of private language can you identify in the case? What functions do you think it serves for Martha, Jack, and Tim? After considering the case, reflect on and list as many examples of nicknames or other private codes you use in your family or friendships. What functions do they serve in your relationships? Hint: think about conflict resolution, playfulness, privacy, secrecy, and/or discussing taboo or uncomfortable topics.

5. What kind of rituals do you have in your own friendships or personal relationship? How about in your family? Make a list of all the "rituals" you can think of in one of these relationships. Don't overlook the mundane ones in favor of the annual or celebratory! As you look at your list, can you identify when and how the ritual developed? Does its origin tell you anything about the shared history and culture of your relationship?

References

Baxter, L. A. & Braithwaite, D. O. (2006). Family rituals. In L. Turner, D. & R. West (Eds.), *The family communication sourcebook* (pp. 259–280). Thousand Oaks, CA: Sage.

Baxter, L. A., Braithwaite, D. O., & Koenig Kellas, J. (2009). Empty ritual: Young-adult stepchildren's perceptions of the remarriage ceremony. *Journal of Social and Personal Relationships, 26*, 467–487.

Bruess C., & Pearson, J. (1997). Interpersonal rituals in marriage and adult friendship. *Communication Monographs, 64,* 25–46.

Bruess, C., & Pearson, J. C. (2002). The function of mundane ritualizing in adult friendship and marriage. *Communication Research Reports, 19,* 314–326.

Fiese, B. H. (2006). *Family routines and rituals.* New Haven: Yale University Press.

Fiese, B. H., Tomcho, T., Douglas, M., Josephs, K., Poltrock, S., & Baker, T. (2002). A review of 50 years of research on naturally occurring routines and rituals: Cause for celebration? *Journal of Family Psychology, 16,* 381–390.

Goffman, E. (1967). *Interaction ritual.* Garden City, NY: Anchor.

Jorgenson, J., & Bochner, A. (2004). Imagining families through stories and rituals. In A. Vangelisti (Ed.), *Handbook of family communication* (pp. 513–538). Mahwah, NJ: Lawrence Erlbaum.

19

Being Similar and Different: Multiethnic-racial Identity and Communication in Personal and Family Relationships

Jordan Soliz

Keywords

communication and identity, ethnic-racial identity, ethnic-racial socialization, family solidarity, ingroups/outgroups, multiethnic-racial

Anissa left her grandparents' house disheartened. She loved her grandparents very much and, for the most part, enjoyed being around her father's family. But not tonight. She was upset about something that happened, which, while not common, was also not isolated. That night, the family was gathered together after dinner in the living room sharing stories, laughing at each other, and having a good time. Anissa was talking with her cousins when she overheard a conversation between her Uncle Mark, Aunt Katy, and some other relatives. Katy was telling the story about how she accidently broke the lawnmower. When one of her relatives asked Mark if he was going to buy a new lawnmower or get it repaired, he replied jokingly, "What I do need a lawnmower for? Have you seen how many Mexicans live in our neighborhood now?" Anissa knew her Uncle Mark had a crude sense of humor but, for her, this crossed the line. There were enough people in the room to hear his comment and Anissa expected some type of reaction. She looked around and, although not everyone was laughing, no one said anything to her uncle or to her, for that matter.

Anissa was upset and decided to excuse herself to collect her thoughts. Sitting in the guest bedroom, she reflected on what was said and became more and more frustrated and upset. Not only was she upset with her uncle, but she was also upset with her family for not confronting her uncle about his remark. If her parents were able to attend that night, she knew—or hoped—that they would have said something to the family. Given that they were not there, Anissa decided to talk with her grandparents. After she told them why she was upset, her grandmother replied, "Anissa, we agree that Uncle Mark's comment wasn't in the best taste. But, he was just joking. You know him. He wasn't serious." Anissa replied, "But Nana, he was joking about my mom's family! He was joking about my mom! He was joking about me! They are Mexican. *I* am Mexican." "Well, yes. But, you're only part Mexican," her grandfather replied, "and sometimes Uncle Mark doesn't see you that way. He just sees you as a member of our family. You know he wasn't talking about you or your family specifically." Their defense of her uncle made her even more upset. Anissa decided to drop the matter and, after a few minutes, left after saying some reserved good-byes.

Driving home, she replayed the incident in her mind time and time again including the conversation with her grandparents. Many thoughts were going through her mind. *What does that mean—he just sees me as family? Is that supposed to excuse the comment or make it so I am not offended? Was I being too sensitive? Was it fair to my grandparents to be so upset with them? Why am I so frustrated?* This was not the first time something like this had happened with her dad's family. In fact, similar incidents had happened with her mom's family. Anissa remembered last Easter when some of her cousins on her mother's side were making fun of "white people" and her cousin, Ricky, told her, "Oh, don't be offended Anissa. We know you can't pick your family. Besides, your old man is alright, know what I'm sayin'? Anyway, we love ya'! You're our little *güera*!" Although she knew he was joking, she still remembers how much that comment "stung" because she actually did feel different from her mom's family from time to time just as she did from her father's family. When she arrived home, Anissa sat down on her couch and pulled out her journal. Whenever Anissa was frustrated, worried, or confused, she wrote in her journal as writing out her thoughts helped her make sense of things. She often wrote about her love life, her relationships with friends, future aspirations, and daily stressors. Tonight, she decided to reflect on what happened at her grandparents' house and, in doing so, decided to focus on growing up with parents from different ethnic groups.

Anissa's Reflections

Anissa started writing the first entry in her journal initially reflecting on her childhood:

> Was it like this when I was a child? Hmm. When I was a kid, I didn't think too much about the differences between other family members and me. Mostly, I just enjoyed being around my grandparents, aunts, and uncles, and playing with my cousins. Of course, I noticed some differences like how parents would use words like "mija" and "mijo" in mom's family but never on dad's side. There were typically different types of food served at each family's house and the older family members on mom's side spoke Spanish. But, I just thought all of this was normal—at least, it was normal for me. Of course, my dad does remind me that, as a young girl, I used to always ask why his family "looks different" from mom's family. Other than that, I know I didn't feel any different.

Anissa sat for awhile, continuing to ruminate on the experiences with her dad's family that day. Starting a new page in her journal, she began writing about her teenage years when she had started to recognize some of the complexities in her family and, more importantly, her identity:

> I remember when I was 13 and we moved to a new house leaving me with two sets of friends at school—one from my new neighborhood and the other from the old neighborhood. All the girls from the old neighborhood had the same background as my mom's family—they were names like Ruiz, Chavez, Santoyo and I had grown up with them. However, as I got older, I started to feel a little out of place. When I went to their houses, they would often speak Spanish with their parents or use a lot of slang that I was only somewhat familiar with. Although I certainly grew up around Spanish speakers and could speak a little Spanish, I was not fluent. But, all my friends in this group were fluent. I noticed that their heritage became more important to them as we got older like when Elena had her Quinceañera ceremony when she has 15. It was becoming important to me too. But, I remember feeling that I was not identifying with my Hispanic background to the same extent that they were. I also noticed that the older we got, the more they spoke in Spanish to each other or used words and phrases that I didn't always understand. They didn't do this to exclude me. In fact, I remember Julia or maybe it was Valeria saying something like, "Oh, hey, someone explain what that means to Anissa," after a joke was made in Spanish. Although they said this to include me, I remember that moment specifically because I felt kinda' out of place. These were my friends since childhood. Yet I felt I didn't quite belong all of the sudden. Our families—at least my mom's—shared the same heritage, ate the same types of food, spoke the same language as these friends. However, I remember thinking I was different. All of us—me included—would joke about my lighter complexion and lighter hair. For the most part, this was just part of our friendship as we always teased each other. But, during this time, it became an issue for me because I remember not

> feeling "Mexican enough." Thinking back on it, that was ridiculous. This is my heritage, this is who I was—who I am. But, at that time, I felt out of place.
>
> Unfortunately, it was the same with my friends from the new neighborhood. All of my friends in this group were "white." While I was the "lighter" one with the group of friends from the old neighborhood, we always referred to me as the "Little Latina" with this new group of friends. They always commented on how I wore my hair, dressed, and some of the expressions I would say. Plus, some of the music, shows, and other things I liked that obviously came from mom's family seemed foreign to this new group of friends. None of these difference was because of any prejudice or anything like that—simply different backgrounds. Regardless, like my other friends from the old neighborhood, I didn't feel as comfortable around them as I did when we first got together. It was a tough time. I started noticing similar issues with cousins on each side of my family. When we were younger, I never really thought about or noticed these differences. But, they seemed to be more evident at that time in my life and I remember feeling really confused about who I was and where I belong.

Once she finished, Anissa read her entry. She was surprised by what she had just written. *Wow! That makes it sound like I was really struggling at that point in my life.* Anissa knew that, despite what happened at her grandparents' house, she definitely did not have the same issues today. In fact, she was very secure in who she was and perceived her mixed heritage as a blessing. Anissa strongly believed that having a mixed heritage provided her with a more astute view of the world, made her more tolerant and respectful of others, and provided her with the skills to adapt to different people and situations. Of course, she sometimes had to deal with people who often challenged her identity. Anissa started reflecting about one specific experience during her senior year in high school when she applied for and received a small scholarship for students of color. She began writing in her journal about this:

> I remember being so nervous about this scholarship. It wasn't a lot of money. But, it really wasn't about the money. I worked really hard in school and this scholarship was based on academic merit and extracurricular scholarly activities like the debate club I was involved in. If I won, it would show my parents and family how hard I have been working. In our homeroom that week, they announced the three winners. When it was announced that I received the scholarship, I was ecstatic. My teachers and most of my friends and classmates were very happy for me. Yet, I still remember the comment I overheard from—oh, I can't remember her name. Anyway, as I was receiving my congratulations, I heard, "Well, I guess today she's Hispanic! How convenient." To this day, I still regret not saying anything to her. I don't know why I didn't. After all, who was she to question me and my heritage or how I choose to identify?

After she wrote these two entries, Anissa realized there was definitely a shift in how secure and comfortable she was in her mixed background from when she was 13 years old to her senior year in high school. *What changed? What happened?* Anissa continued to ruminate on this. Then, it became apparent and she was surprised she did not think about this before because it now seemed so obvious. She began to write:

> When I was a kid, mom and dad didn't talk to us about their relationship or how they reconciled any differences from their different backgrounds. Mom's family is from Mexico and she was born and raised in the Bay area. Grandma and grandpa moved around a lot with my dad but mostly in smaller towns in the Midwest until he was in high school and they moved to the suburbs of Chicago. They couldn't be more different in their upbringing, cultural backgrounds, or personalities for that matter. Even to this day, his Spanish is absolutely horrible and Dad can't stand Mom's molé and won't touch menudo! Of course, Mom is just as critical—in a fun way, mostly—of Grandma's cooking. Like I said, they never really talked about the ethnic differences in the family. Okay, not to sound cliché, but they seemed to operate under the idea that "love transcends difference." Like all couples, they had their arguments but most of them had nothing to do with having different backgrounds. Well, I do remember a few occasions when some issue would arise and create tension usually resulting in a brief fight between the two. In most cases, this would relate to a comment a friend or

> family member would make about immigration or Hispanics, in general. Mom would be offended and upset with Dad for not contesting the comment or perhaps Mom and Dad had different views on these issues. But, these incidents were few and far between. Basically, Mom and Dad had a great marriage and their different backgrounds didn't seem to have any negative effect. Our family was the most important thing and they both tried to make sure we embraced customs and rituals from each side of the family. But, I think that, because the differences didn't seem to be important to them, they never really addressed my mixed background with me until they started seeing some of the issues I was dealing with once we moved. At that point, they started asking questions and we had more direct conversations about my background.

As she continued to write, Anissa reflected on some of the specific conversations she could remember. Specifically, she thought about those conversations that had a significant impact on how she thought about herself and how she dealt with some of the issues that were arising as ethnic-racial identity seemed to be more important with her peers.

> I came home one day from school and Dad was home early from work. He immediately knew something was wrong and asked me about it. I told him that I just felt like I didn't quite belong with my groups of friends. He listened to me talk about some of my experiences and conceded that he and Mom maybe didn't realize some of the issues I was dealing with and apologized for it. I told him he didn't need to apologize. After all, it's not like they did anything wrong—it was other people or maybe even me. And then, Dad said something to me I can remember almost word for word. He said, "Anissa, yes you are different from your friends. But in the best way possible! You are unique but don't ever feel like you don't belong or fit in. Are people going to say things that are insensitive? Yes. Unfortunately, that is the world that we live in. And people you talk with including friends and even family might say or act in ways that make it difficult at times. But, Anissa, those are your opportunities. If you want, you can ignore it and try to forget about it. Or you can let people know how you are feeling and give them something to think about. Challenge them to re-think how they view the world." Okay, what Dad said wasn't earth-shattering. But, it was so important that he recognized some of my struggles and made me start thinking about my mixed background not so much as a burden, but as a source of pride.

Anissa remembered leaving that conversation feeling much better and also thought about a conversation with her mother that was similar in its influence. She wrote:

> One time I asked Mom if her parents loved me as much as they loved their other grandchildren. She replied, "What are you talking about?! Of course they do! Why would you even ask that?" I told her that I knew the answer and I knew the question was ridiculous. But, as I started getting older, I always felt that my cousins connected with my grandparents more than I did. They were all mostly fluent in Spanish like my grandparents and would speak to them in Spanish at times. I wasn't fluent and often would feel left out. They shared all the same customs and rituals with my grandparents because all of my aunts and uncles married people with the same background. With my dad's family, I grew up with additional customs and rituals. I knew my feelings were mostly stemming from internal insecurities but it was a question I had to ask my mom. She replied, "You need to stop thinking of yourself as half this and half that because when you say half, you think incomplete. You are just as much a part of me as you are a part of your father including everything about our backgrounds. You have double of everything—not half of anything. Double the family history, double the rituals, double the heritage. Start thinking about it that way and start thinking about how your background really puts you at an advantage because in you and in your family, you have experiences and insight most people do not have. That will make you a better person!"

> Throughout some of my formative years, I continued to receive these types of messages from my parents and it truly changed the way I felt about who I was and how I responded and internalized any feelings of difference.

As Anissa finished thinking about the influence of her parents' messages, she thought to herself: *I can't forget about Justin!* Justin was one of Anissa's best friends. She met him during the second semester of her freshman year in high school. Again, she began to write:

> I remember that everyone thought Justin and I were into each other when we were really just good friends. We clicked after being paired up as partners in Biology class with another student, Craig. Craig was a nice kid and all of us had a good time in class. After a few weeks, out of nowhere, Craig asked Justin, "Hey Justin. Quick question—what are you?" I knew exactly what Craig was trying to ask. I had similar questions asked to me throughout my life especially when I was in less diverse groups once we moved to our new neighborhood. I knew that Justin also had a mixed-background—his mom was white and his dad was African-American. Craig was trying to get at Justin's racial background. But, that question—"What are you?" sounds so awkward. Justin also knew my background and gave me a wink and shot Craig a very inquisitive look. "What do you mean?" Craig responded, "You know, like, what are you? What are your parents? Just curious." Like me, Justin knew what Craig was trying to get at but kept acting confused. Finally, Justin answered Craig and did so politely even though he could have been offended by how he asked it. In these situations, I was always curious as to why people asked the question in the first place. What motivates people to want to know that and what is it that makes them ask some people but not others. Equally annoying was when people would say, "Oh, you don't look Mexican." How was I supposed to respond to that? Am I supposed to apologize or feel relieved?
>
> Anyway, Justin and I continued to bond over the next few years. Our friendship was based on a lot of things that had nothing to do with our backgrounds. But, we also did share in the experience of having mixed heritages. I also felt that, being African American, Justin had to deal with a bit more disapproval from some circles in society than I did. Although I certainly had experiences with friends, family, and other situations where people didn't take into account my background and how I identified, Justin had to deal with people who actually disapproved of his parents' marriage. Yet, he seemed to handle it in stride. One night, we were having an in-depth conversation about our backgrounds. I asked him one time if he ever felt like he maybe didn't belong to certain groups or felt kinda' on the margins. He replied something like, "My parents told me that I am equally made up of what they are. They were different races and I am both. They told me that society will often categorized me as 'black' but to be proud of all I was and to be proud of being biracial. My father told me that some people from all racial groups will not accept my claiming to be biracial and that I should always have the mindset that biracial does not mean rejecting one identity over the other. But accepting both." So, he said that helped him any time he had issues with feeling like he was being accepted or not accepted in certain social groups. Conversations like that one with Justin were just as important as the conversations with my parents because they showed me that I had shared experiences with others and perhaps there was something to claiming a multiethnic or biracial background.

Annisa put her pen down and took a deep breath. She always loved writing in her journal. The process of writing down her thoughts and thinking about the past was always worthwhile. But, it could be exhausting and she was tired. After reading her entries, she felt much better. Reflecting on these reminded her of some of the experiences that made her the person she was today.

For Further Thought and Reflection

1. Based on Anissa's reflections, describe the process of her ethnic-racial identity development. Focus on critical moments—positive and negative—that you believe shaped her identity. You may want to research models of racial or ethnic identity development to compare how the process you identified differs, if at all, from these models. What role does communication play in the process you identified?
2. Reflect on *your* ethnic-racial identity. Is your ethnicity or race important to you (i.e., is it a salient part of your identity)? What memorable messages can you recall from family or friends that influenced how you perceive yourself in terms of ethnicity or race? In what ways are your experiences similar or different from Anissa's experiences?
3. The number of marriages between people from different ethnic-racial groups and the population of multiethnic-racial individuals both have grown considerably the last few decades. However, our culture and society is still primarily characterized by monoethnic-racial norms in that our assumptions are that families and individuals have one dominant ethnic-racial heritage or identity. How are these norms reflected and manifested in the interactions Anissa has with family members and friends?
4. When our interactions in personal relationships (e.g., friends, family) are influenced by group differences such as ethnicity or race, are the interactions still considered *interpersonal* communication or are they interracial-ethic communication?

References

Hughes, D., Rodriguez, J., Smith, E. P., Johnson, D. J., Stevenson, H. C., & Spicer, P. (2006). Parents' ethnic-racial socialization practices: A review of research and direction for future study. *Developmental Psychology, 42*, 747–770.

Orbe, M. P. (1999). Communication about "race" in interracial families. In T. J. Socha & R. C. Diggs (Eds.), *Communication, race, and family: Exploring communication in black, white, and biracial families* (pp. 167–180). Mahwah. NJ: Lawrence Erlbaum.

Root, M. P. P. (2003). Bill of Rights for racially mixed people. In M. P. P. Root & M. Kelly (Eds.), *The multiracial child resource book: Living complex identities* (p. 32). Seattle, WA: Mavin Foundation.

Shih, M., & Sanchez, D. T. (2005). Perspectives and research on the positive and negative implications of having multiple racial identities. *Psychological Bulletin, 131*, 569–591.

Soliz, J., & Rittenour, C. E. (2012). Family as an intergroup arena. In H. Giles (Ed.), *The Handbook of intergroup communication* (pp. 331–343). New York: Routledge.

Soliz, J., Thorson, A., & Rittenour, C. E. (2009). Communicative correlates of satisfaction, family identity, and group salience in multiracial/ethnic families. *Journal of Marriage and Family, 71*, 819–832.

PART IV

Series Challenges in Interpersonal Communication

20

"It Can't Be Domestic Violence; We're Not Married!" The Many Faces of Intimate Partner Violence

Loreen N. Olson
Emily A. Rauscher

Keywords

dating violence, abuse, aggression, domestic abuse, intimate partner violence, relational violence

Emma and Jason had been moving their stuff into their new apartment all day and were just getting ready for dinner. Their move to Springfield, while a lot of work, was exciting. They both had graduated college in the spring and were looking forward to starting their careers. Since they first met, they spent almost all their free time together and counted down the minutes until they could be together again. It didn't take long for Emma and Jason to know they loved each other and were looking forward to living together for the first time. Emma had gotten a teaching job at the local high school, and Jason was starting work as an IT systems manager at the community college. On that first night, Emma and Jason settled onto the couch with dinner to watch the new episode of *Bones* on Hulu. They were both fans of the show and had been watching it together since they started dating. They could think of no better way to spend the first night in their new apartment.

That night's episode saw the show's main characters, Booth and Brennan, investigating the murder of a young woman. Jason and Emma watched the crime fighting duo unearth a violent relationship the young woman had with her boyfriend that led to her untimely death. Medical records and neighbors' reports noted the young woman had suffered multiple broken bones, bruises, lacerations, and verbal abuse at the hand of her live-in boyfriend. One scene showed a flashback of a fight a neighbor witnessed that involved the boyfriend hitting the young woman so hard she fell down the stairs in their apartment complex and broke her arm. When the show was over Emma said, "Wow, that scene when the neighbor was talking about that couple's fighting was really disturbing. Can you imagine what it would be like to be in that kind of physically violent relationship?"

"No, that would be awful. I can't imagine ever being able to hit a woman the way that man was hitting his girlfriend. But I'm not a violent person and neither are you, so we could clearly never have one of those type of relationships," Jason replied.

Several weeks later, Emma and Jason had started their new jobs and were becoming acclimated to their new city. Emma was making new friends at work and was really enjoying being a teacher. Jason, on the other hand, was more of an introvert and had a more difficult time settling in. Soon Emma's new friends wanted her to start going out with them. While Emma was thrilled about these new relationships, Jason was jealous of Emma's social life, which often did not include him. Since they had spent so much time together alone, it was very difficult for Jason to adjust to this change in their relationship. He was especially jealous of one of

Emma's male colleagues, Eric. Emma swore Eric had a girlfriend and there was no cause for Jason's jealousy, but Jason remained suspicious of Eric. Up to this point in their relationship, Jason and Emma had spent most of their time alone together, which was just the way they had both wanted it to be. However, with their new move, new home, and new jobs, things were changing. Many evenings when Emma was supposed to be meeting with her new friends, Jason would guilt her into staying home with him.

Jason would say different things to convince Emma not go out with her friends: "Please don't go out tonight, Emma. The last few weeks have been so hectic at work for both of us; we've hardly seen each other," "I'd really like to stay in and do something together," or, "Don't tell me you're going out again, Emma? Don't you think two nights in one week is a bit much?" Occasionally he would even insult her upbringing with things like, "Geez, Emma, this place is getting as dirty as your mother's house. You really need to stay home and help me clean this pigpen!"

Most of the time Jason convinced her to stay home. When she thought about what he was saying, Emma realized that he was often right. She probably was spending too much time with her friends and not enough time with Jason. She did love him, and he was only looking after her best interests. She made a promise to Jason and herself that she wouldn't go out with friends as often as she had been.

One evening, however, Emma made a quick decision to go out with her friends immediately after work instead of going home to see Jason first. There was a new "chick flick" she really wanted to see and several of her female work colleagues were going. She texted Jason to let him know of her plans and to tell him she would be home around 9 p.m. Jason was livid when he read Emma's text! He couldn't believe she was breaking the promise she had made. Besides that, he was just sure Emma was out alone with Eric, not out with female co-workers as she claimed. Jason quickly responded to Emma's text saying, "Is Eric there?! I cannot believe you're going out without me! I bet you're cheating on me with him! If you are, we're through!"

Emma was shocked at Jason's text. He had never said anything like this to her before. She didn't want to ruin their relationship over a silly movie with friends, so she made up an excuse and went home to Jason. Upon arriving home, Emma sat down to talk with Jason about the text message he had sent.

"Jason, I just don't understand why you got so angry. I've told you a million times, there's nothing going on between me and Eric," Emma said.

"I may have overreacted, Emma, and I'm really sorry for that. I get worried I'm going to lose you," Jason responded.

"You're not going to lose me, Jason. But please understand that I like to spend time with my friends on occasion. That doesn't mean I love you any less," said Emma. They made up and went to bed happy that night.

Unfortunately, the matter did not remain resolved. Over the next few months Jason and Emma continued fighting the same battle. Emma would mention going out with her work friends and Jason would convince her not to. Slowly Emma's friends started leaving her out of their plans. One day her friend, Stephanie, approached her at school and asked her why she never wanted to spend time together after work anymore. "I know. I hate it. But, I just haven't had the time because of prepping for classes and grading," responded Emma.

"Come on, Emma, I know that's not true. What's the real reason? You can talk to me, I promise I won't tell anyone what we talk about," said Stephanie.

"Okay, to be honest, Jason is really insecure about me hanging out with you all, especially Eric. I really love him and don't want to upset him, so when he asks me not to go out I don't. I just don't feel like it's worth the fight," said Emma.

"Emma, I'm not a relationship expert, but spending all your time together and never doing things with other people just doesn't sound like a healthy relationship. In fact, it sounds like he's a bit too possessive. People in relationships need their own space. For whatever it's worth, just know that I'm always here for you if you need anything," Stephanie responded.

After that conversation, Stephanie and Emma became closer. They talked at school, became Facebook friends, followed one another on Twitter, and texted frequently. One night while Emma was watching television with Jason, she and Stephanie were texting back and forth. At one point Stephanie said something funny and Emma giggled out loud. "Who are you talking to on that thing all the time? What's so funny that you're interrupting the show?" Jason asked.

"Oh, I'm just talking to my friend Stephanie from school. She's really funny" responded Emma.

"Yeah, right, Emma. Who are you really talking to? It's Eric isn't it? The way you're attached to that phone all the time and grinning right now just tells me it's a guy. Just admit it!" demanded Jason.

Finally feeling like she had been pushed too far, Emma shouted, "I'M NOT TALKING TO ERIC, YOU IDIOT! I'M TALKING TO STEPHANIE! Now leave me the f_ _ _ alone."

"THEN WHY DON'T YOU SHOW ME THE TEXTS?" Jason yelled back, throwing a pillow at the couch close to where Emma was sitting.

Picking the pillow up, she exclaimed, "Because I shouldn't have to; you should trust me. I'm not going to show you my private text messages with my friend," as she threw the pillow back at Jason.

With that, Jason stormed off to bed. Emma stayed up for another hour watching TV and texting Stephanie about the fight she'd just had with Jason. She just didn't understand why Jason was so jealous and suspicious of her texting. Stephanie suggested that maybe Jason was just a really controlling person and cautioned Emma about remaining in the relationship.

Emma and Jason went to work the following day without talking about their fight. Emma thought about it all day at school and decided that when she got home, she would initiate another conversation about their relationship. However, when she arrived home she found Jason sitting at the kitchen table waiting for her; he was clearly upset. "What's up, Jason?" Emma asked.

"What's up? I'll tell you what's going on. You're a liar and a blabbermouth!" Jason accused.

"What are you talking about, Jason?"

"I'm talking about the fact that you were telling 'Stephanie,' who I really think is Eric by the way; you just put his name in your phone as Stephanie to keep me from knowing. Anyway, you were telling 'Stephanie' about our fight last night! That's OUR private information; you shouldn't be telling other people about it!" at this point Jason was yelling. "Also I saw on your Facebook, Twitter, and Instagram accounts that you ARE friends with Eric. Why are you even friends with him? I just knew something was up between you two!"

Emma slowly asked, gritting her teeth, "First of all, how do you know I was talking to Stephanie about our fight last night? Second of all, how do you know I'm friends with Eric on all those accounts? You're not on Twitter or Instagram." Then a light bulb went off for Emma. She had accidentally left her phone home today. Jason had clearly been snooping through it. "You went through my phone didn't you?! How dare you! You trust me so little that you felt the need to snoop through my texts, Facebook, Twitter, and Instagram accounts?!"

"Yeah. So what? I did go through your phone, and I'm not sorry about it. I knew you were fooling around with him and what I found confirms it! One thing's for sure—if there is any hope of us staying together, you'll have to delete him from all of those accounts," demanded Jason.

Emma didn't know what to do; she was in complete shock that he had invaded her privacy like this. "Jason, I think I need some time to think. I'm going to go to the gym." She left the apartment, slamming the door as she left.

It took Emma quite a while to regain her composure. Finally, her head cleared enough to process what had just happened. Emma thought about how much she loved Jason and what a good match they were *most* of the time. But, on the other hand, she also thought about how violated she felt by his snooping through her phone. She also thought about how much meaner their fights had become. They didn't seem bothered by the fact that they were yelling at each other more and more, throwing pillows, and slamming doors. They didn't physically hurt, but they were doing things in anger that neither of them had ever done before.

By the time she was done with her workout, she decided that, while she was still very angry with Jason, they needed to discuss privacy boundaries and the way they were fighting. She would do what Jason asked and delete Eric from her social networking sites. She couldn't risk her relationship with Jason just to keep Eric as a Facebook friend. She walked out the front door of the gym with renewed faith in her relationship with Jason. However, just as she was getting into her car, she caught a glimpse of Jason's car leaving the parking lot. She quickly came to the conclusion that he had followed her to make sure she had really gone to the gym. She got into her car and started to cry. Not only was he keeping tabs on her online, he was now following her to the gym? She just didn't know what to do anymore.

That night Emma slept in the spare bedroom. She didn't feel like she could be in the same room with Jason right now. By the time she left for work in the morning Jason was already gone. He had left her a note on the kitchen table, "We need to talk tonight." Indeed, they did need to talk. But what was she going to say to him? How were they going to get through this? How could she make him understand that she loved him and wanted to be with him, but also wanted to have a life outside of their relationship?

When Emma got to school, her day started like any other day. Yet, she couldn't stop thinking about her relationship problems. After her students got back from lunch, she began to lecture to her junior students. About halfway through the lecture, one of her female students stood up, slammed her fist into her desk, and started yelling at the male student next to her. It was widely known at Emma's school that these two students were a couple. "Jackie just texted me to tell me Sarah told her you were out with another girl this weekend!" yelled the female student.

"Well Jackie and Sarah are both liars! Baby, you know I would never cheat on you," responded the male student.

"Screw you, Kris! Don't lie to me. All you are is a big, worthless, cheating, ugly, stupid liar! I'm done with you. I hate you! I hope you die!" yelled the girl.

"Screw you right back, Lucy! You are the ugliest girl I've ever dated, which makes it surprising that you're such a slut at this school. I only went out with you because I knew you would be an easy lay," Kris fired back. At this point, Lucy picked up her textbooks and started throwing them at Kris. Luckily he blocked or dodged them all.

Initially, Emma stood at the front of the room in shock, unable to move. However, after the throwing of the textbooks started, she snapped out of it. "Kris! Lucy! STOP! This is NOT a way to behave in a classroom!" she exclaimed. At that moment the bell ending class rang. Emma's next class period was free, so she escorted Kris and Lucy to the principal's office. The four of them sat through Emma's retelling of events to the principal. When the tale was complete, the principal required Kris and Lucy to schedule a one hour session with the guidance counselor for later that afternoon. The principal also asked Emma if she would attend the meeting to explain to the counselor what happened.

After Kris, Lucy, and Emma all told their side of the story, the counselor, Ms. Norstrom, asserted, "Thank you, Emma, for coming with the students. It's helpful to have a third person describe what happened. As for you, Kris and Lucy, you have a very serious situation here. Your relationship has become very unhealthy. You don't seem to be able to handle your anger with each other and you both respond aggressively when you get into fights. Your name-calling and put downs are also very mean. These types of actions hurt the other partner, and they certainly aren't a way to show someone you love them. Domestic violence is never to be tolerated. Never! If you do not work on improving your treatment of each other, things will probably get worse rather than better."

Lucy jumped in, "wait a minute! What do you mean domestic violence? We're not married. Only married people have that crap in their relationships. Besides, Kris and I don't hit each other. We just get mad and yell at each other. Yeah, sure we call each other bad names and say really mean things to each other, but we don't hit each other. How is that domestic violence? That's just crazy!"

Emma was thinking the same thing and was beginning to question this counselor's professional skills when Ms. Norstrom responded, "Actually, Lucy, domestic violence doesn't happen just in married relationships. It can happen in any romantic relationship. Dating violence, intimate partner violence, and relational violence are all terms people use to describe what you two are experiencing. There are many names for the same behavior—acts of aggression that harm (intentionally or not) the other partner. Relational violence doesn't just involve only physical acts either. Verbal aggression, emotional abuse, and attempts to control the other partner are also all considered part of it. Both males and females can be aggressive as well. Too often people think that the only real domestic violence is when a woman frequently and severely gets beaten by her male partner. Don't get me wrong—this happens, and it's very serious when it does. But, other less severe, yet also unhealthy, kinds of aggression exist in some relationships—similar to what you two are experiencing. There is just a big variety of violent couples—even ones that include no physical violence but a lot of verbal, psychological, and emotional abuse."

Lucy and Kris glanced at each other and then looked at Ms. Norstrom, not saying anything. Ms. Norstrom continued, "Given what happened today, you two are going to have to be suspended for a couple of days. The school just cannot tolerate such behavior. Neither of you should tolerate such behavior in your relationship either. While you're away, I want you to really think about what I've said. I'll see you back here on Monday. We'll get to work on seeing how we can help you relate to each other in a healthier way." With that, Emma, Kris, and Lucy all got up, thanked Ms. Norstrom, and walked back to their classrooms.

When Emma got home, she found Jason sitting on the couch, waiting for her. Jason said, "Emma, I think we need to talk about what happened between us last night. I think we crossed a line."

"Yeah, Jason, I think you're right. I'm not proud of anything I did or said last night. And after seeing a young couple at school get in a fight today and talking with the counselor about it, I've come to realize what we're doing is not healthy. We're not handling our anger well or communicating in productive ways. In fact, given what the school guidance counselor, Ms. Norstrom said today, I think our relationship would be considered an example of dating violence. She told the students that relational aggression can look different in different types of couples. Domestic violence, for example, isn't just something that married couples experience nor does violence involve only physical behaviors. Words can be a way of hurting a partner too. Even controlling a partner's every move and being overly jealous about what they're doing, can be an unhealthy pattern in a relationship. I think we know a bit about that, huh, Jason?"

"Yeah, you're right, Emma. I need to work on being a better partner. I don't like the idea of dating violence being a part of our relationship. I definitely lost my temper, and I think you did too. We need to promise each other that when things go a little wrong, we won't resort to violence ever again," Jason said.

"I really do regret what happened. I'm very sorry. I won't ever do anything like that again. I don't want to be that kind of couple," said Emma.

For Further Thought and Reflection

1. What forms of unhealthy communication patterns between partners do you see in this case?
2. Do you think Emma and Jason's conflicts are aggressive? Why or why not? Do you think they are violent? What do you think is the difference between aggressiveness and violence? How do you think their conflicts compare and contrast to the young couple in the school or the relationship portrayed in *Bones*?
3. Many times, people think that domestic violence happens in marital relationships and often involves physical abuse. Aggression in dating relationships can be overlooked or ignored since the partners are "only dating." However, researchers have identified a variety of violent couples. Terms such as domestic violence, intimate partner violence, and dating violence have been used to describe relationships characterized by aggression. With this in mind, do you think that Emma and Jason have a violent relationship? Why or why not? What term, if any, do you think best applies to Emma and Jason's relationship? What term would you use to describe Kris and Lucy's? The couple on *Bones*?
4. It can be difficult to change patterns of behavior in relationships. Can we be sure that Jason and Emma won't become "this type of couple"? If you could make a prediction about the teenagers' relationship, what would it be? Do you think either couple will be able to change their behavior and start treating each other well? If not, why not? If so, how would change occur and what would it look like?
5. If you or someone you know were involved in a violent relationship, what would you do? What advice would you seek/give? To whom would you turn for advice or help? Would change be possible?

References

Cahn, D. D. (Ed.). (2009). *Family violence: Communication processes.* Albany, New York: SUNY Press.

Johnson, M. P. (2008). *A typology of domestic violence: Intimate terrorism, violent resistance, and situational couple violence.* Boston, MA: Northeastern University Press.

Levy, B. (2006). *In love and in danger: A teen's guide to breaking free of abusive relationships* (3rd ed.). Seattle, WA: Seal Press.

Olson, L. N. (2004). Relational control-motivated aggression: A theoretically-based typology of intimate violence. *Journal of Family Communication, 4,* 209–233.

Olson, L. N. (in press). Violence, aggression, and abuse. In C. Berger & M. Roloff (Eds.), *International encyclopedia of interpersonal communication*. Hoboken, NJ: WileyBlackwell.

Spitzberg, B. H., & Cupach, W. R. (Eds.). (2011). *The dark side of close relationships II.* New York: Routledge.

Waldal, E. S. (2011). *Tornado warning: A memoir of teen dating violence and its effect on a woman's life.* Encinitas, CA: Sound Beach Publishing.

21

Unilateral Union: Obsessive Relational Intrusion and Stalking in a Romantic Context

William R. Cupach
Brian H. Spitzberg

Keywords

stalking, obsessive relational intrusion, privacy invasion, unrequited love, jealousy

Alex and Anna, now 27 and 26 years old, respectively, worked together in the information systems division of a large insurance company. After knowing each other at a distance for about a year, they were both assigned to work on a large development project. Alex and Anna enjoyed working together, and, about six months into the development project they started dating. That was almost two years ago. Now, they don't speak to one another and each is extremely uncomfortable if they run into the other. In their own words, Alex and Anna each provide a perspective on what happened between them, and why.

Alex's Story

From a distance, I always thought that Anna was cute. She seemed bright and friendly, precisely the type of woman I would want to spend time with; in fact, I saw her as the type of woman I might eventually want to marry. I wanted to ask her on a date, but it never seemed to work out. Our encounters at work were cordial, but infrequent and brief. I was dating other women off and on, and I figured someone as attractive as Anna must have lots of boyfriends. I almost got up the nerve to ask her out when I struck up a conversation with her at a division picnic, but suddenly other people were part of the conversation and the opportunity slipped away. Then, one day I suddenly found myself assigned to work on the same project as Anna. I secretly felt really excited, figuring I would now be able to get to know her better and lay the groundwork for dating her.

As soon as we began working together, things really seemed to click between us, both professionally and personally. We made great strides on the project and our skills seemed complementary. We often had to work late together, but neither of us seemed to mind. In our conversations, I tried to find out as much as I could about her, though I was never satisfied that I knew enough. I Googled her, checked her Facebook page, and asked some colleagues at work about Anna's social life, trying to figure out if she was "available" for more than just a working relationship.

Anna was very friendly toward me. She always smiled at me, listened to me intently when I talked, and offered sincere words of encouragement and support whenever I talked about personal problems. We teased and joked quite a bit, and I could tell that she really liked me. I started to feel like we were destined to be together, so I felt I had to make my move. Confident that she found me attractive (she had given me numerous compliments), I decided to ask her out on a "real" date. We started seeing each other every weekend, and, within a month, we got together a couple of times during the week as well.

For the most part, I enjoyed our times together. We laughed, talked, and enjoyed each other's company. Sex was great! When we were not together, I thought about Anna constantly. The first few months were the best of my life. But I started getting suspicious that Anna didn't feel the same way about me as I did about her. She wanted to cut back a bit, saying she needed time for other things in her life. Whatever those other things were, I couldn't understand why I couldn't be a part of them—unless of course she was seeing someone else. I did what I could to confirm my suspicions on my own, but ultimately I simply raised the issue with her. This led to our first big fight, where I accused her of dating other men and hiding the fact from me. She denied it, but her anger made me wonder why she was being so defensive if there really was nothing to hide.

Although I was upset that Anna might be seeing other guys, I wanted to smooth things over with her. I apologized to her for not trusting her (though I had lingering suspicions). If anything, I felt I had to work even harder to win her loyalty and affection. I redoubled my efforts to show her how much I cared for her. I frequently would leave messages on her desk and bought her flowers and greeting cards. I called her or texted her almost every night, but about half of the time she wasn't available or wasn't answering. When I would ask her later what she had been doing, she sometimes told me, but often seemed evasive. If I couldn't get a hold of her until late at night, she seemed annoyed that I called.

The more I pursued Anna, the more she seemed to play hard to get. This simply fueled my desire for her. I told her I loved her on several occasions, but she never said it back to me. When I asked her whether or not she loved me too, she said she wasn't sure. I was convinced that, even if she had been seeing other guys, she loved me and was simply afraid to face such a deep commitment and admit it.

Anna seemed to be less and less available by phone. The gaps in time before she responded to my text messages grew longer. She starting making excuses for not being able to go out on nights we normally would see each other. I became very frustrated as we were now seeing each other maybe once every week or two outside of work. After awhile I figured out that Anna had unfriended me on Facebook, which led to a big fight between us. The strain in our personal relationship began to take its toll at work.

Then one Friday afternoon, without warning, Anna broke up with me. We met for a drink at one of our favorite places, and she calmly told me that she thought our relationship had "run its course." She said she thought I was a "nice" person, but that we were incompatible. She claimed we were both unhappy and that it was adversely affecting work. She said something vaguely about remaining friends.

I was devastated. I begged her for another try, but she was steadfast. I went home that night, feeling numb and humiliated. What would everyone at work think? What would my family think? What would Anna tell people behind my back? How could she do this to me! I got drunk that night and called Anna, hoping to reconcile. She was pleasant as always, and I got a glimmer of hope when she said we should at least put things on hold.

I knew Anna just needed some time. But I also knew that persistence was the key. You don't obtain valuable things in life without effort; sometimes you have to struggle and push to get what you want. If I did nothing, Anna and I would never be together. If I pursued her vigorously, I had a good chance of winning her over. After all, Anna left the door open for a relationship between us, and I've seen persistence pay off so many times before in life.

All I could think about was getting back with Anna. I felt I couldn't be happy unless I restored our relationship, so I spent lots of time plotting my strategy to win her over. I sent her cards, poems, flowers, and little gifts just to let her know I was thinking about her. I continued to call and text Anna several times a week. When she didn't (or wouldn't) answer the phone, I left her voice mail messages. When she did answer, our conversation was cordial. I felt like she was trying to be "nice" to me—but nice is not what I wanted. I was happy to talk to her, but I missed the intimacy and closeness in our talk, the physical contact, and hanging out together.

Anna posted for and got a job in a different division and she seemed pleased to be transferring to a different building. I couldn't understand why she would want to change jobs when she was so good at the one she already had. Since she still wouldn't go out with me, and since we no longer saw each other at work, I devised what I considered to be safe ways to see or communicate with her. I sent her humorous e-mail messages and interoffice notes and cartoons that I thought she would enjoy. I knew some of the bars and restaurants Anna and her friends liked to visit. I would sometimes casually show up, hoping to make brief contact with her. Sometimes I went alone, sometimes with my friend, Randy. I increasingly wondered what she was doing and where she was going. Once or twice at the end of a work day, I even waited in my car and followed her when she drove away to see where she was going.

I also would occasionally drive by Anna's house—thinking I might see her coming or going. Finally, I noticed a car parked in front of her place I hadn't seen before. *My God!* She *was* seeing someone else and she hid the fact from me. When I called to confront her, she first said it was none of my business. Then she admitted she was dating someone else, and told me that I needed to get on with my life. She said not to call her anymore. I was outraged. How could she betray me like that?!? I felt angry and hurt. Apparently I wasn't good enough for her.

Anna was now screening all of her calls and ignoring my text messages, so I had to settle for leaving messages on her voice mail. Once a man answered her phone—presumably her new boyfriend—and I just hung up. I no longer wanted to get back with Anna. I wanted to get back *at* her. I wanted her to know the grief she had caused me, and I wanted to punish her for hurting me. I wanted to scare her a little, so I made some empty threats, such as "You'll be sorry if you don't come back to me—I'll make sure you regret it." Because she never responded to my notes I left her, one day I left a letter opener in her mailbox to let her know I wanted her to respond to my messages. The next thing I knew, the police visited me and served me with a Temporary Restraining Order. I was told that they could send me to jail if I tried to contact Anna in any way.

Now, Anna and I are bitter enemies. I feel ashamed and embarrassed for behaving foolishly, but I am still deeply resentful toward Anna because I feel she led me on, humiliated and betrayed me. I would like to see her suffer in some way for how she hurt me.

Anna's Story

Alex seemed like a good guy—until I got to know him. Although I apparently met him a few times before, I never really noticed him until we were assigned to work together on the development project. At first I found him to be charming and attractive. I could tell he was infatuated with me, and I enjoyed the attention he showered on me. Our personalities seemed to mesh and this fostered a good working relationship between us. I respected his contributions to the project, and I felt that he admired what I had to offer as well. When Alex asked me out on a date, I wasn't surprised. In fact, some of my friends told me he had been asking all kinds of questions about me for several weeks. I was concerned that dating someone at work could pose problems if it didn't work out, but I decided to take the risk.

The first few weeks were a whirlwind. We both got caught up in the excitement of a new relationship. But it didn't take long for me to realize that Alex was not the sort of guy I wanted to spend my life with. Early on, it was apparent that Alex was very controlling. He insisted on making decisions about where we went, when, and with whom. He seemed constantly to test my loyalty to him. The attention he paid to me quickly became smothering and needy. I liked Alex as a person, and I enjoyed our dates, but I didn't like the fact that he was so jealous and suspicious of my private life. I thought to myself, *how can he be so possessive when we've only been dating six weeks?!* One time when I returned from the bathroom, I found him looking through my mail lying on the kitchen counter. This angered me and sent up a red flag that I would have a difficult time trusting him.

I thought of breaking it off with Alex after a few months, but I kept putting it off. I didn't want to hurt him, and I didn't want the ordeal of defending my desire to break up. I also knew it could become complicated dealing with him at work. So I decided to simply scale back the relationship. I made excuses so that our dates were less frequent. He compensated by calling and texting me more and more frequently, despite the fact that I would see him every day at work. If I was unavailable or didn't answer the phone, he apparently kept calling until he could reach me. One night I just refused to answer the phone and it rang every 15 minutes. I finally couldn't stand it anymore and around 1:00 in the morning I answered the phone. I asked him to please not call me so late, but he continued to do so. I finally started turning off my phone at night so I could get some sleep. Whenever I did this, it angered him and he would make sarcastic and snide remarks to me at work the next day. His frequent posts on my Facebook page became so awkward and embarrassing that I unfriended him. When he discovered this he was furious.

Alex began to be more of a pest than a dating partner. The more I got to know him, the more apparent it became that he had a very fragile ego. I wanted out of the relationship completely, but I feared he would go into a rage, or sabotage me at work, or worse. The more I withdrew from him, the harder he pressed. It became increasingly difficult to work with him, but it was essential to the project that we collaborate. The relationship was costing me time, sleep, productivity at work, and more, and I was getting nothing but aggravation out of it.

Because I had cooled off the relationship, Alex assumed that I was dating someone else behind his back. I wasn't, and I told him so. Nevertheless, Alex undertook a campaign of spying on me to find out for himself. He would drive by my house frequently, and sometimes come to the door, especially if I had told him earlier over the phone that I was busy. He really just wanted to see if I was with another man. He also annoyed my friends by asking them my whereabouts all the time. He seemed to follow me everywhere. He started showing up at social gatherings and public places he normally wouldn't have gone to, just to "run into" me. I had this creepy feeling he might be following me or waiting for me around the next corner. He made some comments that led me to believe he was monitoring the Facebook pages of some of my friends in order to keep track of me.

I jokingly mentioned to my friend Karla that I sometimes felt as if Alex were stalking me and that I must be paranoid. But Karla wasn't so sure I was paranoid. She told me about a recent article she read on the Internet about stalking and obsession with relationships. The researchers cited in the article reported that stalking is not all that uncommon, and that it can be dangerous. I was surprised to learn that nearly two million people in the U.S. are the victims of stalking each year. I always thought that stalkers were "sociopaths" harassing celebrities. But Karla told me that the most common type of stalker is a former intimate partner, and that the vast majority of victims are female. My annoyance regarding Alex was turning into serious concern.

I finally decided enough was enough. I tried to break it to Alex gently because I knew he would be hurt. I wished him no ill will—I just wanted my life, my privacy, and my freedom back. I told him that we could still be friends, but that I didn't want to date him anymore.

After I broke up with Alex, he seemed to push even harder than before. He called me constantly—sometimes six or eight times in an evening. I avoided him as much as I could. Work became intolerable so I explained the circumstances to my manager and asked for a transfer, which I got, even though I hated to leave the work I was doing. Moving to another building made it difficult for Alex to badger me at work—although he managed to clog my computer in-box with unwanted e-mail even after I set-up filters for his e-mail address, and he incessantly pestered me with unwanted text messages.

One day I answered the phone when Alex called, and I firmly told him never to call me again. After that I would not answer the phone when he called or respond to his texts. He eventually figured out I was screening his calls and started using his friends' phones to call me. So I just stopped answering any calls that I didn't recognize and told my friends to leave a message when they called because I was screening.

I started dating another man that I met through my cousin. About this time, Alex was driving by my house frequently and he started leaving threatening messages on my answering machine. He would call me nasty names, like "frigid bitch," and tell me that I would pay for making him miserable. He also made derogatory remarks about my new boyfriend, though Alex really knew nothing about him. One of the things that angered me the most was that Alex tried to spread rumors about me to co-workers and friends. He told people that I was a slut and that I gave him a sexually transmitted disease—an embarrassing outright lie! I couldn't believe I ever saw anything attractive about this guy. How could I have been so wrong?

One day I came home to find a dagger in my mailbox. It really scared me. Alex's messages had become increasingly threatening, and I always had the feeling I was being watched. He would show up unexpectedly almost anywhere I went—including dates with my new boyfriend. So I finally called the police. Because I kept track of Alex's recent threatening behaviors, and because I had some of his threats recorded on my cell phone, I went to the police and was able to get a restraining order against him. But it didn't keep me from being afraid.

I've read too many stories where a restraining order can send the restrained person "over the edge" with anger. I really feared Alex would do harm to me. I changed my phone number and my locks. I don't walk my dog alone at night anymore. I frequently change my routine so that my schedule is not predictable.

Alex said he'll "get" me. But I haven't seen him since I took out the restraining order, except once at work, where he flashed me a sick smile and glared at me. I am anxious. I am resentful. I am angry. My life has been completely disrupted. I am less trusting of people, and men in particular. I wonder why I waited as long as I did to break up with Alex. I wonder why I couldn't see sooner that he had an obsessive personality. I wonder what I could have done differently before and after the break up to prevent his anger from escalating. Now I wonder, how can I protect myself? How can I get back to leading a normal life? Will he pop up again unexpectedly and do harm to me?

For Further Thought and Reflection

1. In what ways does Alex's communication with Anna reveal that his interest in her is obsessive and his pursuits are excessive? Are there early warning signs in Alex's behavior that, in retrospect, Anna might have relied on to alter how she communicated with Alex? In what ways does Anna's communication foster Alex's persistence in pursuing a relationship with her?
2. Our culture seems to promote a script that says persistence in pursuing relationships and potential partners pays off. Where does this "script" or societal message come from? What factors perpetuate and reinforce the belief that persistence ultimately leads to success, particularly where relationships are concerned?
3. At what point does pursuit of a relationship become obsessive? How do you know when you should abandon the goal to have a relationship with someone? Where is the line that divides normal persistence in a relationship pursuit versus obsessive and inappropriate pursuit?
4. Many people enjoy seeing their partner be a little jealous. When is jealousy productive and when is it unproductive in relationships? How can you manage your own jealousy so that it doesn't become destructive?
5. Anna struggled with deciding when "enough was enough," and when Alex's behavior had become excessive. At that time, she broke it off, avoided contact, and eventually called the police and took out a restraining order. What, if anything, would you have done differently in her place? Why? What advice would you have given Anna at various points of her relationship with Alex? Why is hindsight, or the view of a friend, so much clearer than when we are directly involved in the relationship?
6. How do new and evolving communication technologies increase the risk of unwanted contact? How might they improve our ability to manage or cope with unwanted contact? Is our fascination with social networking sites making unwanted relationship pursuit more or less likely to be a problem?

References

Cupach, W. R., Spitzberg, B. H., Bolingbroke, C. M., & Tellitocci, B. S. (2011). Persistence of attempts to reconcile a terminated romantic relationship: A partial test of relational goal pursuit theory. *Communication Reports, 24*, 99–115.

Davis, K. E., Swan, S. C., & Gambone, L. J. (2012). Why doesn't he just leave me alone? Persistent pursuit: A critical review of theories and evidence. *Sex Roles, 66*, 328–339.

Dutton, L. B., & Winstead, B. A. (2011). Types, frequency, and effectiveness of responses to unwanted pursuit and stalking. *Journal of Interpersonal Violence, 26,* 1129–1156.

Ménard, K. S., & Pincus, A. L. (2012). Predicting overt and cyber stalking perpetration by male and female college students. *Journal of Interpersonal Violence, 27*, 2183–2207.

Nguyen, L. K., Spitzberg, B. H., & Lee, C. M. (2012). Coping with obsessive relational intrusion and stalking: The role of social support and coping strategies. *Violence and Victims, 27*, 414–433.

Schultz, A. S., Moore, J. & Spitzberg, B. H. (2013). Once upon a midnight stalker: A content analysis of stalking in films. *Western Journal of Communication* [online first].

Spitzberg, B. H., & Cupach, W. R. (2014). *The dark side of relationship pursuit: From attraction to obsession and stalking* (2nd ed.). New York, NY: Routledge.

22

Muslims, Head Coverings and Fantasy Football: Moving Beyond the Stereotype

Timothy M. Muehlhoff

Keywords

stereotype; Jihad; language as reflection, selection, and deflection; hijab; reducing uncertainty; labels; categorization, characterization, and correction

In an introduction to interpersonal communication course at a Midwestern university students are assigned a listening project that requires them to learn about themselves and others by selecting a representative of a group whose perspective they would not ordinarily listen to.[1] *Two days after the project is assigned the news is dominated by the Boston Marathon bombing where one bomber, Dzhokhar Tsarnaev, before his capture leaves a hastily scribbled note stating that an attack against one Muslim is an attack on all. Reports link Tsarnaev to a mosque with ties to the Muslim Brotherhood and suggest the attack was payback for American military action in Muslim countries. Deeply disturbed by this incident, Michael, a Christian student in the class, decides to visit the Muslim Student Center on campus and listen to the perspectives of a Muslim student.*

Before visiting the Muslim Center, Michael stumbled across an online study discussing current views of American Muslims. The report stated that ten years after 9/11 American Muslims overwhelmingly reject any form of Muslim extremism. However, more than 40% of the general public believes there is a great deal of support for extremism within the Muslim American community. When asked, 56% of American Muslims reply that they desire to embrace American values and participate in American customs, while only 33% of the general public agree that Muslims entering our country want to adopt American values and lifestyle.[2]

Walking to the Muslim Center Michael decided spontaneously to ask students he passed what they thought of when they heard the word, *Muslim*. He was shocked at the responses. Some of the words people said: *angry*, *war*, *hatred*, *upset*, *terrorists*, *Allah*, *religious*, *head covering*, *devout*, and *9/11*. While his impromptu survey was hardly scientific, it confirmed key parts of the study he'd read before coming to the center. Michael wonders what words the guy he's going to interview would use to describe Christians?

Michael walks into the Muslim Student Center and is introduced to Amon, an American-born Arab who is a devout Muslim majoring in religious studies and psychology. They grab coffee and settle into two large leather chairs in the lounge. Amon notices Michael's Detroit Lions football cap and congratulates him on his team winning two games this season. Michael laughs and responds that after going winless the previous year two victories is a huge success! Michael asks if Amon likes football, and Amon explains that while his dad grew up playing soccer in Saudi Arabia, he's a huge football fan and is a fantasy football junkie. Michael says he is too, and soon they are comparing how their fantasy teams and players fared the previous Sunday. After a complete rundown of stats, the interview begins with Michael pulling out a tape recorder and asking the first question.

Michael: On my way over, I asked students to tell me the first word they thought of when they heard the word, *Muslim*. They used words like, *angry*, *war*, *hatred*, *Allah*, *religious*, *terrorist*, *head covering*, *devout*, and *9/11*. As a Muslim, how does that make you feel?

Amon: Well, it saddens me, but I'm not surprised. While not all Arabs are Muslim, many of the same stereotypes would apply to both. At the very least, Arabs and Muslims are seen as angry or unstable people.

Michael: (attempting to make a joke) You did get angry when I said my fantasy team would *crush* yours if we went head-to-head.

Amon: (in a deadpan tone) Hey, don't *ever* mess with my team. My religion, yes, my fantasy team, never.

Michael: Go back to something you just said, that all Arabs are not Muslim. To be honest, I make that assumption all the time.

Amon: That would be like saying all Americans are Christian.

Michael: Seriously, where do you think that impression of Arabs or Muslims comes from?

Amon: It might be helpful to separate the two. Arabs often take a beating in how they are portrayed in films and TV shows. It comes from a million different voices. Movies like *True Lies*, *Raiders of the Lost Ark*, *The Mummy*, *Father of the Bride 2*, and TV shows like *JAG*, *The West Wing*, and *The Agency*, all present Arabs and Muslims in a negative light. In fact, a media scholar named Jack Shaheen—I think that's his name—documented over 900 Hollywood films that portrayed Arabs in an offensive manner. When you see a negative or menacing image of something or someone over and over you can't help but form an impression of it and even grow fearful of it.

Michael: But don't you think we watch those shows, we know they're fiction?

Amon: I hope so. But what about kids who are perhaps less discerning? What happens when an image is placed before them at a young age? Did you ever see Disney's movie, *Aladdin*?

Michael: Of course. I remember my teacher showing it in school.

Amon: Remember the opening song? Don't worry, I won't sing it. It's something about a barbaric place where people cut off parts of your face if they don't like you! People sing it and don't even consider the racist lyrics! They get caught up in the catchy tune and watch Aladdin and Jasmine, two light-skinned heroes, fight off sinister Arabs. When they hear this song and watch the movie it perpetuates an offensive stereotype of Arabs being barbaric and angry. *Look at me in the wrong way and I'll cut off your ear*. So, no, it doesn't surprise me that students responded that Muslims are upset or angry. However, the other words the students used—*war, terrorists, 9/11*—really is scary and deeply discouraging. This view of Arabs as terrorists has even found its way into my favorite comedy, *The Office*.

Michael: (laughing) *The Office* is a riot. I love it. Remember the episode where Dwight unexpectedly punched Michael Scott in the gut and then they fought during their lunch break at Dwight's karate school?

Amon: (laughing with him) Yes, absolutely hilarious. Do you remember the show in which Michael as the boss decides to do diversity training? He has everybody in the office put Post-it notes on their foreheads that have different ethnicities written on them such as Black, Asian, Mexican, Jewish, and so on. They then are to treat each other according to the stereotype; Asians don't care about food and Jews only care about money. At the end of the exercise, Michael says into the camera: "Nobody was an Arab—that would be too explosive. No pun intended." It's said for laughs, but we all know what he means.

Michael: Look at an Arab in the wrong way, and he'll cut off your ear.

Amon: (pointing to himself) Or, look at *me* in the wrong way and I'll put a bomb in your office.

Michael: You mentioned that having fellow students use words like, *hatred*, *terrorists*, and *9/11* to describe Muslims is scary. Could you elaborate?

Amon: Sure. Every time there is an incident involving a person of Arab ethnicity the entire Arab community holds its collective breath and fears an anti-Islamic backlash. For example, I remember reading somewhere that after the Fort Hood massacre in Texas, a mosque in Dearborn, Michigan, found a disturbing package left on its doorstep. It was a hardbound copy of the Quran which had been defaced with spray paint. Inside was a note that read something like: "Islam is a disease. Muslim immigrants are the virus. Every Muslim should be kicked out of the USA."[3] I know that such talk is crazy and should be ignored. When events like Fort Hood or 9/11 happen my community feels a type of double shock—shock at the tragedy itself and shock at the possible retaliation against us by people who view us negatively. Knowing that people have such twisted views of us can also make listening to the news a nerve-racking experience.

Michael: How, so?

Amon: As an Arab living in the States, when you are listening to the news and hear of a shooting or bombing your first thought can be: God, don't let the shooter be a Muslim. Did you know that right after the bombing of the federal building in Oklahoma City news outlets quickly reported suspicious Middle Eastern individuals had been seen in the area before the bombing? Of course, later we learned that it was Midwestern Caucasians that were responsible.

Michael: I don't mean to offend you, but let me ask you a delicate question.

Amon: Fire away.

Michael: Hasn't Islam kind of earned its reputation of being violent? Doesn't Islam in fact believe in something called a holy war?

Amon: Yes, we do. However, let me say two things about holy war, or as we call it, Jihad. First, not all Muslim theologians agree on what the Quran—our holy book—teaches about this topic. You are a Christian. Not all Christian scholars or pastors agree on every doctrine or passage of the Bible?

Michael: Uh, no. We have plenty of lively and heated disagreements.

Amon: Well, we do, too. It's impossible to boil all of the richness and diversity of Muslim perspectives into one monolithic voice. When it comes to a controversial idea like holy war, you are going to get very different ideas coming from the Muslim community. Second, most Muslims I know believe that when Jihad was started by Muhammad—the leading prophet of Islam—it was done only as a form of self-defense. As I and most of my friends understand the Quran, it teaches that holy war should only be waged in defense of life and property and never to oppress or dominate another. So, six days after the terrorist attacks of 9/11 dozens of leading Islamic scholars issued a statement that said they were grief-stricken at such horrifying events and the murder of innocents could never be justified nor tolerated by true followers of Islam. However, because the idea of Jihad is so controversial, it's all people think of when it comes to Islam.

Michael: My communication professor said that all language simultaneously *reflects*, *selects*, and *deflects*.[4] If I hear what you are saying, when people talk about Muslims and Islam, all they select is the most violent view of the holy war aspect.

Amon: That's right. In talking about Muslims people reflect the media's representation of us as violent people and then selectively only focus on the so-called violent aspects of Islam such as Jihad.

Michael: What do you think is deflected or neglected by this pervading stereotype of Muslims as being violent or terrorists?

Amon: Wow, a lot. First, to me, Islam is a religion of peace, not war. The Quran teaches that peace is one of the names of Allah and many Muslims end their daily worship with the simple prayer: "O God, you are Peace." Also, when Arabs or Muslims are seen through the limiting lens of oil barons or nomads herding camels, then all the great accomplishments of Arab culture are deflected and glossed over. Few people realize that geometry, algebra, and Arabic numerals are all linked to the medieval Arab world as well as our modern understanding of astronomy. As a fellow believer in God, you may be interested to know that one of the key arguments for God's existence, the cosmological argument, was developed by Islamic theologians and is often used by Christian philosophers to debate atheist thinkers. But all of this is passed over, or deflected when individuals select one aspect of my community such as how we look or dress and ignore the rest.

Michael: (smiling) This is just my opinion, but if you're trying to win people over to the Muslim perspective—particularly teenagers— I wouldn't take credit for helping create Algebra. Just a thought.

Amon (chuckling): I'll bring it up at our next meeting.

Michael: You mentioned that when people just focus on how some Arabs dress, so much else gets glossed over. I found it interesting that some students in my survey, particularly female students, mentioned *head covering* in describing Muslims. Thoughts?

Amon: They were most likely refereeing to a *hijab*—an Islamic covering—that some women choose to wear. The word *hijab* is an Arabic word that literally means *curtain* or *covering* and is not mandated by the Quran. Some women wear them as a sign of modesty and others wear them simply because they like how they look. I have one friend who has over 100 of them and she started wearing them after the attacks of 9/11 as a sign of pride in her culture and religion. I know of another woman who wears miniskirts to school and a *hijab* to the mosque. I have a good friend who is Arab but not particularly religious who wears one made by the fashion designer Yves St. Laurent because she thinks it looks cool.

Michael: That makes me think of a stereotype I have that's become clear during this interview—all Arabs are Muslims or are religious.

Amon: That'd be like saying all Americans are Christians. People tend not to fit into one neat category.

Michael: Why do you think we like to do that, fit people into predictable, neat categories?

Amon: Good question. I think most of us—myself included—like to keep life simple, organized, and predictable. Trying to figure out the world is tough work and we are all looking for shortcuts. In my religion class, I remember my prof saying that on average one new mosque opens each week in the United States and that Buddhism is now the fourth most practiced religion in America. Well, imagine how messy, chaotic, and exhausting it would be to take time to form an opinion of every Muslim and Buddhist individually. It's easier to form an opinion about the group as a whole and then apply that general judgment to all the people in the group.

Michael: So, all Muslims are angry and violent individuals who will cut off your ear if they don't like your face . . .

Amon: And all Christians are intolerant and supported the Crusades.

Michael: Touché. That reminds me of something we studied in one of my classes. We just had a test on it last week. One expert argued that in order to break a complex world up into more manageable, predictable pieces we continually work through a three-stage process when encountering people.[5] What was it? I know it started with three Cs. Categorization, characterization, and . . . what is the third one? . . . Nuts, what was it?

Amon: "Nuts" doesn't start with a "C".

Michael: You're not helping. *Correction*. That's it. Categorization, characterization, and correction. When we first meet a person we immediately place him or her into broad categories such as liberal or conservative, Christian or Muslim, and so on. Once we place them into a category, we assign specific characteristics to that person based on the category. The correction stage, which my professor said was the *most* neglected stage, only occurs if we get to know individuals and address initial judgments. The problem is our categories often keep us from getting to know people on an individual basis. To be honest, if it weren't for this listening assignment, I would never have come into this center and met you.

Amon: Don't feel bad, I can count on one hand the number of serious conversations I've had with Christians outside of my religious studies classes.

Michael: One last question, it's kinda off the wall. What do you think God thinks about stereotypes?

Amon: (laughing) What made you think of *that*?

Michael: One of my favorite writers, Eugene Peterson, says that with God there is no ditto among souls. What I think he means by that is that each person is created uniquely by God and could not possibly be contained by a one-size-fits-all label.

Amon: Well said. While labels or categories can help us organize life, they can also blind us to the unique qualities of individuals within a particular group. With each person we should, like God, seek to see the uniqueness inherent in them.

Michael: Okay, that's a perfect place to end this interview. Hey, this has been really helpful.

Amon: God's peace to you and good luck next Sunday with your fantasy team.

Michael: Thanks, I need both.

Surprising. That's the word Michael used to describe his interview with Amon at the Muslim Center. He was surprised that Amon liked fantasy football, watched *The Office*, and even joked about being able to diss his religion but not his fantasy team—he didn't see that coming. All in all, he liked him even though he doubted they would run into each other again. After the interview he was troubled by the story of the defaced Quran being left on the doorstep of the Mosque in Michigan. How would he feel if someone did that to the Bible? He wondered if stereotypes aren't always about merely organizing a chaotic world, but sometimes about fueling hate and wanting to feel superior to others? He also wondered if meeting Amon would make a difference in how he viewed Muslims on campus or if he'd just see Amon as an exception?

Endnotes

1. Thank you to my colleague Dorothy Alston Calley who regularly challenges her students to engage in such a meaningful listening assignment and shared her idea with me.
2. http://www.people-press.org/2011/08/30/a-portrait-of-muslim-americans/
3. Ghosh, B. (2009). In America's most Muslim city, fears of a backlash, *Time*, November 30, p. 6.
4. Burke, K. (1966). *Language as symbolic action*. Berkeley, CA: University of California Press.
5. Quattrone, G. A. (1985). On the congruity between internal states and actions. *Psychological Bulletin*, 98, 3–40.

For Further Thought and Reflection

1. How did Amon's noticing of Michael's sport's cap and their mutual enthusiasm for fantasy football help set the tone for their conversation?
2. If Michael were to have passed *you* on his way to the student center and asked: "What's the first word you think of when you hear, *Muslim*?" how would you have responded? Would your response have been positive or negative? Where does your idea of a Muslim/Arab come from? What role do the media play in forming it? How do events like the Fort Hood shooting or the attacks of Sept. 11 shape how you view Arab/Muslim students on your campus?
3. Michael brings up a three-stage process—categorization, characterization, and correction—and mentions that *correction* is often the most neglected stage. Why do you think correcting our stereotypes of others is often neglected or difficult?
4. In his closing observations of the interview, Michael writes: *Wonder if meeting Amon will make a difference in how I view Muslims on campus or if I'll see him as an exception?* What do you think? When you meet someone who breaks a stereotype you have of a group does that change how you view the group as a whole or merely that individual?
5. Are stereotypes more about helping us organize a chaotic world, being lazy in our perceptions of others, or perpetuating hate and superiority through language?

References

Allport, G. W. (1979). *The nature of prejudice*. Reading, MA: Perseus Books.

Perry, B. (2001). *In the name of hate: Understanding hate crimes*. New York: Routledge.

Wingfield, M., & Bushra, K. (2002). Arab stereotypes and American educators. *Social Studies and the Young Learner*, *7*, 7–10.

Wood, J. T. (1998). *But I thought you meant . . .: Misunderstandings in human communication*. Mountain View, CA: Mayfield Publishing.

23

(When and How) Should I Tell? Disclosing Social Identity in Personal Relationships

Brenda J. Allen

Keyterms

self-disclosure, relationship development, friendship, social identity, secrets

Jayla Brown sighed as she closed the door to her suite in the first-year students' residence hall. She was relieved that her roommate Lisa wasn't there; she could have some time to herself. Lisa was such a ball of energy that Jayla barely had time to hear herself think. But, that didn't really bother Jayla because Lisa was a positive person and basically a sweet girl. So far, she had been a great roommate, especially compared to other roomies she'd heard about. Jayla plopped on her bed and began to reflect on her first two and a half months at Northeastern State University. She and Lisa had hit it off from the first day they moved in. They had so much in common it was crazy. They both were middle children, and had been on the honor rolls and the cheerleading squads at their high schools. Plus, they were raised in Christian households, although neither of them had gone to church since they came to NESU. They both had a sick sense of humor, which meant that they laughed a lot, and had similar taste in movies and TV shows. They even had the same favorite color: purple, which meant that their bedding and accessories complemented each other. In fact, they both had bought the exact same lavender desk set from Target! They each had gone with one guy during their last two years of high school, and had broken up with him right before coming to college. Most important of all, they both were reluctant pre-med majors, mainly because of parental pressure. Jayla was glad to have a roommate who really understood her ambivalence about becoming a doctor. Some days she knew that's what she wanted to do; other days she wished she felt free to choose her career path. But her older sister Leila already had disappointed her folks by becoming a professor, and Jayla knew they were counting on her. The way things were going, she and Lisa might become best friends.

Sure, they also were different from one another. For one thing, Lisa was white and Jayla was black. That didn't bother Jayla. She had gone to a predominantly white private school, and some of her best friends were white. Jayla smiled at the cliché. "Really, they are," she said aloud, and laughed to herself. Lisa, on the other hand, had never been friends with anyone black, and she sometimes relied on media stereotypes when she talked with Jayla. She assumed that Jayla liked hip hop, which she did, but she also liked other types of music, as her iPod playlist showed. Right after they met, Lisa had tried to "talk black" to Jayla, using phrases like, "Yo! What up?" Jayla was frustrated at first, but she decided to be patient. She thought Lisa was trying too hard to relate to her based on her race. She gently explained that all young blacks didn't talk like that. Lisa seemed to understand, and she apologized to Jayla. To be fair, Jayla also had stereotyped Lisa, who was from California. She had figured that Lisa would talk like the Valley Girls she had seen on TV and movies, but Lisa didn't. Still, Jayla sometimes teased Lisa. One time when Lisa asked her opinion about an outfit, Jayla replied in her best impression of Valley Speak, including the trademark uptalk that made her statement sound like a question: "You look, like, totally awesome?" She and Lisa had cracked up. They both would occasionally joke with each other by using this type of language.

Jayla didn't think their racial difference was a big deal in her budding friendship with Lisa. They had confided in each other about topics like being homesick, and their apprehensions about their careers. However, Jayla never felt fully open with Lisa because she was holding back an important piece of information about herself that she'd told only one other person. And, she didn't know if, when, and how she would ever tell Lisa.

Jayla exhaled deeply as her thoughts turned to the main reasons she had come to NESU. In addition to having a great pre-med program, NESU touted its racially diverse student body. This appealed to Jayla because she wanted to develop more friendships with students of color. More important to Jayla, NESU was listed online as a "gay friendly campus." Jayla had struggled for years with her sexuality, and she had only recently become comfortable with being attracted to females. However, no one but her older sister Leila knew about that. And, she had promised not to tell Jayla's secret, even though she had encouraged Jayla to tell their parents. Jayla just wasn't sure how her parents would react, since their church had such a strong stance against homosexuality. Indeed, one reason Jayla had tried to suppress her feelings and to be "normal" was because she didn't want to be a sinner, and she didn't want to disgrace her parents. Thanks to Leila, she didn't feel like a bad person, but she still couldn't face her parents yet.

When Jayla was a junior in high school, she visited her sister Leila at her college. They were walking on campus when two girls passed them, walking hand-in-hand, and gazing at one another lovingly. "That is so cool," her sister said. "I'm glad they feel comfortable enough to show their relationship in public." Jayla seized the moment. "I hope I can show that side of myself one day, too," she murmured. Leila stopped abruptly. "What did you say?" she gasped. "You heard me," Jayla said more firmly. "I'm pretty sure that I'm gay." "Oh, Jay," Leila said softly, as she gathered her sister in her arms. "That must be so hard for you." Jayla choked back tears as she nodded slowly. They talked all night about Jayla's feelings and fears, and her sister had fully supported her. Since that night, they'd had many conversations about Jayla's sexuality.

And, Leila had given Jayla lots of resources, including books and articles about black lesbianism. Jayla especially cherished a book by Audre Lorde called *Sister Outsider* because it discussed complex challenges of being female, black, and lesbian. Some authors referred to a "triple consciousness" of these three identities that made it hard for black lesbians to find a community of people who would accept them fully. Jayla's religious identity as a Christian further complicated these challenges.

Jayla also had found a wealth of information online, including blogs and discussion groups written by young gay people of varying races. She realized that she wasn't alone and that she wasn't some kind of freak. She hadn't found the nerve yet to form friendships or to explore intimate relationships online, but she was comforted to have those options. Thank goodness she had come out to her sister. Jayla hoped that everyone she would eventually come out to would be as supportive and caring as her sister. But, based on what she'd read, she knew it would be hard to predict how people would react. *It's just not fair,* she sighed. She knew she would have to come out again and again and again and again, for the rest of her life. She hoped only that the process would get easier as she repeated it.

Jayla sighed loudly again. *How naïve was I?* she thought. She had fantasized about having a multiracial network of gay and straight friends at NESU with whom she could be herself. She had read that many young people came out when they went to college. And, she figured that once she established an "out" life at school, it would be easier to tell her parents about her sexuality. She was desperately tired of feeling guilty about passing as straight. Her mom asked her almost every time they talked if she had met a nice young man, and Jayla would say she was too busy studying to think about dating. Jayla knew that her parents wanted her to have a positive, loving marriage like theirs, and they were looking forward to becoming grandparents. She dreaded letting them down, and she hated feeling like she was deceiving them. She was feeling more and more urgency to tell them the truth.

Her dad had really wanted her to go to his alma mater, a black university. She had decided against that, because she had read online about the challenges that often confront black gay students at historically black colleges and universities (HBCUs). And, she had witnessed homophobia and heterosexism in their family's church, which was mainly black. She knew that not all black folks were against homosexuality, and she had read that some HBCUs were becoming more welcoming to gays and lesbians. However, she hadn't found anything on her dad's college's website that led her to believe that it would welcome her. In contrast, NESU's site included sexual orientation in its diversity statement, and it had a GLBTQ student service center, which her dad's school didn't. However, Jayla felt conflicted about not going to an HBCU, because she also realized that the odds of her finding a black girlfriend would probably be higher at her dad's alma mater. Yet, she was open to dating girls outside of her race.

Jayla smiled at the thought, since she hadn't dated ANY female yet. She basically had pretended to be heterosexual throughout high school, and she'd had a boyfriend during her junior and senior years. Mark hadn't pressured her for sex because he had taken an abstinence pledge in his church. They had kissed and made out and she had pretended to enjoy that, but she had known since at least middle school that she was attracted to girls. She and Mark had agreed to remain friends after they both decided to go to colleges that were far away from each other. Mark was one of her best friends, and he was high on the people she planned to come out to.

However, her plan to begin a new life by being out at NESU wasn't working out at all. She hadn't anticipated the complex challenges that now confronted her. First of all, she was having a hard time finding the so-called gay-friendly environment at NESU. During orientation, the director of Jayla's residence hall cautioned girls about having boys in their rooms. She seemed to be trying to be inclusive when she said, "The same rules apply for heterosexuals and homosexuals." However, she blew it by adding: "No one wants to wake up seeing two girls in bed where a man is supposed to be." In Jayla's Interpersonal Communication class, all of the examples of intimate relationships in the textbook referred to heterosexual couples, and whenever her professor gave examples of couples, he used female and male names. She hoped that the communication and diversity class she was taking next semester would be more inclusive. Even more discouraging, every time she walked by the GLBTQ center on campus, she saw only white males. She sure didn't feel comfortable entering that space to talk about her sexuality. She wondered if white females or males of color who identified as GLBTQ felt the same way.

Then there was the race thing. Jayla had been so optimistic about meeting students of varying races, especially other black students. When she attended a Black Student Alliance, shortened to BSA by students, meeting, a guy had smiled at her, and said, "Welcome, my sister." Jayla wondered if he would be so warm if he knew she was gay. She met another black girl named Erika who seemed nice. Erika was a sophomore, and she told Jayla that she would help her get acclimated to NESU. Jayla wanted to take her up on the offer, but she was unsure of how and if she should tell Erika about her sexuality. She noticed another girl at the meeting with a short-cropped haircut who was dressed in masculine clothes, and she wondered if she was gay. *Shut up* she told herself. *You know you shouldn't assume.* After all, she certainly didn't *look gay.* Her relaxed hair was shoulder length, and she wore the latest feminine fashions. She even had been named "Best Dressed" in high school. After attending the first BSA meeting, Jayla wasn't sure if she would become an active member. Most of the students seemed to know one another very well, even though they were friendly to Jayla and the other new students who were there. However, during the meeting, someone responded to a suggestion by saying, "That's so gay," and almost everyone laughed.

Despite the high percentage of students of color on campus, Jayla had been the only black student or student of color in many of her classes. Some of the white students seemed awkward around her, and some of her white professors seemed to single her out when race-related topics arose. Her political science professor asked for her comments on whether she thought the United States was post-racial after electing Barack Obama as president. Shouldn't the white students in the class be expected to weigh in on this topic too? Was she supposed to have special knowledge just because the President and she were both black? Even worse was when her sociology professor once asked her for the "black perspective" on urban crime. How was she supposed to represent the perspective of all black people? And why single out a black student to comment on urban crime? She knew the professor meant no harm, but his blindness to the bigotry in asking her was frustrating. She found herself feeling self-conscious about her race in ways that she'd never experienced, although some of her black friends at church had accused her of being an Oreo (black on the outside and white on the inside) because she went to a private, predominantly white, high school. They really got on her case when she started dating Mark, who was white. The good news was that Lisa was receptive when Jayla expressed some of her frustrations about race at NESU. She seemed genuinely concerned about Jayla's feelings, which she didn't dismiss or downplay. Jayla was learning to depend on Lisa to try to understand her. She had reciprocated when Lisa talked about being uncomfortable about sexist comments that one of her science professors often made in class. And, they had discussed concerns about being females among mainly male pre-med majors on campus.

Jayla exhaled deeply once again as she turned her mind back to her dilemma.

Should she or should she not come out to Lisa? She had been hopeful that her roommate would be open to her sexual identity. After all, Lisa had grown up near San Francisco, which Jayla had heard was one of the most gay-friendly cities in the world. Following advice from one website, Jayla had tried to gauge Lisa's attitudes toward homosexuality by asking her about her interests and experiences. During one of their first conversations, she had said, "Sooo, I understand that San Francisco is a really diverse city." Lisa had replied, "Yes, it is. We have so many different cultures there, and the city is so dynamic." "What do you mean," Jayla probed. "Oh, you know," Lisa said, "a lot of different ethnic groups and all kinds of food and music." Jayla wanted to push further, but she didn't want to seem too obvious.

Jayla knew that if she was going to come out to Lisa, her timing was crucial. From what she'd read, if she waited too long, Lisa might feel hurt and betrayed that Jayla had withheld something so important from her. Lisa might not trust her as much. But, if she told her too soon, Lisa might not have gotten to know other things about Jayla. "It's just not fair," Jayla groaned. Why did she have to worry about disclosing her sexual identity when straight people don't have to even think or talk about it? Of course, Lisa assumed she was straight because Jayla had a boyfriend in high school. One day when they were walking across campus, Lisa had pointed out a tall black guy, and said, "Ooooh, look at him, Jayla. You should try to get with that." Jayla sucked her teeth, and replied, "Lisa, how many times do I have to ask you not to talk like that?" Lisa grinned, and said, "OK. Sorry, girl, but you know I'm right." Jayla shook her head. In a way, she was glad that she could focus on Lisa's lame attempts to talk black as a way to deflect responding to her logical assumption that she would be interested in a guy—a black guy at that. She hadn't told Lisa yet that her high school boyfriend was white. Lisa had gone out on a couple dates with guys since they had become roommates, and she always wanted to talk about them with Jayla. Jayla had managed to avoid or minimize talking about dating, boyfriends, and sex, but she knew that she couldn't do that much longer. After all, these were "normal" topics for female friends their age.

Jayla propped up on her elbows, dropped her head into her hands, and exhaled loudly once again. What might happen if she told Lisa? Lisa might be so repulsed that she would ask for another roommate. Or, she might shrug it off as no problem. Or, she might act like it was OK, but then become cold toward Jayla. Or. . . . Jayla knew that guessing was fruitless. However, her brain started churning about the consequences of NOT telling Lisa. How could they deepen their friendship and freely discuss important topics like dating and intimate relationships or other topics that Jayla would have to either avoid or flat out lie about?

Jayla pounded her fist on her pillow. She knew she shouldn't let much more time pass. She had read lots of advice about how, when, and where to have a "coming out" conversation with friends and family, and she had rehearsed a couple of opening lines. She even had printed out an article about living with a gay roommate to give Lisa. Lisa was going home for Fall Break, so this might be a good time to tell her and give her time to think about it away from campus. Hmmmm. Maybe she could text Lisa while she was gone, instead of talking to her face-to-face. That might be easier for both of them. *Nah,* she thought. That just didn't seem right. As Jayla asked herself one more time, *What should I do?* the suite door opened, and Lisa bounded in. She smiled broadly and said, "What up, Jay?"

For Further Thought and Reflection

1. What communicative challenges does Jayla face in developing new relationships at NESU and in maintaining relationships in her family?
2. What communicative challenges might Lisa face when Jayla comes out to her?
3. Are there certain topics that friends should expect to discuss and confide in one another as they develop their friendship? If so, what are examples? Might those topics vary according to the friends' gender, age, race, sexuality, religion, and other aspects of social identity? Why or why not?
4. How do you decide when is "the right time" to disclose personal, private information to a new friend?
5. Should Jayla tell Lisa about her sexuality? Why or why not? If she should, how and when should she tell her? Should she already have told her?
6. Should Jayla tell her parents about her sexuality? Why or why not? If so, how should she tell them? Should she already have told them?
7. Do you agree that Jayla has an especially complex challenge with forming friendships at NESU (and other contexts) because of her social identities (i.e., female, black, lesbian, and Christian)? Why or why not?

References

Allen, B. J. (2011). *Difference matters: Communicating social identity,* 2nd ed.. Long Grove, IL: Waveland Press.

Caughlin, J. P., & Vangelisti, A. L. (2009). Why people conceal or reveal secrets: A multiple goals theory perspective. In T. Afifi & W. Afifi (Eds.), *Uncertainty and information regulation in interpersonal contexts: Theories and applications* (pp. 279-299). New York: Routledge.

Goldstein, S. B. (2013). Predicting college students' intergroup friendships across race/ethnicity, religion, sexual orientation, and social class. *Equity & Excellence in Education, 46*, 502– 519.

Holland, L., Matthews, T. L., & Schott, M. R. (2013) "That's so gay!" Exploring college Students' attitudes toward the LGBT population. *Journal of Homosexuality, 60*, 575–595.

Lorde, A. (1998). Sister outsider: Essays & speeches by Audre Lorde. Freedom, CA: The Crossing Press.

Matthews, C. H., & Salazar, C. F. (2012). An integrative, empowerment model for helping lesbian, gay, and bisexual youth negotiate the coming-out process. *Journal of LGBT Issues in Counseling, 6*, 96–117.

Savage, D., & Miller, T. (2012). *It gets better: Coming out, overcoming bullying, and living a life worth living.* New York: Plume.

Spradlin, A. (1998). The price of passing: A lesbian perspective on authenticity in organizations. *Management Communication Quarterly, 11*, 598–605.

24

What Happened? Naming and Talking about Acquaintance Rape

Kate Lockwood Harris

Keywords

ambiguity of language, consent, intimate partner violence, pragmatics, rape myths

I love him. I do. He has this goofy, sideways grin. No matter where you are in the room, it always looks like he's smiling just at you. Whenever he makes a peanut butter and jelly sandwich, he measures out three tablespoons of peanut butter—exactly—for each slice of bread. He sings the Beatles non-stop, especially "Love, Love Me Do," and the words are just a little bit different every time. He's got four skateboards, and he always leaves them in random places in his apartment. He tells the worst jokes, I swear. And he's smart like it's nobody's business. He can have a conversation with just about anyone, anywhere, and make a friend. I love him.

My friend, Maya, can't believe that I love him. Sure, she sees all those things that I see: the charming smile and the neurotic sandwich-making technique and his wit and smarts and penchant for forgetting the words to songs. But she can't believe that I love him. Not after what happened.

It was pretty bad, for sure. And it was wrong, no doubt about it. It shouldn't have happened, but it did.

I talked to one of my friends about it the next day. The first thing she said was, "Why didn't you just kick him or something?" I couldn't answer her question. I figured I'd done something wrong. So I just shut up about it.

I didn't tell anybody about it for a couple of years after that, actually. I didn't know what to say or how to talk about it. I couldn't find a way to explain it. And I was afraid that everybody would blame me for it.

I was so messed up afterwards. Later the night it happened, I cried a lot. I was bleeding and raw. It was so confusing. I ended up drinking a lot for about a year afterwards. I mean, not just a Smirnoff on a Friday night. I had three or four drinks most nights. Margaritas were my favorite, and on weekends I'd just drink until I fell asleep. I was miserable, so depressed that I couldn't get out of bed some mornings.

At the time it happened, he and I had been dating for six months. We were definitely in love, and we told each other so. The day it happened, he and I got together at about 11 a.m. We ran some errands, saw a movie with some of our buddies, and then had dinner. I told him then, over our three-tablespoon peanut butter sandwiches, that I didn't want to have sex that night.

I was as clear as I could have been. Plain as day, really. I said, "I don't want to have sex tonight." I had some really important reasons why I didn't want to, and I told him about them. I'm pretty sure he understood them.

We went back to my place and started to make out. I didn't say no when we got in bed. I didn't say yes either. I was so turned on. Who wouldn't be? He's cute and passionate and smart and sensitive, and he knew—for sure by that point—what got me going. I wanted him, but I didn't want to have sex.

We kept making out for a while, then everything stopped feeling right. I remember clearly what happened next. I was on my back on the bed, staring. I wasn't there. Not emotionally, not mentally. It was like I was watching a movie, and I couldn't believe what was happening. I remember looking so hard at the wallpaper. There was this repeating flower pattern on it, the kind that anybody's mom would have thought was perfect for decorating, but the kind that I found nauseating. It was just a little too happy.

I don't think he was there either. At least not the guy I know. I mean, he was there, but he wasn't. That's part of what's tough about it, I guess. He seemed like a machine on top of me. I usually felt connected to him, but not then. I just lay there, not moving, not saying anything. He just kept going and going and going, fast, hard. Like it was the only thing in the world to him, just like those flowers on the wallpaper were to me in that moment.

Maya says he raped me. I don't know. I mean, yeah, he had sex with me when I hadn't agreed to have sex. And that's pretty much the definition of rape, right? Any sex without consent. But it just seems more complicated than that. I mean, if I call it rape, that makes him a rapist. Yet he's my boyfriend. Yeah, what happened sucked, and what he did was definitely wrong. But rapists belong behind bars. And there's no way I'd be friends with, much less date, a rapist.

I guess most people think if it's rape, you've got to be kicking and screaming. I wasn't doing anything. I was just so shocked that he was doing this after I'd told him I didn't want to. It was like I was totally frozen. He didn't hold me down, but I was pinned to the bed; shock at his behavior, disbelief at his disconnection, and a sense of unreality were weights on my body. Since it happened I've thought about the million things that could have been different. I could have stayed home that night. I could have screamed when I was in bed with him. I'm pretty sure he would have listened. But I thought he had listened earlier in the day when I'd said no. If I made my wishes clear earlier, did I have to restate them? Why didn't he ask if I'd changed my mind?

Maya says I'm blaming myself. I don't think it's my fault that this happened. It takes two to tango, right? So it's at least 50 percent him. I do think there are specific things I could have done differently, like saying something at the time. That's different from thinking I caused it to happen.

Maya thinks it's his fault. In some ways, I agree. He could have made sure I wanted to have sex. And he darn well should have paid attention to what I'd said earlier in the day. I can't figure out why he didn't.

But then again, we'd had sex so many times before. Really, really good sex. I mean, the kind of sex where you're grinning for three days afterwards and you're afraid your grandma is going to be able to tell you got laid because you're so in love with the whole world afterwards.

And we'd gotten into this routine where we read each other's bodies—all that nonverbal stuff. We hardly ever said anything directly about what we wanted. It was like in the movies; we looked into each other's eyes and we could read each other. The way we touched each other said a lot. So that was kind of the norm, just communicating without words.

He wasn't reading me that night, though. Yeah, I was turned on, but when he got on top of me, I totally stopped moving, and that wasn't normal. I have no idea why he didn't notice and why he didn't find out what was going on. I trusted him, you know? I expected him to be paying attention to how I was feeling, and he always had before, even if we weren't talking about it.

Maya took a course about violence in relationships, and she told me that by the time we're done with college, one out of every four women in our class will have been raped. I couldn't believe it. I mean, when I hear "rape" I think about soldiers at war raping women, really brutal stuff. That's definitely rape. Or when someone breaks into your house in the middle of the night and holds a knife or a gun to your neck. That's definitely rape. Or those awful stories you hear about when a whole group of men takes turns on a woman—gang rapes. That's awful. Or maybe even in some really abusive relationship where the guy is threatening to kill his wife, or not let her have any money, or not let her go out to visit her friends, where he's just got total mental control over her. Even that I can see being rape.

So when Maya says one in four of the women I go to college with will be raped, I just have a hard time believing it. Maya has asked me a lot of questions about what I think rape means. And, like I said, seems like if someone doesn't agree to get it on and then it happens anyway, that's rape.

My friend, Jan, had a similar, confusing experience. A bunch of us went to a party the first month of our first year on campus. Everybody was having fun, and we all had a few drinks. Jan started flirting with this hot guy we'd all been drooling over. He had nice muscles, his eyes always seemed to be smiling, and he had been so considerate to all of us since we met. That made him even hotter, I think. He was definitely a nice guy. Anyway, he and Jan really hit it off. Eventually the two of them disappeared, and we all thought, "Hey, great, they're going to make out for a while." I can't remember how the night ended, but a few months later I talked to Jan. The party was at his place, and she had gone upstairs with the guy to his room. They'd talked and flirted for a while longer. They started kissing and touching, and she said she was into it. After a while the drinks started to have a serious effect on her. She said that she started getting really tired, and eventually she passed out. She woke up naked and he was on top of her, in her. She said she was still a little drunk so she just tried to push him off. She eventually fell back asleep, and she said the details were hazy.

"Did he use protection?" I asked.

"No, I don't think so," she said. "And I think he might have given me herpes. I broke out, and I've got to go to the doctor."

"Oh my gosh, Jan. I'm sorry that happened." I asked her what she was going to do about it. "What am I going to do about what?" Jan asked.

"Well, he raped you!" I said to her.

"Well, if he raped me then that means it's all his fault and I don't think that's right," she said.

"You were passed out. How could it not be his fault?" I asked.

"I was drunk. I chose to drink."

"Yeah, but it's not *your* fault."

"No, I don't think it is," said Jan, "But I could have done things differently."

"He *should* have done things differently," I said, angry that this guy had taken advantage of my friend. "Even if you had not passed out, you still can't give consent if you're that drunk."

"He was drunk too. How come I can't be responsible for consenting when I'm drunk but he can still be responsible for initiating sex when he's drunk?" she asked.

"Because drunkenness is not a free pass to assault people. He used alcohol as a weapon against you." I was uncomfortable. Clearly he'd done something wrong, and it seemed like Jan didn't want to admit it, but I guess she had a point. I mean, he definitely raped her, and I thought she should press charges against him. That's what you do when you're raped, right?

That's what Maya did. One of her friends raped her our first year on campus. Maya is very straightforward when she talks about what happened: It was rape, it was a crime, she's not at fault, and he should be punished. She reported the incident to the school, but nothing happened. Well, something happened. Even though Maya had an e-mail from him in which he admitted to raping her, the school administration found him innocent. He had to write a four-page paper about "respect." Maya had to get a new group of friends—the people she was close to sided with him and thought she was making it all up.

Maya was telling a group of us about everything that had happened. Our friend Jim listened then chimed in. "Are you sure it wasn't just bad sex? I mean, I have a friend who didn't want her boyfriend to know she was cheating so she called it 'rape' to get out of trouble." Maya rolled her eyes in response.

Our other friend, Sam, challenged Jim: "Oh please, stop that. You're saying that women often use the term 'rape' to manipulate people, and that seems sexist to me. When women say they've been raped, people aren't exactly sympathetic. They'll be like, 'What were you wearing?' Or, 'You probably wanted it anyway.' That's so demeaning. Maya and I took a violence class together last semester. You know what we learned? That false reports of rape are so rare—around one percent—and no more frequent than false reports for any other crime. But you know what's different about rape? Most rapes are *never* reported to the authorities, and many women never say *anything* about it at all—to anyone. Maya's courageous for coming forward."

Jim got defensive. "So what am I supposed to do, just assume that anytime someone cries rape that they're telling the truth?"

Sam continued: "I'm saying that the idea of 'crying rape' is a myth. Someone tells me that they've been raped, or they think they've been raped, or even just something went really wrong, and I'm going to assume they are telling me the truth. Because 99% of the time they are. What kind of ass would I be if someone I know tells me about a violent trauma they experienced and I hint that they are lying? Especially when I know the real numbers about rape."

Jim retorted: "So you're saying all men are rapists, huh?"

Sam: "Where'd you get that idea? It's not true. Most men never rape, but those few men who do rape do it repeatedly. Haven't you ever heard of rape myths? You're talking about a lot of them." The conversation ended there.

I wish I had Maya's clarity. For me there seem to be so many more factors to consider. I know how easy it is to blame victims for this stuff. They say, "Oh she was asking for it. She wanted it and she just didn't know it." I don't want my story to be read that way. And for me it's extra complicated: If I speak out against my boyfriend, I'm also speaking out against my community. Black people already have so many stereotypes put on us, and there are already so many Black men in jails.

What happened to me was wrong. And what happened to Jan and to Maya was wrong, too. I worry that if we don't call it rape—or even if we do—people won't take us seriously.

Jan and Maya and I all got together for a picnic lunch the other day. Jan brought fruit salad, Maya brought drinks, and I brought the sandwiches, of course. He made them for us, with three tablespoons of peanut butter each. The three of us talked about all of this. Maya thinks that if we call our experiences rape, people will understand that what happened was horrible and terrible. I can't imagine that I'm dating a rapist. And Jan doesn't want to put the guy who violated her behind bars. All of our perspectives make sense to me. Is what happened to Jan really the same as what happened to me? And is what happened to us the same as what happens to women who are raped during wars? Or by multiple people at once? I'm just not sure we have enough words to describe all of this stuff.

The fictional characters in this chapter and their statements are based on themes that emerged from approximately forty interviews that the author conducted with young women who had an experience of unwanted sex. Some of those women called their experience rape, and others did not.

For Further Thought and Reflection

1. How is consent communicated? How do people know if a partner agrees to have sex?
2. Based on these characters' descriptions, what are the consequences of experiences of nonconsensual sex?
3. When describing experiences like the ones in this story, what does naming them with the word "rape" accomplish? In what ways is the word "rape" limited?
4. Rape myths are false but popular ideas about the nature and prevalence of rape. The narrator and other characters in this story refer to a couple of these myths, for example that women often make false reports of rape and that victims of rape are to blame for their own assaults. How do you think these myths influence whether a person or a community labels an episode of nonconsensual sex as rape? What impact do you think rape myths have on preventing and responding to rape?
5. Imagine a friend or loved one tells you that he or she has been raped. Based on what you have learned about good communication skills, what would you say or do? What interpersonal responses would be unhelpful or even harmful? How would your response compare to the supportive interpersonal communication you would offer to friends and loved ones who have experienced other kinds of trauma?

References

Belknap, J. (2010). Rape: Too hard to report and too easy to discredit victims. *Violence Against Women, 26*(12), 1335–1344..

Beres, M. (2010). Sexual miscommunication? Untangling assumptions about sexual communication between casual sex partners. *Culture, Health & Sexuality, 12*(1), 1–14.

Carmody, M., & Ovenden, G. (2013). Putting ethical sex into practice: Sexual negotiation, gender and citizenship in the lives of young women and men. *Journal of Youth Studies, 16*(6), 792–807.

Deming, M. E., Covan, E. K., Swan, S. C., & Billings, D. L. (2013). Exploring rape myths, gendered norms, group processing, and the social context of rape among college women: A qualitative analysis. *Violence Against Women, 19*(4), 465-485.

Fisher, B. A., Daigle, L. E., & Cullen, F. T. (2010). *Unsafe in the ivory tower: The sexual victimization of college women.* Thousand Oaks, CA: Sage.

Gavey, N. (2005). *Just sex?: The cultural scaffolding of rape.* New York, NY: Routledge.

Harris, K. L. (2011). The next problem with no name: The politics and pragmatics of the word *rape. Women's Studies in Communication, 34*(1), 42–63.

Peterson, Z. D., & Muehlenhard, C. L. (2011). A match-and-motivation model of how women label their nonconsensual sexual experiences. *Psychology of Women Quarterly, 35*(4), 558–579.

25

Starting a New Family Legacy: Transitioning from High School to College as a First-Generation Student

Tiffany R. Wang

Keywords

first-generation students, identity, autonomy/connection

Dani's TRiO Blog

About me: My name is Daniela, but most people think that's hard to pronounce so you can call me Dani. I am a first-year chemistry major who has two dreams in life: to be the first in my family to finish college and to gain acceptance into medical school. I'll be blogging on behalf of TRiO, an on-campus program that helps first-generation students like me succeed in college. Join me as I share the ups and downs of college life as I make the jump from high school senior to college freshman.

Goodbyes and Hellos

Move in day is finally here! I can't believe that I'll be leaving my hometown and moving into a dorm with a potluck roommate I've never met. Let's hope that roommate survey I filled out actually does pair you with a complementary roommate like the housing people promise it will. I have my doubts, but I'm cautiously optimistic right now. I looked my new roommate up on Facebook and she seems nice enough from our Facebook chats. Although I'm excited about the freedom I'll have in college, I'm not sure I'm ready for this big move. Let's face it: it's hard to leave your family, friends, and hometown behind. My family is really close and we do everything together, so living in a different town will be a new experience for me.

Since you don't know me, let me give you some background information. I'm the oldest child in my family. My sister Ximena is sixteen and my brother Juan is fourteen. I'm moving here from a small farming town. Although I've lived in my hometown for most of my life, I spent my early years in Mexico. My parents moved to the United States to follow the proverbial American Dream. Unfortunately, life here hasn't been a complete dream for my family. My parents work minimum wage jobs as a factory worker and a custodian. Even though both of them work, we still struggle to pay the bills.

My parents have always told me that education is the key to a better life. As I started high school, I knew that I had to do well on my ACT exam so I could get a scholarship and afford to go to college. Throughout high school, I spent most of my time studying and made honor roll every semester. After anxiously checking the mail for a week, I received my acceptance letter and it was the most wonderful piece of paper I've ever received! This letter was the first step to my future and I felt like I had proved the doubters wrong. Now that I'm here, I really don't want to disappoint my parents. They're constantly telling their friends how excited they are that they have a daughter who's going to college. It's quite fun being the center of attention, but I also feel like I have the weight of the world on my shoulders: my parents are counting on me to set a good example for my younger siblings and cousins. Hopefully, I'll be able to do that over the next four years, but first I just need to get through New Student Orientation and my first week of classes. I'm sure I will face many obstacles here, but I'm ready to start this new chapter of my life.

New Beginnings

Life has been crazy! I thought starting college would be fun, but it's actually been quite overwhelming. Although I've declared my major, know what I want to do with my life, and even managed to get a class schedule with no 8 A.M. or night classes, I don't quite feel like a college student just yet. At New Student Orientation, I walked around campus with my roommate, Ashley, and her parents, because my parents had to go back to work after they unloaded my stuff. Although Ashley and I basically have the same personality and are a lot alike, we're different in a lot of ways too. She went to a really elite prep school nearby and took many Advanced Placement classes. I'm pretty sure she is almost a sophomore already because she transferred in a lot of credit hours. Her family is really well off and her parents both graduated from here and went on to complete graduate degrees. Ashley's family has football season tickets on the 50-yard line so she's been coming to campus since before she could even walk. It's almost like she already has the answers and that she's always known she was going to graduate from college because that's just what her family does. It's different for me. College is really new and really scary. Words like credit hours, General Education, and Panhellenic just make my head hurt. It's like learning a whole new language that everyone else already knows. I have a lot of catching up to do!

I'm taking four classes (composition, chemistry, public speaking, and a study skills class just for TRiO students) and they seem to be going pretty well so far. I especially like my composition professor. On the first day of class he came in dressed completely casual: shorts, school t-shirt, and flip-flops. The first thing he asked us to do was address him by his first name rather than Dr. I'm confident I could ask any question in his class without feeling stupid or intimidated. After class, I decided to chat with him for a few minutes. I was surprised to find out that he is of Mexican heritage and came to the United States at a young age as well. We really connected over our similar stories and I felt an unspoken bond with him. He knew exactly what it was like to struggle and go against all of the challenges I have faced and continue to face today. I really think we were able to connect because he understood my story and I understood his story. I didn't have to explain my story, because he just got it. I was really inspired talking to him, and seeing a person like him go from rags to riches makes me believe that I will be able to achieve my own American Dream some day and be able to go back to my hometown and open my own medical clinic. If my composition professor is any indication of what my professors will be like here, this should be a great semester.

As I look back on all of the classes I have attended this week, some seem to be harder than the ones I took in high school, but being a student in the classroom feels familiar. I've always excelled at school, so hopefully I will be able to succeed in college as well. I guess I'll truly know if I'm cut out to be a college student after my first chemistry exam next week. I'm spending the weekend hitting the books so I should do fine on the exam.

Disappointments

I spoke too soon in my last blog. I'm enjoying most of my classes, but this has not been my week! I took my first chemistry exam and it was really hard. I didn't know how to study for it and I completely bombed it. I got the exam back and there was a giant F at the top and big red Xs all over the exam. This is especially distressing because I should be good at chemistry. This is my major after all and this is just the introductory class. I can't imagine how hard the other chemistry classes will be. My whole world feels like it's been turned upside down. I was an honor roll student all throughout high school and I never got an F on anything in my life. I tried to hold myself together in class, but I completely broke down when I got back to my dorm room. I wish I could just drop this class and not worry about bringing up my grade, but I have to have this class for my major. Even if I pass this class, I can't really get a bad grade, because I need a really high GPA if I want to get into medical school. Fortunately, my roommate was there when I broke down and she encouraged me to go and see my professor during his office hours. I'd heard a lot of great things about this professor so I was sure that talking to him would help me improve my grade in his class.

I took my roommate's advice and went to see my professor during his office hours yesterday. My professor, who shall remain nameless in this blog, was quite rude to me and I left his office feeling disappointed and defeated. I've always respected my high school teachers and even consider some of them to be my mentors, but it's hard to respect my chemistry professor after what happened yesterday. He made me feel like a complete idiot and was not helpful at all. When I went to talk to him I felt like there was a huge power distance between the two of us. He made it quite clear that he was the professor who knew everything and that I was the student who didn't know nearly enough. He said that he didn't have time to help me because he was working on a very important research grant proposal and that I really should have learned this material in high school chemistry. As he shooed me out of his office, he suggested I read the book more carefully and seek out remedial tutoring. My chemistry professor's comments really irritated me because I went and visited him during the office hours he listed on his syllabus. I thought professors were supposed to reserve office hours for meeting with students. My chemistry professor doesn't seem to be particularly interested in students. He just seems to care about his research. My conversation with him really bothered me. I couldn't believe that someone could bog me down like that just because I did not understand how lipids, acids, and bases worked. These concepts might seem simple to him, but he has a Ph.D. in Chemistry from an Ivy League school and I'm just starting out and taking my very first college chemistry class.

I wish I could just let things go and move forward with my life without worrying about what's happened to me in the past. If I don't have a good interaction with a professor, I'm not the type of person who can just suck it up and move on. I just become really discouraged and allow the doubts that have haunted me before to creep in again. I keep thinking that maybe my chemistry professor is right and I should have learned all of this material in high school. Talking to him makes me doubt my abilities and intelligence. These doubts raise even more questions for me. Should I be in this field? Should I be in this major? Am I pursuing the right path? To make matters worse, I'm going to have to tell my family about this grade when I go home this weekend. I've always done well at school, so I'm sure they'll be disappointed in me.

Home Cooking

Going home over the weekend was bittersweet for me. I really enjoyed getting to eat some of my mom's home cooking, catch up on what's happened at home since I started college, and spend time with my siblings and closest high school friends. Telling my family about my failing grade wasn't as bad as I thought it would be. We sat down and had dinner and talked about what happened. My parents have never really been into science or really school in general, so they shared some stories from high school about times when they hadn't done so well on their tests. My siblings, Ximena and Juan, filled me in on some exciting news. Ximena got the lead in the high school musical and Juan made the school soccer team. Although I was more interested in what was happening in their lives, they kept asking me questions about what college life was like. They wanted to know all about my dorm room, roommate, classes, teachers, and friends. I really think that they'll want to follow in my footsteps and go to college some day. After my siblings left the dinner table to start homework, my parents assured me that I would do better on the second exam and that I could bring up my grade before the end of the semester. They kept reminding me that this was just one class and that I was doing just fine in all my other classes. While my parents' faith in me was quite encouraging, I really wish they could have given me some specific advice on how to improve my performance on the second exam. When I asked them what they suggested I should do to improve my grade in chemistry, they just told me study more, do your best, and everything will work out in the end. It's frustrating that they've never been to college so they don't really know what it takes to make good grades in college. College is five times harder than high school and I really wish there was someone I could talk to who could speak from firsthand experience about what college is like and tell me what I need to do to bring up my grade in chemistry.

Unfortunately, my friends couldn't give me any better advice than my parents did. Many of them started jobs right after high school rather than going to college and they seem to be making pretty good money and are definitely less stressed than I am. They keep telling me that I shouldn't be wasting my money on classes that I'm not doing well at and that I should just move back home and start a job like they did. As I go back to college after a weekend home, I'm left with a couple more questions. What should I do if I continue to struggle with my chemistry class? Maybe college just isn't my thing and I should get a job instead. At least I'll be making decent money rather than going into debt for school. Is going to college really worth the money and time I'm putting in? My friends seem to be much happier than I am and they're not in college. Maybe my dream is unattainable and I should have stayed in my hometown where it's safe and comfortable.

Mid Semester Blues

We're at the halfway point in the semester. My composition class is going well. My professor has encouraged us to write about our personal experiences and it's been really fun to share my essays with my peer review partner. My public speaking class is quite interesting. We're starting persuasive speeches soon and professor has asked us to pick a nonprofit organization or cause we want to advocate for. I'm going to pick a topic related to healthcare because I want to be a doctor. While I've enjoyed my composition and public speaking classes, I've enjoyed my study skills class the most. What makes this class different from my other ones is that I have a lot in common with many of my classmates. Some classmates immigrated to the United States from a different country. Other classmates have told me how important it is to them to be the first person in their family to graduate from college. My professor and TRiO advisor actually participated in TRiO when she was in college so she's a great role model for all of us. Although I've managed to improve my grade in chemistry by doing well on the lab reports, this class is still definitely a struggle for me. I did pass my second chemistry exam, but I still have a lot of work to do if I want to make a decent grade in this class.

As I look back on my semester thus far, I've realized that college success is not just about textbooks and classes. It's also about finding a balance in my life. Right now I'm struggling to balance many different worlds: my college life and my home life, my Mexican roots and my desire to fit in with my new American friends, and my classes and my desire to go out and have fun. Most days I feel like I haven't quite found the balance yet. I feel caught between my past and my future. I love my family and want to remain close to them, but I also want to make some decisions for myself and be an independent person apart from my family. I want to create a new legacy of higher education for my family, but I am not sure whether the personal or financial cost will be worth it. So many questions and not enough answers.

My world was thrown further out of balance today at the worst possible time: midterm week. As I was walking back to my dorm room after my lab for my chemistry class, I saw I had a missed call and voice message from my mom on my cell phone. I quickly called my mom back and she told me that my uncle had died from a massive heart attack that day. He was in his mid 40s and left behind my aunt and my young cousins. It was devastating to realize that I wouldn't have the chance to say goodbye to him and that I couldn't be there to support my extended family during this difficult time. The funeral is happening this week. My roommate thinks I should stay on campus because midterms are happening and skipping them will mean that my grades will suffer. She says I need to look out for myself and do what's best for me. My family is pressuring me to come home for the funeral, because I should be there for my aunt and my cousins as they grieve the loss of my uncle. They say that our family sticks together no matter what. I'm really not sure what to do. Both my education and my family are important and I hate that I'll have to make a choice between the two. Life just keeps getting more complicated.

The Puzzle

After much thought and consideration, I decided not to go home for the funeral so I could take my midterms last week. Part of me thinks I made the right decision to put my own goals and my education first. Part of me wishes I had put my family first and gone home. College is starting to feel like a puzzle that I can't quite figure out how to put together. It's complex and challenging and I'm hoping I actually have all the pieces I will need to finish the puzzle and graduate. Some days, I feel like I'm trying to complete the puzzle without the picture on the box to reference. Some small sections of my puzzle are starting to come together. I've made some new friends. While my TRiO Program and Hispanic Student Association friends remind me of my friends back home, this college is a lot less diverse than my high school so I'm also trying to be more open to meeting some new people who are different from me. I've also started to build a relationship with some of the advisors who work in the TRiO Program. However, there are many sections of the puzzle that aren't yet completed. In fact, some of the puzzle pieces seem to be missing. Despite the academic and personal obstacles I have faced this semester, I don't want to be a statistic and drop out. I want to prove my chemistry professor wrong and show him that I have what it takes to earn my diploma. I want to make my parents proud and myself proud so I can show my younger siblings and cousins that they can go to college and succeed. I want to be a positive role model for others in my hometown. I'm just not sure what I need to do to be more successful. I think I'm going to have to make a decision on whether college is right for me very soon. Should I keep working at this puzzle or start a completely new one?

For Further Thought and Reflection

1. Dani mentions that she had an unspoken bond with her composition professor. What common experiences do Dani and her composition professor share? How do these commonalities influence the way Dani perceives her composition professor?
2. In relational dialectics theory Baxter discusses the autonomy/connection dialectical tension, which reflects the struggle to balance the simultaneous needs to be independent and have ties with others. How did Dani experience this dialectical tension in this case?
3. Orbe and Groscurth (2004) discuss how liaisons, helpful individuals on campus, can help first-generation students adjust to college. What liaisons are already in Dani's life? What liaisons should Dani consult to determine whether college is right for her?
4. If you were a liaison in Dani's life, what advice would you give to her as she decides whether or not college is right for her?
5. Wang (2012) outlines memorable messages, brief prescriptive commands that are remembered for a long time, first-generation college students receive from on-campus mentors. What memorable messages would help Dani succeed in college? What memorable messages is Dani not receiving from her parents and friends in her hometown because they lack the firsthand college knowledge needed to help her?

References

Baxter, L. (1990). Dialectical contradictions in relational development. *Journal of Social and Personal Relationships, 7,* 69–88.

Benmayor, R. (2002). Narrating cultural citizenship: Oral histories of first-generation college students of Mexican origin. *Social Justice*, *29,* 96–121. Retrieved from http://www.socialjusticejournal.org/Backiss.html

Orbe, M. P. (2004). Negotiating multiple identities within multiple frames: An analysis of first-generation college students. *Communication Education*, *53,* 131–149.

Orbe, M. P. (2008). Theorizing multidimensional identity negotiation: Reflections on the lived experiences of first-generation college students. *New Directions for Child and Adolescent Development*, *120,* 81–95.

Orbe, M. P., & Groscurth, C. R. (2004). A co-cultural theoretical analysis of communicating on campus and at home: Exploring the negotiation strategies of first generation college (FGC) students. *Qualitative Research Reports in Communication*, *5*, 541–547. Retrieved from http://www.tandfonline.com/toc/rqrr20/current

Wang, T. R. (2012). Understanding the memorable messages first-generation college students receive from on-campus mentors. *Communication Education*, *61,* 335–357.

Wang, T. R. (in press). Formational turning points in the transition to college: Understanding how communication events shape first-generation students' pedagogical and interpersonal relationships with their college teachers. *Communication Education.*

Wang, T. R. (in press). "I'm the only person from where I'm from to go to college": Understanding the memorable messages first-generation college students receive from parents. *Journal of Family Communication.*

PART V

Change and Continuity in Long-Term Relationships

26

The Queen and Her Bee: Social Aggression in Female Friendship

Erin K. Willer

Keywords

social aggression, bullying, popularity, social dominance, social identity theory

Fire in the Hive

Mia desperately smiled with her eyes at Nathaniel, willing his baby browns to connect with her own as he talked to her. *What I wouldn't give to—*

Nathaniel's incessant chatter interrupted her daydreaming, "Just look at her. Not only is she gorgeous, but every girl in the bar wants to *be* her and every guy wants to be *with* her." They both looked across the bar at Layla who was surrounded by a group of their guy and girl friends who were focused intently on her. "Do you think she likes me?" he asked.

Mia rolled her eyes, "Oh please, what's the huge fascination with Layla?"

Nathaniel looked surprised, "Come on, you know Layla better than anyone. You are best friends. How can you even ask me that question?"

Mia thought, *I'm going to throw up if I have to spend another minute of my life talking about Layla. In sixth grade it was, "Do you think Layla is going to invite me to her birthday party?" Sophomore year it was, "What's Layla wearing to homecoming?" Last week it was Dr. Rifken talking about how Layla is the perfect team leader for her Sudan awareness fundraiser, and now I have to listen to the hottest guy on campus plan their future together. People only like her because they don't know how two-faced she is.* "Whatever, Nathaniel, just make sure you wear a condom." *Whoops, I probably shouldn't have said that.*

Nathaniel looked back at Mia confused, "But I thought Layla had only been with one—"

At that moment Layla caught Mia's eye from across the dance floor and motioned with her head toward the ladies' room. Saved from having to respond to Nathaniel, Mia jumped up to meet Layla in the restroom.

When Mia walked in, Layla was talking to Olivia, a member of Alpha Rho, their rival sorority. *Why is Layla talking to that phony? Look at her with her fake tan and her fake personality.*

Olivia seemed to brace herself at the sight of Mia who gave her usual look of disdain anytime the two crossed paths. Before Mia had the chance to make her usual snide comments, Layla said, "Hey, Mia! I was just talking to Olivia about the fundraiser next weekend."

Mia rolled her eyes and responded in a tone that clearly communicated her lack of interest as she headed into the bathroom stall, "Greaaat."

Olivia excused herself so as not to have to be the target of Mia's passive aggressiveness and backstabbing. The whole Greek system had come to call her the *Green* Goddess. Her slimy antics and propensity to glob on to Layla reminded them more of the goopy salad dressing of the same name as opposed to someone with the traits of a *Greek* goddess.

When Mia came out of the stall, Layla was pulling her hair into a ponytail. "What the hell is your problem?" she snapped.

"What do you mean?" Mia asked innocently.

"Why were you so rude to Olivia?"

"I just can't stand her or any of the Alpha Rhos. They're *so* nice; it's disgusting. Nobody's *that* nice. They're not like us Omegas—we might be mean but at least we are real."

"You are really ugly when you act like that," Layla quipped.

How can she say that? She's the one who is the queen of cruelty, Mia thought.

Smiling now, Layla's tone was more understanding, "I hear you though. Those girls *are* fake. And did you get a look at Olivia's shoes? Hideous!"

They both laughed and Mia watched Layla as she applied a thin layer of gloss to her lips. *How can I love her and hate her so much?*

"So I saw you out there talking to Nathaniel. It looked like you were about to plant one on him the way you were staring at him. What's up with that?"

Should I tell her I'm in love with him? No, she'll steal him away like she does with every guy I like.

Before Mia could answer, Layla said, "He is so hot. Too bad he's from Rockport Valley. My dad would kill me if I went out with someone who's from that part of town! What were the two of you talking about?"

"Nothing much. He said you looked fat though, so I had to set him straight." *Just a little lie will keep her away from him.*

"What?! He must have had too many drinks. He usually is telling me how hot I am."

The two checked themselves in the full-length mirror one more time. Mia looked at Layla's reflection and then back at her own. *I am hideous.*

"So is my gorgeous best friend accompanying me to after hours?" Layla asked.

Maybe I'll have a chance with Nathaniel if she's not here. "Na, I think I'm going to stay here a little longer."

"Please? I don't want to go without my BFF."

"No, I'm just not feeling it tonight."

"Ug, you are so lame," Layla scoffed as they headed out of the bathroom and back into the bar.

A group was halfway out the door when their roommate Avery yelled, "Hey, you two coming?"

Layla hollered over the music, "I am, but this loser is staying here."

On her way out the door she yelled at Mia, "See you at home! That is if you can avoid the walk of shame for once!"

Mia nervously laughed as everyone in the bar turned to look her way, snickering as they whispered to one another. Her mind flashed back to last spring when one of her sorority sisters posted an unflattering picture on Facebook of Mia walking home the morning after hooking up with a guy she had met that night. She watched out the window as her friends piled into cabs while Layla ran around to the drivers giving them directions to the party. *Why does she have to say stuff like that?! It makes me look like such a skank. Why am I even friends with her?* Mia looked around the bar to see if she could find Nathaniel. Maybe talking to him would get her mind off of Layla and her comments. After doing a lap around the dance floor and still not finding him, she bellied up to the bar and ordered a cocktail.

A couple of hours and a few cosmos later, Mia tried to concentrate on walking in a straight line down the sidewalk that led to her house. She was still frustrated with Layla but thought that maybe she was being too sensitive. *Layla has been my best friend since we were little kids. Sure she can be mean, but she was there for me when I was so depressed I couldn't even get out of bed two years ago.* Mia stumbled a little which interrupted her thought. She realized that she was about to pass Nathanial's apartment. Although her conscience told her she should head straight home to bed, she still was disappointed that she did not have a chance to talk with him because he apparently had left the bar to go to an after-hours party. *Maybe I'll just see what he's up to. There's no harm in that.* She knocked on the door and Nathanial's roommate answered the door. "Hey Griffen is Nathaniel home?"

Surprised to see her, Griffen responded, "Hi Mia. I'm not sure. I just got home. You can go check his room if you want."

Oh my goodness, his bedroom! "Ok, thanks!" Mia headed down the hallway, running her fingers through her hair and popping a mint into her mouth. She lightly knocked on the door. No one answered but she heard the T.V. murmuring inside. "Hey Nath you in here?" she said while turning the doorknob. As soon as she did, she wished she didn't. The room was a flurry as the sheets torpedoed up to cover the bodies on the bed. "Oh my goodness, sorry!" Mia screeched. *He has a girl in here. Run!*

Although she wanted to slam the door, she stood frozen after catching a glimpse of a tattooed Omega that matched the one on her own midriff. Mia's mind drifted back to freshman year when her pledge class headed to Tenacious Ink to have their letters branded on their bodies after receiving bids from Epsilon Omega. The other girls got their tattoos on their ankles, but she and her best friend thought it would be classier to have the letters on their stomachs where they could cover them.

"Mia, GET OUT OF HERE!" Her fond trip down memory lane was interrupted, snapping her back to reality. She looked up and the tattoo was now covered but Layla's face was not.

Sweetening the Sting

Layla slinked out the front door of Nathaniel's apartment, hoping no one would hear her leave. As soon as the door clicked shut behind her, she madly texted Mia, "OMG, that was so awkward! So sorry you had to see that! ☺" *Please God let Mia see the humor in the situation. She's been so stressed out lately about her parents. Please don't let her have one of her usual freak-outs*, Layla thought. She stared at her phone but got no response. *I hope this means she is sleeping and not sitting up waiting to lecture me about my inappropriate behavior.* As she turned the key to the front door of her house, Layla could see a silhouette lying on the couch inside watching T.V. When she walked in, she was relieved to find that it was Avery and not Mia.

"Look who it is coming home at 4 a.m.!" Avery teased.

"Yeah, yeah. I was at—" Layla began.

"Oh I KNOW where you were. Mia came stomping in about an hour and a half ago. She filled me in on your little 'run in,'" Avery said while making air quotes with her fingers.

"She wasn't mad was she? Wait, where is she? In her room sleeping?" Layla whispered.

"Oh no, she came in fuming about how you always steal every guy she likes away from her."

"Wait, she really likes Nathaniel? Not that she really has a chance with him, but she can *have* him. He's fun, but not exactly my type."

"Well, apparently she is in love with him."

"Oh great," Layla said rolling her eyes. "Where did she go? I have to talk to her and try to smooth things over before she refuses to talk to me."

"Why do you even care? Nobody likes her. She's just plain nasty. Why do you think everyone defriends her on Facebook and calls her Green Goddess? She said she had to get out of here because she wasn't sure what she would do, and I quote, 'if I have to see that whore.'"

Whore? She better not have told Avery about Jamie and Dillon. "What else did she say?"

Tentatively, Avery said, "Ah, nothing much."

Sensing Avery was lying, Layla thought, *I knew Mia couldn't keep a secret about what happened with the guys.*

"She just got her backpack and left."

Exhausted, Layla said, "I'm going to bed. I am not going to try to track her down at this time of the morning." On her way to her room she noticed something was missing from the wall in the hallway. *She took down the picture of us in Cancun? Oh boy, this is not going to be pretty.*

Lying in bed thinking about what she was going to say to Mia, Layla decided to text her one more time. "I'm really sorry about Nathaniel. I had no idea how you felt about him." She paused before pushing send. "Let's talk tomorrow. Love you."

Layla woke up and checked her phone immediately. Still no response or call from Mia. *I need a latte before I can deal with her.* She walked around the corner to the Coffehouse.

As soon as she walked in, Carson, Layla and Mia's chemistry lab partner from two semesters ago, shouted "Hey LAY-la, late night last night?!"

Shocked, she turned looking at him confused. *What the...* Without answering she made a beeline toward the barista's counter to avoid his question. *He's just being an idiot right? He couldn't possibly know about what happened last night.*

Not wanting to have to see him on her way out the door, Layla decided to drink her coffee there and waste some time on the Internet. After checking her e-mail and the latest totals for the Sudan awareness fundraiser, she glanced over to see if Carson had left yet. *Darn, why won't that moron leave?* Needing to waste some more time, she logged onto her Facebook account. As she scrolled down her homepage, she saw the typical status updates—pictures of last night's dinner, selfies taken before going out to party, complaints about the score of last night's football game, ridiculous posts about mundane activities. *Who cares? Why do people write—*

Her complaining was interrupted by a status update that slapped her in the face: "Mia Wallace is disgusted by what she has just seen." Carson had commented in response to Mia's post, asking what had disgusted her. Mia's response read, "My slut of a best friend."

Layla's mouth hung open and her eyes began to well. *She didn't! Oh my goodness, how many people have seen this?* She clicked on Mia's profile so that she could look at the list of Mia's Facebook friends. *Oh no, not Jose, my secret crush! And Dr. Rifken!* Layla also noticed that Mia's profile picture was no longer a shot of the two of them at last week's tailgate, but a photo Mia had taken of herself looking sullen. After clicking around on Mia's profile some more, Layla found that Mia had untagged her in all of her pictures and that all of the ones of the two of them had been deleted completely. *I am going to make her pay. Doesn't she know she has messed with the wrong person?* Layla stood up with purpose and headed toward the door.

"Leaving so soon LAY—," Carson began.

Before he could finish Layla pointed her finger at him and said, "Shut. Up."

Cowering, Carson replied with his voice cracking a bit, "I'm s-s-sorry Layla."

As soon as she was out the door, she thought, *Poor Carson. He is just an innocent bystander*. She turned around and went back inside where Carson still had a shocked look on his face. "Look Carson, I'm sorry I snapped at you. I'm just really angry right now."

"I'm sorry for giving you a hard time Layla," he said remorsefully. "And I'm sorry about Mia's status update. I figured she was joking since the two of you are so close."

"Thanks Carson. I have to go see if I can fix this mess."

On her way home Layla's phone incessantly chattered with text message alerts. One from her friend Jasmine read, "Girl, sounds like you had fun last night!!!"

Oh great the gossip queen knows?!

Another one from her sorority president said, "You need to get Mia to remove her Facebook post ASAP."

Oh my gosh, the reputation of the sorority! I've worked so hard for people to see us as the smart girls who are committed to community service, not the ones who are always drunk and sleeping around! I have to make this right!

Layla was on the phone. As she listened she thought to herself, *Be assertive, but don't flip out; be understanding, but don't act like a pushover.* Just as she suspected, Mia's phone went to voicemail. Layla cleared her throat and left a message: "Mia it's me. I wanted to tell you one more time that I am very sorry about Nathaniel. I also wanted you to know that even though I understand that you are hurting, it was totally uncool for you to post what you wrote about me on Facebook. You need to remove what you wrote immediately. I know I can forgive you for what you have done, and I hope you can forgive me. This is the last message I am going to leave. I hope you don't make a stupid decision and end our friendship over this. Goodbye." *Whoops, I was doing so well until that last part. Oh well, at least she knows I am serious.*

Bumbled Bee

Three weeks after Layla had left the message, Mia lay in the dark room of her dad's house where she had been staying. She tried ignoring the sound of him screaming at her brother to do his homework while she listened to what Layla had to say in her message one last time. She then pushed delete. *Who does she think she is? She hopes I "don't make a stupid decision." Man, she is SO stuck up. Whatev. I can't stand her or any of those Omegas anymore.* All of them had taken Layla's side and refused to speak to Mia. She had not been to an Epsilon Omega function since the night of their falling out. Although she had been spending a lot of time in bed sleeping, when she did go out she hung out with a new group of friends who, despite their reputation for skipping class and their propensity for using designer drugs, accepted her for who she was. As she lay alone in the dark, she replayed everything that happened, not only on that night, but also over the course of their friendship. *The time when we were 12 and she teased me about my bubble butt in front of everyone and they then for a year made popping sounds with their lips every time they passed me…In high school when she told Jackson Jones about my crush on our English teacher…Last winter when she invited Avery to her parent's condo in the mountains but not me.* The more she thought, the angrier she got. She picked up her phone thinking, *It's time for me to teach that little backstabber a lesson.*

Bee Keeping?

Layla was sitting at the kitchen table when her mom walked in from the garage, "Oh, hi sweatheart. I didn't know you were coming home today."

"I just needed to get away." Before her mom could ask her what she needed to get away from, Layla's story of what had been going on with Mia flooded out of her mouth. She of course edited this version, saying that Mia had burst in while she was watching T.V. with Nathaniel rather than having sex with him.

When Layla stopped to catch her breath, her mom shook her head and said, "Why are girls so mean? Just yesterday two of those Rockport Valley women drove by in a big old fancy Land Rover. I swear they were laughing and pointing at my Nissan parked in the driveway. And then at work Justine told my boss I took an extra half an hour lunch break. What can I say? Girls will be girls."

"Mom. This is about me," Layla snapped.

"Sorry dear. What are you going to do?"

"I don't know. At first I just wanted to get back at Mia for what she wrote on Facebook about me. But now I am starting to feel sorry for her. I know she has had to go through a lot in her life with her parents constantly fighting and being so demanding of her. Plus, she's got really low self-esteem. She's ruined so many friendships over the years. I never thought ours would be one of them. For now, I just think it's best if I stay away from her."

"I would just hate for your relationship with Mia to be ruined over this, Layla. You've been friends your whole life. Why don't you just try calling her one more time," her mom said picking up Layla's phone that was laying on the table. Mia stared at the phone for a few seconds, and then to her surprise, it rang. Her mom looked at the phone and then said, "Speak of the devil."

For Further Thought and Reflection

1. Socially aggressive communication includes those messages that are damaging to a person's sense of self and/or her relationships with others. Mia and Layla both communicate in ways that are socially aggressive. How is their social aggressiveness both similar and different? Why do you think each of them communicates in the mean ways that she does?
2. Mia and Layla are not the same in regard to their degree of popularity within their social network. What characteristics do you think contribute to their social status? How do you think their social aggressiveness potentially factors into their popularity?
3. Mia compares herself to others inside and outside of her social network. How do these comparisons relate to her social aggressiveness?
4. Mia and Layla respond differently to one another's social aggression both mentally and communicatively. What factors do you think contribute to these different emotional and behavioral responses?
5. Layla's mom suggests that "girls will be girls," a common answer to the question "Why are girls so mean?" Researchers suggest that there are not significant differences between males and females when it comes to perpetrating indirect forms of aggression. Why do you think people perceive females as more socially aggressive than males?

References

Hawley, P. H. (2007). Social dominance in childhood and adolescence: Why social competence and aggression may go hand in hand. In P. H. Hawley, T. D. Little, & P. C. Rodkin (Eds.), *Aggression and adaptation: The bright side to bad behavior* (pp. 1–29). Mahwah, NJ: Lawrence Erlbaum Associates.

Miller-Ott, A. E., & Kelly, L. (2013). Mean girls in college: An analysis of how college women communicatively construct and account for relational aggression. *Women's Studies in Communication, 36*, 330–347.

Willer, E. K. (2011). 'My stomach was upset, like when I eat vegetables': Coping with social aggression via a narrative metaphor intervention. In R. H. Shute, P. T. Slee, R. Murray-Harvey, & K. L. Dix (Eds.), *Mental health and wellbeing: Educational perspectives* (pp. 331–334). Adelaide, Australia: Shannon Research Press.

Willer, E. K. (2012). Drawing light(ning) from the clouds of social aggression: A visual narrative analysis of girls' metaphors. *Qualitative Communication Research, 1*, 347–383.

Willer, E. K., & Cupach, W. R. (2008). When "sugar and spice" turn to "fire and ice": Factors affecting the adverse consequences of relational aggression among adolescent girls. *Communication Studies, 59*, 415–429.

Willer, E. K., & Cupach, W. R. (2011). The *mean*ing of girls' social aggression: Nasty or mastery? In W. R. Cupach & B. H. Spitzberg (Eds.). *The dark side of close relationships—II* (pp. 297–326). New York: Routledge.

Willer, E. K., & Soliz, J. (2010). Face needs, intragroup status, and women's reactions to socially aggressive face threats. *Personal Relationships, 17*, 557–571.

27

College is Just Not the Same: Communicating and Managing Identity on Social Media

Jenna Stephenson Abetz
Amanda Holman

Keywords

transition to college, identity, Facebook, long-distance romantic relationships

It was finally here—college freshman move-in day. Jayda had barely slept in anticipation of the big day ahead. With the uncertainty of what she needed, Jayda decided to air on the side of caution and pack anything in question, evidenced by the plastic bins overflowing with clothes, shoes, and accessories in the back seat. Jayda bounded down the stairs, antsy to get on the road. She stepped outside to find her dad triple checking the bungee cords that secured heaps of clothes, bedding, and school supplies to the car. Just then her boyfriend Max pulled his pickup truck into the driveway and greeted her with a big smile and hug, while her mom was snapping pictures and taking video on her iPhone. "This is Jayda leaving for college," she narrated. "Jayda, how are you feeling, honey?" "Jayda and Max get together for a picture," she requested. Jayda gave her mom a goofy smile and grabbed Max's hand as they both hopped in the car. She pulled out her phone and excitedly updated her Facebook status to *My college adventure is about to begin #nextchapter #superexcited #state.*

Jayda's parents piled into the family car and drove the six hours north to her school. It was the perfect fit for her, not too big, not too small, nestled in the mountains—a beautiful place for a fresh start. While several other students from her high school were also attending State, Jayda was not very interested in sticking close to them. In some ways the coziness and the familiarity of the small town she grew up in comforted her and she knew she would miss the connections she had made here, but Jayda simultaneously felt smothered by this close knit community where everyone knew everyone. Although she would miss Max, she was eager to move on and experience life outside her small town upbringing. Unlike Max, who was a popular and outgoing football player during their high school days, she was more introverted and preferred hanging out with him and her three close friends to having a hundred acquaintances. To her, college was a chance to start over, to grow, explore, make new friends, and figure out who she was away from the familiarity of home. Jayda kept checking the clock on her phone, resisting her childlike urge to ask her parents if they were almost there. Her parents took this opportunity to share stories of their own college experiences, stories that had been told repeatedly throughout her childhood and adolescence. College sweethearts, they told her stories of studying together and eventually bringing one another home to meet each other's families. Jayda's mom often joked that her dad partied a bit too much, using her dad's behavior as a lesson in making responsible choices. Although Jayda was more reserved, she enjoyed hearing about her dad's transgressions—particularly the time he climbed a rockface near his campus as a freshman pledge to spray paint his fraternity letters on the side and the legendary parties he threw with his lacrosse buddies. Just then her phone tweeted, signaling a post from her roommate on Facebook: "Can't wait to meet you soon!" it read. Jayda excitedly responded "Me too!"

Throughout the afternoon, Jayda, Max, and her parents worked steadily at moving her in to her new home. Her mom made Jayda's bed, smoothing out the wrinkles and fluffing the pillows while her dad and Max worked diligently setting up the computer and assembling a bookshelf. She thought to herself, *I'm going to be okay*, but felt a tightness in her throat remembering that she was just hours away from leaving the security of her parents and Max. Jayda and her parents had always been close, although they sometimes bordered on being too involved in her life. They were the kind of parents who pinned her childhood drawings on the refrigerator and adorned their cars with "proud parents of a Cambridge Middle School Honor Student." When it came to Max, she had secretly hoped he would also attend State, but ever since they started dating during their sophomore year of high school she knew his dream was to take over his family farm and that meant staying in their small town. Watching him assemble the bookshelf she still couldn't believe that over two years ago Max asked her on a date. They were so different. He loved the outdoors, hosting big parties at his parents' lake cabin, and probably was the most popular guy in their school. Jayda on the other hand liked to keep a low profile and spent most of her time going to art galleries with her three best friends or at Max's farm horseback riding. Even their families were different. Being an only child, Jayda's parents always referred to their family as the "three amigos." Her parents' romantic history began in college and they always reflected on their college days as some of the best times of both their lives. Max's family was big in comparison, with his parents and five younger siblings. His parents met in high school, his dad took over the family farm at age 19, married his mom, and started their happy family. Jayda loved his family and knew she would miss seeing them too. As excited as she was for a new adventure, it hit her in that moment that soon she would be all on her own in a new place—without three of the people she loved the most.

That first night, Jayda's head was spinning from meeting so many new people and introducing herself so many times. Her introverted self was over-stimulated from all the interaction and craved some alone time and a good night's sleep. She logged onto Facebook to unwind for a few minutes. The first post in her newsfeed was her mom's recent announcement "Dropped Jayda off at college…missing our baby girl" complete with a picture of Jayda standing outside her dorm. While Jayda was slightly embarrassed at her mom's post, she also loved hearing from her and decided to send her a private message so others would not see. "I really miss you too and I'll call you soon" she typed as she crawled into her bed, hugging her childhood bear that smelled of her old room. Just then Max messaged her:

Max: Got back home alright—riding with your parents sure was fun lol, missing you—how was your first day?

Jayda: Overwhelming, so many new people, I got lost finding the bookstore, but I am excited to explore campus tomorrow and get my bearings.

Max: Well I'm just here hanging out with some of the old crew and wishing you were here. We're planning to make a trip down to visit you after harvest is over.

Jayda: That would be so great!

Max: Love you.

Jayda: Love you more!

The next weeks were filled with classes, dorm activities, new clubs, and meeting new people. Surprisingly, Jayda loved it. She found herself making an effort to be outgoing and take others up on offers to get together—she played Ultimate Frisbee with some guys from the second floor, joined a poetry club, and began taking kick-boxing classes at the Rec Center with her suitemates. After Bio class, she returned to her dorm to find her lab partner, Copeland, and three guys from her poetry club had sent her friend requests on Facebook. Jayda smiled, proud of all the connections she was making so quickly. It typically took her a long time to develop friendships and the sense of belonging she already felt at State gave her a sense of instant community. She posted a new status: "Having a great time at State" and updated her profile picture to one with her suitemates posing on the Quad—a picture previously occupied by Football and homecoming dance pictures with Max for the past two years. A few minutes later, a message popped up from Max.

Max: I see how it is...1 month away at school and you've replaced me :-)

Jayda wasn't sure if Max was actually upset or was just teasing her the way he liked to, but she felt the need to respond.

Jayda: haha, you know I would never replace you, let's talk tonight, love you!

Max: Love you too :-)

October

After less than half a semester, Jayda had a group of good friends, part of an artsy and musical crowd, who had a shared interest in slam poetry and alternative music and spent Friday nights hanging out and throwing small parties. She had developed a good friendship with her lab partner, Copeland, and they often spent time hanging out and studying together. When he caught a cold she took notes for him and e-mailed them to him after class. "Thanks for being so awesome, you're the best!" he wrote on her Facebook wall. Jayda smiled and replied "Never would've survived the quiz on Biomes without you!"

Later that evening, Max called to catch up. "I've really been missing you, Jayda" he admitted. "Me too, Thanksgiving will be here before we know it" she responded. "Hey, who is this Copeland guy?" he asked casually, but with a hint of suspicion. "Oh he's just a friend, why?" Jayda asked, wondering how Max even knew about Copeland given that she had not mentioned him. "I just saw he wrote on your Facebook wall and you've never talked about him." Jayda felt a bit defensive, "Am I not allowed to have friends you don't know about? I just took notes for him in class this morning since he was sick and missed class." Max quickly responded "Look I wasn't trying to start something with you, he just seemed a little flirty, that's all." "He's not flirting, we are friends, I was being a good friend" said Jayda, adding "Look I gotta go," in an attempt to stop this conversation. "Fine, I'll talk to you tomorrow" Max said with a sense of defeat. Jayda flopped onto her bed and sighed in frustration. She knew Max was having a hard time with the distance between them but she made a conscious effort to message him and text him most nights to let him know she was thinking about him. But he had to understand that she was just trying to adapt to her life at college and she was still trying to figure things out. What did Max expect from her? Did he just want her to go away and not make any new friends and have life remain exactly the same way it was when they used to put notes in each other's lockers and goof around in the hallway between classes? Things were going to change and he needed to understand that. He was always such a confident person and initially seemed to be adjusting well to the fact that she was going away, but his new questioning surprised her. She wished Max would realize that she was going to make friends and that did not change how she felt about him.

The next week when Copeland tagged a picture of the two of them goofing around at her suitemate's Halloween party, Jayda quickly went to her computer to delete it in order to avoid a discussion about it with Max. *We are just friends, but pictures can really give the wrong idea,* she thought. Before she could delete the picture, her phone buzzed with a text from her mom: "you look like you're having fun in your pictures, but remember why you are in college—make smart choices." Jayda rolled her eyes, realizing the top of her beer was evident in the picture. She sighed, internally conflicted, *this is not how college used to be,* she thought to herself. She remembered all the stories her parents would tell of their college days and how they could make mistakes and get away with things because their choices did not unfold in real time to their families back home.

Winter Break

Nearing the end of her first semester, Jayda couldn't believe she'd been away from home for nearly four months. The bonds she was forming with her new friends already made college feel like a new sort of home, but she was still so eager to see Max, eat her mom's cooking, and sleep in her old bed. Things seemed different with Max and even though it had only been one semester, there was a tension brought on by the time spent apart. She hurriedly packed up some winter clothes, cautious not to keep the sophomores giving her a ride waiting. The drive home was dragging and Jayda kept fidgeting in her seat, passing the time by making casual chit-chat with the girls. She gave them directions to Max's house and bought herself some alone time with him by telling her parents a final exam had run late and she'd be home after dinner.

Jayda rang Max's doorbell and bounced into his arms when he answered. "I thought we'd never get here" Jayda sighed, exasperated. "Well I'm so happy you're actually here—do you want to stay in or go get some pizza or what?" Max said as he hugged her tight, Jayda smiled and pulled out a bag of popcorn, Twizzlers, and the DVD "Friday the 13th". While they were both very different people, one thing the couple initially bonded over was the thrill of horror movies. Max smiled back, "I guess some things don't change" he laughed. Sitting on the couch together, Jayda thought about how much she loved being away at State but missed this closeness with Max; missed what was happening right here in this moment—all the texting, Facebook, and phone calls couldn't replace this.

After the movie, the tensions she had been feeling before subsided and she and Max felt like their old selves again. Maybe that's all they needed, just some alone time to be together and forget about the distance that separated them. Out of the blue, Max said, "I knew that this would be hard, but I feel like we talk less and less about our future together." Jayda responded, "I'm just trying to figure out who I am now that I'm away at school and meeting some great new people, but that doesn't change who we are." "Well, it just feels different now; you have a whole new group of friends that I don't even know besides what I see on Facebook." Jayda sighed, wanting to comfort Max at the same time feeling uncertain of how to reassure him. "Well how about if I try to make a better effort to fill you in and maybe you can come visit more often now that it's winter and you won't be as busy with the farm stuff. You'll have more time to make trips to come see me the next few months." Just then Jayda's phone buzzed, her parents eager to see her and wondering why her trip was taking so long. "Look, I gotta get home, my parents are dying to see me and I told them I'd be home an hour ago, can you drive me?" Max held Jayda's hand in the car, just happy to be with her but knowing the holiday break would be short. He felt like he had so much more he wanted to say to her but also wanted to just enjoy the time he had with her.

The next day while out with her parents, Jayda ran into three classmates from high school. "Oh hey Jayda, how are you? How's college?" one of the girls responded. "Good" Jayda responded, struck by the awkwardness of interacting with people she hadn't seen in months and was never really close friends with. Old connections already mattered less than she thought they would, but Jayda still wanted her classmates to see her as someone who had a great life away at college. "Seems like you're having a good time without Max" the other responded with a bit of a snarky tone. Caught off guard, Jayda felt the need to defend her relationship but was at a loss for words. "I actually ran into him the other weekend at Christy's party." Jayda tried to cover up her surprise, "Oh right, yeah he said it was fun" and then said she had to go. *This doesn't make sense,* Jayda thought to herself. *Max had posted on Facebook that he was working on the night of Christy's party.*

It had almost been three weeks and Jayda was anxious to get back to her college life. The walls of her small town felt like they were steadily closing in on her so she decided to pack up and head back to State a day early since Max had agreed to drive her. "Alright, well I wish you could've stayed longer" her mom replied longingly to Jayda's assertion that she needed to get things together for the start of the next semester. Always studious and organized, Jayda knew her mom would buy that argument even though the real reason she wanted to get back was to see her friends. Packing up her stuff while Max was making the drive over, she saw that he had texted her. "I'm almost there, do you mind if we stop by my buddy's party first? A bunch of the old crew are getting together tonight." She would have preferred if Max had just wanted to make the drive and spend some time with her new friends, but she agreed and responded "That's fine as long as we're not there too long."

After making an hour of small talk with people who were mainly Max's friends in high school, Jayda was getting anxious to get on the road and feeling out of place. Jayda just wanted to start the drive with Max, but he kept asking for a few more minutes. Sensing her frustration, he asked "Don't you want to be here? These are your friends too" "It's just that I want us to go so you can meet some of my friends before you head back in the morning." "I wouldn't fit in with them, from what I've seen of them, they're not people I really want to hang out with!" he blurted. "What is that supposed to mean?" Jayda asked, continuing "I don't want to be spending any more time hanging out with these people who seem like they are still stuck in high school." Looking offended, Max countered "Is that what you think of me—that I'm some loser who never moved on from high school?" Jayda looked away. "Fine let's just go," Max said, "maybe let me know if you're going to change into another completely different person next time you come home!" The six hour drive to State was filled with silence, Jayda wanted to say something, just couldn't find the right words, so she stared numbly out the passenger side window, wondering what was going to become of their relationship.

For Further Thought and Reflection

1. How do the educational and familial backgrounds of Jayda and Max inform and shape their understandings of love, commitment, and relationships?
2. In this case, Jayda noted the ways social media, Facebook in particular, helped her transition to college, but also brought its own unique challenges. Drawing on your own experience and observation, can you point out the ways in which communication on social media brings both relational benefits and challenges to students transitioning to college?
3. Facebook and other social networking sites have changed the way we communicate in long-distance romantic relationships. How do you see Facebook helping and hindering Jayda and Max's long-distance relationship. How, if at all, do Facebook and other social media complicate romantic relationships?
4. Write the end of this story. Is a future relationship possible between Jayda and Max? How might they communicate to rebuild their relationship?

References

Maguire, K. C., & Kinney, T. A. (2010). When distance is problematic: Communication, coping, and relational satisfaction in female college students' long-distance dating relationships. *Journal of Applied Communication Research, 38*, 27–46.

Pempek, T. A., Yermolayeva, Y. A., & Calvert, S. L. (2009). College students' social networking experiences on Facebook. *Journal of Applied Developmental Psychology, 30,* 227–338.

Sahlstein, E. M. (2004). Relating at a distance: Negotiating being together and being apart in long-distance relationships. *Journal of Social and Personal Relationships, 21*, 689–710.

Stafford, L., & Merolla, A. J. (2007). Idealization, reunions, and stability in long-distance dating relationships. *Journal of Social and Personal Relationships*, *24*, 37–54.

Stephenson Abetz, J., & Holman, A. (2012). Home is where the heart is: Facebook and the negotiation of "old" and "new" during the transition to college. *Western Journal of Communication, 76,* 175–193.

28

Who's the Parent Now? When Adult Children Become Caregivers for Parents

Julia T. Wood

Keywords

parent-child relationships, gender roles, emotional conflicts, venting, honesty, sandwich generation

When I was nine years old, I was very sick with mumps. I was miserable—achy, uncomfortable, and feverish. I couldn't speak without strain and even swallowing was painful. I remember my mother sitting with me for hours on end. She rubbed my forehead with a cool washcloth to ease the fever and she stroked my swollen neck gently. Although I didn't realize it then, mother was neglecting other things she'd planned to do in order to care for me. Perhaps she resented me (or my illness) for intruding on her plans; perhaps she felt frustrated at having to nurse me; perhaps she was worried about what she wasn't getting done while she sat by my bedside. If so, she didn't show those feelings. I never sensed any resentment as she sat patiently with me.

The scene I've just described was replayed 32 years later, only the second time, our roles were reversed: I was the one sitting by my mother's bedside, trying to ease her pain from a terminal disease that would too soon take her from me. As I cared for her, I felt sadness and deep love for this woman who had given birth to me and nurtured me all of my life. Yet, I also felt resentment, frustration, and anger. I resented her needs because they interfered with my family plans and my professional responsibilities. I was frustrated by the unpredictability that her illness injected into my world. And I was angry at her for not acting like my mother—not taking care of me, putting her needs aside for mine—and for reversing our roles so that I was now acting like a mother to her and she was acting like a needy child.

Most of all, I felt guilty—horribly, wrenchingly guilty for feeling resentment, frustration, and anger toward my mother. I despised myself for not lovingly giving her unbounded time and comfort. Why couldn't I be as selfless for her as she had been for me?

During the process of taking my mother through her final passage and recovering from her death, I learned many things about what was happening in me and between us. I learned that the mixture of feelings I had—love, sadness, resentment, frustration, anger, guilt—were typical of many children who become caregivers for sick or dying parents. I learned that what I felt didn't make me a horrible person, and that my feelings were normal. The case that follows illuminates what I discovered about relationships in which children assume the role of parents with their own parents. The case, however, is about far more than my personal experience. It reflects insights from counselors and research on general patterns in relationships in which adult children care for parents.

* * * * *

"It's not that I don't want to take care of her; it's that I don't have the time," Kate says in an effort to explain to her therapist what she is feeling about her mother who moved into her home two months ago. "I mean, I still have my job and my marriage to Mark and our two children—those responsibilities haven't gone away just because mother is living with us and needs constant care."

"Are you saying that if you had more time, you'd be happy to take care of your mother?" Sylvia asks.

Kate nods. "Yes, of course. I'm not a selfish person."

"Is that what it feels like to you—that it would be selfish not to want to care for your mother?" Sylvia asks. Sylvia anticipates that Kate will equate not wanting to do everything for her mother with being selfish. The role of women in Western culture is so firmly tied to caring for others that it's hard for any woman not to feel she's selfish if she doesn't want to do that.

"Of course. I'd want to do it if I had the time." Kate feels compelled to answer this way, but part of her is relieved that her job and family limit how much she can do for her mother. She doesn't mind fixing meals and doing laundry or talking with her mother. Other parts of caregiving, however, do bother her. She dreads helping her mother in the bathroom and despises cleaning up when her mother loses control in her bed. That disgusts her, but she berates herself for these feelings. They seem so heartless.

"Do you think your mother never resented taking care of you?"

"Of course not. She was always there for me."

"So maybe she did what you needed even if she resented it," Sylvia suggests. "Does that mean she was somehow less caring or less loving?" Kate ponders the question. She's a mother now, too, and there are times when she is frustrated by her children's needs, or resents their demands on her time and energy. She tries to hide those feelings, but sometimes she does resent her children, just as she sometimes resents her mother.

"If love is doing only what we want to do, it's not very admirable," Sylvia says. "Perhaps a more mature, authentic kind of love is doing what others need even when we don't enjoy it."

"Maybe," Kate allows. "But it seems dishonest to act like you don't mind doing something when really you do."

"Okay, let's play that out. What would be the point of telling your mother you don't like doing some things—like changing her bed when she's soiled it? Would that do you any good? Would it do her any good?"

"No," Kate admits. "But sometimes I just feel the need to express my anger or frustration about all of her needs and how they fall on me."

"Nothing wrong with that," Sylvia replies. "And this is a safe place for it. You need somewhere where you can vent your anger and frustration without hurting your mother and without feeling guilty yourself. You can do that with me; you can do it with your friends; you can do it with Mark. And you should."

"It just seems so selfish to feel anything but a desire to help her," Kate says. "I feel like a terrible person if I get angry when I have to rearrange my schedule for her or when I get disgusted about cleaning up after her. Those aren't nice feelings."

"So who says all of our feelings are nice?" Sylvia asks. "Does it mean you don't do what she needs? Of course not. You do it, in spite of anger or disgust. That's real love, not the storybook kind. Give yourself permission to have those feelings and express them in safe places where they won't hurt your mother."

"What I'd really like to do is express that anger to Sandy," Kate mutters. Her brother, Sandy, lives in the same town, but he never invited their mom to move in with him. Actually, it would have been easier for him because his and Alice's children are older—both in high school—and their home is larger. But when she and Sandy talked about the fact that their mom couldn't take care of herself anymore, both of them had just assumed Kate and Mark would make room in their home. When Kate had suggested tentatively that maybe their mom could live 6 months of the year with each of them, Sandy had dismissed the suggestion, saying it was better for their mom to live in one place.

Since their mom moved in with Kate's family, Sandy has stopped by once a week for a short visit, and he sometimes calls between visits. What infuriates Kate most is how much her mother appreciates the little that Sandy does for her. Just last week he stopped by for only 30 minutes. After he left, Kate remembers her mother said, "It's so good of Sandy to make time out to visit me. I know how busy he is." Kate had thought "He gets praised for giving her thirty lousy minutes, and I spend hours every day taking care of her!"

Sylvia nods. Kate's situation is like that of many adult women who are caring for parents. Often there are brothers, but most don't volunteer for caregiving. Sometimes they help with expenses, but they seldom take much responsibility for the day-to-day nursing and personal care. Almost always, that responsibility falls on daughters or daughters-in-law whose husbands don't provide hands-on care for their own parents.

Sylvia reflects on the lack of change in gender roles regarding caring for others. Although the feminist movement enlarged women's political, economic, and professional opportunities, it hasn't transformed the traditional expectation that women are the primary caregivers of young children and anyone else who needs care. Both women and men continue to expect that women will do it. This sometimes creates extraordinary pressures on women in what's been dubbed the "sandwich generation"—those people who are caring for children at the same time they are caring for parents and parents-in-law. When those people are also engaged in full-time work outside of the home, the strains can be overwhelming. When more women were full-time homemakers and mothers, it was less of a strain for them to take care of relatives. Then too, Sylvia realizes, life-spans have expanded significantly, so more people are living to ages when they require assistance.

The problem is not just men who don't assume equal responsibility for caring for parents and in-laws. It's equally women who expect so much of themselves. Kate is like many of her clients, who are stretched to the breaking point to meet their responsibilities to jobs, children, husbands, and elderly parents. And still they often feel guilty for feeling strained, angry, or resentful. Sylvia wishes she could do more to help her women clients challenge the internalized feelings that they not only should care for others, but should always feel happy to do so.

"We can't control what Sandy does—or doesn't do, so let's focus on what we can control," Sylvia redirects the conversation. "Tell me more about what your resentment and frustration and anger are like?"

"Well, I just feel like I can't do it all and like I shouldn't have to," Kate begins. "It's like I have to fix all of her special meals and keep track of her medications and make sure she gets to her doctors' appointments, and everything, and nobody is taking care of me."

That's what Sylvia had been waiting to hear. Sylvia imagined Kate probably felt some sense of betrayal that her mother is no longer mothering her.

"So, not only do you have the responsibility of taking care of someone who is needy, but that person is the very one who is supposed to take care of you," Sylvia says.

"I miss my mother so much. She always took care of me, even after I was grown up and married. She was the one who would always support me and make time for me and help me."

"And now she can't do that for you and you have to do it for her? Is that what it feels like?"

Kate nods, dabbing her eyes with a tissue. "I feel like I don't have a mother anymore. It's like she's another of my children, and that feels so strange."

Sylvia nods. One of the most difficult issues when children become caregivers for parents is role reversal. Suddenly, they have to watch and protect the parents and oversee daily schedules in the home.

"Sometimes I feel like I've *become* my mother," Kate continues. "I take her dinner to her room and start talking to her, but it's her voice—not mine—that comes out. I sound like she did when she was mothering me—her words, her tones, even her gestures and facial expressions."

"That makes sense. She's your primary role model for caring. When you step into that role, it's natural for you to act like she did," Sylvia says. "Do you also hear your mother in yourself when you're mothering your children?"

"Yes, but they are children and I am *their* mother. I'm not my mother's mother; I just act like it, and she acts like my child." Kate thinks about what happened this morning before she left for her session with Sylvia. After helping her mother bathe, Kate explained that she would be gone until about 5 or 6 PM that evening. Her mother had asked if she could have tomato soup and a grilled cheese sandwich for lunch. Kate cringed, thinking about that interaction. Why would a 72-year-old-woman have to ask permission to have what she wants for lunch? Yet, the incident wasn't unusual. Her mother often asked permission for the most ordinary things as if Kate were the parent who controlled her activities.

"That's the hard part. Being with her but not having her be the person she's always been for you," Sylvia empathizes. She knows that Kate is experiencing both the loss of her mother as a mother and of her own role as her mother's child. It's a double whammy. "And it's really hard to become that person for her, to be her mother when you so much still want her to be yours."

"It really is," Kate agrees. "After more than 40 years with our roles one way, it's so hard to deal with turning them upside down. I don't want to lose our mother-daughter relationship just because she needs a lot of help now."

"Okay, that's a good thought. Let's build on it by talking about ways you might let go of the mothering role with her," Sylvia says. "Can you define the parts of your relationship with your mother in which you feel most pushed into the mother role?" Working together over the next two sessions, Kate and Sylvia figured out that helping her mother with personal care (baths, shampoos, changing clothes) made Kate feel like her mother's mother. Fixing meals didn't make her uncomfortable because Kate or Mark fixed meals for the family anyhow. In conversation with Sylvia, Kate also realized there were benefits to having her mother live with them. She liked talking with her mom about daily life, and enjoyed seeing her mother interact with the children.

Following her discussions with Sylvia, Kate talked to Mark and then the two of them talked with her mom and Sandy and Alice. Together, they decided that they could afford to hire a nurse's aide who would come to the house for three hours each day to provide personal assistance to her mother. This relieved Kate of some of the responsibilities she disliked and allowed her to spend more time with her mother in ways that both of them enjoyed.

There are still days when Kate feels some resentment or anger. Sometimes the aide has to cancel and Kate is back to juggling her schedule and providing personal care to her mother. Sometimes she still resents Sandy. And there are moments when she deeply misses having a mother who puts aside everything for her. Even so, letting go of the bulk of mothering tasks has reduced the strain on Kate and revived parts of their mother-daughter relationship.

For Further Thought and Reflection

1. This case raises questions about whether honesty is always advisable when communicating in personal relationships. Do you think Kate should tell her mother she sometimes feels resentful, frustrated, disgusted, or angry? Is not telling her mother about these feelings dishonest?
2. This case points out that women continue to assume primary responsibility for caregiving. What aspects of socialization and education might be used to foster more balance in caregiving in our society?
3. In Kate's situation, it was possible to hire professional help to reduce the burdens on Kate and to diminish Kate's need to be a mother to her mother. How might Kate have coped if hiring help had not been feasible?
4. Sylvia suggests that an admirable, mature love is based on more than doing what one feels like for another person. To what extent do you think "real" love includes meeting obligations even if doing so creates resentment and frustration?

References

Gleckman, A. (2009). *Caring for our parents.* New York: St. Martin's Press.

Gross, J. (2012). *A bittersweet season: Caring for our aging parents—and ourselves.* New York: Vintage.

Wickert, K., Dresden, D., & Rumrill, P. (2013). *The sandwich generation's guide to elder care.* New York: Demos Health.

Wood, J. T. (1994). *Who cares?: Women, care and culture.* Carbondale, IL: Southern Illinois University Press.

29

"I'm Sorry for Your Loss": Communicating with Those Who Are Bereaved

Paige W. Toller

Keywords

self-disclosure, grief, social support, dialectical tensions

It was a beautiful spring day in May. The tulips and daffodils were blooming in brilliant shades of yellow, pink, and red. The sky was robin's egg blue and full of fluffy, white clouds. For 20-year-old Libby Jamieson, it may as well have been a cold December day. Libby was standing in Oak Park Cemetery, trying to pay attention to their pastor's reading of the 23rd Psalm. Her mother's casket was only a few feet away, draped in dozens of red roses, her mom's favorite flower. Libby's dad stood next to her, tightly gripping her hand in his. To Libby, her father's face looked as numb and cold as she felt on the inside. The pastor finished reading and friends and family lined up to offer their condolences to Libby and her father. People began shaking her hand or hugging her, whispering phrases such as "at least she's not in pain anymore" or "I'm so sorry for your loss." Libby tried to say "thank you" but her throat was dry and her lips seemed to be glued shut. She just silently nodded her head as if to agree with what people were saying. Next to her, she noticed that her dad struggled to talk and was nodding his head as well.

Toward the end of the line, Susan Lawrence stood and waited to hug Libby, her best friend for more than 15 years. Susan and Libby had known each other since they were in the same kindergarten classroom. Through games of hop-scotch, braces, first crushes, homecoming dances, and the college application process, Susan and Libby had been inseparable friends. Over the years Susan had grown close to Libby's parents as well. Libby's mom, Marianne, had spent many afternoons baking cookies and giggling with the two girls about the cute neighbor boy down the street. Marianne had always been there to cheer them on during their volleyball games or yell right along with them at varsity football games. Six months ago while on break from college, Susan had been at Libby's house, helping Libby and her mom bake Christmas cookies when the doctor called and told Marianne she had late stage ovarian cancer. For the rest of that afternoon, Susan, Libby, and Marianne sat in the living room, holding each other and crying. From that day until the end of winter break, when Susan was not with her own family, she was at the Jamieson home.

Although Marianne's type of cancer was aggressive, she told Libby and Susan that she was going to "beat this thing" and for nearly six months, she courageously went through chemo and radiation. Her shiny black hair fell out in large clumps and her bright, green eyes began to sink back into her face. Her petite frame became even smaller as she shrunk down to barely 95 pounds. To Susan, Marianne's bubbly personality seemed to wither as well. Susan also watched her friend Libby change. Normally adventurous and out-going, Libby became quiet most of the time. Instead of going back to the university for the spring semester, Libby moved back home and spent every minute by her mother's side. Susan visited the Jamieson house as much as she could, but she was also a college student and her school was nearly two hours away. At least every other day Susan texted Libby to see how things were going. Sometimes Libby responded within a few minutes; other times Susan's texts went unanswered.

The line of people had shrunken and Susan finally reached Libby. Susan was trying to think of something to say to Libby but nothing came to mind. Susan swallowed the huge lump in her throat and managed to croak out "Hey, Libbers." Libby's eyes began to spill over, "Hey Susie-Q. I'm glad you're here." They both stood there for a few seconds before Susan opened her arms and reached out to Libby. Grabbing on to each other, they held one another and cried for what seemed like a very long time. Noticing that there were others waiting to speak to Libby, Susan mouthed "call me" and began to walk away. Libby nodded and began shaking the next person's hand.

Two months had passed and summer was in full swing. Except for a few texts, Susan and Libby had not been in contact since the funeral. The Fourth of July was in two days and Susan was looking forward to a weekend of cooking out and boating. She had recently reconnected with Jeff, a former high-school sweetheart, and was excited that they were going to spend the weekend together. Jeff and Susan had dated for two years in high school before Jeff graduated and went away to college. Although Susan had dated other guys while in college, none of them seemed to measure up to Jeff. Apparently Jeff felt the same way about her and had contacted her via Facebook a few months ago. Things were going well between them.

As excited as she was about the upcoming weekend, Susan was concerned about Libby. She had stopped over at the Jamieson house a few days ago to see if Libby wanted to go boating with them during the holiday weekend. She thought maybe it would do Libby some good to get out of the house and hang out with people her own age. It seemed that Libby and her dad were attached at the hip these days. Libby rarely went anywhere and, if she did, her dad was usually with her. Jeff was bringing Mark, his college roommate, home with him for the weekend and Susan thought Mark and Libby might hit it off. As she walked up the sidewalk, Susan noticed Mr. Jamieson mowing the yard. Always thin, he had lost even more weight. Susan wasn't sure but she thought his hair even looked a little grayer. Susan waved to him and he stared at her for a few seconds before finally waving back. "That's odd. Doesn't he recognize me?" thought Susan, as she rang the doorbell.

Libby opened the door to Susan's smiling face. "Hey Libbers, what's up?" Susan cheerfully chirped. "Not much" Libby said dully. "Come on in. I'm just doing some laundry." "Lib, I can't believe you have any laundry to do. Every time I see you you're in the same pair of pajama pants!" Susan joked. Libby smiled weakly as Susan continued talking, "Anyway girlfriend, you'd better make sure your cutest tank top and shorts are clean, because I know someone who's dying to meet you. His name is Mark Walters and he is super cute. He's a communication studies major at Eastern Tech and is on the rugby team. Oh, did I mention that he's Jeff's roommate and that he's super cute? Lib, are you listening? Hey Lib, I'm talking to you!" Libby was staring off into the corner, something Susan had noticed her doing a lot the last two months.

"Huh? What? Oh yeah, Suz, um, I don't know if I'll be able to go with you or not. I'm not sure what Dad's got going on this weekend." Trying to hide her disappointment, Susan said softly, "Well, why don't you come out with us for a little while." "Okay Suz. Well, I'll think about it. I gotta go; I need to go put stuff in the dryer. Guess I'll see ya around." "Uh, yeah, sure Lib. See you around. I'll let myself out." As Libby went into the laundry room, Susan walked toward the front door. What was up with Libby? Sure, Susan realized that her mom had died just two months ago and both Libby and her dad were really missing Marianne, but it wasn't like Libby to not be excited about going boating. Libby was a fantastic water skier and usually was out on the water as much as possible in the summer. Libby just wasn't the same person anymore and Susan wished she knew how to get her old friend back.

Tossing clothes into the dryer, Libby was angry. Her best friend Susan had just left after nagging her to go on a boating date with some new guy this coming weekend. Dating! As if Libby cared about dating these days! Frankly, Libby didn't care much about anything except spending time with her dad and taking care of him. "I can't believe Susan thought I'd want to go boating. Gosh, my mom's only been gone two months and she acts all upset because I don't want to drop everything and go hang out with her and some guy I don't even know. Boy, she's got a lot of nerve!"

Libby continued to angrily hang clothes in her parents' closet until she ran across one of her mom's old bathrobes hanging toward the back. As her eyes began to swell with tears, Libby lifted the nightgown to her nose, hoping that it might still smell of her mom's favorite lotion. She breathed in deeply, and rubbed the soft cotton against her cheek. Tears began to spill onto the nightgown and that all too familiar ache began to spread through Libby's chest. God, if she could only hug her mom one more time. If she could only sit and talk with her mom just once more. She would give anything just to have one more minute with her mom; one more second even.

In some ways, her mom was still with her as Libby felt her presence everywhere. Everything at home somehow reminded Libby of her mom. Her mom's garden in the backyard was blooming with the perennials her mom planted years ago. Every time she cleaned up the kitchen, Libby thought of the many hours she and her mom spent cooking and laughing. Even going through the Starbucks drive-thru made Libby think of her mom and how much her mom loved coffee. Although Libby was glad she could still feel her mom's presence, sometimes it made that ache inside hurt even more.

Many times Libby would talk to her mom throughout the day. As she cleaned the bathrooms or cooked dinner, Libby would often say out loud, "Well Mom, looks like the china cabinet needs a good dusting" or "What do you think Dad wants for dinner tonight?" While her dad was at work, she would sometimes go into their bedroom and sit in her mom's favorite rocking chair. She would grab one of her mom's favorite sweaters, hold it close, and sob and sob until she had no tears left. Even though she and her father had cleaned out her mother's closet and taken things to Goodwill, there were a few items that were just too hard for her or her dad to donate. Libby was so glad she had kept one of her mom's old sweaters. It was almost like her mom was still there. Almost . . . but not quite.

Libby wished she could talk to Susan about her mom and some of the things she was feeling, but she didn't think Susan would understand. Susan would probably think something was wrong with her if she knew that Libby talked out loud to her dead mother. Heck, sometimes Libby thought it *was* crazy to talk to her mom. Sane people didn't talk to dead people, or cry into their old sweaters, right? All Libby knew was that it made her feel better to talk to her mom throughout the day and hug her things and right now she was willing to do anything to make the pain a little less.

Susan had a great time boating with Mark and Jeff, although it wasn't the same without Libby there. In the weeks that followed, Susan texted Libby every now and then, but she didn't really know what to talk to Libby about. About a month after they went boating, Susan ran into Libby at the grocery store. As they greeted each other Susan couldn't help but notice how awkward it was between them. "Hey Lib, how's it going? What are you up to these days?"

"Oh hey Suz, not much. How are things going with you?"

"Oh, pretty good I guess. I've been working at Forever 21 this summer. Great employee discount you know."

"Oh yeah, I bet so. Are you still dating, uh, um, gosh, sorry. I forgot his name."

"Jeff. Yeah, we're still together. He's a really great guy."

"I bet so. Well, it was good to see you."

"Yeah, Lib, it was good to see you too. Well, gotta run. See ya around."

As she walked toward the checkout, Susan couldn't believe that she'd just had a conversation with her best friend. It was like talking to a stranger. Libby used to be so bubbly and talkative, but now she was so quiet and withdrawn that it made Susan uncomfortable to be around her. Susan just didn't know what to say to her. What do you say to someone who seems completely lost and heartbroken? How do you talk to someone that you don't even know anymore? Would it be okay to bring up Libby's mom in front of her? Susan really missed Libby and wanted to spend time with her again but she didn't know how to connect with Libby anymore.

At the other end of the store, Libby was also upset about their conversation, but she was glad that Susan had at least spoken to her. Over the past few weeks, Libby felt like people she knew were avoiding her. Just last Friday one her high school classmates had seen her at the mall and acted as if she didn't know her. At least Libby thought that's what happened. Maybe the girl really hadn't recognized her, although they had been on the cheerleading squad together for two years. Good grief, what was wrong with her? Was she becoming paranoid?

Anyway, what was the deal with Susan? Before her mom had died Susan was incredibly supportive and was around a lot. Now that her mom was gone, it seemed that Susan rarely stopped over and was always nervous around her. Of all of the people that she thought would have been there for her, Susan was at top of her list. Now it seemed like Susan didn't even know her anymore. Jeez, not only had she lost her mom, but now she'd lost her best friend too. Libby wished she could talk to Susan about their friendship, but frankly, she didn't have the energy to do so. Most of the time, it was major effort to even get out of bed and get dressed. It had only been a few months since her mom died, but it felt like an eternity. Libby wished someone would talk with her about her mom, or at least mention her name. Libby felt like others wanted her to just forget about her mom. Just because a loved one dies, that doesn't mean you have to forget they existed, right? Or maybe you were supposed to forget them? Libby just didn't know.

The rest of the summer passed and it was time to start the fall semester. Susan had already returned to her college two hours away, while Libby started classes again at the local junior college while continuing to live at home. As Susan was finalizing her schedule for the fall semester she noticed a death and dying class still had a few seats. On a whim, Susan enrolled in the course. She wasn't sure why she was taking this course, but she thought maybe it might help her understand Libby better. She hadn't seen Libby since that day in the grocery store over a month ago. She really missed hanging out with Libby and wanted to find some way to reconnect with her, if that was possible.

The first two weeks of class went smoothly and so far Susan really liked her death and dying class. The course was being taught by Dr. Harrison, a clinical psychologist with a background in grief counseling. A warm, soft-spoken woman in her early 40s, Dr. Harrison struck Susan as compassionate and knowledgeable. After class on Thursday Susan approached Dr. Harrison to see if she could talk with her about Libby. Susan figured if anyone could understand what was going on with her best friend, it would be Dr. Harrison. "Dr. Harrison, I was wondering if you had a few minutes to talk with me?" "Oh yes. Susan, right? I would be happy to talk. What's on your mind?"

Susan spent the next hour in Dr. Harrison's office, talking about Libby's mom and how Libby was acting since her mother's death. She told Dr. Harrison how much she missed the "old Libby" and how awkward she felt around her. Dr. Harrison was very understanding and helped Susan better understand what the grieving process is like. Apparently, losing someone you are very close to, like a parent, really impacts who you are as a person. According to Dr. Harrison, most people who go through a huge loss become different people and part of grieving for them is to create a "new normal." That didn't mean that Libby would never be a fun person again; it just meant that for some time she would be sad and withdrawn.

Dr. Harrison suggested that one way Susan could support Libby would be to accept the fact that Libby was not going to be herself for awhile. Another way Susan could support Libby would be to listen to Libby talk about her mom and her feelings, if that was something that Libby wanted to do. Most of all, Susan could really help Libby by just letting her be wherever she was in her grief. As Dr. Harrison said, grief is not a step by step process where someone "gets over it" in just a few months. Instead, grief was something that ebbed and flowed. Sometimes a grieving person would feel better for awhile and then out of the blue they would feel intense sadness again. Susan was really glad she had talked with Dr. Harrison. She realized that it was normal that Libby wanted to spend a lot of time at home with her dad. Rather than encouraging her to go out and have fun, Susan could spend time with Libby and her dad. In time, Libby might feel like going out again.

A few more weeks passed and soon it was the first Saturday in October. Susan had driven home for the weekend and was headed to Oak Park Cemetery. Today would have been Libby's mom's birthday, and Susan was pretty sure Libby would be at the cemetery. As she walked toward Marianne's grave, she saw Libby putting red roses by her headstone. Libby looked up and seemed surprised to see Susan. "Suz, what are you doing here?"

"Hey Lib, I thought you would be here. Today is your mom's birthday isn't it? I bet you really miss her." Libby began to cry and Susan wrapped her arms around Libby's small shoulders. "Oh Suz, I miss her so much." "I can't imagine Lib. I really can't. Lib, I'm really sorry I haven't been there for you. Can we talk?"

For Further Thought and Reflection

1. What are some of the reasons that Susan is having difficulty communicating with Libby following her mom's death? What are some of the reasons that Libby is having trouble communicating with Susan as well?
2. If you were in the same situation as Susan, how easy or difficult would it be for you to talk with Libby? As Libby's friend, how would you try to communicate caring and support?
3. What, if anything, could Libby do to help Susan better communicate with her?
4. Some communication scholars have found that grieving individuals often experience the relational dialectics of openness-closedness and presence-absence. Relational dialectics is a theoretical framework that says that people in relationships often experience competing needs or goals simultaneously. For instance, the dialectic of openness-closedness is characterized by wanting to disclose information and not wanting to disclose information at the same time. Likewise, the tension of presence-absences occurs when people continue to feel the emotional presence of someone, even though the person is physically absent. What instances of openness-closedness and/or presence-absence did you see in this case study?

References

Baxter, L. A., Braithwaite, D. O., Golish, T. D., & Olson, L. N. (2002). Contradictions of interactions for wives of elderly husbands with adult dementia. *Journal of Applied Communication Research, 30*, 1–26.

Dyregrov, K. (2005–2006). Experiences of social networks supporting traumatically bereaved. *Omega, 52*, 339–358.

Goldsmith, D. (2004). *Communicating social support*. Cambridge, UK: Cambridge University Press.

Knight, K. H., Elfenbein, M. H., & Capozzi, L. (2000). Relationship of recollections of first death experience to current death attitudes. *Death Studies, 24*, 201–221.

Lehman, D. R., Ellard, J. H., & Wortman, C. B. (1986). Social support for the bereaved: Recipients' and providers' perspectives on what is helpful. *Journal of Counseling and Clinical Psychology, 54*, 438–446.

Rando, T. A. (1988). *Grieving: How to go on living when someone you love dies*. San Franciso: Jossey-Bass Inc.

Schulz, R., Newsom, J. T., Fleissner, K., Decamp, A. R., & Nieboer, A. P. (1997). The effects of bereavement after family caregiving. *Aging and Mental Health, 1*, 269–282.

Servaty-Seib, H. L. & Burleson, B. R. (2007). Bereaved adolescents' evaluations of the helpfulness of support-intended statements: Associations with person-centeredness and demographic, personality, and contextual factors. *Journal of Social and Personal Relationships, 24*, 207–223.

Toller, P. W. (2005). Negotiation of dialectical contradictions by parents who have experienced the death of a child. *Journal of Applied Communication Research, 33*, 44–66.

Toller, P. W. (2011). Bereaved parents' experiences of supportive and unsupportive communication. *Southern Journal of Communication, 76*, 17–34.

30

Friends of the Heart: Communication between Long-Term Friends

Mary E. Rohlfing

Keywords

friendship, familial bonds, sex differences in friendship, cross-sex friendship

Sophie had stood alone in her father's now empty house for close to fifteen minutes. Knowing she'd never return to this place again, she wanted to allow herself time to experience the feelings of relief and sadness pulsing through her heart and gut. She visualized her father as she had often seen him during her annual visits "back home," seated at the kitchen table, bathed in a low light, smoking cigarette after cigarette. She remembered the ever-present stacks of now discarded magazines and newspaper clippings he piled neatly on the floor near his feet. As she blinked back the tears filling her eyes, she turned one last time to look out the window overlooking the creek and meadow where just this morning she had seen three deer grazing in the knee-high grass. She tried futilely to remember the names her father had given each one, remembering how nearly every time he had called her, he'd talk endlessly about them, and how she almost invariably would tune him out. Now, she wished she'd paid closer attention and knew which was which. Realizing that this thought, too, was hopeless, she began to sob.

Sophie realized that nothing would ever be as it had been, and she simultaneously ached to bring her father back and struggled to let him go. Dabbing at the tears that had begun to flow less freely, Sophie knew there was nothing now to do but go on. She sighed and said aloud, "That's it." Her own voice startled her in the quiet as she quickly and definitively strode to the back door, opening it and shutting it tightly behind her.

Stepping outside, Sophie squinted and blinked as her moist eyes adjusted to the bright sun. She saw Jay leaning comfortably against the driver's door of the rented moving truck parked in the driveway, noticing that at his feet were three stubbed cigarette butts. "Now's a good time to quit that nasty habit," she called out as cheerfully as she could. "We have 2,000 miles of highway ahead of us, and you are NOT going to smoke in that truck!"

"Please," Jay muttered sarcastically. "Is there anything more annoying than a holier-than-thou ex-smoker? I don't think so. After all I'm doing for you, you won't let me smoke in the truck? It's going to take us three weeks to get to Oregon, because we're going to have to stop every fifty miles so I can have a fix." Sophie laughed, and as she did, made a noise like a horse. Realizing what she'd done, she laughed harder. "There you go, snorting already." Jay shook his head in mock disgust. He reached toward her to take her suitcase. "You think I'm kidding? This provokes a lot of anxiety for me, Sophie. Driving and smoking go together like Justin Timberlake and Jimmy Fallon, baby. Great alone? Oh, hell, yes! Together? Perfection."

Sophie had walked around to the passenger door of the truck and Jay noticed that she was tugging at the locked handle to let herself in. He pulled the keys from his pocket and tossed them in a high arc over the cab of the truck to her. Sophie snatched the keys from the air, unlocked the door and got in. As they settled into their seats and Sophie handed him the keys, she said, "That reference, Jay, is tired and old, just like you and smoking. It's time for you and smoking to break up."

Ignoring her, Jay said, "Perish the thought," and dramatically revved the engine. Then, turning to her, he said, "Let's go, Thelma. Time to get this show on the road, hit the bars, pick up Brad Pitt, blow up an oil truck, and drive off the cliff." Sophie giggled as she thought of her partner Melissa's parting comments as she dropped them off at the airport four days before. Hugging Sophie, Melissa looked over her shoulder and spoke to Jay, "Now don't go pulling any 'Thelma and Louise' crap out there. Don't stop at bars, don't blow up any oil trucks, stay away from Brad Pitt, and for God's sake, don't go near any cliffs." The comment had humored them for the last three days. The night before they left Oregon for Pennsylvania, the three of them had curled up on the couch and watched the classic, "Thelma and Louise" for their weekly movie night. As they worked cleaning out Sophie's father's house, they frequently referred to one another as Thelma or Louise.

As Jay adjusted the mirrors, Sophie poured herself a cup of coffee from the thermos and reached for her phone on the seat between them. Looking for some music to play, Jay muttered, "If I hear a single Beyonce song before noon, I will throw that iPhone of yours right out of this truck. I haven't had enough coffee for that kind of crazy yet."

"What makes you think I would have Beyonce downloaded?" she asked incredulously. As the engine began to purr, the first strains of a Beyonce song cranked loudly through the speakers. Sophie stared at Jay, waiting for him to answer.

Jay caught her gaze then looked out over the meadow, "Well, let's see. Maybe because I've known you for, what? Thirteen long, painful years? Maybe because your musical taste is more predictable than a 'Fast and Furious' remake? Gee, Sophie, I don't know, how could I have known?" They smiled and he barked, "Now pour me a cup of coffee, woman. We out!" Sophie snorted again as she poured, then pretended to nearly spill the cup in his lap as she handed him the steaming mug. "So help me, I'll kill you," Jay sneered as he took the cup from her.

Jay placed the cup on the dashboard then leaned forward to lower the volume. Gently placing his hand on her knee, he looked at Sophie and asked, "Are you really ready?" Sophie smiled weakly and nodded her head. "You sure?" She looked away, knowing if she kept his gaze a moment more she would burst into tears. "OK," Jay said, realizing it was time. "Thelma," he yelled, as he turned up the music to a near deafening-volume, "let's drive off this cliff!"

As he maneuvered the over-loaded truck out of the driveway and onto the street, Jay began to sing along, and Sophie couldn't suppress a smile. Minutes before she had been ready to break down, but was now light-hearted and excited. Aside from Melissa, who couldn't come along since she was just two weeks into the school year as a high school principal, Sophie could imagine no one she'd rather be with. "Hey, wait a minute," she said watching her father's house disappear in the side mirror behind them. "Did you call me 'Thelma,' Thelma?" Jay nodded affirmatively. "I thought I was Louise and you were Thelma. We need to get this straight."

Jay beamed. "To tell you the truth, Louise, I don't know which one's which. I do know, though, that Brad Pitt was a hottie when he was young. You be whoever you need to be, dear. You be Angelina, I'll be Brad. Hell, you be Brad, I'll be Angelina."

Sophie thought of how they often delighted themselves arguing over pop culture trivia, and the great lengths to which each would go to prove the other wrong. They had dubbed these disagreements, the "culture vulture" wars. She recalled how they had gotten into arguments at parties over who had written a particular song or directed a cult classic movie. Invariably, they would notice that they had cleared the room and were left alone. "Well," Jay would say at such moments; "we've once again run off the competition with our superior knowledge of all things popular and all things cultural."

For the next few hours, they barely spoke, but Jay could tell that Sophie was restless. He noticed her open the glove box to retrieve the insurance and rental agreement, which she dropped to the floor. Cursing, she scooped it up and fished a rubber band from her pocket to bind the papers together before putting them back. Next, she thumbed through her phone, talking to herself as she deleted old text messages. Finished with that task, she reached under the seat for a water bottle, setting it on the seat between them. Seeming to have run out of chores, she momentarily leaned back in her seat, then quickly jerked forward to adjust the speakers. With the sound just right, she settled in again, but not for long. Once more she opened the glove box, this time removing a crisp, new pocket notebook and pen. Shifting in the seat to face Jay, she asked, "How many miles have we gone?"

He shrugged his shoulders and coughed. "Eighty miles? One hundred? I don't know."

Sophie admonished him. "Jay, look at the odometer. What's it say?"

Jay looked crossly at her. "It reads," he said elongating the word to indicate that she had misspoken, "1,982 and six tenths of a mile." Sophie sighed and rolled her eyes.

"Didn't you zero out the odometer at the beginning of the trip?" Jay shrugged again. Perturbed, Sophie whined, "Jay, I need to keep track of this shit."

"What?" he asked. "What are you keeping track of?"

Sophie made no attempt to hide her irritation. "The miles, the gas, the hotel bills, how much we spend on food. That's what!"

Exasperated, Jay asked, "Why? First, who cares how many miles we go, how much gas we use, or what the rooms cost? Second, can't your phone keep track of that? Are you channeling your father? Don't go anal on me." He looked away from Sophie to avoid her glare.

Sophie responded, "I'm not anal. I have to keep track to be reimbursed. You know how my brothers are." Jay was unconvinced. The two times he'd met Josh, he seemed like an easy going guy, albeit tough to get to know. Her older brother, Nick, lived in California and had never ventured to Oregon to see his sister, nor had she ever gone to see him. He didn't think Nick or Josh would be counting pennies under the circumstances. After all, she had saved them both a lot of grief by taking on the task of dealing with their father's house and belongings.

Sophie yanked open the glove box and tossed the notebook inside. She remained silent as they drove west on the Pennsylvania Turnpike passing one farm after another. Jay considered apologizing, but he wasn't sure why. He knew Sophie was trying to maintain her generally jovial demeanor, but the events of the last three weeks were beginning to wear on her. Although she'd sworn she could handle the aftermath of her father's death alone, and claimed that she would relish "driving solo" in the rental truck across country, Jay had insisted on coming along. No way would he or Melissa let Sophie face all the emotional and physical work that had to be done by herself. Since he was between jobs, Melissa and Jay decided he was the best choice to accompany her. Jay knew, though, that Sophie was too proud to admit she needed him, so instead, when they talked about the trip, he would say he was coming along because he'd never had the chance to visit the east coast with someone who had grown up there.

In their 13 years of friendship, Sophie and Jay had been through a great deal. They first met when both were 20-years-old and enrolled in the same math class. One day, Sophie approached Jay to ask if he'd share his notes since she'd missed the last class. He invited her to his house to get them, and they became instant friends. Sophie liked to say that had they been heterosexual, theirs would have been a classic case of love at first sight.

As Jay got to know Sophie better, he revealed that his lover, Zach, who was five years older than Jay, had recently died of a drug overdose. Since Zach's death, Jay had remained single and celibate. He told anyone who asked that Zach had been his "one and only," and that he couldn't be "replaced." As the years passed, Sophie saw Jay's reluctance to become involved romantically with anyone new was strategy for protecting himself from being hurt so deeply again. A few years back, she had begun to encourage him to date, summoning the courage to tell him what she thought was at the root of his long spell of solitude. Doing so had been a mistake. Jay stormed out of Sophie and Melissa's house half-way through the birthday dinner they had prepared in his honor. He accused them of meddling in his life and told them both to "fuck off!" For three weeks, he refused to return their calls, and once, when Sophie stopped by his house to try to talk things out, he yelled at her through the closed door that he wanted to be left alone. She stood outside his door, telling him how much he meant to her and how deeply she missed his friendship. Realizing he was not going to let her in, she finally walked away, unsure that she'd ever see him again. Then, a week later, he stopped by her office and asked her to lunch. As she tried again to apologize, he cut her short. "You did that already. Don't belabor the point." After that, Sophie never raised the issue with Jay again.

As he drove, Jay remembered how early in their friendship, Sophie had faced her first real heartbreak when her lover left her for another woman. When she told Jay that what she missed most was having someone to say goodnight to, he called every night for the next six months to "tuck" her in. He happily stopped doing so, when, one night, Melissa answered the phone. He had known her for years and had long thought that she and Sophie would make a great couple. Now that the two of them had been going strong for seven years, he knew he'd been right.

Jay looked at Sophie and noticed she looked tired. He moved the water bottle and told her to lie down on the seat to sleep. She shook her head and continued staring out the window.

Sophie had known for years that her father's health was fragile. Still, she was shocked when he died. Three days before his death, she had phoned to tell him that she and Melissa were off for a week-long hike in the wilderness. When she asked how he was, he said he was "a little under the weather," but it was "no big deal." As they bid each other goodbye, he told her to have a great time and to send his "love to Mel." While Sophie and Melissa were hiking, Sophie's father had "slipped away" due to a massive infection in his lungs.

Sophie's big brother, Nick, was the first to hear of their father's death, and after two days of failing to reach his sister, Josh advised Nick to call Jay to find out where they were. Jay told Nick that Sophie and Melissa weren't due home for four days and that they were 30 miles from where a phone might work. He volunteered to hike in and tell Sophie what had happened, but Nick refused Jay's offer, thinking it best that they enjoy their trip. Their father had been cremated and there would be no funeral. Nick was assured that their father's attorney could handle the other details. Since none of the children wished to return to Pennsylvania and live in the home their father had bought after their parents' divorce, all that remained to be done was for the house to be cleaned out and put up for sale.

Talking with Nick, Jay understood why Sophie found him so difficult. While Nick was friendly, he was terse and officious, offering no hint that he felt much sadness about his father's death. Nick, Sophie said, thought their father had "lacked ambition" and was to blame for their parents' divorce. In his eyes, their father was not a "real" man. Despite knowing all of this, Jay thought it odd that Nick could be so cool. Before the conversation, he'd always thought Sophie was too hard on her brother. After talking with Nick, he understood why she was.

Sophie loved her brothers, but was not as close to either of them as she was to most of her friends. Nick's values, she felt, were exactly opposite of her own. He was a staunch and vocal conservative whose conversations were frequently laced with homophobic and racist remarks. He'd been married three times, and each wife was younger than the last. On those rare occasions when they spoke, Nick answered her questions about how he was in financial terms. Sophie, on the other hand, didn't much care about money. She didn't make much at the homeless shelter where she worked, but Melissa was well-paid as a school administrator. They had plenty. Still, Sophie thought Nick believed she was less than successful in life. That she was a lesbian didn't sit well with him either, and it hurt that he never asked her about Melissa. Jay knew Sophie thought Nick was a bigot and tried to dismiss him, but also that she was hurt by her brother's disapproval of her.

Josh, Sophie's younger brother was nearly ten years her junior. He admired Sophie, but since he and his girlfriend lived three hours away from Sophie, they saw each other only once or twice a year. Sophie felt closer to Josh, but he had been only eight years old when she left home for good. In her mind, it was as though they had grown up in two different families.

Hoping to break the silence that had engulfed them, Jay picked out some new music to listen to. He noticed Sophie tapping her foot to the beat of the song. Although he'd known her for over a decade, and felt more comfortable with her than anyone else, he realized it wasn't until he made this trip back to where she had been raised that he felt he had real insight into her life. He asked Sophie about her favorite places, what she had done as a teenager, and what it was like, at eighteen years of age, to drive cross-country alone to go to college in Oregon. Sophie warmed to the questions, providing details she had never before shared. She was animated as they made their first stop for food and gas, and told him a funny story about traveling with her family when she was ten, and how at this very Howard Johnson's, her mother had absent-mindedly driven off without Nick before he returned from the men's room. It wasn't until they were three miles down the road that Sophie realized Nick wasn't in the car and screamed loudly for her parents to go back to get him.

After they ate and filled the truck with gas, Sophie took over driving as Jay curled into a fetal position, using his wadded up sweatshirt as a makeshift pillow. Sophie drove for close to four hours when she realized that she was too sleepy to go any further. She pulled off the highway and stopped at the nearest hotel. As she parked, Jay awoke and asked what was going on. She told him it was time to stop for the day. Jay rubbed his eyes and looked at the hotel sign. "Let me wake up, and I'll go in and register with you," he said quietly as he tried with little success to flatten his mussed hair. Stretching his mouth so as to regain feeling in his face, he asked what time it was. Sophie told him and he asked, "Have I really been asleep that long?"

"Yes. Thelma," Sophie answered. "And by the way, you're fabulous company on a road trip. Your insightful remarks, pointed questions and generally interesting patter are really making the miles fly by, pal."

Jay blinked his eyes and rubbed them, "I'm sorry. I should have stayed awake to talk to you." He yawned and stretched his arms. "I just couldn't. These last few days have been rough on this old queen. Packing this truck and carrying all that heavy furniture is more labor than I'm used to. You would have done better bringing some big, butch dyke, my darling." Sophie laughed as he continued, "Now, when we get to Oregon and start trying to figure out how to mix your dad's furniture with that funky, Bohemian college student decor of yours and Mel's, I'll be fabulous help. At the moment, though, I'm just a warm body."

Sophie stroked his hair helping to smooth down a stray strand or two he'd missed. She then reached up to the dashboard and grabbed Jay's cigarettes. She shook one loose from the pack and put it between her lips. "Got a light?" she asked. Saying nothing, he reached into his pocket and pulled out his lighter. Sophie took it from him and lit the cigarette. He noticed that although she had quit two years ago, she didn't cough as she inhaled. Before handing it to him, she took another drag. Exhaling, she said, "This will help you wake up."

Jay was genuinely confused and quickly turned to roll down the window so the smoke could escape. "I thought this was a non-smoking truck."

"It was. I can't ask you to go all day without smoking. You stay here and enjoy it." Before he could thank her, she had opened the door and jumped out.

After showering, writing postcards, and clicking through the channels on the television, Jay popped up from his bed and announced, "I'm going to get a six pack and some burgers. Please take advantage of my absence to call your sweetie and do that kissy-face thing. I don't want to be subjected to that crap."

Sophie smiled and waved as he walked to the door. "Wait," she said. "I have to tell you something." Jay turned back to look at her. She continued, "I've been a jackass today. I just, I just, oh, Jay, how can I repay you? You're so good to me. You've been such a huge help these last few days. I could never have gotten all that done without you."

When it appeared that she might tear up, Jay cut her off. "Sophie, you know I despise this kind of verbalized sentimentality. Stop before I vomit."

"No," she said seriously. "Most of time I honor your inability to link words to feelings. Just shut up and hear me out." Jay rolled his eyes and sat down. As he did, she said simply, "I love you, friend."

Jay sat looking at her, expecting Sophie to continue. Realizing that she was through talking, he exclaimed, "That's it? That's all you have to say to me?" They laughed. "You are so incompetent as a woman sometimes, Sophie." Standing to leave, he said, "So, that was the big heart-to-heart? You're pathetic."

As he opened the door, he turned back. "Tell me again, which am I? Thelma or Louise?" She shrugged, unable to recall. "OK, well, whichever one slept with Brad Pitt is the one I'm going to be; got it?" As he walked out the door, he called over his shoulder, "I love you, too, Sophie. And when you call Melissa, tell her I only thought about killing you twice today."

She knew he wouldn't hear her but called after him anyway. "You have to love me, I'm your best friend, Thelma!"

For Further Thought and Reflection

1. Some researchers have claimed that men and women enact friendship in different ways. Can you see differences in how Sophie and Jay communicate their feelings of friendship and love for each other?
2. Many people believe that men and women cannot have successful friendships. What has been your experience with cross-sex friendships? How do those friendships differ from ones you have with same-sex friends?
3. Identify aspects of Sophie and Jay's communication that reflect the history of their friendship. How might their communication be different if they had been friends only a short time?

References

Braithwaite, D. O., & Kellas, J. (2006). Shopping with friends: Everyday communication at the shopping mall. In J. T. Wood and S. Duck (Eds.). *Composing relationships: Communication in everyday life* (pp. 86–95). Belmont CA: Wadsworth.

Ledbetter, A. M. (2009). Family communication patterns and relational maintenance behavior: Direct and mediated associations with friendship closeness. *Human Communication Research, 35*, 130–47.

Metts, S. (2006). Hanging out and doing lunch: Enacting friendship closeness. In J. T. Wood & S. W. Duck (Eds.), *Composing relationships: Communication in everyday life* (pp. 76–85). Belmont: Wadsworth/ Cengage.

Rohlfing, M. E. (1995). "Doesn't anybody stay in one place anymore?" An exploration of the under-studied phenomenon of long-distance relationships. In J. T. Wood, & S. Duck (Eds.) Under-studied relationships: Off the Beaten Track (pp. 173–196). Thousand Oaks, CA: Sage.

Spencer, L., & Pahl, R. (2006). *Rethinking friendship: Hidden solidarities today*. Princeton, NJ: Princeton University Press.

Wood, J. T., & Inman, C. C. (1993). In a different mode: Masculine styles of communicating closeness. *Journal of Applied Communication Research, 21*, 279–295.

CPSIA information can be obtained
at www.ICGtesting.com
Printed in the USA
FSOW03n0634261017
40313FS

9 781524 946869

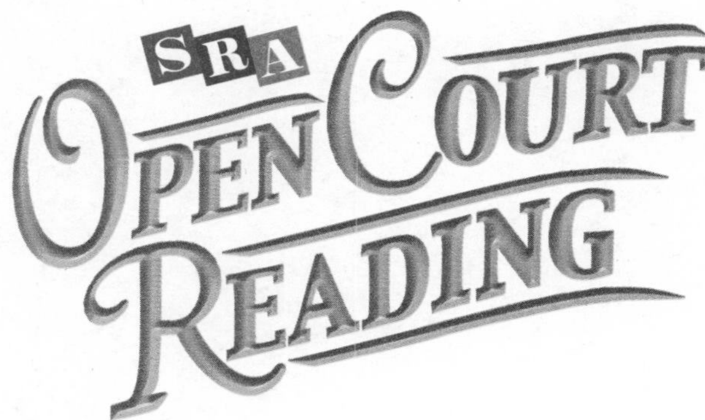

Pre-Decodable and Decodable Takehome Books

Level K
Pre-Decodable Books 1-15
Decodable Books 1-20

A Division of The McGraw-Hill Companies

Columbus, Ohio

SRA Open Court Reading

www.sra4kids.com

SRA/McGraw-Hill

A Division of The ***McGraw-Hill*** *Companies*

2005 Imprint

Printed in the United States of America.

Send all inquiries to:
SRA/McGraw-Hill
8787 Orion Place
Columbus, OH 43240-4027

ISBN 0-07-572303-4
13 14 15 16 17 18 19 QPD 06 05 04

Contents

Level K

Pre-Decodables

Decodables

About the Takehome Books

The *SRA Open Court Reading Pre-Decodable and Decodable Books* allow your students to apply their knowledge of phonic elements to read simple, engaging texts. Each story supports instruction in a new phonic element and incorporates elements and words that have been learned earlier.

The students can fold and staple the pages of each *Pre-Decodable Takehome Book* to make books of their own to keep and read. We suggest that you keep extra sets of the stories in your classroom for the children to reread.

How to make a Takehome Book

1. Tear out the pages you need.

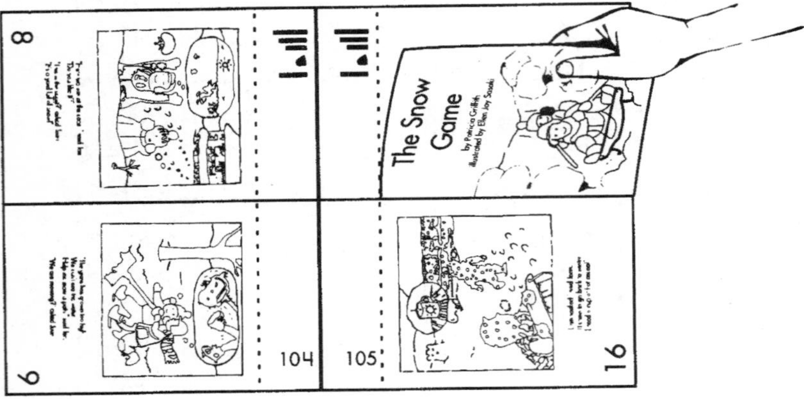

2. Place pages 4 and 5, and pages 2 and 7 faceup.

3. Place pages 4 and 5 on top of pages 2 and 7.

4. Fold along the center line.

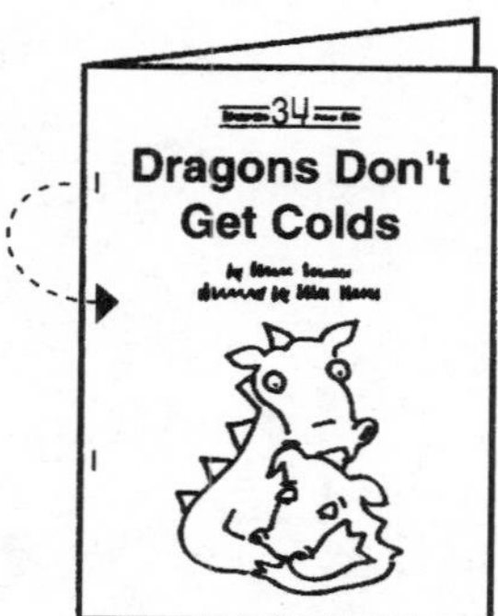

5. Check to make sure the pages are in order.

6. Staple the pages along the fold.

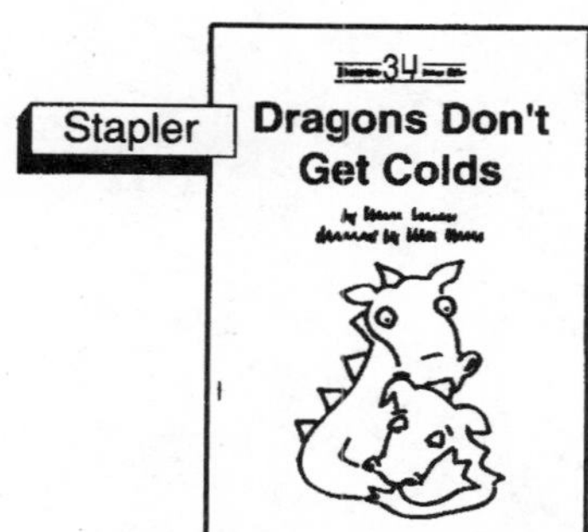

SRA Open Court Reading

6

Just to let you know...

A message from ______________________________________

Help your child discover the joy of independent reading with *SRA Open Court Reading.* From time to time your child will bring home his or her very own *Pre-Decodable* or *Decodable Takehome Books* to share with you. With your help, these stories can give your child important reading practice and a joyful shared reading experience.

You may want to set aside a few minutes every evening to read these stories together. Here are some suggestions you may find helpful:

- Do not expect your child to read each story perfectly, but concentrate on sharing the book together.
- Participate by doing some of the reading.
- Talk about the stories as you read, give lots of encouragement, and watch as your child becomes more fluent throughout the year!

Learning to read takes lots of practice. Sharing these stories is one way that your child can gain that valuable practice. Encourage your child to keep the *Pre-Decodable* or *Decodable Takehome Books* in a special place. This collection will make a library of books that your child can read and reread. Take the time to listen to your child read from his or her library. Just a few moments of shared reading each day can give your child the confidence needed to excel in reading.

Children who read every day come to think of reading as a pleasant, natural part of life. One way to inspire your child to read is to show that reading is an important part of your life by letting him or her see you reading books, magazines, newspapers, or any other materials. Another good way to show that you value reading is to share a *Pre-Decodable* or *Decodable Takehome Book* with your child each day.

Successful reading experiences allow children to be proud of their new-found reading ability. Support your child with interest and enthusiasm about reading. You won't regret it!

the 
park

The Park

by Lynn Edwards
illustrated by Kersti Frigell

Pre-Decodable Book 1

A Division of The McGraw-Hill Companies
Columbus, Ohio

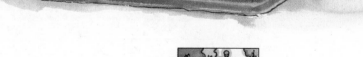

www.sra4kids.com

SRA/McGraw-Hill

A Division of The McGraw-Hill Companies

Printed in the United States of America.

Send all inquiries to:
SRA/McGraw-Hill
8787 Orion Place
Columbus, OH 43240-4027

the sandbox

the 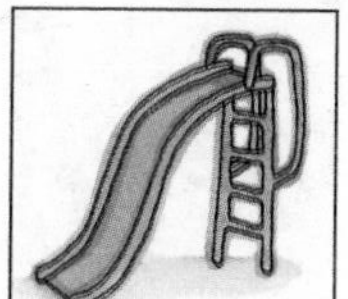 slide

the  trees

the  children

the  swings

13

Here is the lunch.

Lunch

by Lynn Edwards
illustrated by Kersti Frigell

Pre-Decodable Book 2

A Division of The McGraw-Hill Companies
Columbus, Ohio

www.sra4kids.com

SRA/McGraw-Hill

A Division of The McGraw-Hill Companies

Printed in the United States of America.

Send all inquiries to:
SRA/McGraw-Hill
8787 Orion Place
Columbus, OH 43240-4027

Here is a [napkin] .

napkin

Here is an  apple.

Here is the  lunchbox.

Here is a [sandwich] .

sandwich

Here is an 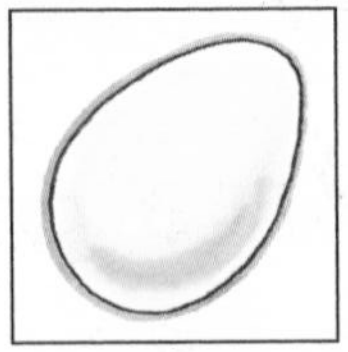 [egg] .

egg

17

Here is the school.

School

by Linda Cave
illustrated by Gary Undercuffler

Pre-Decodable Book 3

A Division of The McGraw-Hill Companies
Columbus, Ohio

www.sra4kids.com

SRA/McGraw-Hill

A Division of The McGraw-Hill Companies

Printed in the United States of America.

Send all inquiries to:
SRA/McGraw-Hill
8787 Orion Place
Columbus, OH 43240-4027

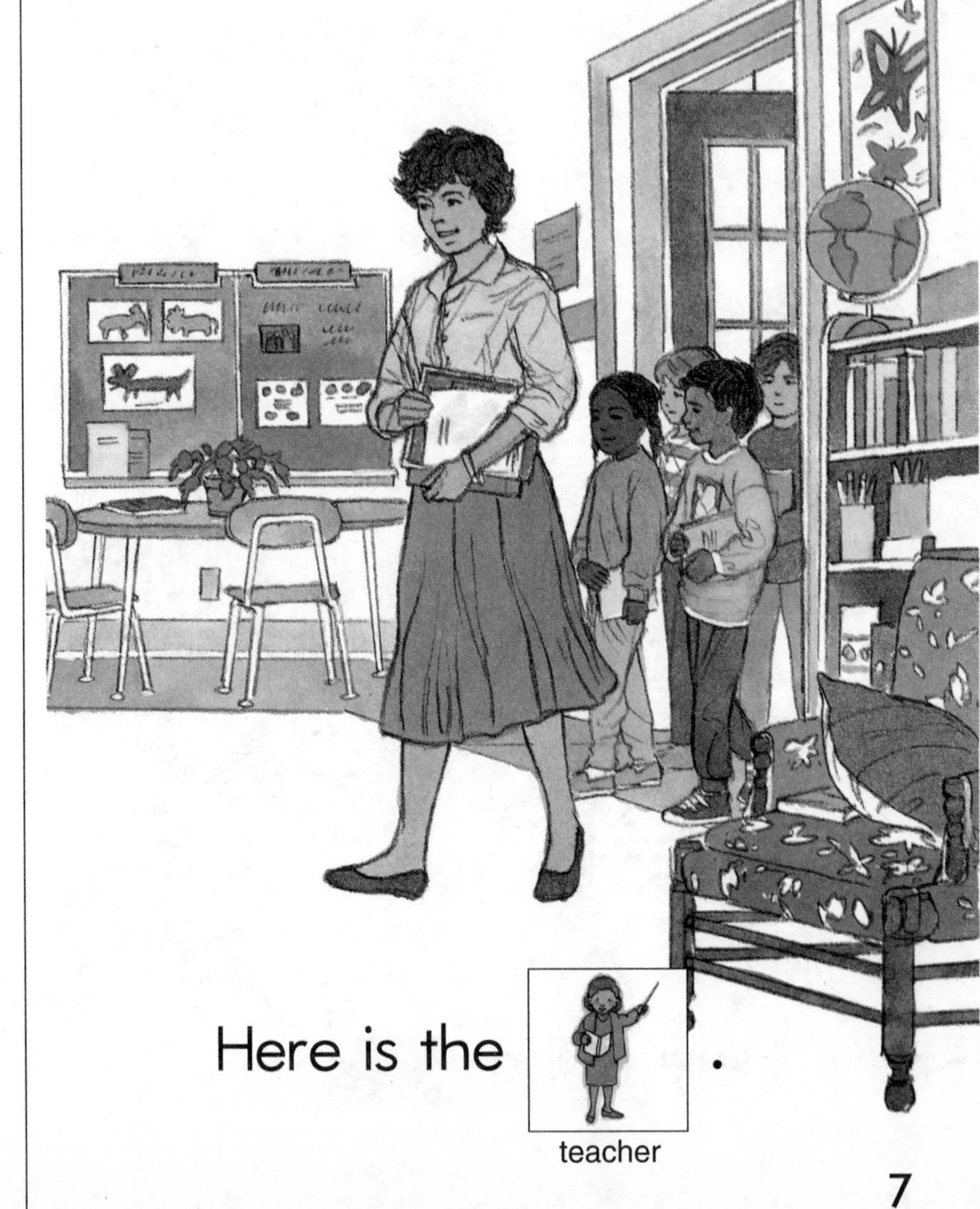

Here is the [teacher].

I see the  [books].

I see the [crayons].

Here is the  [flag].

I see the boys.

I see the girls.

I see the  tables.

I see the chairs.

We see 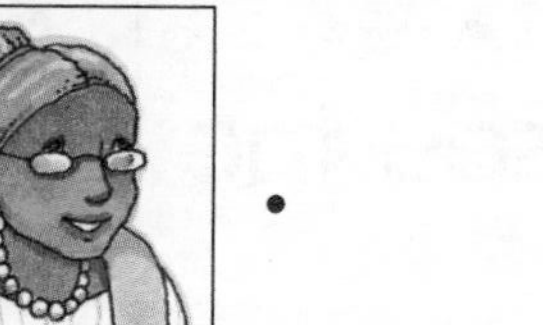 

.

We See

by Elsie Sidney
illustrated by Anthony Accardo

Pre-Decodable Book 4

SRA
A Division of The McGraw-Hill Companies
Columbus, Ohio

www.sra4kids.com

SRA/McGraw-Hill

A Division of The McGraw-Hill Companies

Printed in the United States of America.

Send all inquiries to:
SRA/McGraw-Hill
8787 Orion Place
Columbus, OH 43240-4027

We see the [bus] and the [bicycle].

bus

bicycle

We see the truck .

The van is here.

We see the  .

stop sign

We see the  and the  .

cow

pig

crowns and capes

He is a king. She is a queen.

A Trunk

by Ed Casey
illustrated by Anthony Accardo

Pre-Decodable Book 5

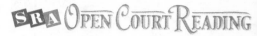

A Division of The McGraw-Hill Companies
Columbus, Ohio

www.sra4kids.com

SRA/McGraw-Hill

A Division of The McGraw-Hill Companies

Printed in the United States of America.

Send all inquiries to:
SRA/McGraw-Hill
8787 Orion Place
Columbus, OH 43240-4027

overalls and a hat

She is a farmer .

boots

He is a firefighter .

a  trunk

a  wig

He is a clown.

a  badge

She is a police officer.

We have a  .

farm

A Farm

by Meg Dandino
illustrated by Gary Undercuffler

Pre-Decodable Book 6

SRA
A Division of The McGraw-Hill Companies
Columbus, Ohio

www.sra4kids.com

SRA/McGraw-Hill
A Division of The McGraw-Hill Companies

Printed in the United States of America.

Send all inquiries to:
SRA/McGraw-Hill
8787 Orion Place
Columbus, OH 43240-4027

I have a small [lamb] .

lamb

I have a small  duck.

I have a big  pig.

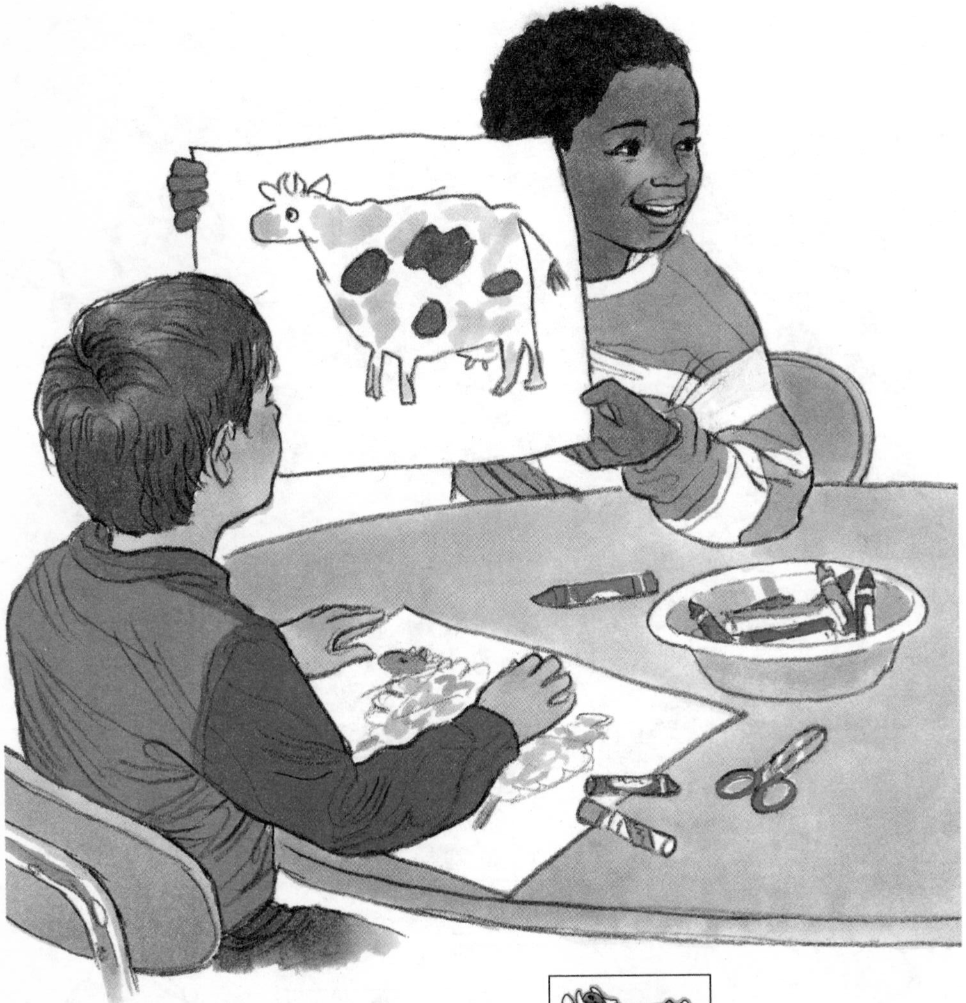

I have a big  cow.

I have a big  horse.

No, it is a  .

space shuttle

SRA Open Court Reading

This Is

by Megan Shawn
illustrated by Meryl Henderson

Pre-Decodable Book 7

SRA
A Division of The McGraw-Hill Companies
Columbus, Ohio

SRA OPEN COURT READING

www.sra4kids.com

SRA/McGraw-Hill

A Division of The ***McGraw-Hill*** *Companies*

Printed in the United States of America.

Send all inquiries to:
SRA/McGraw-Hill
8787 Orion Place
Columbus, OH 43240-4027

This is a  .

box

No, it is a  [space suit] .

space suit

This is a  [jug] .

jug

No, it is a 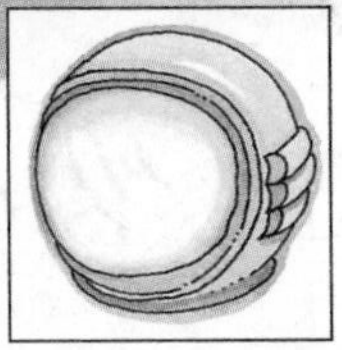 space helmet.

This is a bag.

We go down, down, down.

We Go

by Margaret Ahn
illustrated by Meryl Henderson

Pre-Decodable Book 8

A Division of The McGraw-Hill Companies
Columbus, Ohio

SRA Open Court Reading

www.sra4kids.com

SRA/McGraw-Hill

A Division of The ***McGraw-Hill*** *Companies*

Printed in the United States of America.

Send all inquiries to:
SRA/McGraw-Hill
8787 Orion Place
Columbus, OH 43240-4027

We go up a big  .

hill

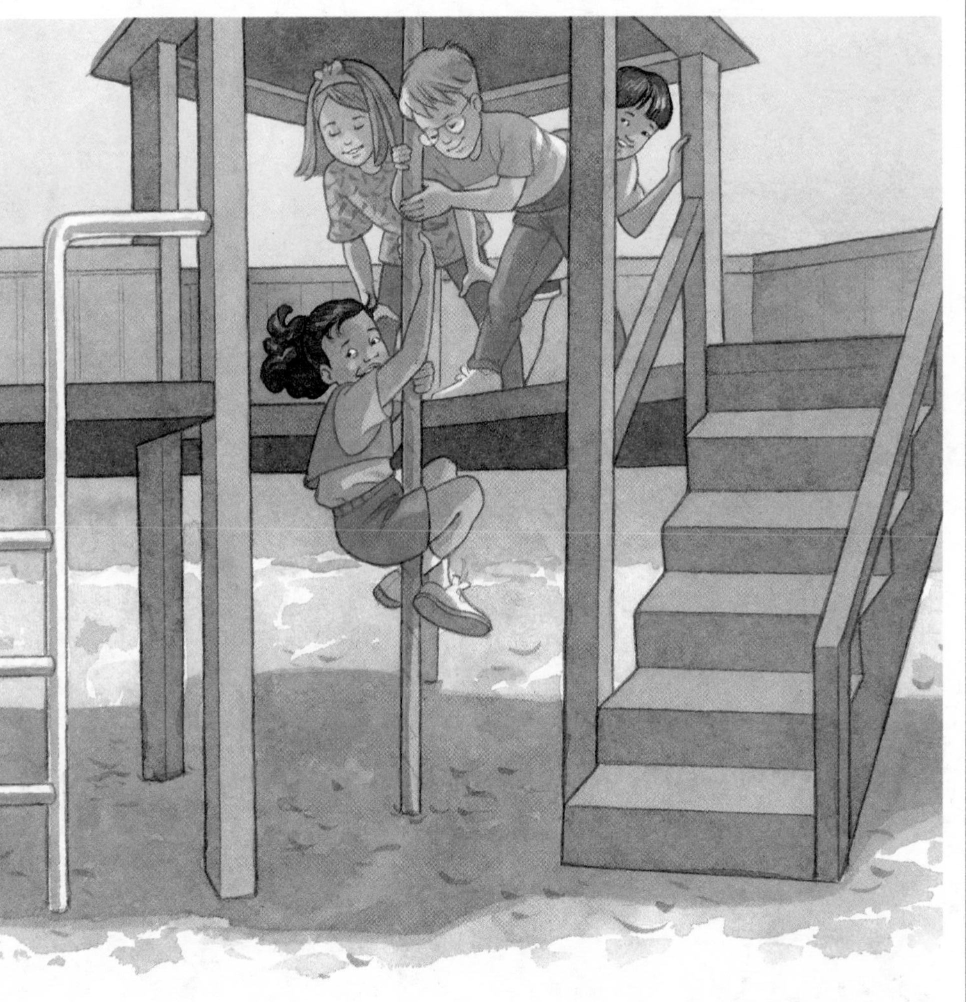

We go down a big pole.

pole

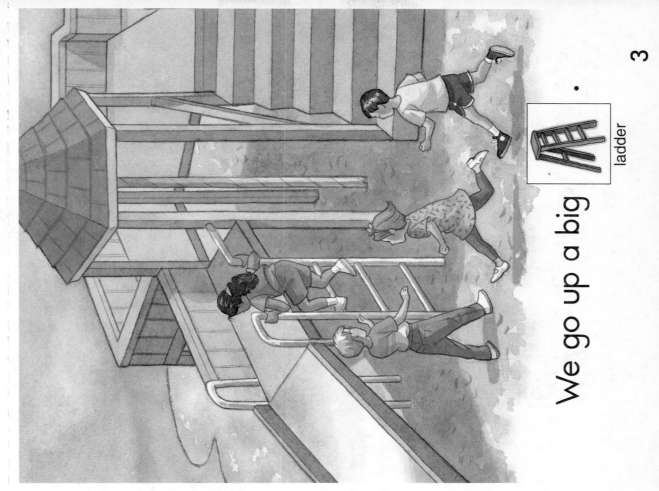

We go up a big ladder.

ladder

We go down the big 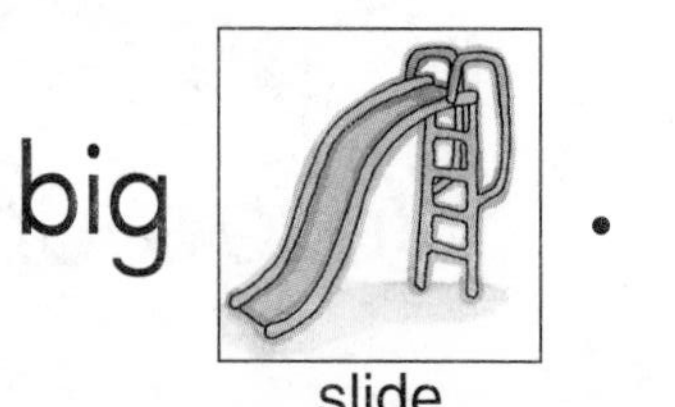 .

slide

We go up the big 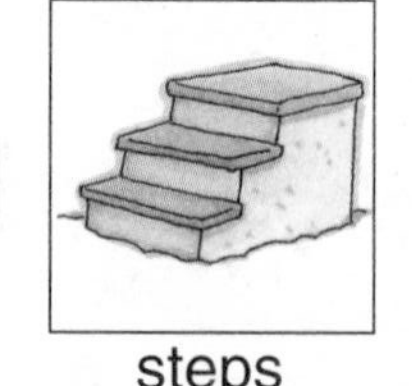 .

steps

We do!

Who Has a Hat?

by Linda Cave
illustrated by Kersti Frigell

Pre-Decodable Book 9

A Division of The McGraw-Hill Companies
Columbus, Ohio

www.sra4kids.com

SRA/McGraw-Hill

A Division of The McGraw-Hill Companies

Printed in the United States of America.

Send all inquiries to:
SRA/McGraw-Hill
8787 Orion Place
Columbus, OH 43240-4027

I have a (green) (hat).

Who has a (rainbow) (hat)?

I have a yellow  hat.

Who has a green  hat?

Who has a red  hat?

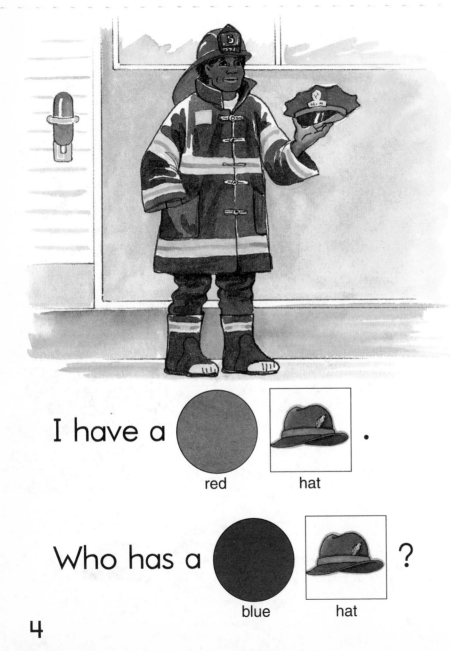

STOP

I have a red hat.

Who has a blue hat?

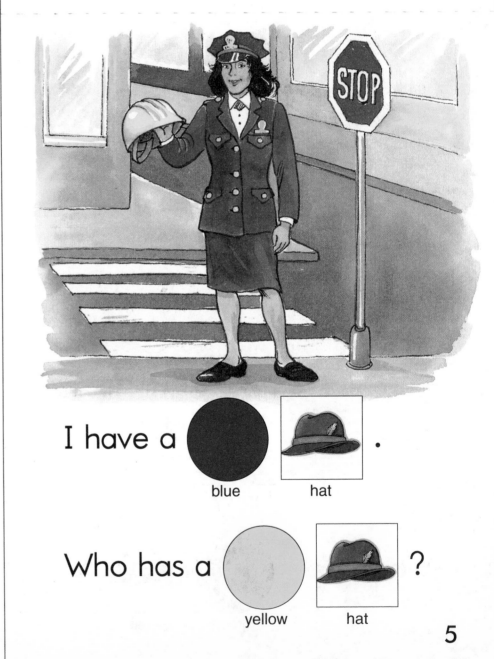

I have a blue hat.

Who has a yellow hat?

Here are  six  bowls 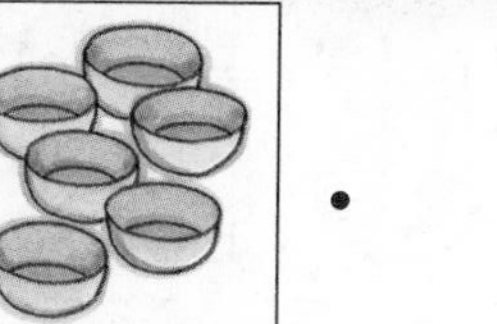 .

The Pot

by Chris Meramec
illustrated by Deborah Colvin Borgo

Pre-Decodable Book 10

SRA
A Division of The McGraw-Hill Companies
Columbus, Ohio

www.sra4kids.com

SRA/McGraw-Hill

A Division of The McGraw-Hill Companies

Printed in the United States of America.

Send all inquiries to:
SRA/McGraw-Hill
8787 Orion Place
Columbus, OH 43240-4027

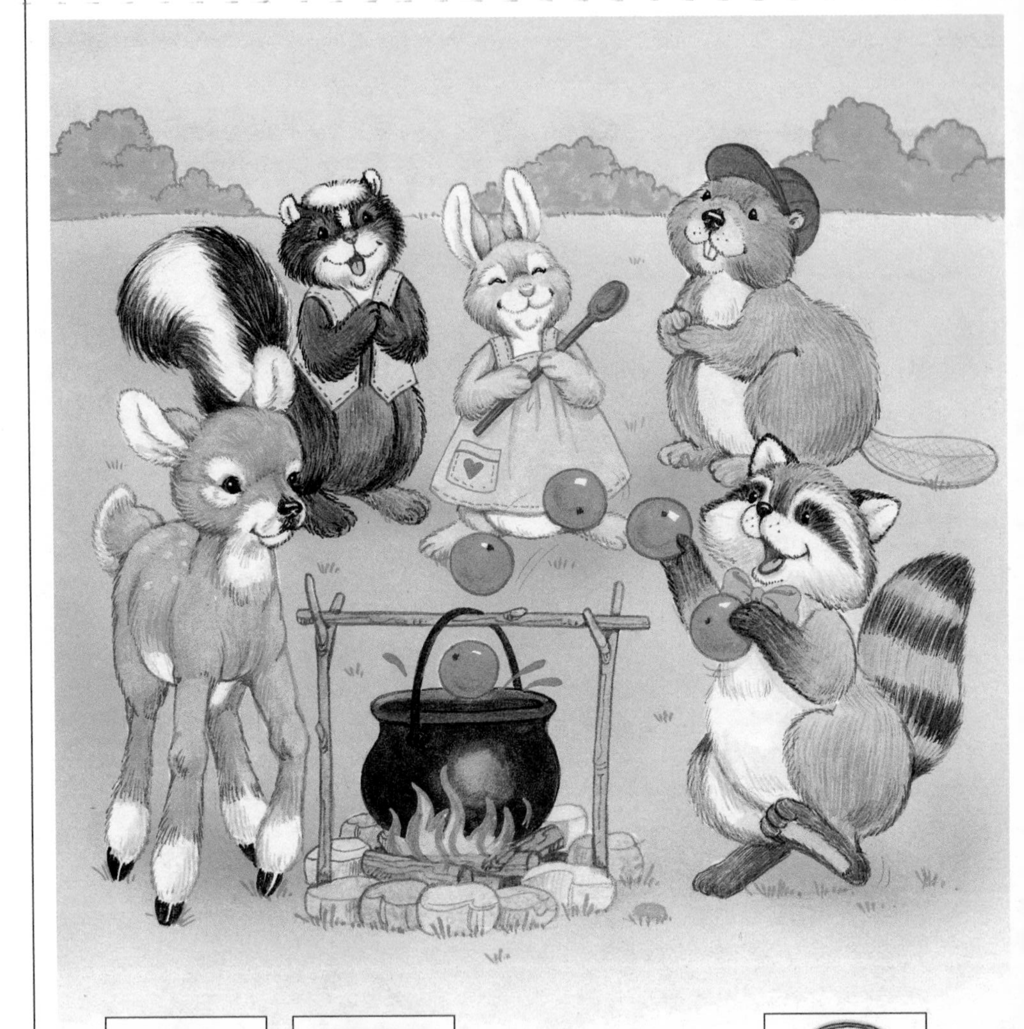

5 Five | tomatoes are in the | pot .

Four potatoes are in the pot.

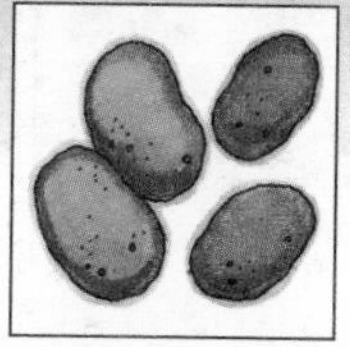

Here is one pot.

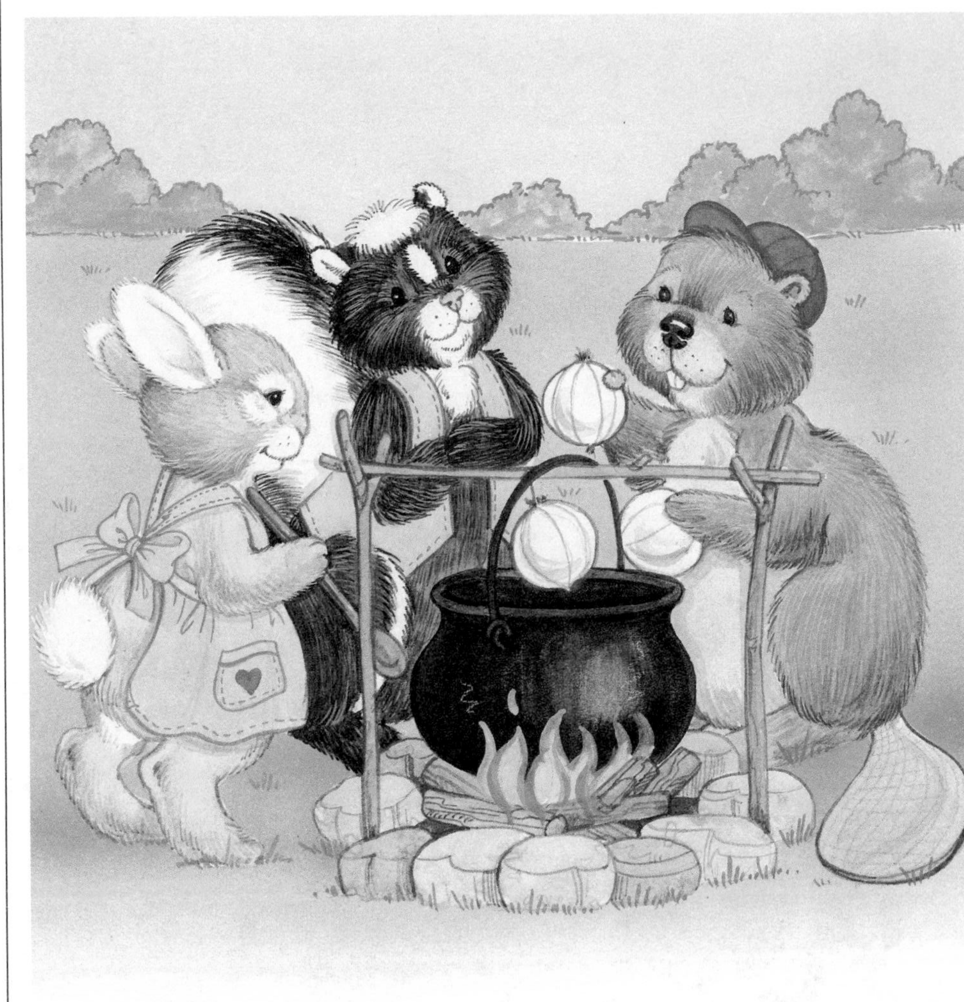

2 carrots are in the pot.

Two carrots pot

3 onions are in the pot.

Three onions pot

No!

SRA Open Court Reading

The Bug, the Duck, and the Frog

by Lynn Edwards
illustrated by Kersti Frigell

Pre-Decodable Book 11

SRA
A Division of The McGraw-Hill Companies
Columbus, Ohio

www.sra4kids.com

SRA/McGraw-Hill

A Division of The **McGraw-Hill** *Companies*

Printed in the United States of America.

Send all inquiries to:
SRA/McGraw-Hill
8787 Orion Place
Columbus, OH 43240-4027

No!

The  frog is on the  alligator !

The frog is on a log.

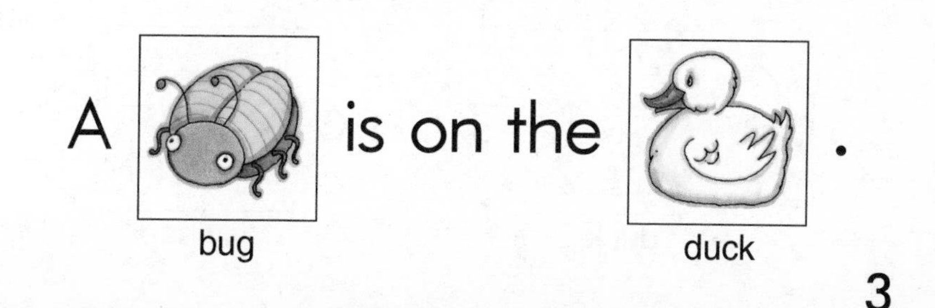

A bug is on the duck.

The  duck is on a  lily pad .

No!

The  duck is on a  frog .

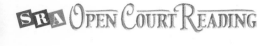

I can [eat]. You can [eat].

We can [eat].

What Can We Do?

by Ed Casey
illustrated by Kersti Frigell

Pre-Decodable Book 12

A Division of The McGraw-Hill Companies
Columbus, Ohio

www.sra4kids.com

SRA/McGraw-Hill

A Division of The **McGraw·Hill** *Companies*

Printed in the United States of America.

Send all inquiries to:
SRA/McGraw-Hill
8787 Orion Place
Columbus, OH 43240-4027

What can we do?

You can   run . I can  run .

We can run .

What can we do?

I can  [hop]. You can [hop].

We can [hop].

What can we do?

This is what we see at the zoo!

zoo

What Do We See?

by Tim Paulson
illustrated by Kersti Frigell

Pre-Decodable Book 13

A Division of The McGraw-Hill Companies
Columbus, Ohio

SRA OPEN COURT READING

www.sra4kids.com

SRA/McGraw-Hill

A Division of The McGraw-Hill Companies

Printed in the United States of America.

Send all inquiries to:
SRA/McGraw-Hill
8787 Orion Place
Columbus, OH 43240-4027

We see [monkeys] .

monkeys

We see [zebras].

zebras

We are at the . What do we see?

zoo

We see a  giraffe.

We see  elephants.

We can throw ! We can catch !

We can bat !

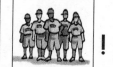

We have a baseball  team !

We Can Have a Team

by Lisa Trumbauer
illustrated by Meryl Henderson

Pre-Decodable Book 14

A Division of The McGraw-Hill Companies
Columbus, Ohio

SRA Open Court Reading

www.sra4kids.com

SRA/McGraw-Hill

A Division of The **McGraw-Hill** *Companies*

Printed in the United States of America.

Send all inquiries to:
SRA/McGraw-Hill
8787 Orion Place
Columbus, OH 43240-4027

We like [baseball], too!

Can we have a [team]?

Do you like 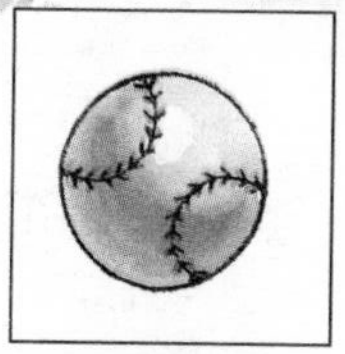 [baseball]?

I like  [baseball].

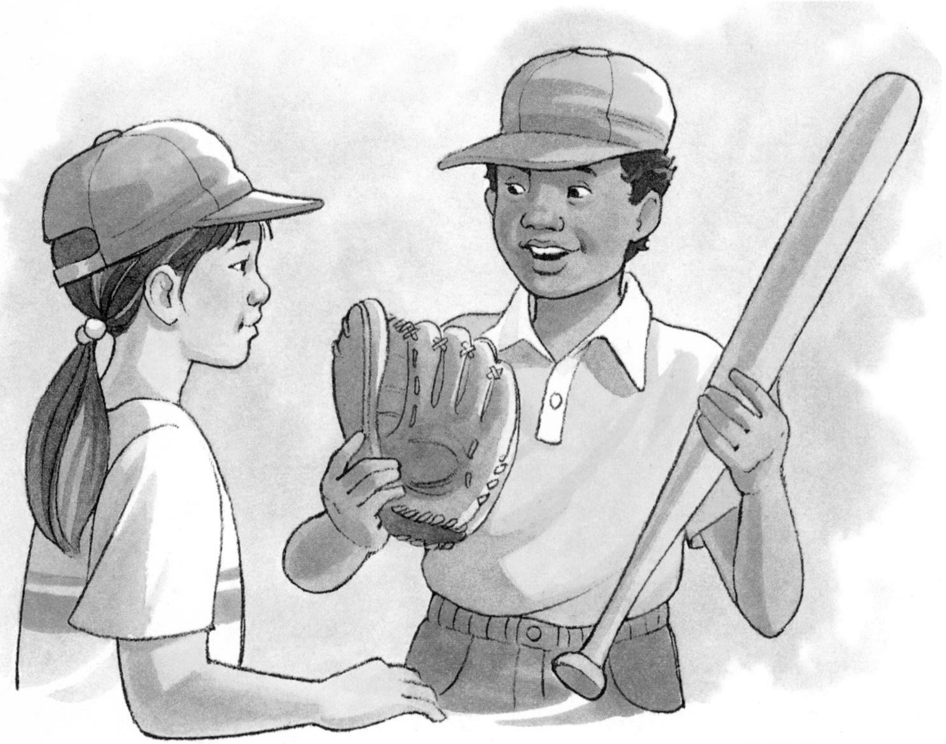

I like  [baseball], too. I can [catch].

I can [bat].

I can 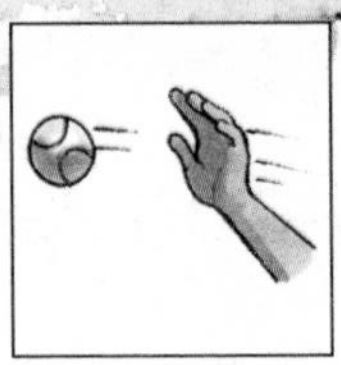 [throw].

I have a  trumpet ! We have a  band !

We Have a Band

by Linda Taylor
illustrated by Deborah Colvin Borgo

Pre-Decodable Book 15

SRA
A Division of The McGraw-Hill Companies
Columbus, Ohio

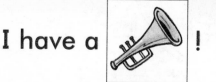

www.sra4kids.com

SRA/McGraw-Hill
A Division of The McGraw-Hill Companies

Printed in the United States of America.

Send all inquiries to:
SRA/McGraw-Hill
8787 Orion Place
Columbus, OH 43240-4027

No, we do not have a  !

band

We do not have a  .

trumpet

No, I do not have a  [trumpet].

I have a [trombone]. We have a [band]!

I can have a  [band].

Do you have a [trumpet]?

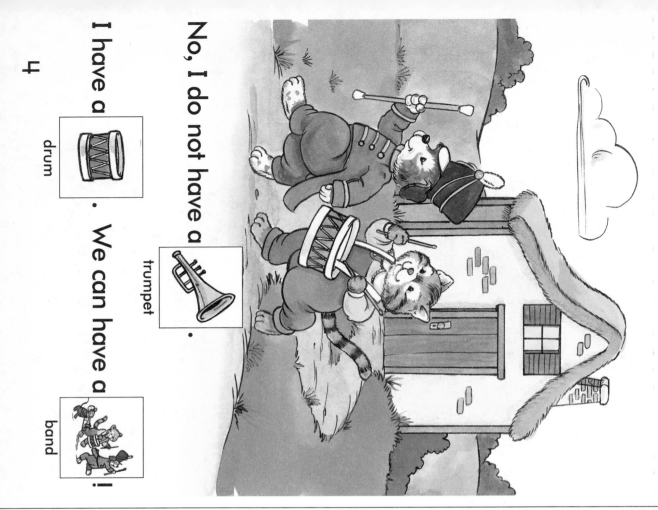

No, I do not have a  trumpet.

I have a  drum. We can have a  band!

We can have a  band. We have a  drum.

Do you have a  trumpet?

Sam sat on a mat.

Sam Sat

by Kris Ward
illustrated by Jan Pyk

Decodable Book 1

A Division of The McGraw-Hill Companies
Columbus, Ohio

SRA Open Court Reading

www.sra4kids.com

SRA/McGraw-Hill

A Division of The McGraw-Hill Companies

Printed in the United States of America.

Send all inquiries to:
SRA/McGraw-Hill
8787 Orion Place
Columbus, OH 43240-4027

a mat

Sam sat here.

Sam

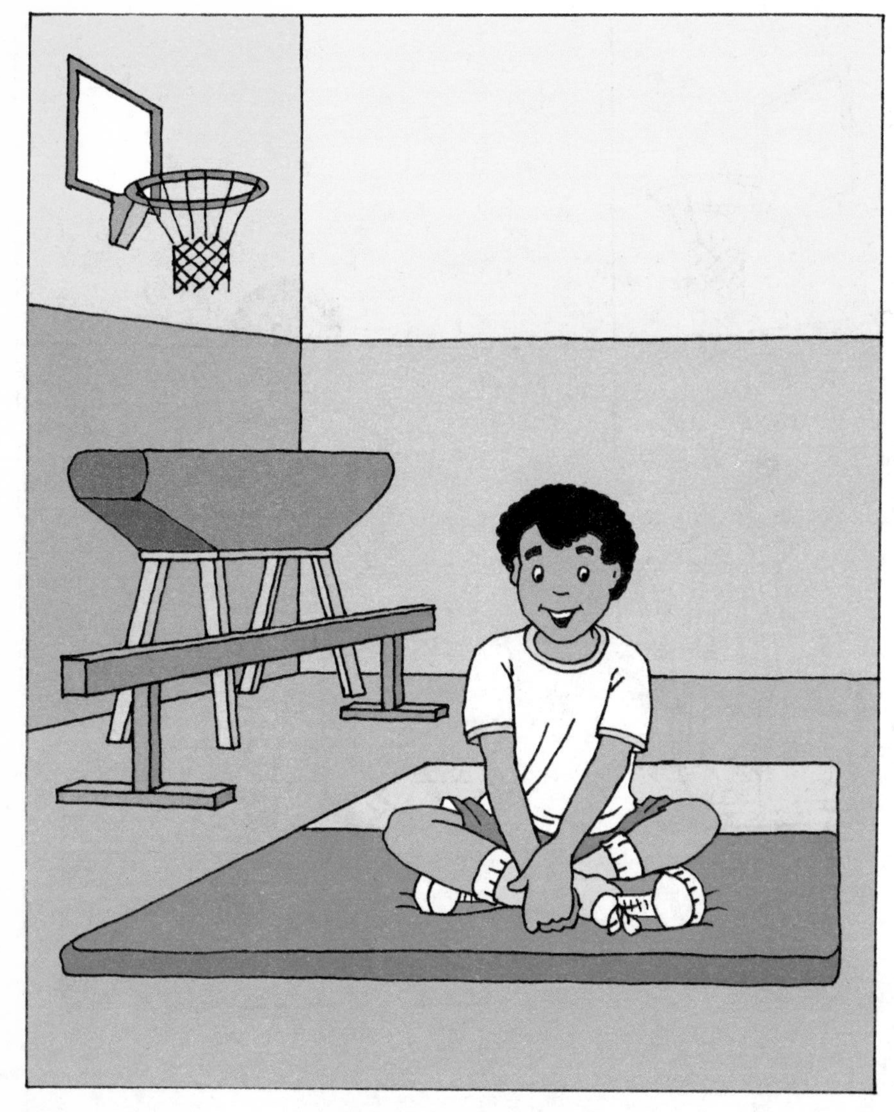

Sam sat.

here

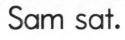

Pam has a hat.

Hat

by Mike Stewart
illustrated by Olivia Cole

Decodable Book 2

A Division of The McGraw-Hill Companies
Columbus, Ohio

www.sra4kids.com

SRA/McGraw-Hill

A Division of The McGraw-Hill Companies

Printed in the United States of America.

Send all inquiries to:
SRA/McGraw-Hill
8787 Orion Place
Columbus, OH 43240-4027

Pam

a hat

Pat

a hat

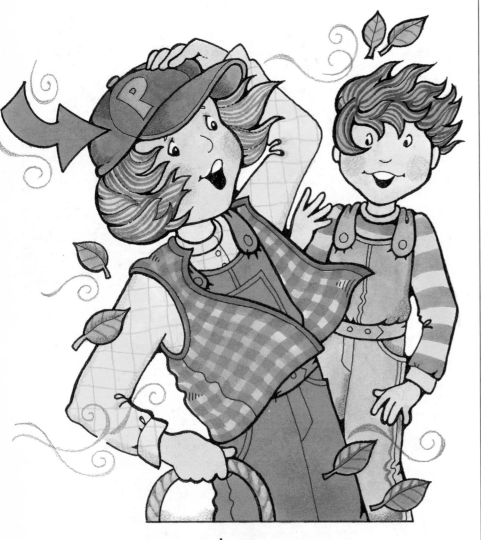

Pat has a hat.

my pal Lil

Sit, Lil

by Dennis Fertig
illustrated by Deborah Colvin Borgo

Decodable Book 3

A Division of The McGraw-Hill Companies

Columbus, Ohio

SRA Open Court Reading

www.sra4kids.com

SRA/McGraw-Hill

A Division of The McGraw-Hill Companies

Printed in the United States of America.

Send all inquiries to:
SRA/McGraw-Hill
8787 Orion Place
Columbus, OH 43240-4027

Sit here.

SRA Open Court Reading

Sit, Lil.

Lil

pal

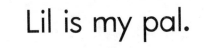

Lil is my pal.

Matt hits the lamp.

Sam and Matt

by Jennifer List
illustrated by Kersti Frigell

Decodable Book 4

A Division of The McGraw-Hill Companies
Columbus, Ohio

www.sra4kids.com

SRA/McGraw-Hill
A Division of The **McGraw-Hill** *Companies*

Printed in the United States of America.

Send all inquiries to:
SRA/McGraw-Hill
8787 Orion Place
Columbus, OH 43240-4027

a lamp

Matt

Sam

a lamp

Sam hits the lamp.

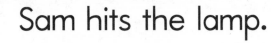

Dad naps.

The Nap

by Rita Blake
illustrated by Gary Undercuffler

Decodable Book 5

A Division of The McGraw-Hill Companies
Columbus, Ohio

www.sra4kids.com

SRA/McGraw-Hill

A Division of The McGraw-Hill Companies

Printed in the United States of America.

Send all inquiries to:
SRA/McGraw-Hill
8787 Orion Place
Columbus, OH 43240-4027

Dad stands.

Dan naps.

Dad stands.

Dad sits.

Dan

A bib is on Bob.

SRA Open Court Reading

A Bib

by Jim Kurtz
illustrated by Olivia Cole

Decodable Book 6

A Division of The McGraw-Hill Companies
Columbus, Ohio

www.sra4kids.com

SRA/McGraw-Hill

A Division of The McGraw-Hill Companies

Printed in the United States of America.

Send all inquiries to:
SRA/McGraw-Hill
8787 Orion Place
Columbus, OH 43240-4027

a bib

Bob

a cat

a bib

A cat is on a bib.

Dot can bat.

Sad Dot

by Dennis Fertig
illustrated by Meryl Henderson

Decodable Book 7

A Division of The McGraw-Hill Companies

Columbus, Ohio

www.sra4kids.com

SRA/McGraw-Hill

A Division of The McGraw-Hill Companies

Printed in the United States of America.

Send all inquiries to:
SRA/McGraw-Hill
8787 Orion Place
Columbus, OH 43240-4027

Dot is not sad.

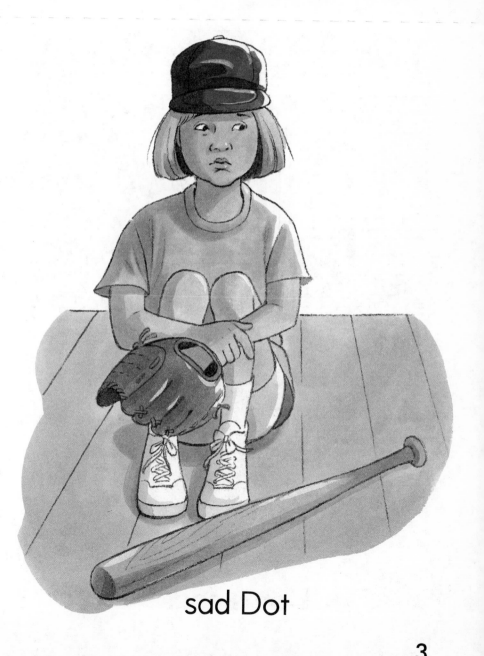

Dot can sit.

sad Dot

Dot is sad.

Dot cannot bat.

Ron can sit in a bus.

Run, Ron

by Linda Sutton
illustrated by Kersti Frigell

Decodable Book 8

A Division of The McGraw-Hill Companies
Columbus, Ohio

www.sra4kids.com

SRA/McGraw-Hill

A Division of The **McGraw-Hill** *Companies*

Printed in the United States of America.

Send all inquiries to:
SRA/McGraw-Hill
8787 Orion Place
Columbus, OH 43240-4027

a bus

Ron cannot run.

run

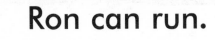

Ron can run.

Ron can still run.

Mom can hug a bug.

Hug a Bug

by Dennis Fertig
illustrated by Pat Lucas-Morris

Decodable Book 9

A Division of The McGraw-Hill Companies
Columbus, Ohio

SRA Open Court Reading

www.sra4kids.com

SRA/McGraw-Hill

A Division of The McGraw-Hill Companies

Printed in the United States of America.

Send all inquiries to:
SRA/McGraw-Hill
8787 Orion Place
Columbus, OH 43240-4027

Jan is a big bug.

a bug

Jan

Mom has a bag.

in the bag

Gus got a hug.

Gus

by Sandra Stewart
illustrated by Kersti Frigell

Decodable Book 10

A Division of The McGraw-Hill Companies
Columbus, Ohio

www.sra4kids.com

SRA/McGraw-Hill
A Division of The McGraw-Hill Companies

Printed in the United States of America.

Send all inquiries to:
SRA/McGraw-Hill
8787 Orion Place
Columbus, OH 43240-4027

Gus got a rag.

Gus did.

Gus ran.

a cup, a jug, a mug

Did Gus tip a cup, a jug, a mug?

Ten men and Fred can fit.

Ten Men

by Kent Wilson
illustrated by Len Epstein

Decodable Book 11

A Division of The McGraw-Hill Companies
Columbus, Ohio

SRA Open Court Reading

www.sra4kids.com

SRA/McGraw-Hill
A Division of The McGraw-Hill Companies

Printed in the United States of America.

Send all inquiries to:
SRA/McGraw-Hill
8787 Orion Place
Columbus, OH 43240-4027

Fred can fit.

Can Fred fit?

ten big men

Ten big men fit.

Fred

The Jets win!

SRA Open Court Reading

Liz Wins

by Jan Webster
illustrated by Meryl Henderson

Decodable Book 12

A Division of The McGraw-Hill Companies
Columbus, Ohio

www.sra4kids.com

SRA/McGraw-Hill

A Division of The ***McGraw-Hill*** *Companies*

Printed in the United States of America.

Send all inquiries to:
SRA/McGraw-Hill
8787 Orion Place
Columbus, OH 43240-4027

Liz zips it in.

Liz zags.

the Jets

Liz is six.

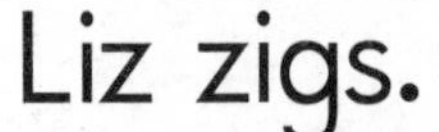

Liz zigs.

Max did fix it.

Fix It

by Jill Bennet
illustrated by Jan Pyk

Decodable Book 13

A Division of The McGraw-Hill Companies
Columbus, Ohio

www.sra4kids.com

SRA/McGraw-Hill
A Division of The McGraw-Hill Companies

Printed in the United States of America.

Send all inquiries to:
SRA/McGraw-Hill
8787 Orion Place
Columbus, OH 43240-4027

Max is wet.

Zip up, Max.

It is wet.

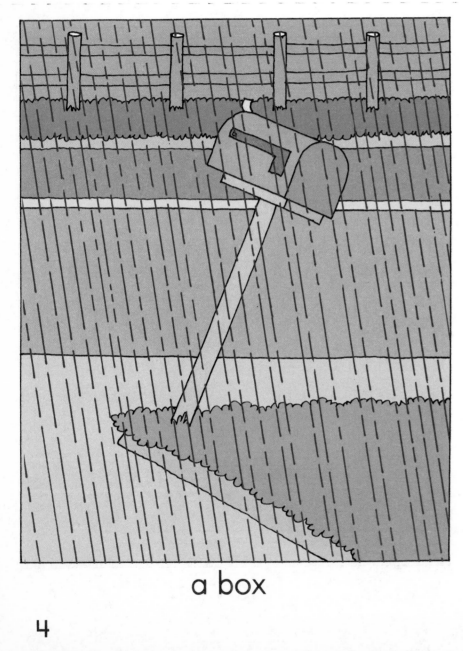

a box

Can Max fix it?

Quint and Kit did the job.

Quint and Kit

by Dennis Mathews
illustrated by Olivia Cole

Decodable Book 14

A Division of The McGraw-Hill Companies
Columbus, Ohio

www.sra4kids.com

SRA/McGraw-Hill

A Division of The McGraw-Hill Companies

Printed in the United States of America.

Send all inquiries to:
SRA/McGraw-Hill
8787 Orion Place
Columbus, OH 43240-4027

Quint and Kit did not quit.

Kit and Quint did not sit.

Quint and Kit

Kit dug.

Quint cut.

Yes, Vic is in the van.

Vic in the Van

by Dennis Fertig
illustrated by Kersti Frigell

Decodable Book 15

A Division of The McGraw-Hill Companies
Columbus, Ohio

SRA Open Court Reading

www.sra4kids.com

SRA/McGraw-Hill
A Division of The McGraw-Hill Companies

Printed in the United States of America.

Send all inquiries to:
SRA/McGraw-Hill
8787 Orion Place
Columbus, OH 43240-4027

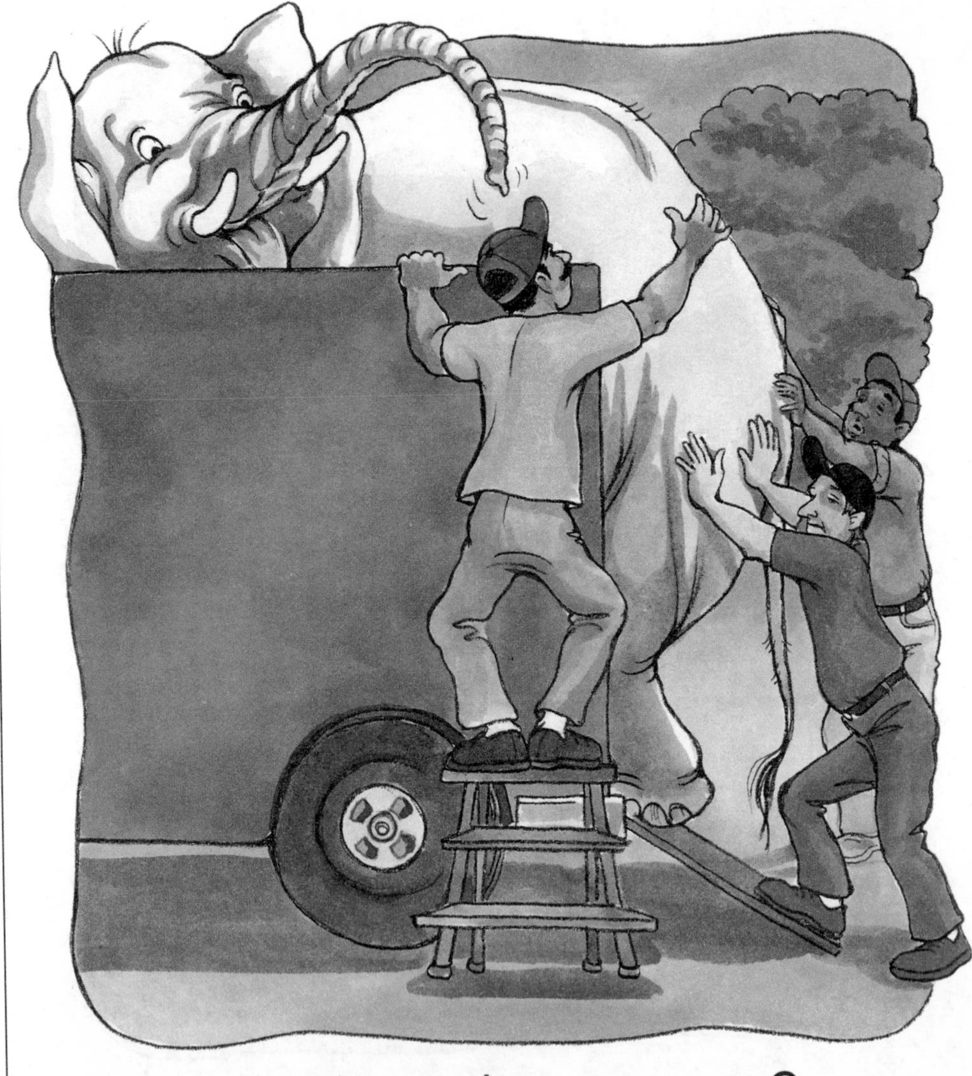

Is Vic in the van yet?

Not yet.

Vic

the van

Is Vic in the van yet?

Kim wins the quiz!

The Quiz

by Pam Ward
illustrated by Mark Corcoran

Decodable Book 16

A Division of The McGraw-Hill Companies
Columbus, Ohio

www.sra4kids.com

SRA/McGraw-Hill

A Division of The **McGraw-Hill** *Companies*

Printed in the United States of America.

Send all inquiries to:
SRA/McGraw-Hill
8787 Orion Place
Columbus, OH 43240-4027

Yes!

A vet can fix pets.

a quiz

Kim can win.

Can a vet fix hats? Pets? Jets?

It is Mugs.

A Bump

by Ken Masters
illustrated by Jan Pyk

Decodable Book 17

A Division of The McGraw-Hill Companies
Columbus, Ohio

www.sra4kids.com

SRA/McGraw-Hill

A Division of The ***McGraw-Hill*** *Companies*

Printed in the United States of America.

Send all inquiries to:
SRA/McGraw-Hill
8787 Orion Place
Columbus, OH 43240-4027

The bump can wag.

The rug has a bump.

Mugs

Mugs is not here.

The rug is flat.

Down.
Viv and Dad zip down.

A Ramp

by Dennis Fertig
illustrated by Meryl Henderson

Decodable Book 18

A Division of The McGraw-Hill Companies
Columbus, Ohio

www.sra4kids.com

SRA/McGraw-Hill

A Division of The **McGraw·Hill** *Companies*

Printed in the United States of America.

Send all inquiries to:
SRA/McGraw-Hill
8787 Orion Place
Columbus, OH 43240-4027

Viv sits on his lap.

Dad can zip up.

steps

Dad must sit.

a ramp

Kip is just as snug.

SRA Open Court Reading

The Quilt

by Dennis Fertig
illustrated by Gary Undercuffler

Decodable Book 19

SRA
A Division of The McGraw-Hill Companies
Columbus, Ohio

SRA Open Court Reading

www.sra4kids.com

SRA/McGraw-Hill
A Division of The McGraw-Hill Companies

Printed in the United States of America.

Send all inquiries to:
SRA/McGraw-Hill
8787 Orion Place
Columbus, OH 43240-4027

Gramps is snug.

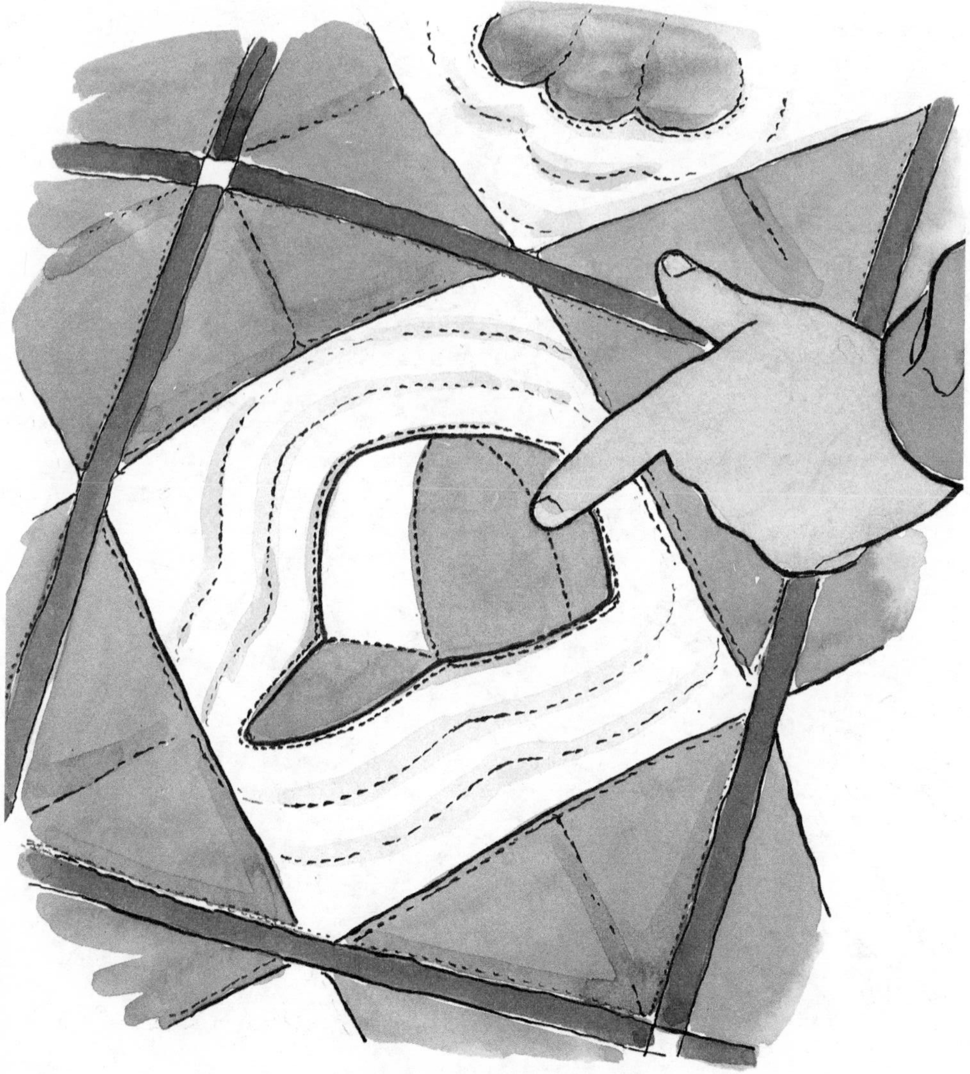

It has red caps.

Gramps

Gramps has a quilt.

It has tan bats.

Puff can rest.

Puff

by Dennis Fertig
illustrated by Barry Mullins

Decodable Book 20

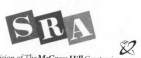

A Division of The McGraw-Hill Companies
Columbus, Ohio

www.sra4kids.com

SRA/McGraw-Hill
A Division of The McGraw-Hill Companies

Printed in the United States of America.

Send all inquiries to:
SRA/McGraw-Hill
8787 Orion Place
Columbus, OH 43240-4027

Yes, Mom can fix Puff.

Mom can stuff Puff.

sad Puff

a rip

Puff has a rip.